ELITE HUNTING CULTURE AND
MARY, QUEEN OF SCOTS

St Andrews Studies in Scottish History

Series Editor
Professor Emeritus Roger Mason (Institute of Scottish Historical Research, University of St Andrews)

Editorial Board
Professor Dauvit Broun (University of Glasgow)
Professor Michael Brown (Institute of Scottish Historical Research, University of St Andrews)
Dr David Ditchburn (Trinity College, Dublin)
Professor Emerita Elizabeth Ewan (University of Guelph)
Professor Clare Jackson (Trinity Hall Cambridge)
Dr Catriona MacDonald (University of Glasgow)
Dr Malcolm Petrie (Institute of Scottish Historical Research, University of St Andrews)

Sponsored by the Institute of Scottish Historical Research at the University of St Andrews, St Andrews Studies in Scottish History provides an important forum for the publication of research on any aspect of Scottish history, from the early middle ages to the present day, focusing on the historical experience of Scots at home and abroad, and Scotland's place in wider British, European and global contexts. Both monographs and essay collections are welcomed.

Proposal forms can be obtained from the Institute of Scottish Historical Research website: http://www.st-andrews.ac.uk/ishr/studies.htm. They should be sent in the first instance to the chair of the editorial board at the address below.

Professor Emeritus Roger Mason
Institute of Scottish Historical Research
St Andrews University
St Andrews
Fife KY16 9AL
UK
ram@st-andrews.ac.uk.

Previous volumes in the series are listed at the back of this book.

ELITE HUNTING CULTURE AND MARY, QUEEN OF SCOTS

John M. Gilbert

THE BOYDELL PRESS

© John M. Gilbert 2024

All Rights Reserved. Except as permitted under current legislation
no part of this work may be photocopied, stored in a retrieval system,
published, performed in public, adapted, broadcast,
transmitted, recorded or reproduced in any form or by any means,
without the prior permission of the copyright owner

The right of John M. Gilbert to be identified as the author of this work
has been asserted in accordance with sections 77 and 78 of the Copyright,
Designs and Patents Act 1988

First published 2024
The Boydell Press, Woodbridge

ISBN 978 1 83765 229 7

The Boydell Press is an imprint of Boydell & Brewer Ltd
PO Box 9, Woodbridge, Suffolk IP12 3DF, UK
and of Boydell & Brewer Inc.
668 Mt Hope Avenue, Rochester, NY 14620-2731, USA
website: www.boydellandbrewer.com

A catalogue record for this book is available
from the British Library

The publisher has no responsibility for the continued existence or accuracy
of URLs for external or third-party internet websites referred to in this
book, and does not guarantee that any content on such websites is, or will
remain, accurate or appropriate

To Myrtle

Contents

List of illustrations		viii
Preface and acknowledgements		xi
A note on the text		xiii
List of abbreviations		xiv
	Introduction	1
1	Hunting culture, conditions, and contexts	13
2	A hunting education	41
3	The hunting couple	56
4	Hunting at the Scottish renaissance court	76
5	Diana the huntress	96
6	Royal huntings	118
7	Hunting for reconciliation	139
	Envoi: Hunting for hope: captivity in England, 1568–87	156
	Conclusion	164
Appendix I: Fieldwork		169
Appendix II: Equestrianism		181
Glossary		189
Bibliography		195
Index		213

Illustrations

Plates

1 Virgil Solis: hunting frieze (BM, ID 01613891287. © The Trustees of the British Museum)   65

2 Frontispiece of *La Vénerie* by Jaques du Fouilloux, printed in 1561 (BnF RES M-S-33, fo. 2r and bpt6k 101300 76)   67

3 Site of James V's hunting lodge or 'palice' in Glen Tilt   86

4 The surrender of Mary, Queen of Scots, at Carberry Hill on 15 June, 1567 (National Archives MPF 1/366/2 extracted from SP 52/13)   99

5 The Lunkarts in Glen Tilt, looking east   130

6 An extract from Pont's map of Glen Tilt, *c*. 1583–96 (Reproduced with the Permission of the National Library of Scotland)   170

7 The location of the ruined building near Dalclathick   175

Diagrams

1 A *par force* hunt   15

2 Drives in France   19

3 Drives in Scotland   23

Maps

1 Blois and Chambord   43

2 Progress of Mary and Francis from 23 October to 18 November 1559, and other places mentioned in the text   63

ILLUSTRATIONS

3	Royal hunting grounds in Scotland from the fourteenth to the sixteenth century	77
4	Falkland Park in the sixteenth century	103
5	Mary, Queen of Scots, in Fife from 14 February to 18 May, 1563	111
6	Glenfinglas Forest	123
7	The Glen Tilt area	129
8	Glenartney Forest	145

Plans

1	Sketch plan of the Lunkarts in Glen Tilt	133
2	Sketch plan of the ruined building in Glenartney near Dalclathick	176

The author and publisher are grateful to all the institutions and individuals for permission to reproduce the materials in which they hold copyright. Every effort has been made to trace the copyright holders; apologies are offered for any omission, and the publisher will be pleased to add any necessary acknowledgement in subsequent editions.

The author and publishers are grateful to the Strathmartine Trust for
generous financial support towards the costs of this volume

Preface and acknowledgements

After retiring in 2010 I spent an enjoyable eight years as a volunteer guide in Falkland Palace. My time there coincided with a series of projects which researched both the palace and the surrounding area. The Living Lomonds Landscape Partnership and Falkland Stewardship Trust supported an excavation of the park pale and an historic woodland assessment of the Falkland Estate. At the same time the National Trust for Scotland explored the history and development of the palace and commissioned a dendrochronological study of its older timbers. As a medieval historian specialising in hunting reserves and woodland management I found it an exceptionally interesting time and it inspired me to research the history of the park in more detail. As I returned to serious historical research I appreciated the encouragement of Christopher Dingwall, John Fletcher, Richard Oram and Simon Taylor. As my research expanded I realised that the hunting activities of Mary, Queen of Scots, could throw new light on her life in France and on her time as queen regnant in Scotland. It also became clear that Mary's career would serve as a good example of the social and political role which hunting could play at court. Thus, the idea of writing a book emerged.

While pursuing this research I have approached numerous people with a variety of questions. I have acknowledged their help at appropriate points in the text and footnotes but in alphabetical order they are Kate Anderson, Michael Ansell, Amy Blakeway, Agnes Bos, Piers Dixon, Christopher Fleet, John Guy, John Harrison, Rachel Hart, Oliver O'Grady, Richard Oram, Norman Reid, Simon Taylor and Ulrike Weiss. I would also like to thank the staff of the various libraries and repositories which I have visited, namely, the National Records of Scotland, the National Library of Scotland, the National Collection of Aerial Photography, St Andrews University Library and their Department of Special Collections, Edinburgh University Library's Centre for Research Collections and the Library of Historic Environment Scotland. Farther afield e-mail communications with Thierry Crépin-Leblond of the Musée national de la Renaissance at Écouen, Jean Vittet at the chateau of Fontainebleau and Severine Lapape and Caroline Vrand of the Department of Prints and Photographs in the Bibliothèque nationale de France were most helpful. Closer to home I am indebted to Ninian Crichton Stuart, Andrew Bruce-Wooton, factor of the Atholl Estates, and to David Wallace, the depute factor of the Drummond Estates, for assistance and permission to access sites in the Falkland Estate, Glen Tilt and Glenartney respectively.

My thanks also go to Rosalind Marshall, Michael Brown and Piers Dixon, who kindly agreed to read over individual chapters at an early stage of their development; but my particular thanks go to Roger Mason, the series editor, whose patience and wise counsels have helped me to turn a vision into reality. Nonetheless I must stress that the views expressed in this book and any remaining inaccuracies are my responsibility alone.

Last but by no means least I would like to take this opportunity to express my heartfelt thanks to my wife for tolerating the time I have spent working on this project. I am also indebted to her for casting her keen eye over my text in order to turn it into more readable English. Without her help, understanding and support this book would never have been written.

John M. Gilbert
Cupar, March 2024

A note on the text

Dates between 1 January and 25 March are given in their modern form as, for instance, 1 January 1565 rather than as 1 January 1564/5. Names of French monarchs are given in their anglicised forms as are sixteenth-century Gaelic names. Gaelic quotations are given in translation but some individual Gaelic words are translated in brackets. Scots quotations are given in the original and in translation when individual words are not close enough to modern English to be readily understood. Quotations and individual words in Latin and French are translated in footnotes, in brackets or as part of the text. Grid references to places in Scotland relate to Ordnance Survey maps and are recognisable as two letters followed by six or eight numerals, e.g., NN13054817. On maps and plans the metric scale is always given but on maps miles are also shown. Where sources have been consulted online the website/url and the date of consultation is usually given in the footnotes, but where a site has been used regularly over several years these details are given in the Bibliography. However, where books have been accessed online, for instance on Google Books or through a university-library website, these details are not given.

Abbreviations

Adams, 'The Queenes Majestie'	Simon Adams, '"The Queenes Majestie … is now become a great huntress": Elizabeth I and the Chase', *The Court Historian*, 18 (2013), 143–164
Almond, *Daughters of Artemis*	Richard Almond, *Daughters of Artemis: the Huntress in the Middle Ages and Renaissance* (Woodbridge, 2009)
Almond, *Medieval Hunting*	Richard Almond, *Medieval Hunting* (Stroud, 2003)
Anthenaise, *Chasses princières*	Claude d'Anthenaise and Monique Chatenet (eds), *Chasses princières dans l'Europe de la Renaissance* (Arles, 2007)
Bellenden, *History* (1821)	*History and Chronicles of Scotland written in Latin by Hector Boece and translated by John Bellenden*, ed. T. Maitland, 3 vols (Edinburgh, 1821)
BL	British Library
BnF	Bibliothèque nationale de France
Boece, *Historiae* (1527)	Hector Boethius, *Scotorum Historiae* (Paris, 1527)
Broomhall, *Women and Power*	Susan Broomhall (ed.), *Women and Power at the French Court 1483–1563* (Amsterdam, 2018)
Carpenter, 'Performing diplomacies'	Sarah Carpenter, 'Performing Diplomacies: The 1560s Court Entertainments of Mary Queen of Scots', *SHR*, 82 (2003), 194–225
Catalogue des Actes	*Catalogue des Actes de François II*, ed. Marie-Thérèse Martel, Centre Nationale de la Recherche Scientifique (Paris, 1991)

ABBREVIATIONS

CDS	*Calendar of Documents relating to Scotland*, ed. J. Bain, 4 vols (Edinburgh, 1881–8)
Chatenet, *La Cour de France*	Monique Chatenet, *La Cour de France au XVIe Siècle* (Paris, 2002)
Contamine, 'Dames à Cheval'	P. Contamine, 'Dames à Cheval', in P. Contamine and G. Contamine (eds), *Marguerite d'Écosse* (Paris, 1999), 201–217
Crépin-Leblond, *Marie Stuart*	Thierry Crépin-Leblond, 'Marie Stuart à la cour de France', in Crépin-Leblond et al. *Marie Stuart: le destin français d'une reine d'Écosse* (Paris, 2008), 33–52
CSPF	*Calendar of State Papers Foreign, Elizabeth*, ed. Joseph Stevenson et al. 26 vols (London, 1865–1950)
CSPS	*Calendar of State Papers relating to Scotland and Mary Queen of Scots*, ed. Joseph Bain et al. 12 vols (Edinburgh, 1898–1952)
CSPV	*Calendar of State Papers Venice and Northern Italy*, ed. Raymond Brown and C. Cavendish Bentinck, 38 vols (London, 1864–1947)
Cummins, *The Hound and the Hawk*	John Cummins, *The Hound and The Hawk, The Art of Medieval Hunting* (London, 1988)
Donaldson, *All the Queen's Men*	Gordon Donaldson, *All the Queen's Men, Power and Politics in Mary Stewart's Scotland* (London, 1983)
DOST	*Dictionary of the Older Scottish Tongue*, ed. W. A. Craigie and A. J. Aitken (London, 1937–2001)
Duanaire Finn	*Duanaire Finn, The Book of the Lays of Fionn*, ed. Eoin McNeil (London, 1908)
Excerpta e Libris Domicilii	*Excerpta e Libris Domicilii Jacobi Quinti*, Bannatyne Club (Edinburgh, 1836)
ER	*Exchequer Rolls of Scotland*, ed. George Burnett et al. 23 vols (Edinburgh, 1878–1908)
Ferrières, *Roy Modus*	Henri de Ferrières, *Le Livre du Roy Modus et de la Royne Ratio*, ed. Gunnar Tilander (Paris, 1932)

ABBREVIATIONS

Fittis, *Sports and Pastimes*	Robert S. Fittis, *Sports and Pastimes of Scotland* (Paisley, 1891)
Fouilloux, *Vénerie*	*La Vénerie de Jacques du Fouilloux ... et L'Adolescence de l'Autheur* (Poitiers, 1561)
Furgol, 'Itinerary'	Edward M. Furgol, 'The Scottish Itinerary of Mary Queen of Scots, 1542–8 and 1561–8', *PSAS*, 117 (1987), 219–32
Gilbert, *Hunting*	John M. Gilbert, *Hunting and Hunting Reserves in Medieval Scotland* (Edinburgh, 1979)
Gobry, Francis II	Ivan Gobry, *François II 1559–60* (Paris, 2012)
Groundwater, 'Afterword'	Anna Groundwater, 'Afterword: What Now?', in Wormald, *Mary Queen of Scots*, 207–238
HES	Historic Environment Scotland
HMSO	His Majesty's Stationery Office
Houwen, *A Palace in the Wild*	L. A. J. R. Houwen, A. A. MaDonald and S. L. Mapstone (eds), *A Palace in the Wild* (Leuven, 2000)
Inventaires de la Royne	*Inventaires de la Royne d'Écosse*, ed. J. Robertson (Edinburgh, 1863)
Knox, *History of the Reformation*	John Knox, *History of the Reformation in Scotland*, ed. W. C. Dickinson, 2 vols (London, 1949)
Langton, *Forests and Chases*	John Langton and Graham Jones (eds), *Forests and Chases of Medieval England and Wales c.1000-c.1500* (Oxford, 2010)
Lesley, *History* (1570)	John Lesley, *History of Scotland from the death of King James I in 1436 to the year 1561*, ed. Thomas Thomson, Bannatyne Club (1830)
Lesley, *De Origine* (1578)	Johanne Leslaeo, *De Origine, moribus et rebus gestis Scotorum* (Amsterdam, 1675)
Leslie, *Historie* (1596)	*Historie of Scotland by Jhone Leslie*, trans. Father J. Dalrymple in 1596., ed. Father E. Cody and William Murison, 2 vols, Scottish Text Society (Edinburgh, 1888 and 1895)

ABBREVIATIONS

Master of Game	*Master of Game by Edward second duke of York*, ed. William A. and F. Baillie-Grohman (London, 1904)
Lynch, *Mary Stewart*	Michael Lynch (ed.), *Mary Stewart Queen in Three Kingdoms* (Oxford, 1988)
Lynch, 'Queen Mary's Triumph'	Michael Lynch, 'Queen Mary's Triumph: The Baptismal Celebrations at Stirling in December 1566' *SHR*, 69 (1990), 1–21
Mickel 'From Bourgeois Wife'	Lesley Mickel, 'From Bourgeois Wife to Renaissance Monarch: The royal Entertainment and Imperial Ambition of Mary Stewart (1561–66)', *Review of Scottish Culture*, 27 (2015), 48–61
Montaiglon, *Latin Themes*	Anatole de Montaiglon (ed.), *The Latin Themes of Mary Stuart* (London, 1855)
Nau, *Memorials*	Claude Nau, *History of the Reign of Mary Stewart from the murder of Riccio until her flight into England*, ed. J. Stevenson (Edinburgh, 1883)
NCAP	National Collection of Air Photographs
Neighbors, 'Elizabeth I Huntress'	Dustin Neighbors, 'Elizabeth I "Huntress of England" ', *The Court Historian* (2023), 49–79
NGR	National Grid Reference
NMRS	National Monuments Record of Scotland
Noirmont, *Histoire de la Chasse*	Dunoyer de Noirmont, *Histoire de la Chasse en France, depuis les temps les plus reculés jusqu'à la Révolution*, 3 vols (Paris, 1867)
NRAS	National Record of the Archives of Scotland
NRS	National Records of Scotland
NSAS	*New Statistical Account of Scotland*, 15 vols (Edinburgh, 1834–45)
NWDG	Native Woodlands Discussion Group
OS	Ordnance Survey
OSAS	*Old Statistical Account of Scotland*, ed. John Sinclair, 21 vols (Edinburgh, 1791–99)

ABBREVIATIONS

Parkinson, 'A Lamentable Storie'	David Parkinson, '"A Lamentable Storie": Mary Queen of Scots and the inescapable *querelle des femmes*', in Houwen, *A Palace in the Wild*, 141–160
Phoebus, *Livre de Chasse*	Gaston Phoebus, *Livre de Chasse*, ed. Gunnar Tilander (Karlshamn, 1971)
Pitscottie, *Historie*	R. Lindsay of Pitscottie, *The Historie and Cronicles of Scotland*, ed. A. J. G. Mackay, 3 vols (Edinburgh, 1899–1911)
PSAS	*Proceedings of the Society of Antiquaries of Scotland*
RCAHMS	Royal Commission on Ancient and Historical Monuments
Richardson, 'Riding like Alexander'	Amanda Richardson, '"Riding like Alexander, Hunting like Diana": Gendered Aspects of the Medieval Hunt and its Landscape Settings in England and France', *Gender and History*, 24 (2012), 153–70
RMS	*Registrum Magni Sigilli Regum Scottorum, Register of the Great Seal of the Kings of the Scots*, ed. J. Thompson *et al*. 11 vols (Edinburgh, 1882–1914)
RPC	*Register of the Privy Council of Scotland*, ed. J. H. Burton *et al*. First Series, 14 vols (Edinburgh, 1877–1933)
RPS	*Records of the Parliaments of Scotland to 1707*, ed. K. M. Brown *et al*. (St Andrews, 2007–10) at http://www.rps.ac.uk
RRS, ii	*Regesta Regum Scottorum*, ii, *The Acts of William I, 1165–1214*, ed. G. W. S. Barrow (Edinburgh, 1971)
RSS	*Registrum Secreti Sigilli, Register of the Privy Seal of the Kings of the Scots*, ed. M. Livingstone *et al*. 8 vols (Edinburgh, 1908–1982)
Ruble, *La Première Jeunesse*	Alphonse de Ruble, *La Première Jeunesse de Marie Stuart* (Paris, 1891)
SAS	Society of Antiquaries of Scotland
SHR	*Scottish Historical Review*

ABBREVIATIONS

SHS	Scottish History Society
TA	*Accounts of the Lord High Treasurer of Scotland*, ed. T. Dickson *et al.* 13 vols (Edinburgh, 1877–1970)
TAFAJ	*Tayside and Fife Archaeological Journal*
Veauvy, *Cavalières Amazones*	Isabelle de Veauvy, Adélaïde de Savray and Isabelle de Ponton d'Amecourt, *Cavalières Amazones* (Paris, 2016)
Walton, *Catholic Queen*	Kirsten P. Walton, *Catholic Queen Protestant Hierarchy* (Basingstoke, 2007)
Warnicke, *Mary Queen of Scots*	Retha M. Warnicke, *Mary Queen of Scots* (London, 2006)
Watson, 'Deer and Boar'	W. J. Watson, 'Deer and Boar in Gaelic Literature (Aoibhinn an Obair an t-Sealg)', in John Ross, *The Book of the Red Deer* (London, 1925), 75–100
Watson, 'Obair an t-Sealg'	W. J. Watson, 'Aoibhinn an Obair an t-sealg', *Celtic Review*, 10 (1913–4)
Wormald, *Mary Queen of Scots*	Jenny Wormald, *Mary Queen of Scots: A Study in Failure* (London, 2017)

Introduction

Over the years much has been written about Mary, Queen of Scots, but remarkably little has been said about her sporting activities. In some ways this is hardly surprising, given the nature of the evidence. There is no direct reference to her playing royal tennis, which was called *jeu de paume* in France or 'caiche' in Scotland, and there is only one reference to her playing golf and *jeu de maille* or pall mall, an early form of croquet. This lack of evidence, however, has not hindered numerous writers from crediting her with playing golf throughout Fife and East Lothian.[1] Although there is slightly more evidence relating to her falconry and archery, it is with her horse riding and hunting that the body of evidence, although not voluminous, does improve. Her biographers recognise Mary's love of hunting but do little more than mention the location of some of her hunts or note that she tried to ban the use of guns to kill deer or wild fowl.[2] Those historians who do delve into a little more detail make use of the near-contemporary account of Mary's hunt in Glen Tilt in 1564, which was made readily accessible by R. S. Fittis in 1891.[3] Antonia Fraser described it and briefly considered its exact location.[4] Duff Hart Davis wondered about the accuracy of the surviving account, and W. J. Watson was concerned to describe the Gaelic hunting methods which are illustrated by that hunt.[5] These writers did not attempt to examine the political and social significance of that or of any other hunt. In terms of assessing the importance of Mary's hunts in Scotland, only Retha Warnicke has shown awareness of the social importance of hunting by briefly recognising that the king was expected to entertain the nobility with sports.[6] In France the position is no better. Only one nineteenth-century historian, Hector de

---

[1] These imaginings have been brought to a close by Neil S. Millar, *Early Golf: Royal Myths and Ancient Histories* (Edinburgh, 2022), 59–70.

[2] Wormald, *Mary Queen of Scots: A Study in Failure*, 123; Walton, *Catholic Queen*; John Guy, *My Heart is My Own. The Life of Mary Queen of Scots* (London, 2004), 152, 271; Robert Stedall, *The Challenge to the Crown*, 2 vols (Brighton, 2012), i, 147, 262.

[3] Fittis, *Sport and Pastimes*, 54–5.

[4] Antonia Fraser, *Mary Queen of Scots* (London, 1970), 218–19, 326.

[5] Duff Hart-Davis, *Monarchs of the Glen* (London, 1978), 25–6; Watson, 'Obair an t-Sealg'; Watson, 'Deer and Boar'.

[6] Warnicke, *Mary Queen of Scots*, 88.

la Ferrière, has paid any attention to Mary's hunting, but he made no attempt to analyse what that evidence tells us about Mary's experience in France.[7]

What has been lacking is the realisation that Mary's hunting is a topic worthy of serious study for its own sake. Previous biographers, scholarly and otherwise, seem to have subscribed to the outdated view that hunting was little more than a pastime. As we will see, the large amounts of time spent on hunting and the huge allocation of resources to provide the facilities and equipment necessary to enjoy this pastime at an elite level can only be explained if hunting carried a political and social significance in royal and noble society. Hunting has been well researched throughout medieval and early modern Europe, but that is not the case for sixteenth-century Scotland.[8] What is intriguing about Mary, Queen of Scots, in this context is not only that she is a woman and a ruler, but for the first time there is just enough evidence to determine the significance of hunting in renaissance Scotland and to explore how a Scottish monarch could employ the hunt to his or her advantage.

While many still write about Mary's intriguing personal story, modern scholars tend to focus more on her role as a monarch by examining the implications of her upbringing, how she governed in Scotland, how she formed policy, and what these policies were.[9] Historians have expanded our understanding of Mary's government and statecraft by studying various aspects of her reign, such as gender issues, court performance, and the literary and material culture of the court, but they ignore the role of hunting in her social and political milieu.[10] Similarly, historians who have studied hunting and related issues in sixteenth-century England and Europe have failed to explore the relevance of Mary's career to their studies.[11]

In fact, it has long been recognised that hunting as an elite activity had a political dimension throughout the medieval and early modern periods. In

---

[7] Hector de la Ferrière, *Les Grandes Chasses aux XVI Siècle* (Paris, 1895), 66–68, and *Les Chasses de François Ier* (Paris, 1886), 74–6.

[8] The works by Corvol, Anthenaise, Almond, Cummins, Dalby, and Lindner given in the bibliography are examples of research into hunting in Europe.

[9] Donaldson, *All the Queen's Men*; Lynch, *Mary Stewart*; Wormald, *Mary Queen of Scots*; Julian Goodare, 'Mary [Mary Stewart] (1542–1587) queen of Scots', *Oxford Dictionary of National Biography* (Oxford, 2007) at https://doi.org/10.1093/ref:odnb/18248 [accessed 15 September 2019]; Warnicke, *Mary Queen of Scots*; Crépin-Leblond, *Marie Stuart*.

[10] For example: Groundwater, 'Afterword', 209, 221–7; Walton, *Catholic Queen*; Warnicke, *Mary Queen of Scots*, 8–15; Parkinson, 'A Lamentable Storie'; Carpenter, 'Performing Diplomacies'; Mickel, 'From bourgeois wife'; I. B. Cowan, 'The Roman Connection: Prospects for Counter-Reformation during the personal Reign of Mary, Queen of Scots', in Lynch, *Mary Stewart*, 105–22, at 116–19; Clare Hunter, *Embroidering Her Truth* (London, 2022).

[11] Almond, *Daughters of Artemis*; Valerio Zanetti, 'Breeched and Unbridled Bifurcated Garments for Women in Early Modern Europe', *Costume*, 55 (2021), 163–85; Veauvy, *Cavalières Amazones*; Contamine,'Dames à Cheval'; Ulrike E. Weiss, 'Backwards in high heels; a brief history of the sidesaddle', in Ulrike E. Weiss and Claudia P. Pfeiffer, *Sidesaddle 1690–1935* (Middleburg, 2018), 1–18.

INTRODUCTION

the early medieval period the act of creating hunting reserves and developing a forest law politicised hunting because areas where it had once been considered to be the right of all free men to hunt were turned into reserves for the enjoyment of one man, whether king or magnate.[12] From their inception in the Frankish kingdom in the seventh century, these reserves, *foresta* as they were called in Latin, represented the power of the king to regulate activity within that area.[13] The king could then enjoy this pastime undisturbed, with a plentiful supply of game, and offer excellent hunting to favoured nobles and barons.[14] French historians considered that both the overall size and number of the hunting reserves which a king held and his ability to control the formation of private reserves related directly to the power of the monarch.[15] In England, deer forests entered the political arena because of the grievances which they created. Regulation extended not only to the game and the hunting but also to other uses of the reserve, such as cutting and collecting wood, clearing lands for agriculture, and grazing domestic animals such as sheep, cattle, pigs, and horses.[16] This control was summarised as control of the *vert*, the vegetation, and the *venison*, the game. In England these feelings of grievance stemmed not so much from the harsh punishments provided for breaking the rules, since they were seldom enforced, but from the limitations and duties placed on those lands which barons and the Church held within royal forests.[17] As a result, in the twelfth and thirteenth centuries the extent of the forests became a political issue in a struggle against what was seen as royal despotism.[18]

[12] William Perry Marvin, *Hunting Law and Ritual in Medieval English Literature* (Cambridge, 2006), 82.

[13] Graham Jones, 'A common of hunting? Forests, lordship and community before and after the Conquest', in Langton, *Forests and Chases*, 36–7. For more information on the origin of the word *foresta*: Charles Petit-Dutaillis, 'De la signification du môt "forêt" à l'époque franque; Examen critique d'une théorie allemande sur la transition de la propriété collective à la propriété privé', *Bibliothèque de l'École des Chartes*, 76 (1915), 97–152, at 141–3; Nicolas Schroeder, '"In locis vaste solitudinis". Représenter l'environnement au haut moyen âge: l'example de la Haute Ardenne (Belgique) au VIIᵉ siècle', *Le Moyen Âge*, 116 (2010), 10–11, 31–35.

[14] Eric J. Goldberg, *In the Manner of the Franks: Hunting, Kingship and Masculinity in Early Medieval Europe* (Philadelphia, 2020), 79–80.

[15] Ernest Jullien, *La Chasse, son Histoire et sa Legislation* (Paris, 1868), 88–91, 97–9; Charles Petit-Dutaillis and Georges Lefebvre, *Studies Supplementary to Stubbs Constitutional History*, 2 vols (Manchester, 1908–29), i, 95, 117, 200, 203, 208.

[16] Piers Dixon, 'Settlement in the hunting forests of southern Scotland in the medieval and later periods', in G. De Boe and F. Verhaege (eds), *Rural Settlements in Medieval Europe*, Medieval Europe Brugge 1997 Conference (Zelik, 1997), vi, 345–54.

[17] G. J. Turner, *Select Pleas of the Forest* (London, 1901), lxv–lxvi, 58, 60; Charles R. Young, *The Royal Forests of Medieval England* (Leicester, 1979), 30, 44–8, 65, 102–3; Oliver Rackham, *The Last Forest* (London, 1993), 89–90; John Langton, 'Medieval forests and chases: another realm?', in Langton, *Forests and Chases*, 14–35 at 15, 28.

[18] See for example: Austin Lane Poole, *From Domesday Book to Magna Carta 1087–1216* (Oxford, 1954), 28–35; W. L. Warren, *King John* (Harmondsworth, 1966), 169–70; W. L. Warren, *Henry II* (London, 2000), 200–5.

The considerable area of royal forests in the medieval period has raised the question as to why these royal reserves were so large and numerous.[19] While the supply of venison for court occasions and the revenue to be obtained from reserves by way of fines, fees, and confiscations were important, the main reason for the large extent of hunting forests lies in the varied demonstrations of power and authority which they created in the localities. In view of all the activities which had to be controlled to protect the *vert* and the *venison*, forests were, at least potentially, the most intensively governed areas of the kingdom.[20] As the middle ages progressed, the personnel enlisted to regulate these activities expanded and royal government became a clear and obvious presence in the vicinity of these reserves.[21] Forests and hunting progresses have been described as 'instruments of royal rule', since they demonstrated the king's lordship and highlighted his control of the land and of the game.[22] Moreover, nobles who were invited to join the king's hunt were sharing his power, his sport, and his largesse. Such patronage also extended to grants of forest resources, such as timber and venison, the right to hunt in royal forests, the grant of part of a royal forest to a favoured magnate, or indeed the right to create the private equivalent of a royal forest.[23] Hunting and hunting reserves not only demonstrated royal power but helped to create and sustain it. The study of hunting is not simply a question of describing cynegetic techniques and exciting chases but requires the historian to consider a variety of aspects of government including the creation and management of the reserves, the means by which the loyalty of nobles and barons was secured, the enforcement of forest rules through the judicial system at central and local level, and how royal authority was maintained throughout the kingdom. The hunts themselves, therefore, whether royal or baronial, were only the tip of the iceberg.

The royal hunt in the early middle ages has been described as 'a theatre of royal power and display'.[24] When the Crown depended on the support of

[19]   Judith A. Green, 'Forest laws in England and Normandy in the twelfth century', *Historical Research*, 86 (2013), 416–31, at 418, 422–5; Oliver Rackham, *The History of the Countryside* (London, 2000, orig. 1986), 133–8; Oliver Rackham, *Woodlands* (London, 2006), 158–9.

[20]   David Rollason, 'Forests, parks, palaces and the power of place in early medieval kingship', *Early Medieval Europe*, 20 (2012), 428–49, at 436–7.

[21]   Paul Warde, *Ecology Economy and State Formation in Early Modern Germany* (Cambridge, 2006), 22, 162–7; John Langton and Graham Jones, 'Deconstructing and Reconstructing the Forests: Some Preliminary matters', in Langton, *Forests and Chases*, 1–13, at 11.

[22]   Marvin, *Hunting Law and Ritual*, 96.

[23]   Amanda Richardson, 'Putting the "royal" back into forests: kingship, largesse, patronage and management in a group of Wessex forests in the thirteenth and fourteenth centuries', in Langton, *Forests and Chases*, 125–40, at 127, 132, 140; Gilbert, *Hunting and Hunting Reserves*, 20–1; Langton, 'Medieval forests and chases: another realm?' 33.

[24]   Jones, 'A common of hunting', 37 where the phrase is attributed to David Rollason. Jérôme Buridant, 'La forêt et la chasse au XVIᵉ siècle', in Anthenaise, *Chasses princières*, 159–78, at 165.

INTRODUCTION

the nobility to govern and maintain law and order throughout the country, the monarch needed to know the means by which he could gain their co-operation and their acceptance of his authority. Court rituals and ceremonies in royal palaces, and official entries into towns, were all seen as part of this process – and so too was hunting.[25] These contacts between the ruler and the ruled were extremely important and were managed carefully to ensure that the desired impact was achieved. By the sixteenth century a perfor-mance culture had developed which included tournaments, ballets, firework displays, water spectacles, *al fresco* fetes, masques, and royal entries. In renaissance courts these fetes were performed to demonstrate the supposedly unrivalled power of the ruler. A state entry to a city symbolised its conquest and the submission of its bourgeoisie. When a tournament or the siege of a fort was staged as part of a festivity it was always arranged so that the king would emerge as the victor against evil foes, in order to create the image of the all-powerful monarch as a force for good. Poets, artists, craftsmen, and writers were commissioned to compose masques and poetry and to construct stage sets to contribute to the overall impact of the celebration. No expense was spared on the staging of these festivals, because great expenditure high-lighted the magnificence of the monarch. Likewise, lavish, well-furnished royal *chateaux* surrounded by deer parks and wooded forests served to create a similar impression.[26] The hunt assemblies held before the start of a royal hunt can also be categorised as *al fresco* fetes or *fêtes champêtres* (countryside fetes) and, indeed, large show hunts were organised in the sixteenth century to enhance the image of the monarch.

Many other aspects of hunting have been researched, including the sociology and fieldwork of hunting parks, the impact of hunting reserves on the ecology and economy of an area, references to hunting in literature and art, and the hunting activities of elite women, particularly in early modern Europe.[27] This last topic has come to prominence with the growing academic

---

[25] Janet L. Nelson, 'The lord's anointed and the people's choice: Carolingian royal rit-uals', in David Carradine and Simon Price (eds), *Rituals of Royalty: Power and Ceremonial in Traditional Societies* (New York, 1987), 137–80, at 166–72; David Rollason, *The Power of Place: Rulers and their Palaces, Landscapes, Cities, and Holy Places* (Princeton and Oxford, 2016), 151.

[26] Roy Strong, *Art and Power: Renaissance Festivals 1450–1650* (Woodbridge, 1984), 20–21.

[27] John Fletcher, *Gardens of Earthly Delight* (Oxford, 2011); S. A. Mileson, *Parks in Medieval England* (Oxford, 2009); Robert Liddiard (ed.), *The Medieval Park, New Perspectives* (Macclesfield, 2007); Marie Casset, *Les Évêques aux Champs: Châteaux et Manoirs des Évêques Normands au Moyen Âge (XIe–XVe siècles)* (Caen, 2007), 60–9; François Duceppe-Lamarre, *Chasse et Pâturage dans les Forêts du Nord de la France: Pour une archéologie du paysage sylvestre (XIe–XVIe siècles)* (Paris, 2006), 18–102, 171–81; Michel Devèze, *La Vie de La Forêt Française au XVI Siècle*, 2 vols (Paris, 1961); Oliver Rackham, *Trees and Woodland in the British Landscape* (rev. edn, London, 2001), 164–83; Marvin, *Hunting Law and Ritual, passim*; Marcelle Thiebaux, *The Stag of Love: The Chase in Medieval Literature* (London and New York, 1974); Archibald A. M. Duncan, *Scotland, The Making of a Kingdom* (Edinburgh, 1975), 364–5, 420–3; Richard Oram, *Domination and Lordship*,

interest in the part played by women at various levels of society and the extent to which their lives were defined by what male society saw as acceptable behaviours for women.[28]

As one would expect, hunting, especially chasing game on horseback across country, was seen as a typically male behaviour and, as such, not to be enjoyed by women.[29] It required excellent horsemanship, skill with weapons, self-discipline, and bravery, all of which were seen in the early medieval period as markers of masculinity.[30] It is noticeable that in the fourteenth, fifteenth, and sixteenth centuries hunting treatises written with a didactic intent only occasionally mentioned women.[31] The mid-fifteenth-century Devonshire Tapestries and the early sixteenth-century tapestries, Les Chasses de Maximilien, do not depict noble ladies chasing game but portray them riding sedately on side-facing saddles and holding a hawk. They are presented as decorative ornaments applauding the feats of their male companions and providing an amatory interest at the end of the hunt.[32] In the mid-sixteenth century the engravings of the German artist Virgil Solis do show women chasing deer, but they are riding pillion on a side-facing saddle behind a man, clinging to him for dear life and not riding independently.[33] It was believed that women should not chase game on horseback across open country because it was not safe. If they wanted to hunt, they should do so only in the sheltered confines of a deer park, where the deer were already captured, and so chasing them was not considered to be true hunting.[34] In the medieval and early modern periods there was a publicly presented perception

---

Scotland 1070–1230 (Edinburgh, 2011), 238–48; Zanetti, 'Breeched and Unbridled', 163–85; Martha Moffat Peacock, 'Women at the Hunt: developing a gendered logic of rural space in the Netherlandish visual tradition', in Albrecht Classen and Christopher R. Classen (eds), *Rural Space in the Middle Ages* (Berlin, 2012), 819–64.

[28] Walton, *Catholic Queen*, 25–44 gives a useful summary of the *Querelle des Femmes*, the debate about women. Merry E. Wiesner-Hanks, *Women and Gender in Early Modern Europe* (Cambridge, 2019), 16–35, 305–20.

[29] Rollason, 'Forests Parks and Palaces', 441–2.

[30] Goldberg, *In the Manner of the Franks*, 6–7.

[31] In the late fourteenth century Gaston Phoebus mentions women only when he explains how to make the chase easier for them: Phoebus, *Livre de Chasse*, 195. Ferrières, also in the later fourteenth century, makes no mention of women as hunters: Ferrières, *Roy Modus*. The same is true of the mid-sixteenth-century *La Vénerie et l'Adolescence* by Jacques du Fouilloux. But in the early fifteenth century Edward, duke of York, in his *Master of Game*, makes a single mention of ladies when they are included in the concluding dedication in one of the manuscripts: *Master of Game*, 113.

[32] For the Devonshire Tapestries see Cummins, *The Hound and The Hawk*, 7–8 and figure 9 after p. 150. For Les Chasses de Maximilien, see Almond, *Medieval Hunting*, 151 and illustrations after p. 152.

[33] *Virgil Solis Single Sheet Prints II Holstein's German Engravings, Etchings and Woodcuts 1400–1700* (eds), D. Beaujean and G. Bartrum (Rotterdam, 2004), vol. 64, in which prints nos 525, 526 and 527 show couples.

[34] John Coke, *Débats des Hérauts d'Armes de France et d'Angleterre*, ed. Leopold Pannier (Paris, 1877), 5–6 and BnF, MS. Français 5837, fos 2, 4r, 4v.

INTRODUCTION

that chasing game at speed across country was not an appropriate activity for women. The practice, however, was rather different.

Nineteenth-century French historians were well aware that aristocratic women hunted by chasing game on horseback, but in the later twentieth century some doubt was cast on this by historians who questioned whether they did join the chase in open countryside.[35] Being unaware of the documentary evidence that women hunted, historians also argued that the illustrations in two fourteenth-century manuscripts, *The Taymouth Book of Hours* and *Queen Mary's Psalter*, which showed ladies chasing game on horseback and riding astride, were either humorous drawings of an absurd situation or else allegories of women in pursuit of a man.[36] However, the works of Richard Almond and Amanda Richardson have made major contributions towards redressing the balance, and various aspects of women's hunting such as riding dress and equestrianism have also been researched.[37] All now accept that while many elite women did not hunt, there were skilled, knowledgeable, and brave women who participated in the masculine pastime of chasing deer in open country.[38] They rode astride like men, and in the sixteenth century – and probably much earlier – they did so wearing breeches or some kind of bifurcated garment under a more feminine wrap-around apron or *devantière*.[39]

[35] Noirmont, *Histoire de La Chasse*, i, 129–30; Hector de la Ferrière, *Les Grandes Chasses au XVI Siècle* (Paris, 1884), 60–82. For the doubters see Cummins, *The Hound and the Hawk*, 7; Naomi Sykes, 'Animal Bones and Animal Parks', in Liddiard (ed.), *The Medieval Park*, 53–55.

[36] BL, Yates Thomson MS 13 ('*Taymouth Book of Hours*'), fos 77r, 81v, 82r. Available at: http://www.bl.uk/manuscripts/Viewer.aspx?ref=yates_thompson_ms_13_fs001r [accessed 27 August 2020]; BL Royal Ms 2 B vii ('*Queen Mary's Psalter*'), fos 152v, 153r. Available at: http://www.bl.uk/manuscripts/Viewer.aspx?ref=royal_ms_2_b_vii_f084r [accessed 27 August 2020]. The illustrations are questioned by Veronica Sekules, 'Women and Art in England in the thirteenth and fourteenth centuries', in Jonathan Alexander and Paul Binski (eds), *Age of Chivalry. Art in Plantagenet England 1200–1400* (London, 1987), 41–8, at 47 and by Naomi Sykes, 'Animal Bones and Animal Parks', 54, though she does admit that they could be accurate representations of what did happen in parks.

[37] Almond, *Daughters of Artemis* and *Medieval Hunting* consider the artistic evidence more fully, whereas Amanda Richardson, '"Riding like Alexander, Hunting like Diana": Gendered Aspects of the Medieval Hunt and its Landscape Settings in England and France', *Gender and History*, 24 (2012), 153–70 explores the documentary evidence. Janet Arnold researched women's riding dress in 'Dashing Amazons. The Development of Women's Riding Dress.1500–1900', in Amy de la Haye and Elizabeth Wilson (eds), *Defining Dress: Dress as Object, Meaning and Identity* (Manchester, 1999), 10–29. Several authors who researched the same topics accepted that ladies hunted, though their use of written documentary sources was still limited e.g., Peacock, 'Women at the Hunt', 819–64; Weiss, 'Backwards in high heels', 1–17; Isabelle Veauvy *et al. Cavalières Amazones* (Paris, 2016); Zanetti, 'Breeched and Unbridled', 163–85.

[38] Robin S. Oggins, 'Review of Richard Almond, *Daughters of Artemis*', *The Medieval Review* (2010), review no. 10.06.40.

[39] The evidence for the *devantière* is discussed in Appendix II. Veauvy, *Cavalières Amazones*, 45, 64. Note that Veauvy *et al.* use 'amazon' to refer to riding side-saddle rather than astride.

Although these women were adopting what were seen as male behaviours they were not considered to be challenging behavioural norms and their conduct was accepted in elite society.[40]

What is particularly relevant to this study is that hunting was an extremely useful ability for those women who by inheritance, accident of birth, or untimely death found themselves thrust into the role of queen regnant, governor, or *de facto* regent. Elizabeth I in England, Marguerite of Austria, Marie of Hungary, and Marguerite de Parma as governors of the Netherlands, and Catherine de Medici in France were women who appear not to have struggled to survive in a man's world to any greater extent than their male counterparts. They were all keen huntresses and exercised power in one form or another for twenty years or more.[41] The various ways in which female rulers employed hunting to their political advantage have been examined in recent research relating to Elizabeth I which considers how she hunted and how she used the hunt to promote her authority at court and in the country.[42]

In this context it is important to understand how a woman's riding style in the sixteenth century came to convey an image of control. There were basically three ways in which a female could ride a horse: astride, on a side-facing saddle or seat, or on a proper side-saddle.[43] In the earlier medieval period women commonly rode astride, but from the thirteenth and fourteenth centuries onwards, a side-facing saddle became the accepted riding style for elite women on more formal occasions such as making an official entry into a town.[44] In the fifteenth and sixteenth centuries women are seldom if ever depicted riding astride but are frequently shown on side-facing saddles as in the Devonshire Tapestries, Les Chasses de Maximilien, the engravings of Virgil Solis and *Les Très Riches Heures du Duc du Berry*.[45] This seems to imply that women had willingly changed from riding astride where they had full control of a horse to a style where they could progress only very slowly or had to ride pillion behind a man or have a groom lead the horse.[46] In fact, it reflected the idea of what was considered to be acceptable behaviour for women. Women, men argued, were physically and intellectually their infe-

---

[40] Adams, 'The Queenes Majestie', 63; Richardson, 'Riding like Alexander', 266; Neighbors, 'Elizabeth I Huntress', 49–7; Zanetti, 'Breeched and Unbridled', 166.

[41] Peacock, 'Women at the Hunt', 829–32; Wiesner-Hanks, *Women and Gender*, 306–8; Sharon L. Jansen, *The Monstrous Regiment of Women: Female Rulers in Early Modern Europe* (Basingstoke, 2002), 1–2, 5–6; Broomhall, *Women and Power*, 16–17; Krista de Jonge, 'Le parc de Mariemont. Chasse et architecture à la cour de Marie de Hongrie (1531–1555)', in Anthenaise, *Chasses princières*, 269–88.

[42] Simon Adams, 'The Queenes Majestie', 143–64; Neighbors, 'Elizabeth I Huntress', 49–79.

[43] These styles are discussed in more detail in Appendix II.

[44] Contamine, 'Dames à cheval', 216 and n. 71; *Cavalières Amazones*, 40; Weiss, 'Backwards in High Heels', 3.

[45] Musée Condé (Chantilly), Ms 65 ('*Les Très Riches Heures du Duc de Berry*'), fos 5v (May), 8v (August). Available at: https://les-tres-riches-heures.chateaudechantilly.fr [accessed 4 July 2023].

[46] Weiss, 'Backwards in High Heels', 5.

INTRODUCTION

riors and so they required the assistance, support, and guidance of a man to survive in the world.[47] This side-facing style embodied the modest, passive, and submissive bearing expected of women at the time.[48] Despite the impression given by the iconography, women did continue to ride astride and adopt the side-saddle, thus emphasising the element of control which they sought.

Several historians who have considered gender issues in the sixteenth century have recognised that there is a need to distinguish between the models of gender behaviours which were written or preached and what happened in practice.[49] Historians now recognise that education and social standing could enable women to overcome some of the perceived limitations on women's behaviour.[50] In the late fifteenth and early sixteenth centuries the French court produced a variety of royal and noble women who exercised considerable political power in one form or another in various countries in Europe, and Mary was one of these.[51]

Structure of the book

The foundation of this study of Mary's hunting career is the elite hunting culture of France and Scotland, which embodied their hunting methods, hunting rights, the creation and maintenance of hunting reserves, and the attitude of the hunters towards the game. The political aspects of this culture centred on the role of the hunt at their courts and the use of hunting to promote the image and authority of their monarchs.[52] The first chapter considers the various types of hunt which were common in France and Scotland in the sixteenth century, the limitations placed on the right to hunt in both countries, and the existence of large hunting reserves which required careful management of their flora and fauna. When the systems required to ensure sound woodland management and the survival of game in hunting forests

[47] Wiesner-Hanks, *Women and Gender*, 29–32.
[48] Weiss, 'Backwards in High Heels', 5, 6; Almond, *Daughters of Artemis*, 76; Almond, 'The Way the Ladies Ride', 36–9.
[49] Groundwater, 'Afterword', 215; Kamen, *Early Modern European Society* (London, 2006), 172; Penny Richards, 'The Guise Women: Politics, War and Peace', in Jessica Munn and Penny Richards (eds), *Gender, Power and Privilege in Early Modern Europe* (London and New York, 2003), 159.
[50] Wiesner-Hanks, *Women and Gender in Early Modern Europe*, 308, 326; Broomhall, *Women and Power*, 26.
[51] Broomhall, *Women and Power*, 15–17. General gender issues relating to Mary are discussed by Wormald, *Mary Queen of Scots*, 11, 35–6; Walton, *Catholic Queen Protestant Patriarchy*, *passim* but especially 46–7; Groundwater, 'Afterword', 211–21. Warnicke, *Mary Queen of Scots*, e.g., 78–86 considers how gender affected the need to protect her good reputation and 86–95 considers how she took an active role in government, regardless of gender.
[52] The sources for the information in the following paragraphs are given in the footnotes of the chapters themselves.

were extended throughout the country, a much greater number of people were liable to be affected. The argument that this expansion assisted the growing impact of royal government in the sixteenth century is considered in a Scottish context.[53]

Mary's education and her experience as queen in France form the focus of Chapters 2 and 3. Prior to the sixteenth century, a prince's education concentrated on a traditional training in arms, on the practice of warlike sports, such as hunting, and on reading chivalric literature. By the sixteenth century, however, humanists were proposing a more liberal education for princes.[54] They argued that a study of classical languages and literature would encourage princes to become virtuous rulers less inclined to resort to war and more able to argue and speak convincingly with reason and self-discipline. However, most did agree that it was still essential for future rulers to receive some form of military training. While Mary was never expected to become a queen regnant in Scotland, her education did contain elements of both the traditional and the humanist approaches. The main intention of Chapter 2 is to show how Mary learned to hunt, but it also examines her equestrianism and the attitude of the French court towards women's hunting activities. Francis (r. 1559–60), Mary's husband, became king in 1559 and the evidence presented in Chapter 3 argues that Mary accompanied him on many if not all of his hunting progresses and that Mary was not, as has been suggested, abandoned in one palace while he went off hunting from another.[55] While helpful information comes from the accounts of ambassadors, the *Catalogue des Actes* of Francis II provides an altogether different picture of Francis from that found in most histories.[56] This underused collection reveals a picture of Francis as a young king determined to fulfil his duties conscientiously.[57] As his queen, Mary took her part in the important role which hunting played in royal progresses and also participated in royal fetes and performances. Together, Chapters 2 and 3 argue that her training at the French court did indeed help to prepare Mary for her personal rule in Scotland.

Mary's hunting activities in Scotland need to be examined from several viewpoints: the practicalities of how and where she hunted; how her hunts fit into the wider picture of her reign; and how far she managed to fulfil the role of a Stewart monarch. Chapter 4, therefore, contextualises Mary's reign by examining the role of the hunt in the political and social life of the Stewart renaissance court. While renaissance hunting has been mentioned

---

[53]   Warde, *Ecology and State Formation*, 22, 162–7; Paul Warde, 'Fear of wood shortage and the Reality of the woodland in Europe *c.* 1450–1850', *History Workshop Journal*, 92 (2006), 28–57, at 34, 39, 41–3.

[54]   Aysha Pollnitz, *Princely Education in Early Modern Britain* (Cambridge, 2015), 3–7.

[55]   Fraser, *Mary Queen of Scots*, 135.

[56]   *Catalogue des Actes*.

[57]   Ivan Cloulas, 'Review of *Catalogue des Actes de François II*, Marie-Thérèse Martel (Paris, 1991)', in *Bibliothèque d'Humanisme et Renaissance*, 55 (1993), 189–90 ; Gobry, *François II*, passim.

INTRODUCTION

in some work about James V (r. 1513–42), there has been no attempt to gather evidence about this aspect of sixteenth-century court life in any systematic way. The role expected of the monarch in a hunting context and the various ways in which this activity was employed as an instrument of policy have not been explored. The importance of provisioning for individual hunts, the maintenance of accommodation, and the frequency of hunting progresses need to be examined.[58] This account of hunting in renaissance Scotland provides a yardstick against which Mary's performance during her personal reign can be measured. Her early years in Scotland are the subject of Chapter 5, which examines how her ability to hunt helped her to establish her authority and cast herself in the image of previous Stewart monarchs. Mary used hunting on her progresses around the country to good effect, and her pursuit of this male pastime seems to have produced no hostile reaction, but met with approval. A case study of Falkland Palace and its park makes use of work commissioned by Falkland Stewardship Trust and the National Trust for Scotland and provides, for the first time, a picture of the combined development of the palace and park. It also explains how the park, which Mary visited regularly, operated as a hunting reserve in the mid-sixteenth century.[59] In these early years it begins to be evident how Mary had benefitted from her experience at the French court, and her growing confidence is reflected in her cynegetic activities.

In 1563 and 1564 Mary took part in the two large show hunts which were held in Glen Tilt and in Glenfinglas, a favourite hunting ground of previous Stewart monarchs. Both hunts are examined in detail in Chapter 6. The former hunt, mentioned at the start of this Introduction, was organised by the earl of Atholl, but it has never been researched in any detail, never been linked to her father's hunt in the same area, and never been subjected to fieldwork investigation. Placing the story in the landscape in this manner is important when trying to understand what these hunts involved, and in this the maps of the pioneering late sixteenth-century cartographer, Timothy Pont, are invaluable. The performative nature of these events is amply borne out in the Glen Tilt hunt, where sufficient evidence survives both on the

[58] Andrea Thomas, *Princelie Majestie, The Court of James V of Scotland 1528–1542* (Edinburgh, 2005), 52–4; Felicity Heal, 'Royal gifts and gift exchange in Anglo-Scottish politics', in Stephen Boardman and Julian Goodare (eds), *Kings, Lords and Men in Scotland and Britain 1300–1625* (Edinburgh, 2014); Gilbert, *Hunting and Hunting Reserves*, 44–5, 55, 61.

[59] John Harrison, *Falkland Palace, Some Documentary Evidence, Report for the National Trust for Scotland* (2016); Anne Crone, *Falkland Palace: a dendrochronological study, Report for the National Trust for Scotland* (2017); Tom Addyman, *Falkland Palace. Preliminary Analytical assessment of the roofs of the south range and stables, National Trust for Scotland* (2015). The author is indebted to the National Trust for Scotland for permission to use these reports. Coralie M. Mills and Peter M. Quelch, *Falkland Park: Historic Woodland Assessment Survey, A report for the Living Lomonds Landscape Partnership* (2015), held by Falkland Estate Office, The Stables, Falkland. The author is indebted to Ninian Crichton Stuart for permission to use this survey.

ground and in the written record to paint a picture of how it unfolded. Both hunts demonstrate that even though Mary was away from the court, the business of government was ever present. This chapter also shows that Mary was aware of the need to manage the woodlands of Scotland and that she was familiar with the work required to manage her hunting reserves effectively.

Mary's final documented hunt in Scotland, which is the focus of Chapter 7, occurred in Stirling Park in December 1566 during the celebrations for the baptism of her son, James. This was the last of the three hunts recorded in 1566. The first was in Megget in the middle of August and was followed closely by the second, in Glenartney. This apparent increase in organising what were larger royal hunts reflects both Mary's confidence in her position as queen and a desire to hold together the various rival factions stirred up by her marriage to Henry Stewart, Lord Darnley in July 1565. The original plan for the hunt in Megget falls into the category of a judicial raid/hunt as practised by previous Stewart monarchs. The hunt in Glenartney is intriguing because the exchequer rolls mention that a hunting house was built there for Mary in 1563 and, given her enjoyment of hunting, it seems appropriate that the only building which is known to have been commissioned by her should relate to hunting.

The various studies of the baptismal celebrations at Stirling have been shaped by the seminal work of Michael Lynch, but none has studied the implications of the hunt of a white bull in the midst of the celebrations.[60] The main purpose of these festivities was to celebrate the birth of a son and heir and the continuance of the Stuart dynasty, but other political messages relating to support for the Stewart monarchy have been detected. This chapter will consider the messages conveyed by these celebrations in the light of the way in which hunting permeated the whole performance.

Together these chapters deliver a picture of elite renaissance hunting in France and Scotland in all its magnificence and barbarity. They tell of the considerable infrastucture required to support elite hunting and they touch on the ecological impact of hunting reserves. They also demonstrate the uses to which hunting could be put and highlight the importance of studying elite hunting. At a more personal level, these chapters will show the advantages which the ability to hunt brought to Mary, and they will also illustrate what hunting tells us about Mary herself.

---

[60]   Lynch, 'Queen Mary's Triumph'.

1

Hunting culture, conditions, and contexts

In Scotland and England, as in most of Europe, hunting methods, hunting rights, and hunting reserves were the infrastructure on which elite hunting culture was built. The fourth dimension of this culture, the high status awarded to deer, is reflected in the legends and symbolism surrounding these animals. Hunting treatises reported as matters of fact that stags could rejuvenate themselves, live for a hundred years or more, and that their heads and hearts contained medicinal properties.[1] The stag in allegorical literature was given many roles: the human soul being hunted by human vices, Christ being persecuted by man, the lady being pursued by her lover, or 'King Hart' being captured by 'Dame Plesance'. In the eyes of the elite, red deer stags were thought to possess a kind of otherworldly and miraculous quality and, in medieval romance literature, going off to hunt was used as a device to remove the hero from his normal environment into a place of adventure in unfamiliar surroundings.[2] Deer were seen as the ideal game for nobles and royalty to chase because they were the largest and most iconic of the wild animals, and so it was a privilege to eat their meat. The creation or possession of a deer park around a noble residence highlighted that the owner could control this symbolic animal and thus demonstrate his power and status. The nobility did not hunt simply because they enjoyed the sport. It was a mark of their identity. They may have found hunting to be fun, exciting, and rewarding, but of greater importance to the sixteenth-century nobleman was the status which it conferred.

In the early modern period in France the hunted fauna was categorised as greater and lesser game. Red deer were regarded as greater game along with two other herbivores, fallow deer and roe deer. Boar and wolves, which are carnivores, were also considered greater game.[3] In the sixteenth century in Scotland matters were not so clear cut. The contemporary cleric and historian John Lesley, a staunch supporter of Mary, Queen of Scots, did refer in his *Historie* to 'the gretter beistes … athir the harte or the wolfe',[4] thus indicating

---

[1]   Phoebus, *Livre de Chasse*, 64; *Master of Game*, 20.
[2]   Cummins, *The Hound and the Hawk*, 68–74, 70, 181; *Gavin Douglas, Shorter Poems*, ed. P. J. Bawcutt (Edinburgh, 1967), 90 line 129, 93 line 21.
[3]   Philipppe Salvadori, 'François 1er et le droit de chasse', in Anthenaise, *Chasses princières*, 43–60 at 48–9 ; Duceppe-Lamarre, *Chasse et Pâturage*, 117, 233; Ferrières, *Roy Modus*, ii, 273.
[4]   Leslie, *Historie* (1596), i, 20. This is a Scots translation by Father J. Dalrymple in 1596

Scottish familiarity with the distinction between greater and lesser game.[5] The categorisation of hare, rabbit, otter, badger, and wild cat as lesser game is well evidenced in France and would have been similar in Scotland.[6] In France red deer, fallow deer, roe deer, and hare were also categorised as *bêtes rousses* or *fauves* (the russet or fawn beasts), and bear, boar, fox, and otter as *bêtes noires* (the black beasts).[7] The elite in the sixteenth century hunted by chasing game or by having it driven towards them; and, although these methods had been in use for centuries, they were not unchanging and developed over time. While the focus here will be on how both types of hunt were practised at the French and Scottish courts in the sixteenth century, some reference will be made to their earlier development to explain how and why Scottish and French practice differed.

Chasing game in France

In France the *chasse par force* (hunt by force [of hounds]) started life as a straightforward chase or course of wild game by dogs. The problem with a straight chase of this sort outside a park was that the game might outrun the dogs. Consequently, probably by the late thirteenth century and certainly by the fourteenth century, the practice of adding in relays of extra hounds as the hunt progressed had developed. It is this form of the *chasse par force* which Mary would have learned (Diagram 1).[8] It acquired a variety of names including *chasse à cor* (horn), *chasse à cri* (shouts), and *chasse à courre* (at the run), but the name which will be used here is the *chasse par force*. The best-known description of this type of hunt is that given by Gaston Phoebus, comte de Foix, in his *Livre de Chasse* (Book of Hunting), which he wrote between 1387 and 1389. Henri de Ferrières, writing in Normandy between 1354 and 1377, also described it in his *Livre du Roy Modus et de la Royne Ratio* (The Book of King Method and Queen Reason).[9] Both describe, how in the early morning of a hunt, or sometimes the day before, several expert huntsmen with lymers, scenting hounds trained not to bark, would check out the area of the hunt to locate various deer so that the lord could choose to hunt the finest stag in the area. When carrying out this quest in forests, coppices, and scrubland, the huntsman used signs left by the deer such as branches which

---

of Lesley's longer Latin history which he wrote around 1578.

[5] *RPS*, 1428/3/6 and 1458/3/36. In Scotland wolves were treated as pests to be hunted by everyone.

[6] Duceppe-Lamarre, *Chasse et Pâturage*, 233.

[7] Duceppe-Lamarre, *Chasse et Pâturage*, 233; Ferrières, *Roy Modus*, ii, 273.

[8] Noirmont, *Histoire de La Chasse*, ii, 373–4; Ferrières, *Roy Modus*, i, 36, 43, 79.

[9] Phoebus, *Livre de Chasse*, especially chapt. 39, 172–6 and chapt. 45, 193–211; Ferrières, *Roy Modus*, 14–58 especially 35–55. See also Cummins, *The Hound and the Hawk*, 32–46. Cummins's book is the authoritative work on hunting methods.

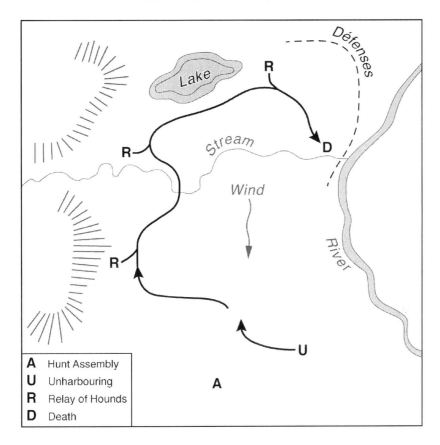

Diagram 1   A *par force* hunt.

it had broken, its droppings or *fumées*, and its scrapings and tracks to try to assess the age and quality of the beast.

Meanwhile the hunters gathered at the hunt assembly to eat and drink and prepare for the day. Most hunts began early in the morning in order to locate the stag before it moved from the spot where it had spent the night. The huntsmen who had been on the quest to find the deer would have returned to the assembly of hunters with the *fumées* of various deer on the basis of which the lord, along with his chief huntsman, decided which stag to hunt. Relays, each comprising two or three couples of greyhounds or scenting hounds, were then sent to positions at some distance from each other along the expected course of the chase, ready to join the hunt as it progressed.[10] Placing the relays was a skilled business requiring familiarity with the terrain

[10] Ferrières, *Roy Modus*, 43; Phoebus, *Livre de Chasse*, 194.

and knowledge of the behaviour of the deer or whatever game was being hunted. Most of the hounds involved in the main pack were running hounds which hunted by scent, because they could follow the deer in woodland when it was out of sight. Towards the end of the hunt the final relay would include larger, heavier dogs and greyhounds which hunted by sight and could hold the deer at bay and pull it down.

When all was ready the huntsman with his lymer led the lord, his companions, and the main pack of hounds to the chosen stag and ensured that the pack picked up the correct scent. The deer was then stirred or unharboured from its resting place and the pack set off after it. The servants who looked after the hounds ran on foot while the noble hunters rode on horseback, though on occasions when hunting smaller game or boar the noble hunters might also follow on foot.[11] The hunt now depended on the skill of the dogs and their handlers. Because the hounds had to follow one deer and one deer only it was important that they should not get the scent confused. The handlers had to be ready for the deer's attempts to throw the dogs off the scent by doubling back, entering a stream, or joining other deer to confuse the scent. All the while the hounds were in full cry and horn signals were blown to let the hunters know what stage the hunt had reached. The handlers with the relays had to uncouple or release their dogs to add fresh impetus to the chase, but in order not to divert the hounds from the scent they had to wait until half the pack of pursuing hounds had passed.

When the stag, exhausted, turned at bay, the hunters blew a signal on their horns and any relays in the area which had not been used were uncoupled to join the rest. After the lord or one of the chief huntsmen killed the deer with a sword there followed an elaborate ceremonial which comprised unmaking or butchering the carcase and then the *curée*, the rewarding of the hounds. The unmaking was carried out in a specific order largely dictated by the practical task of butchery. The hounds may have had a brief taste of the meat at this stage, but their main reward came later when the small intestines, heart, lungs, and meat from the neck or shoulders were prepared for them. While these ceremonies could vary, the unmaking of the deer and the rewarding of the dogs were a recognised ritual which had to be performed out of respect for the game. It also conditioned the dogs to associate hunting with food.[12]

Sometimes, if women or visiting lords wanted a quicker and easier chase or if the terrain was difficult, the lord might set out lines of men or *défenses* to prevent the hunt entering a particular area.[13] These men would not join the hunt but would talk quietly to divert the deer from any escape route such as crossing a river; but if the deer did come straight towards them, they had to cry out and shout and hold their position to stop the stag heading out of the area set for the hunt. Deer, boar, and hares were the main animals hunted

[11] Andrée Corvol, *Histoire de la Chasse, Homme et la Bête* (Paris, 2010), 27.
[12] Marvin, *Hunting Law and Ritual*, 128.
[13] Phoebus, *Livre de Chasse*, 172, 195–6.

HUNTING CULTURE, CONDITIONS, AND CONTEXTS

par force, but other animals could also be hunted in this manner. When chasing hares, no relays were set out, and so they were coursed by the same hounds throughout the hunt.[14]

Chasing game in Scotland

In Scotland the usual method of chasing game is best described as coursing because it involved the pursuit of a single animal by the same hounds throughout the duration of the hunt. Examples of coursing survive in the Gaelic poems relating to the exploits of the legendary Irish hero Fionn Mac-Cumaill (Finn McCoul), who led bands of young men, the Fian, in a life full of hunting and fighting on the edges of noble society.[15] Although many of the surviving versions of these tales were first recorded only between the twelfth and sixteenth centuries, they are thought to date from the post-Roman era. Those tales, current in medieval Scotland, especially in Gaelic-speaking areas, were told and retold over the centuries. While the hunting practices they embody cannot be precisely dated, the style of Gaelic in which the tales are written does give an idea of when they were composed.[16] Coursing is also portrayed on the Pictish stones of the eighth, ninth, and tenth centuries. Although Pictish culture was gradually absorbed into that of the Gaelic-speaking Scots in the ninth century, these stones suggest that Pictish hunting customs had differed from those of the Scots. In contrast with the Gaelic tales, horses figure prominently in Pictish hunting scenes, which show one or more hunters on horseback with spears, chasing a deer which is being attacked by two dogs. When the dogs are shown attacking singly, they attack the deer's hind quarters and side, but when working together, one jumps at the deer's front leg or neck and the other at its hind quarters.[17] While various symbolic interpretations have been placed on these scenes, it is quite clear from the portrayal of the hounds that these hunts, whatever their symbolic significance, are descriptive and do portray how dogs actually attacked deer.[18] Coursing both on horseback and on foot was still common

---

[14] Ferrières, *Roy Modus*, 69–71.

[15] The poems can be found in *Duanaire Finn*, i, e.g., 140 Caoilte's Urn, 163 The Battle of the Sheaves, 195 Three Heroes went we to the chase.

[16] The evidence for this has been examined by various people: *Duanaire Finn*, i, e.g., 130, 140, 188; iii, 29, 36, 59; Andrew E. Wiseman, 'Chasing the Deer: Hunting Iconography and Tradition of the Scottish Highlands', unpublished PhD thesis (University of Edinburgh, 2009), 58–99; John Murray, *Literature of the Gaelic Landscape* (Dunbeath, 2017), 33.

[17] I. Fraser, *The Pictish Symbol Stones of Scotland*, RCAHMS (Edinburgh, 2008), nos 65.2 Kirriemuir 2; 84 Scoonie; 156 Elgin; 124 Nigg; 128 Shandwick; 51.3 Aberlemno 3; 123 Hilton of Cadboll.

[18] Views on the different interpretations of these scenes can be found in George and Isobel Henderson, *The Art of the Picts* (London, 2004), 128–9, 179; David Clarke, Alice

in the sixteenth century when James IV coursed hares in Falkland Park.[19] A later sixteenth-century poem, *Oran na Comhachaig* (The Song of the Owl), relating to Alasdair Carrach, a fourteenth-century chief of the Macdonalds of Keppoch in Lochaber, describes a hunt where hounds course a stag down a glen 'going at him and falling back'.[20] The later visual evidence for chasing deer, which centres on the West-Highland stones of the fourteenth and fifteenth centuries, shows hunting scenes where the dogs hunt in exactly the same way as the hounds on the Pictish stones. The huntsmen, however, like their compatriots in the Gaelic tales, are on foot and not on horseback. On the late fifteenth-century MacMillan Cross at Kilmory in Argyll, hounds like mastiffs are attacking the stag, and the hunter, who is wielding a halberd – a spear with an axe head fitted just below the spear point – follows on to despatch the deer once it has been pulled down by the dogs. Crossbows and swords could also be used for this purpose. To find a portrayal of a noble hunter on horseback with his hound in the medieval period one has to go to the south-east, to the seal of Robert fitz Fulbert of Stenton *c.* 1170, who, accompanied by a smooth-coated greyhound, is carrying a spear, blowing his horn, and presumably chasing game.[21]

Driving game in France

The second main method of hunting, the drive, varied from *par force* hunting in three ways: many animals were hunted; the game was driven to the hunters; and the end point of the hunt, where the archers awaited the driven game, had to be pre-arranged. The form of the drive with which Mary would have been familiar was the *chasse aux toiles* (hunt to nets/screens), which evolved out of earlier forms of the drive, as greater efforts were made to ensure that as few of the game as possible escaped. The predecessors of the *chasse aux toiles* were described by both Phoebus and Ferrières, who explain that a cordon of men known as the *défenses* should be positioned around the area of the hunt

---

Blackwell and Martin Goldberg, *Early Medieval Scotland* (Edinburgh, 2012), 80–3, 154–5; Jane Geddes, *Hunting Picts, Medieval Sculpture at St Vigeans, Angus* (Edinburgh, 2107), i, 119–21.

[19] *TA*, ii, p. ciii, 154, 394, 427. For other references to chasing deer see William Scrope, *The Art of Deer Stalking* (London, 1838), 348–56; Gilbert, *Hunting and Hunting Reserves*, 294, 305–6, 318–19 laws 14 and 15; Johannes de Fordun, *Chronica Gentis Scotorum*, ed. and trans. W. F. Skene (Edinburgh, 1871–72), 59; Pitscottie, *Historie*, i, 324.

[20] *Oran na Comhachaig* (*The Song of the Owl*), ed. and trans. P. Menzies (Edinburgh, 2012), 81 stanza 23.

[21] Wiseman, 'Chasing the Deer', 53; K. A. Steer and J. W. M. Bannerman, *Late Medieval Monumental Sculpture in the West Highlands* (Edinburgh, 1977), 186; Henry Laing, *Descriptive Catalogue of Impressions from Ancient Scottish Seals* (Edinburgh, 1850), no.697. The Stenton seal does not portray any game.

HUNTING CULTURE, CONDITIONS, AND CONTEXTS

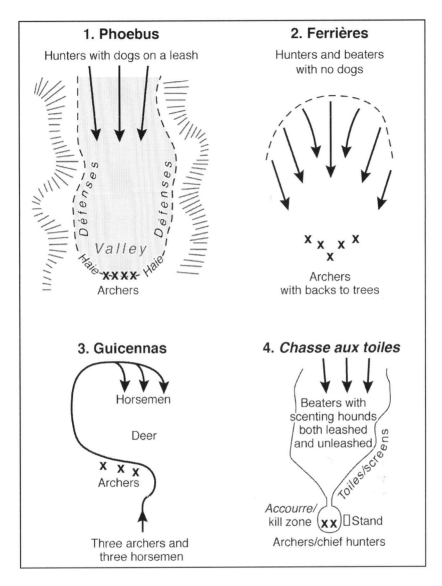

Diagram 2   Drives in France.

(Diagram 2).[22] Their task was to stay still and stop game escaping as the hunters with their dogs drove the game through the woods towards the archers.

[22] Phoebus, *Livre de Chasse*, 255–6; Ferrières, *Roy Modus*, 104–11, 115, 137. This description relates to *bêtes noires* but in subsequent chapters he makes it clear that the same procedures applied to the use of *défenses* when hunting *bêtes rousses*: Ferrières, *Roy Modus*, 115, 137.

19

As they did so the hunters had to make so much noise with horns, shouting, and the barking of their dogs that 'one could not hear God thunder'.[23] Alternatively, as Ferrières describes, when no dogs were involved in the drive the cordon of men was not stationary but acted as *ameneurs* (beaters). The line of beaters, arranged with a curve at each end, then advanced, whistling and talking to each other, with those at each end making more noise and moving more quickly than the rest, thus closing the drive by the time they approached the archers.[24] The archers, the noble hunters dressed in green, waited close to each other with their backs to trees so that they were harder for the deer to spot. Phoebus also pointed out that they had to take care not to shoot towards each other.[25] If a deer passed through them without being hit it should, he said, be allowed to go free, but if it was wounded it should be chased by hunters with scenting hounds.[26] However, to reduce the chance of game escaping at the end of the drive, barriers such as *haies* (fences or hedges) or nets were often used to ensure the game was directed towards the archers.

Because the *chasse aux toiles* was not mentioned in the hunting treatises of Pheobus and Ferrières, nor in the mid-sixteenth-century treatise of Du Fouilloux, and because the *chasse par force* was praised as the ideal form of the hunt, it could be thought that the *chasse aux toiles* was unpopular, but this was not the case.[27] In the *chasse aux toiles* the use of *haies* to entrap game at the end of a hunt was greatly expanded. As with other forms of the drive, the first stage was to check for the presence of game, usually boar, in that part of the wood where the hunt was to be held. The area of the wood where the game had been located was then surrounded with *toiles* (toils or nets) to form the *réserve*, and so in effect the toils were simply a more secure version of the *défenses*. On occasion, ropes with white feathers or men with dogs might be used instead of toils. All this had to be set up without disturbing the game, a major undertaking requiring many men and carts to work quietly down wind of the game as much as possible.[28] At one end of this reserve a smaller enclosure was constructed as a kill zone in a level, open clearing. This was called an *accourre* or a *parc*, not be confused with the larger permanent parks where deer and boar were kept. This kill zone could be linked to the *réserve* by a passage across which there was a screen which could be opened and closed to control the entry of game into the kill zone.

On the day of the drive, huntsmen with scenting hounds and large greyhounds on leashes had to raise the game and drive it to the entrance of the kill zone, where it was held by the dogs. Spectators on a platform could cheer on the hunters and watch the deer or boar being paraded past them

---

[23] Ferrières, *Roy Modus*, 122.
[24] Ferrières, *Roy Modus*, 127.
[25] Phoebus, *Livre de Chasse*, 270; Ferrières, *Roy Modus*, 124.
[26] Phoebus, *Livre de Chasse*, 272.
[27] Claude d'Anthenaise, 'Chasses aux toiles, chasses en parc', in Anthenaise, *Chasses Princières*, 73–100, at 73–9.
[28] Anthenaise, 'Chasses aux toiles', 82–9; Ferrière, *Les Chasses de François 1er*, 49–50.

HUNTING CULTURE, CONDITIONS, AND CONTEXTS

before they entered the kill zone. Sometimes the hunters would confront the selected game in the *accourre* with guns, crossbows, or dogs but, in a form more reminiscent of gladiatorial combat rather than a hunt, they might enter the kill zone on foot to kill a boar with a spear or a wolf with a club. Sometimes the king on horseback could be in the zone with a sword, or he could be on foot like other hunters in the ring. Women did not enter the kill zone but they did shoot the game with arrows from a platform.[29]

Francis I (r. 1515–47) enjoyed the personal combat of the *chasse aux toiles*. In 1527 the English ambassador at the French court wrote from Compiègnes on 28 September that Francis would hunt deer every day and then hunt boar or wolves in the toils while his mother and numerous other ladies of the court watched.[30] Guillaume Budé, in his *Traitté de Vénerie* written *c.*1529 during the reign of Francis I, describes how he watched from a safe distance while Francis went head to head with a boar in the toils.[31] In 1515, in a bizarre episode at Amboise during the wedding celebrations of Antoine duke of Lorraine and Renée de Bourbon, Francis had a four-year-old boar transported to the enclosed courtyard of the chateau. While lords and ladies of the court watched from windows and balconies, the boar attacked various dummies which had been hung there for that purpose. Before the king's planned entry to kill the boar in front of the court it broke into a staircase and charged up to one of the galleries where the court were spectating. Francis, according to Nicolas Sala, a courtier, saved everybody by killing it with his sword, thus displaying his bravery and skill even more effectively than had been planned.[32]

Driving game in Scotland

In Scotland the attempts to confine the game and prevent it escaping took a slightly different form. Instead of stationary *défenses* between which hunters drove the deer to waiting archers, there was a moving line of men on foot called a stable which drove the game towards the archers with the blowing of horns and the barking of dogs. This closely resembled the actions of the mobile *défenses* described by Ferrières in drives when no dogs were involved. The best description of a drive in Scotland occurs in the early fifteenth-century *Ritual Book* of Holyrood abbey, which associates a drive with David I's foundation of the abbey in the twelfth century (Diagram 3).[33] In this hunt, called a *cursus ferarum cum canibus* (a coursing of wild animals with dogs), the game

[29] Anthenaise, 'Chasses aux toiles', 94 n. 34; Hector de la Ferrière, *Les Chasses de François 1er* (Paris 1886), 55–6, 64.
[30] Monique Chatenet, 'Un Portrait du "père des veneurs"', in Anthenaise and Chatenet (eds), *Chasses princières*, 17–42, at 20.
[31] Guillaume Budé, *Traitté de Venerie*, ed. and trans. Henri Chevreul (Paris, 1861), 7.
[32] Noirmont, *Histoire de la Chasse*, i, 156–7.
[33] *Holyrood Ordinale*, ed. F. C. Eeles, in The Book of the Old Edinburgh Club, 7 (1914), 64–6.

was chased to the waiting hunters and not driven quietly. The hunt supposedly took place in what is now the Cowgate in Edinburgh, a valley between two hills, an ideal spot, so the description states, for holding a drive. The animals were chased and driven by dogs through the woods eastwards towards the site of Holyrood abbey. Some of the noble hunters with their dogs, aided by *exploratores* or trackers, drove the game towards the waiting archers between lines of *indagantes* or beaters, who were not stationary but advanced with the hunters to drive the game on.[34] The barking of the hounds, the shouts of the beaters, and the blowing of the hunters' horns are described as filling the air with a certain 'melody', which was presumably akin to Ferrières's thunderous noise. This version of the drive, therefore, shows a preference for a moving line of beaters rather than stationary *défenses*. David and other nobles waited in silence with their dogs, out of sight of the advancing game. The king waited under a leafy tree on horseback, but whether his nobles were also mounted is not clear. In Boece's account of this hunt, written in the early sixteenth century, the word for all those driving the game is the stable or the 'staill'.[35] In Wyntoun's *Chronicle*, written in the early fifteenth century, the component groups of similar hunts are the 'setis' and 'stabile' in one manuscript, and the 'settis' and the 'coursis' in another, giving the idea of the animals being coursed towards the archers.[36] The 'setis' or seats were the places where the hunters awaited the drive, and many of them have given rise to place-names such as King's Seat or Queen's Seat. In this account the stable was definitely involved in driving the game to the chief hunters.[37] In Gaelic the stable were called the *timchoill*, a word which was taken into Scots as 'tinchell' and appears in accounts of hunts in the Highlands in the sixteenth century.[38]

The basic form of the drive as described at Holyrood had altered slightly by the sixteenth century. In his history of Scotland John Lesley, bishop of Ross, wrote about this kind of hunt in the 1570s. He was well known to Mary, having visited her in France and accompanied her on her return. She subsequently appointed him to the bishopric of Ross in 1566. His history, written in Latin in 1578 and then translated into Scots in 1596, gives a description of the drive as it was practised at this time. In the Highlands, especially when the monarch was present, five hundred to one thousand deer could be killed in one massacre, '*una strage*'. Men (often, but not always with dogs) would drive deer and other game from ten to twenty miles away over hills, which

[34] This resembles the hunt described in the fourteenth-century poem *Gawain and the Green Knight*: Cummins, *The Hound and the Hawk*, 54–5.
[35] Bellenden, *History* (1821), ii, 298. This account of the Holyrood hunt exists only in Bellenden's printed edition.
[36] Andrew Wyntoun, *The Original Chronicle of Andrew of Wyntoun*, ed. F. J. Amours (Edinburgh, 1903–14), iv, bk 7, chapt. 1, 328–9 showing the Cottonian MS and the Wemyss MS.
[37] *Master of Game*, 197.
[38] Watson, 'Aoibhinn an Obair an t-sealg', 166.

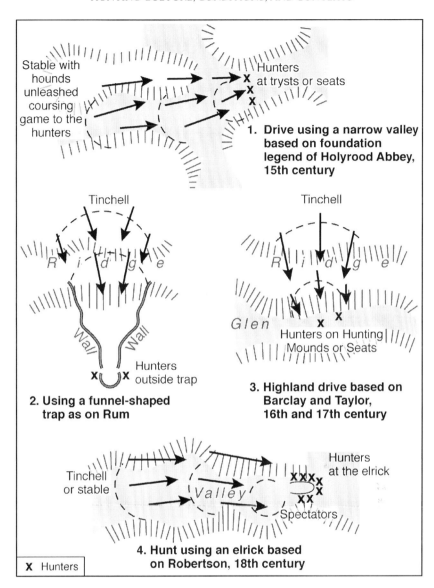

Diagram 3   Drives in Scotland.

may or may not have been wooded, to the 'narrow boundis of a certane valley' where the lords and nobles had made their 'abydeing', *sedes* or seats in the original Latin. From there the hunters released their dogs, shot arrows, threw spears, and used clubs and weapons of all kinds to attack the game, not, as

Lesley says, without great danger to both men and dogs.[39] He also warned that if the leader of the herd was endangered or killed the rest would follow it fearlessly in one mass, threatening the safety of the waiting hunters. In the sixteenth century there seems to have been the same imperative to kill large numbers of game just as there had been in the Gaelic tales of Fionn.[40] The waiting hunters were no longer on horseback, hidden from each other, and there is no clear reference to any sort of enclosure being constructed to trap the deer as in France, although the 'elrick', to be discussed below, could have played this role.

By the sixteenth century there was an increasing stress on the sedentary aspects of the drive. Noble hunters were no longer involved with blowing horns and chasing the game with their dogs towards the waiting archers. That role was left to the tenants of the lord. James IV, when hunting at Ben More in 1501 and Glenartney five years later, waited at the 'sete', where local people brought him fresh butter and cream, no doubt to augment his own provisions.[41] If the king had time to eat and drink, the issue then arises as to whether the king was actually hunting and killing deer or whether he was merely a spectator at his seat. Certainly, in the earliest written description of an elrick, dating to the eighteenth century, 'principal personages and others who did not choose to engage in the chace' observed the hunt from a viewpoint or 'eminence' above the elrick or killing enclosure. While this might suggest that the king was not involved in the killing it must be remembered that the drive could take some time and, in much the same manner as happened in nineteenth-century drives in Atholl, the hunters would know roughly the time required to drive in a certain number of animals.[42] The king and his nobles could have been at or near their seats well before the hunt arrived and anyone not involved in the hunt would have had plenty of time to leave without affecting the drive. This is exactly the position which Mary would have been in when she hunted in the Highlands and it is important to know if she was viewing proceedings from a distance or whether she was in the midst of the action.

In this context the English bow and stable hunt and the Gaelic traditions associated with the drive are helpful. In 1504 Margaret Tudor, James IV's queen, asked Duncan Forester, the forester of Torwood Forest, 'to set the hunting' for her, in other words to arrange a drive.[43] Margaret would have been familiar with drives in England, called bow and stable hunting, where a standing would be arranged for the king and nearby an arbour of branches would be constructed to shelter the king, the queen, and the dogs and to hide them from the game.[44] The standing, as described in the early fifteenth-

---

[39] Leslie *Historie* (1596), i, 19–20; Latin version from Lesley, *De Origine* (1578), 912.
[40] *Duanaire Finn*, ii, 130 The Enchanted Stag, 185 The Magic Pig.
[41] *TA*, ii, 119, 120; iii, 336, 338.
[42] Scrope, *Art of Deer Stalking*, 167.
[43] *TA*, ii, 244.
[44] *Master of Game*, 107–12, 197; Cummins, *The Hound and the Hawk*, 51–2, 64–6.

century *Master of Game*, was not a raised platform, though at a later date it could be.[45] It seems likely that Forester was being asked to arrange the stable along with an arbour where Margaret could await the game, and a standing where she could take an active part in the killing by shooting the game and releasing greyhounds.

Hunting mounds and elricks

Turning to the Gaelic literature, the equivalent of these seats, or standings where hunters awaited the driven game, are referred to in the tales of Fionn as hunting positions and as hunting mounds or hillocks from which Fionn could either direct and watch the hunt or from which he could throw spears at the driven game. In the former sense the poem, *Oran na Comhachaig*, describes Creag Ghuanach, a hill 620m high near Loch Treig, as a 'beautiful hillock of hunting'.[46] In the latter sense these hillocks could also refer to much smaller mounds. When awaiting the hunt each noble had their appointed station called the mound of hunting, '*dumha sealga*', or the site of casting, '*lathair léichte*', from which they threw their spears at the on-rushing game. The hunters could be at risk, and so the hillock was also known as the gap of danger, '*bearna baoghail*'. A fifteenth-century poem refers to the hero going to his 'mound of chase, his site of casting, and his gap of danger'.[47] There was room for more than one person on this mound: later in the same poem Cailte and Oisin are described as being with Fionn in order to protect him when the driven game arrived.[48] Boece was also familiar with this custom and describes the assassination of a king while he was waiting on his 'moitt [motte or hillock]' with only two others for the hunt to arrive.[49] Such hillocks linked to hunting are referred to in less legendary contexts in the twelfth century in a tale about Malcolm III which Ailred of Rievaulx heard from David I, and in the sixteenth-century tale of Alasdair Carrach already mentioned.[50] Given this background, it seems very unlikely that the king

[45]   There is evidence that women did shoot arrows at game while standing on the ground: *Queen Mary's Psalter*, fo. 172r. Elizabeth I shot game from a platform: Ferrière, *Chasses de François 1er*, 55–6.
[46]   *Oran na Comhachaig*, 81 Stanza 19. Creag Ghuanach is at NN299690.
[47]   Kuno Meyer (ed.), *Fianaigecht* (Dublin, 1910), 53 'The Chase of Sid Na Mban Finn'. The Gaelic spelling is taken from Watson, 'Deer and Boar', 86.
[48]   Elizabeth Fitzpatrick, '*Formail na Fiann*: Hunting Reserves and Assembly Places in Gaelic Ireland', *Proceedings of the Harvard Celtic Colloquium*, 32 (2012), 115; Watson, 'Deer and Boar', 81, 88; Meyer (ed.), *Fianaigecht*, 57; Wiseman, 'Chasing the Deer', 69, 83; Ronan Hennesy and Elizabeth Fitzpatrick, 'Finn's Seat: topographies of power and royal marchlands of Gaelic polities in medieval Ireland', *Landscape History*, 38 (2017), 29–62, at 45.
[49]   Bellenden, *Chronicles* (1938), i, 224; Boece, *Historiae* (1527), bk 6, fo.16v, line 75–fo. 17r, line 8, 'monticulum'.
[50]   Aelred of Rievaulx, *Epistola de Genealogia Regum Anglorum* in *Patrologia Cursus*

would have been adopting the passive role of spectator when the traditions all revolved round the lord leading the hunt and demonstrating his prowess as a hunter. The wait for the drive may have been more comfortable than in the twelfth century, but it still led to an active part in the killing. From the accounts which survive from the twelfth, fifteenth, and sixteenth centuries, the waiting hunters do not seem to have been on the other side of an enclosed elrick, nor on an artificial stand overlooking the kill zone. The chief hunters were in the midst of the action, trying either to encircle and kill the game or to shoot it as it rushed past. While they may no longer have been chasing the game, their role still required courage and skill.[51] It is, therefore, not surprising to find that such hillocks featured in at least two of Mary's hunts in Scotland.

To assist the drive, a trap called an elrick, *eileirg* in Gaelic, was used in Scotland in much the same way as *haies* were used in France and hays or *haga* in England (see Diagram 3).[52] The earliest surviving record of an elrick in Scotland is in 1020x29 when 'ind elerc' was granted to the monastery of Deer in the north-east of Scotland. Although there is some debate about the derivation of the word, a link with hunting and a deer trap or ambush is well established.[53] The word survives mainly in place-names but, apart from the above well-known record, the author has encountered no other example of its use in a medieval Scottish document or chronicle. Elrick place-names are scattered over most of Scotland with major concentrations in the central Highlands, the north-east and south-west, but not in Strathmore, Fife and the south-east.[54] There are no elrick place-names in Ireland, nor does the word occur in the Fionn literature, and so the name may be of Scottish origin. Consequently, while the link with deer hunting is not debated it is harder

---

Completus, ed. J. P. Migne, vol. 195 (Paris, 1855), 735; *Scottish Annals from English Chroniclers AD500–1286*, ed. Alan O. Anderson (London, 1908), 113–14; Watson, 'Deer and Boar', 88; *Oran na Comhachaig*, 77 stanza 8 where the Gaelic is *tuim shealga*; 87 stanza 40.

[51] The fifteenth-century accounts from Boece and the Holyrood Ritual book are mentioned above in nn. 32 and 33. The twelfth-century account from Ailred is in n. 48 above, and the sixteenth-century account from Lesley is in n. 37. The other sixteenth-century accounts from Pitscottie and Barclay are mentioned in Chapter 6, nn. 47, 66.

[52] W. J. Watson, *The History of the Celtic Place-Names of Scotland* (Edinburgh, 2011, orig. 1926), 489.

[53] Simon Taylor, 'The Toponymic Landscape of the Gaelic Notes on the Book of Deer', in Katherine Forsyth (ed.), *Studies on the Book of Deer* (Dublin, 2008), 275–308, at 296; Watson, *Celtic Place-Names*, 184, 489; F. Kelly, *Early Irish Farming*, Early Irish Law Series (Dublin, 1997), 277 n. 91.

[54] Michael Ansell, 'Place-Name Evidence for Woodland and Hunting in Galloway and Carrick', *Scottish Woodland History Group Notes*, 11 (2006), 3–10, at 7, prints the south-west section only. The full map is due to be published in T. O. Clancy *et al.* (eds), *Onomastications, A Festschrift for Simon Taylor* (Glasgow, forthcoming). In the south and east the words hay and deer fold or hunt fold may have been used instead: Piers Dixon and John M. Gilbert, 'Dormount Hope: medieval deer trap, park or hay?', *PSAS*, 150 (2021) 201–19, at 214–15, 217 n. 5.

HUNTING CULTURE, CONDITIONS, AND CONTEXTS

to determine exactly what an elrick was. Some elrick place-names relate to areas suited to trapping deer, but others refer to hills or mountains from which, presumably, the lord watched the hunt.[55] (See Map 7) This brings to mind an early eighteenth-century description of a how the highlanders used to hunt which was probably written by Edmund Burt, who worked with General Wade building military roads in the Highlands. The tinchell, according to this account, used to surround a hill and drive a deer upwards gradually closing in till the deer was trapped in a small circle and killed with swords.[56] One wonders if these 'elrick hills' were the locations for this kind of hunt. However, we are on less speculative ground in the late eighteenth century with the first written evidence specifically associated with elricks. James Robertson, in his description of the agriculture of Perthshire in 1799, recorded that, when deer were plentiful, people constructed large enclosures of stakes and brushwood which were high enough to stop deer jumping over them and which had only one opening. Large numbers of men with dogs then drove deer into these enclosures to be slaughtered. These enclosures, he wrote, were often overlooked by a rock or an outcrop from which people could watch the 'whole diversion'.[57] This is reminiscent of the hunt in the sixteenth-century poem *Oran na Comhachaig*:

> the rock [Creag Ghuanach] round which the hunt would circle
> Myself I loved to be roaming there
> where the voice of a sturdy hound was sweetest
> Sending the herd to the narrow trap [*ghabhail chumhann*].[58]

Interestingly, the word for elrick is not used for the narrow trap, although *eileirig* is used elsewhere in this poem to describe a feature seemingly linked to the shelter of deer, perhaps like a hollow: 'the hollow of the brown stag and the elrick of the fairy champions [deer]'; and 'the narrow elrick nurse of the calves and of the fawns'.[59] In 1926 W. J. Watson recorded that long ago he had been told that an '*eileag*' was a v-shaped deer trap which was open at both ends. Deer were driven in at the wide end and killed on their way through the funnel.[60] Whatever their name, various kinds of traps were used to catch driven deer.

The best-known example in Scotland of v-shaped funnels leading to traps

---

[55] Watson, 'Obair an t-Sealg', 163–5.

[56] *Letters from a Gentleman in the North of Scotland to his Friend in London* ... ed. R. Jamieson, 2 vols (London, 1818), ii, 68–70.

[57] James Robertson, *General View of the Agriculture of the County of Perth* (Perth, 1799), 328.

[58] *Oran na Comhachaig*, 79 stanza 14.

[59] *Eileirg* occurs only in the Maclagan Ms and not in any of the other sources of the poem, all of which are mid-eighteenth century in date: Patricia M. Menzies, '*Oran na Comhachaig*. A Study of Text and content', unpublished PhD thesis (University of Edinburgh, 2001), 33 stanza 9, 42 stanza 18; Wiseman, 'Chasing the Deer', 166.

[60] Watson, *The Celtic Place-Names of Scotland*, 489.

is on the island of Rum, where converging stone walls survive high on a ridge between the mountains of Ard Nev and Orval. They start wide apart at the top of the ridge and converge as they descend to a semicircular stone enclosure.[61] These walls are recorded in 1796 but are not mentioned by Donald Monro in 1549 when he described hunting in Rum.[62] He explained that hunting seats needed to be placed high in the hills because the tinchell would drive deer up the mountain. Presumably the deer were driven over the ridge and entered unexpectedly into the v-shaped formation of the dykes on the other side (see Diagram 3).

Comparisons

Some of these techniques used in Scotland when driving deer would have been unfamiliar to Mary when she arrived in Scotland. In sixteenth-century Scotland there were no lines of stationary *défenses* waiting to funnel game towards the waiting hunters. There is no record of hunting at the toils, nor of hunters confronting selected game within an enclosed kill zone. There is no mention of the construction of a stand outside the kill zone from which hunters, both male and female, could shoot at the trapped game. Mary would never previously have waited for deer as they appeared over a ridge above her, nor waited on foot with a bow and dogs in the line of driven deer, nor would she ever have encountered the use of hunting hillocks on the Gaelic pattern. These were techniques and customs which Mary would have had to learn.

Finally, it is noticeable that in Scotland, unlike France, the drive was considered to be more prestigious than the chase. In France, Phoebus and Ferrières considered that chasing stags was the finest form of the hunt, while driving was only for those who did not want the effort of chasing the game.[63] Phoebus, writing near the Pyrenees, recognised that some rough terrain where it was hard to ride after the hounds was unsuitable for *par force* hunting and so *défenses* had to be employed at these points to assist the chase.[64] The *par force* hunt was better suited to wooded spaces or rolling hills and plains such as are found in northern France and the Loire valley, whereas in mountainous areas with steep-sided valleys the drive was an easier and more effective method. Consequently, in France the *par force* hunt assumed priority and by the sixteenth century it was often referred to as hunting in the French style.[65] In Scotland, while chasing a single deer may have been a more common occurrence, it was the drive which Lesley described in some detail and which appears to have been conducted on an altogether grander

[61] *Canmore*, Id 21939 at NM34189928 and Id 21940 at NM23989868.
[62] *Monro's Western Isles of Scotland and Genealogies of the Clans 1549*, ed. R. W. Munro (Edinburgh, 1961), 66; OSAS, xvii, 275. The Rum entry dates to 1796.
[63] Phoebus, *Livre de Chasse*, 61–2, 195; Ferrières, *Roy Modus*, 107.
[64] Phoebus, *Livre de Chasse*, 195.
[65] Corvol, *Histoire de la Chasse*, 32.

HUNTING CULTURE, CONDITIONS, AND CONTEXTS

scale than coursing.[66] Because larger numbers of nobles attended such hunts, they required greater resources and organisation. The feasting following the hunt gave greater opportunities for the lord to share his hospitality, secure friendships, strengthen ties, and discuss policy, whether with kin or with others. In Scotland, therefore, while coursing may have been more common because it did not require large numbers of deer and manpower, the drive provided a greater display of the power of lordship. The continued popularity of the drive can also be attributed to the suitability of driving deer on foot in mountainous terrain and to the survival of sufficient numbers of deer in the Highlands to make it a worthwhile pursuit.

Attitudes

Whatever social and political importance hunting had, there is little doubt that, for the nobility, it was also a pastime. It is less clear whether their pastime contained any idea of fair play, which today would be regarded as an essential part of any sport. They undoubtedly respected nature, the seasons, and the natural reproductive cycle of the game. The timings of the hunting seasons were all determined for natural reasons to allow deer herds to thrive. A 'fence' month, a protected time, was established in July to ensure that fawning hinds were not disturbed. A close season for stags was observed in the winter to let them recover after the rut, and hinds were similarly protected in the summer to enable them to suckle their fawns. Phoebus expressed his dislike of the use of nets because it was, he said, a sport only for old or fat men and prelates involving little skill. He wanted deer to be killed with nobility and gentility, giving the deer what he saw as a fair chance befitting the status awarded to them by elite hunters.[67] Deer and other game were kept in reserves, protected, and allowed to reproduce, but only to ensure that there was a supply of game to hunt in future seasons and not for any idea of preserving a species. They may have been admired, their qualities respected, and attempts made to understand their behaviours and habits, but only insofar as was necessary to facilitate the nobles' pastime. There was no suggestion that it was in any way wrong for the nobility to hunt wild animals.[68] They were fair game. However, the importance attached to the *par force* hunt in France does suggest that the French nobility saw hunting as a sport. If the aim had been to kill game with maximum efficiency, drives and trapping would have been far more popular than the *par force* hunt. In Scotland the predominance

---

[66] Leslie, *Historie* (1596), 18–19.
[67] Phoebus, *Livre de Chasse*, 250–1.
[68] There was an idea that it was wrong for clergy to hunt: Gilbert, *Hunting and Hunting Reserves*, 72–3. In the sixteenth century humanists like Charles de Guise, cardinal of Lorraine, also did not approve of hunting: Stuart Carroll, *Martyrs and Murderers: The Guise Family and the Making of Europe* (Oxford, 2011), 63–4.

ELITE HUNTING CULTURE AND MARY, QUEEN OF SCOTS

of the drive suggests that it was the kill which mattered rather than the sport. This is highlighted by Robert Lindsay of Pitscottie, who wrote a history of Scotland in the 1570s in which he describes a conflict in which one side set an ambush for their enemies 'as they had been settand tinchellis for the murther of wyld beistes'.[69] In Pitscottie's mind this was war, not sport.

Nonetheless there were some signs in Scotland of customs which seem to be derived from what we would now call fair play. In the early sixteenth century, when Boece described the society of the early Scots he created a semi-mythical hunters' paradise which clearly adopted ideas of fair play. Like Phoebus, he despised the use of nets and camouflage and had a mythical king legislate that hares should not be killed when they were lying down at rest but were to be hunted and killed only when being chased by dogs. This king also ordered that if a hare outran the hounds for a certain length of time it should be allowed to go free. Deer hunting was to be banned in winter when there was snow on the ground and deer had to come down to the lower slopes to find food. This king did not want to see such practices destroy the 'honorabill game of hunting, quhilk wes ordanit for his [the king's] nobillis and gentill men'.[70] This was not all a figment of Boece's imagination. In 1401 parliament had enacted that hares should not be killed when there was snow on the ground, and in 1474 this was extended to red deer and roe deer, while fawns were not to be slain until they were a year old.[71]

As in France, such ideas of fair play and sport did not extend to becoming a concern for animal rights. What did exist in some areas was an awareness of the unity of nature. Gaelic literature shows a respect for the deer, for nature, for the seasons, and for the countryside. This is seen in *Oran na Comhachaig* where the speaker expresses his joy at looking after a herd of deer on the hill and then describes the life of a hind with admiration and tenderness.[72] In similar vein, in a twelfth-century poem about Arran the poet describes 'Arran of the many deer' with its mountains, its hills, and its trees. Because the poet regarded the flora, the fauna, and man as one he mentions man's activities with no more attention or prominence than he gives to the deer and the oak trees.[73] Scottish monarchs from the fourteenth to the sixteenth centuries were still in touch with Gaelic hunting culture and it is possible that some of this attitude may have passed on to them. However, one cannot read too much into any inklings of a sense of fair play. While in a course skill may have mattered more than the kill, that was not the case in drives, and it was drives which were the more highly valued events. The chronicles frequently

---

[69] Pitscottie, *Historie*, i, 56.

[70] Boece, *Historiae* (1527) bk 5, fo. 35r lines 21–39; bk 6, fos 16v line 75–17r line 8; Bellenden, *Chronicles* (1838) i, 205, 229. This quote is from Bellenden's print edition: Bellenden, *History* (1821), i, 186.

[71] *RPS*, 1401/2/14, 1474/5/16.

[72] *Oran na Comhachaig*, 82.

[73] 133 Thomas Owen Clancy (ed.), *The Triumph Tree, Scotland's Earliest Poetry 550–1350* (Edinburgh, 1998), 187.

record the number of animals killed, implying that the more animals that were killed, the more successful the hunt.

In France and Scotland as in much of Western Europe these methods were confined to the elite. Only the elite could afford to own and maintain the necessary packs of hounds, retain kennel staff, own horses with the stamina to withstand a long chase, and ensure a supply of food for all their animals. Only the elite could provide the manpower to set up the toils or provide a tinchell, and only the elite possessed the land on which to create hunting reserves. This exclusivity was also embodied in the growing limitation of the right to hunt in the sixteenth century.

Hunting rights

Hunting rights comprised three different but related elements: who could hunt, what animals could be hunted by whom, and where the hunter was entitled to hunt. Of these the most important was the possession of the basic right to hunt, which was by no means universal in the medieval period. Secondly, those with that right needed to know which animals they were allowed to hunt, since not everyone was entitled to hunt all game. Finally, there was little point in being entitled to hunt even the least of the small game if there was no land or territory on which the hunter was permitted to hunt.

The Roman law principle of *res nullius* (the things of no one), which applied to game in both Scotland and France, meant that no one owned the deer on their land. Therefore, under the principle of *occupatio* (taking possession) the game belonged to the person who killed it, regardless of where or on whose land it was killed.[74] Since the first creation of royal hunting reserves in the mid-seventh century this right had gradually become more limited as the extent of the areas where lords held exclusive hunting rights increased. While nobles might control who hunted in their reserves, the principle of *res nullius* did continue to have some currency, because when game entered a lord's reserve it did not become his property but had to be free to leave – unless, of course, the lord lured it into his park. In the early fourteenth century in France nobles could arrange permission to hunt from their own lands on to those of their neighbours, and they would presumably have been allowed to take possession of some or all of the kill.[75] Likewise, in Scotland the medieval forest law allowed hunters to chase game from their own lands into a royal forest.[76] In both countries nobles could hunt greater game in their own reserves, but non-nobles were not allowed to hunt greater game at all and in France after 1396 they could not hunt even lesser game without

[74] *The Institutes of Justinian*, eds John T. Abdy and Brian Walker (Cambridge, 1876), 82 Section II Part I chapt. 12; Gilbert, *Hunting and Hunting Reserves*, 5, 11, 228.
[75] Michel Devèze, *La Vie de la Forêt Française au XVI Siècle*, 2 vols (Paris, 1961), i, 65; Jullien, *La Chasse*, 106–7.
[76] Gilbert, *Hunting and Hunting Reserves*, 305–6 laws 14 and 15.

permission.[77] In Scotland, nobles who held land heritably by charter had the right to hunt as did, free men below that rank, those who rented land but could not pass it on from father to son. This latter group were probably allowed to hunt only lesser game. By the fifteenth century, landholders were increasingly preventing others from entering their lands for this purpose.[78] The sixteenth century saw an increase in feu-ferme tenure, where the tenant paid rent but could also pass the land on from father to son. As the numbers of those who must have felt entitled to hunt grew, the pressure on the nobles' hunting reached the point in 1621 where parliament enacted that only those who held a ploughgate of land heritably were allowed to hunt, otherwise they were subject to a penalty of £100.[79]

Management and governance

To enjoy their exclusive rights, kings created forests and nobles exploited hunting reserves which their families had created in time past or which had been granted to them by the king. In France by the sixteenth century these hunting reserves were called *garennes*, but there were also *buissons*, which were thickets used for driving game, maybe hundreds of square metres in size, and *breuils* or parks where game were held captive with banks, ditches, walls, or fences. *Forêts* by this time referred to large wooded areas which might or might not contain *garennes*. In 1516, however, Francis I decided to limit hunting in royal wooded forests to the Crown and so, in effect, turned these royal woodlands into hunting reserves.[80] In Scotland both 'forrest' in the vernacular and *foresta* in Latin normally meant a hunting reserve, an area where hunting was reserved and which could contain moorland, heath, mountains, and fields as well as woods. By the sixteenth century, however, both words were increasingly being used to describe areas of woodland. The king might also grant free forest rights to a noble which entitled him to create his own hunting reserves, or he might grant free warren rights which conveyed control

[77] Salvadori, 'François 1er et le Droit de Chasse', 46; Jullien, *La Chasse*, 115; Gilbert, *Hunting and Hunting Reserves*, 210, 230–1.

[78] Gilbert, *Hunting and Hunting Reserves*, 230; *Quoniam Attachiamenta*, ed. T. D. Fergus, Stair Society, 44 (1996), 196–7, c34. The author originally thought that this clause of *Quoniam Attachiamenta* also applied to unfree men and that they too were entitled to hunt. Such an interpretation is not borne out by the Scottish Forest Laws 2, 3 and 13 which establish a hierarchy of free men: firstly those who held land by heritable charter; secondly a group called anyone, *aliquis*, and thirdly bondmen. Neyfs or serfs were not free. These laws can be seen in Gilbert, *Hunting and Hunting Reserves*, 304–5.

[79] 139 RPS, 1621/6/43; Norman Macdougall, *James IV* (East Linton, 1997), 156–7, 159; Jane E. A. Dawson, *Scotland Reformed 1488–1587* (Edinburgh, 2007), 174, 182. A ploughgate was around 8 oxgangs of around 13 acres each – approx. 104 acres: A. A. M. Duncan, *Scotland: The Making of the Kingdom* (Edinburgh, 1975), 92.

[80] Duceppe Lamarre, *Chasse et Pâturage*, 145–6; Jullien, *La Chasse*, 157.

HUNTING CULTURE, CONDITIONS, AND CONTEXTS

only over the hunting of lesser game.[81] In both these grants the grantee was entitled to impose the full royal forfeiture of £10 on offenders, which theoretically meant that the king or his sheriff would help him collect the penalty.[82] This was a huge sum in the twelfth and thirteenth centuries and was clearly intended to prevent barons starting a hunt in someone else's reserve.

To maintain an unenclosed hunting reserve required careful conservation of the game and its habitat. These tasks, which involved considerable effort and formed the less glamorous groundwork behind the excitement of the chase, show how hunting involved aspects of governance which could impact upon most of the population. The action taken to preserve the flora and fauna focussed on programmes of management but also revolved around penalties against wood-cutting and poaching, both of which were major problems in France and Scotland.

Francis I in 1516 established that if anyone was caught poaching greater game the punishment would vary from 250 *livres tournois* on the first offence to death on the fourth offence, but there are few examples of the death penalty ever being imposed.[83] For lesser game the fine varied from 20 *livres* or one month's imprisonment for the first offence to whipping and banishment to a distance of at least fifteen leagues from the reserve for the third offence. Those who bought game from poachers were to suffer the same penalties, and if anyone brought a hound into the forest off the leash it would be maimed. Francis was also fairly successful in trying to encourage lords who had forests, *buissons*, and *garennes* to apply the same regulations to their reserves.[84] In Scotland the basic penalty for poaching in royal and private forests was still £10, but Regent Arran in 1551 had added the death penalty for anyone using guns to hunt deer, whether they were poaching or not.[85]

The maintenance of herds of game was also supported by the observance of hunting seasons and of a fence month, but in parks further measures could be taken. In Scotland there are references to feeding deer in winter and trapping foxes, which could prey on young deer calves and on wild fowl.[86] Areas of pasture suitable for deer could be extended both by having cattle crop the rough grasses, leaving finer grass for the fallow deer to graze, and by opening meadows for deer to graze after the hay had been cut.[87] In France

---

[81] Gilbert, *Hunting and Hunting Reserves*, 13, 20–3, 208–10.

[82] Alice Taylor, *The Shape of the State in Medieval Scotland 1124–1290* (Oxford, 2016), 153–4.

[83] *Livre tournois* (pounds of Tour). Coins had been minted in several places in France but the lighter coinage minted in Tours became the basis of the national currency in the thirteenth century. Salvadori, 'François 1er et le Droit de Chasse', 49.

[84] Salvadori, 'François 1er et le Droit de Chasse', 48–9, 56. Devèze, *La Vie de la Forêt*, ii, 64–6; *Ordonnances Des Rois De France; Règne de François I* (Paris, 1902), part 1, 350–3.

[85] Forest Law 13 in Gilbert, *Hunting and Hunting Reserves*, 99, 305; *RPS*, 1504/3/30 and 1551/5/3.

[86] *RMS*, viii, no. 826; *ER*, xii, 288, 448, 528; NRAS, *Scone Palace*, MS 776 (Mansfield Papers), Bundle 1853.

[87] John M Gilbert, 'Falkland Park to c.1603', *TAFAJ*, 19–20 (2014), 69–77, at 88, 92.

within large wooded forests like Retz, which lay around the chateau of Villers Cotterêts, sizeable enclosures of around 42ha were created to act as nurseries where game could be fed and protected and then released into the forest.[88] Both within and outwith deer parks and enclosures it was essential to prevent the overgrazing of pasture by limiting the access of domestic livestock. This limitation was also an essential part of managing woodland.

Deer required a habitat with woods, thickets, grazing, and water, all of which needed to be managed if the deer herd was to survive. Consequently, the ecology of the area had to be altered to suit this particular purpose. Managing woodland was an essential but difficult part of managing a hunting reserve because woods were the major natural resource of the middle ages and there were a huge variety of demands made on them. They provided wood for numerous industrial and domestic uses: from bark for tanning to charcoal for iron-smelting, from spoons for the table to rafters for cathedrals, and for almost everything else in between. Woodlands also provided pasture for livestock as well as being a habitat for the game which the aristocracy wanted to hunt. Grazing and hunting were the two main activities which led to the interaction of men and animals in woodlands, but the people involved had very different goals. In terms of wood, the lord would be looking for a supply of large timbers to construct high-status buildings, while the tenants' main demand would be for the smaller material also referred to as wood. This smaller wood was used for fencing, for agricultural equipment such as harrows and ploughs, for housing, for fuel, and for domestic utensils. The lord liked to hunt both in high forest where tall standard trees grew with room to ride among them and in thickets where deer could shelter, and so he saw the woodlands primarily as his hunting grounds. For that reason, he wished to maintain the woodlands to harbour certain of the wild fauna, such as deer and boar, which lived there. His tenants, on the other hand, wanted to graze cattle, pigs, sheep, and goats in the woods and to clear areas of the forest for agriculture. The forest and its fauna could not withstand unfettered exercise of all these activities. Clearly if the lords wished their tenants to thrive and provide them with labour or rent, they had nothing to gain by limiting the use of the woods solely to their hunting, and so various management practices emerged to try to balance the demands of the different users.

In France, after a period in the fifteenth century when the supply of wood had been able to meet demand, the population in the early sixteenth century started to grow and the issues became acute. Towns like Paris and Rouen suffered from wood shortages, and farmers were again starting to make clearances in forests for agriculture.[89] The story was different in Scotland, where

---

[88] René Collery, 'Evolution de la Forêt de Retz à travers les Âges', *Société Historique Regionale De Villers Cotterêts* (1963), 151–75, at 153. Available at: http://www.histoireaisne. fr/memoires_numerises/chapitres/tome_09/Tome_009_page_151.pdf [accessed 31 August 2019].

[89] Duceppe-Lamarre, *Chasse et Pâturage*, 19, 90, 123; Devèze, *Histoire des Forêts*, 47–9.

there had been shortages of timber since the fourteenth century.[90] Managing these demands raised issues of conservation and sustainability which went far beyond the maintenance of an elite hunting ground. The basics of woodland management were well understood in both France and Scotland, but the legislation of the Scottish parliament was not so clear cut or prescriptive as that of Francis I. In his 1516 ordinance, Francis broke new ground by combining regulations for the hunt with provision for the management of his woods and forests. He was trying to establish a rota of coppicing which was geared to the production of timber as well as the production of the smaller rods and poles which the mass of the population required. When timber merchants were cutting an area of woodland they were required to leave eight to ten young trees per acre (0.4ha) to grow into mature timber trees. If they did not do so they would be fined. The coppice cycle for rods and poles was to be at least ten years. After felling, beasts were not to be allowed into the area until the new tree shoots were large enough to survive grazing animals.[91] In 1544 the ordinance of Henry II (r. 1547–59), the first in France to mention coppices, *taillis* by name, ordered that standard trees should be at least forty years old, but ideally one hundred years old, before felling. He wanted woods to contain high forest in the centre and coppices around the edges. The felling of a complete section or *coupe* of a wood was recommended rather than selectively felling trees of a certain size or age throughout the forest. If a complete *coupe* was felled the assumption was that the old, lesser-quality wood would be removed along with the good wood, thus giving room for new growth throughout the whole of the *coupe*.[92] These ordinances were intended to operate nationwide, not just on the royal domain.

In Scotland the parliament of James V concentrated on limiting the felling of young wood because very little was being left to grow into timber trees. Planting was also encouraged, but no attempt was made to define the length of the coppice cycle for rods and poles or for timber, thus presumably allowing for greater flexibility in different growing conditions. In June 1535 parliament enacted that any lord with £100 worth of land should plant three acres of woods in the next planting season and construct enclosures around their plantations to protect young shoots from grazing animals. The onus for planting was now clearly placed on the lord to ensure that planting occurred and was not simply passed off to the tenant. The penalty for cutting or peeling bark from young trees was increased with each offence from £10, to £20, to the death penalty, which seems somewhat draconian but presumably was aimed at landed offenders in the hope of raising more money by way of remissions.[93] More significantly, however, parliament legislated that

---

[90] John M. Gilbert, 'Woodland Management in Medieval Scotland', *PSAS*, 146 (2016), 242–3.
[91] *Ordonnances Des Rois de France: Regne de François 1er*, i, 360 clause 37, 372 clause 72; John L. Reed, *Forests of France* (London, 1954), 38ff.
[92] Devèze, *La Vie de la Forêt*, ii, 177.
[93] 153 *RPS*, 1535/17. Remissions for offences against the vert and venison were relatively

the king could arrange annual inquisitions to determine whether this law was being observed. Parliament also established that enforcement was the responsibility not of the local lords but of the sheriff or whoever held a royal commission to take action on wood-cutting.[94] While these arrangements applied to the country as a whole, James V was the first monarch to produce more detailed parliamentary legislation relating particularly to royal forests in an effort to improve their provision for hunting. Head foresters had to produce the charters granting them their office and they had to follow the king's instructions concerning the keeping of the forests. No cattle, sheep, or horses were to be grazed in royal forests and any found there were to be confiscated and divided between the king and his forester. James then proceeded to encourage private holders of woods and forests to exact similar penalties for illegal grazing in their reserves.[95] In his efforts to improve the supply of wood and timber in the public interest James continued to make free forest grants but to limit many of them solely to wooded areas. This followed the practice of James IV (r. 1488–1513), but James V's charters, more frequently than in the past, itemised the existence of forest courts to manage these woods.[96]

Enforcing these rules was no easy matter, and in France many royal officials were reluctant to do so.[97] What Francis I wanted most was the facility to hunt around his favoured royal residences, and so he started to improve the management of these reserves by appointing more keepers to catch poachers and by creating *capitaineries des chasses* (captaincies of hunts) at Fontainebleau in 1534, Senart in 1539, and Chambord in 1542.[98] This was not popular because the areas covered by these *capitaineries* included the holdings of other proprietors who, consequently, were banned from hunting or cutting wood freely on their own lands. Because the *maîtres des eaux et forêts* (masters of waters and forests) were corrupt and slow to implement the law, Francis transferred cases relating to poaching to provost marshals who carried out summary justice on the spot. Henry II, who was as determined as

---

common in Ettrick Forest in 1460s and 1470s: Gilbert, *Hunting and Hunting Reserves*, 165–8, 174. Despite legislation in James III's reign the practice continued: *ER*, viii, 587. Although there are no similar surviving records of remissions for offences against the *vert* and *venison* during Arran's governorship it seems likely that they would have continued, given his liking of the revenue which they produced: Amy Blakeway, *Regency in Sixteenth Century Scotland* (Woodbridge, 2015), 166. For procedures of remissions and compositions see Jackson W. Armstrong, 'The Justice Ayre in the Border Sheriffdoms 1493–1498' *SHR*, 92 (2013), 1–37 at 30–1.

[94] Richard Oram, 'Public Policy and Private Practice: Production, Management and Development of Scotland's Woodland Resources from the 12th to 17th Centuries', NWDG *Scottish Woodland History Conference 2016: Notes*, 21 (2022) 1–7, at 5–6.

[95] *RPS*, 1535/18.

[96] E.g., *RMS*, iii, nos 27, 679, 801, 1156 and NRS C2/22 no. 46; *RMS*, iii, no. 2400 and C2/28/1 no.154; *RMS*, iii, no. 1596 and C2/25 no.307; *RMS*, iii, no. 2170 and C2/27 no. 64. There are at least 34 such grants.

[97] Jullien, *La Chasse*, 156.

[98] Salvadori, 'François 1er et la Droit de Chasse', 52–4.

Francis to deal with poachers, confirmed these arrangements. To control the recognised rights of *routiers* (commoners) to use his woods, Francis employed the idea of inquests or *reformations*. Such inquests had started in the fourteenth century as a result of an ordinance in 1341 and Francis continued to use them in his own forests, but after 1535 he applied them to his lords' lands as well.[99] Commissions of foresters and members of local *parlements* were sent into royal and private forests to check documents, to establish the rights to which people were entitled, to hear complaints, to repress abuses, to take back areas of forest wrongly cleared, and to apply the law. Francis did more than any of his predecessors to implement these ordinances on the ground and he was successful in preventing the destruction of many woodlands.[100] Henry II confirmed most of the legislation of Francis I and continued the practice of holding *reformations* in forests which he particularly wanted in good condition for hunting such as Loches, Amboise, Chinon, and Fontainebleau. They focussed on controlling rights of use, extending the bounds of the forest, and ensuring that high forest was not turned into coppices for the smaller wood. The foresters were then required to monitor the quality of the woods which were being turned from high forest into coppice to ensure that the process did not destroy the high forest.[101]

In Scotland in the sixteenth century peripatetic commissioners of Crown lands and the resident *ballivi ad extra*, bailies in charge of an area of royal lands, had to ensure that woods and hunting forests were being maintained. The commissioners held courts in which they leased lands to tenants, tried poachers and cases of illegal grazing, and collected fines. In 1499 in Ettrick Forest, in a manner reminiscent of the French *reformations*, they enquired into poaching, the destruction of young wood, grazing of pigs and goats, and those who used wood for industrial purposes such as tanners, charcoal burners, turners, and coopers.[102] On occasion, circuit judges called justice ayres might also enquire into the cutting of young wood and impose fines, but there is no surviving record of any work carried out by the proposed annual inquisitions relating to the planting of trees.[103]

In both France and Scotland local tenants were encouraged to play their part in the maintenance of the *vert* and *venison*. In 1550 Henry II decided to trust local villagers in and around the park of Chambord to guard the park, stop illegal breaches of the walls, and control poaching. If they did not carry out these duties they were to be held responsible for any offences

---

[99] Devèze, *La Vie de la Forêt*, i, 66 ; ii, 93.

[100] Devèze, *Histoire des Forêts*, 50.

[101] Devèze, *La Vie de la Forêt*, i, 258.

[102] John M. Gilbert, 'The Statutes of Ettrick Forest', Stair Society *Miscellany II* (Edinburgh, 1984), 41–60, at 53 clause 7; *ER*, xi, 393 clauses 9, 14, 16.

[103] NRS RH2/1/6 (Justice Eyre Journal Books for 1508), fo. 144 gives the points of dittay for 1508; Robert Pitcairn (ed.), *Criminal Trials in Scotland from 1488 to 1624*, 3 vols (Edinburgh, 1933), i, part 1, 66.

and be fined accordingly.[104] Such a system of tenant-foresters was also used in several places in Scotland such as the forest of Boyne and Enzie, and the lands of the abbeys of Arbroath and Coupar Angus, but it is the royal forest of Ettrick which gives the best example of how this system operated.[105] The tenants of Ettrick Forest were expected to keep their steads or holdings 'forest-like', which meant that they had to protect the wood and the deer and limit ploughing to recognised areas. Failure to do so could and did result in loss of lease, and in the late fifteenth century fines for grazing, wood-cutting, and poaching were imposed, although many were remitted.[106] The efficacy of this system was adversely affected by the introduction of feu-ferme tenure to Ettrick by James IV. It gave tenants a hereditary right to their lands in return for a greatly increased rent; but many of these feu-ferme grants also gave the tenants the freedom to plough and to sublet, along with freedom from the forest courts.[107] While not all leases were so generous, it is clear that this stress on finance rendered the maintenance of Ettrick as a hunting reserve impossible, and James V's hunt at Catslack in Ettrick in August 1525 is the last known royal hunt within the bounds of the forest.[108]

The growth of royal authority in sixteenth-century Scotland has been linked to an expanding bureaucracy, to the predominance of central instruction over the customs of local nobility, and to the ability of royal bureaucracy to influence behaviour across the entire country.[109] There can be little doubt that regulations on hunting, wood-cutting, and grazing around royal and private forests had the potential to impact on the majority of the population. The historian, therefore, must try to determine the extent to which hunting contributed to this extension of royal authority over local society in Scotland. Matters that had previously been the focus of attention within forests were now also being tackled outside forests by the commissioners of royal lands, by justices-on-ayre, and, potentially, by the proposed tree-planting inquisitions. Dealing with thefts of wood and deer was now a matter of public policy and it was no longer left entirely to local lords to initiate action. The lords sitting in parliament were familiar with these problems, and so parliament had expanded its role by legislating to improve woodland management, to control stalking, and to ban hunting with guns. This legislation was intended to operate throughout the country and was not to be dependent on the whim of particular lords. However, it has been suggested that parliament's laws were

---

[104] Monique Chatenet, *Chambord* (Paris, 2001), 139.

[105] Gilbert 'Woodland Management in Medieval Scotland', 246.

[106] Gilbert, 'The Statutes of Ettrick Forest, 1499', 52–3, 57; *ER*, xi, 460; Gilbert, *Hunting and Hunting Reserves*, 165–8.

[107] *RSS*, i, e.g., nos 1858, 1859, 1867, 1872.

[108] *Excerpta e Libris Domicilii Jacobi Quinti* (Edinburgh, 1836), 3. Mary's hunting in Traquair is discussed in Chapter 7, but she may have made incursions into the lands of Ettrick Forest.

[109] Julian Goodare, *The Government of Scotland 1560–1625* (Oxford, 2004), 195–6, 283–5.

not meant to be fully enforced but were enacted as 'enabling legislation' so that they could be enforced when required.[110] In the context of poaching and woodland management, such an approach to enforcement would inevitably lead to a reduction in the size of deer herds and in the supply of timber. In this context, therefore, it can be argued that while the laws may have operated as enabling legislation, that cannot have been the intention of the legislators.

The government, however, simply did not have the administrative or coercive capacity to stop these activities either on a permanent or on a countrywide basis. Attempts to control poaching in royal forests were much greater in those reserves where the king wanted to hunt. Hence the stern reminders to the foresters of Glenfinglas in 1508 and of Glenartney in 1518 to carry out their most basic duties.[111] Attempts by the government to enforce regulations on illegal felling were, so far as the surviving evidence tells, intermittent to say the least, amounting to one justice ayre in 1510. In the late fifteenth and sixteenth centuries an active landlord such as Coupar Angus abbey or an active royal administration as in Ettrick Forest must have increased their tenants' awareness of the wishes of royal government, but this was not a nationwide experience.

It has been suggested that in parts of Europe there was no need for legislation on wood-cutting because there was a plentiful supply of wood and, consequently, it is argued that the true purpose of such laws was to extend central bureaucracy and state control. Problems with wood supply arose because of the difficulty of transporting wood at a reasonable price to where it was needed and not because of any overall shortage. The purpose of these laws on wood-cutting, therefore, was not primarily to protect woodlands. When such laws were passed, it is said, they had alarmist and lengthy preambles trying to justify what could be seen as unnecessary legislation.[112] There were only two possible examples of such preambles in Scottish legislation, but both are very brief, one relating to wood-cutting in 1504 and the other to guns in 1551. Neither shows any signs of being a cover for a desire to extend the bureaucracy. The act of 1504 increasing the penalties for cutting young wood considered, wrongly, that the 'wod of Scotlande is uterlie destroyit', and the 1551 act which banned hunting with guns considered that all wild animals and wild fowl 'ar exilit and banist' by the use of guns, which again was clearly not the case.[113] Otherwise, the acts dealing with wood-cutting and poaching were all very matter of fact and were tackling real practical situations and shortages. Although wood shortages in Scotland were to a certain extent local, there was no suggestion that the aim of the Scottish legislation was to expand the Crown's bureaucracy. Their primary aim was to improve the

[110] Goodare, *The Government of Scotland 1560–1625*, 120.
[111] *RSS*, i, no.1637; NRS GD160/528/9.
[112] Warde, *Ecology and State Formation*, 2, 162–7; Warde, 'Fear of wood shortage', 34, 39, 41–3.
[113] 173 *RPS*, 1504/3/33, A1551/5/3.

supply of wood for all throughout the country and to maintain the supply of deer for royal hunting by controlling relevant behaviours, but it was an aim they were never able to realise. Nevertheless, this aim did have an effect on the role of government.

Since the thirteenth century localised systems had been in place to control hunting in royal and private reserves and to manage woodland throughout the country, but by the sixteenth century, as we have seen, attempts were being made to replace this localised control with central regulation and central enforcement. Many of the nobles who had power in the localities supported these attempts when working as commissioners of royal lands, as royal bailies, or as justices on ayre and when passing legislation in parliament. Not unreasonably, therefore, the Crown must have expected their co-operation not only when they were acting as royal officials but also when they were acting as private landlords. Where this worked best, of course, was when royal and private interests coincided, as is evidenced by the number of cases of illegal woodcutting brought to the justice ayres of James IV in 1510. Together the inquisitions into tree planting, the inquests of the commissioners of Crown lands, the points of dittay of justice ayres, and the attempts to have similar penalties applied in both private and royal woods and reserves mark a distinct departure from the localised medieval past. However, the intention to treat these matters on a nationwide basis for the public good was only partially realised. Whatever these countrywide regulations contributed to the wider effectiveness of royal government in Scotland was a result of accidental evolution rather than planned development.

2

A hunting education

Mary's departure to France on 29 July, 1548 resulted from the political, territorial, and religious ambitions of the Tudor and Valois dynasties. In 1543 Henry VIII (r. 1509–47) promoted the idea of a marriage between Mary and his son Edward, an alliance which the governor of Scotland, James Hamilton, earl of Arran, initially supported. Henry VIII pursued this alliance by releasing those Scottish lords whom he had captured at Solway Moss in 1542, the so called 'assured lords', on condition that they argued for this English marriage for Mary. However, under the influence of Cardinal Beaton, archbishop of St Andrews, Arran soon returned to James V's more traditional policy of the 'Auld Alliance' with France. The ensuing struggle known as the 'Rough Wooing' led to English invasions of the south-east of Scotland, during which Henry VIII attempted unsuccessfully to beat the Scots into submission. After Henry's death in 1547 Protector Somerset, regent for Edward VI, inflicted a heavy defeat on the Scots at the battle of Pinkie. He then pursued a policy of military occupation and created an English pale in order to further what was now openly proclaimed as a Protestant British union. Despite its attractions to reformers, most Scots did not support such a union and so Arran turned to France for aid. The death of Francis I and the accession of his son Henry II in 1547 rendered French intervention in Scotland more likely. Marie de Guise, Mary's mother, was still politically active in Scotland and she hoped to maintain Scotland's pro-French-Catholic stance. Her brothers, François duke of Guise and Charles cardinal of Lorraine, used their influence with Henry to persuade him to support their sister's position in Scotland. When the Scots asked Henry for assistance he realised the dynastic possibilities of such a marriage and spared no expense in its pursuit. He sent a fleet and troops to Scotland, recaptured St Andrews Castle from the reformers who had seized it, and provided lavish pensions to secure the support of key Scottish nobles. As English power in Scotland collapsed, the Scottish parliament met at Haddington on 7 July, 1548 and accepted the offer of a French marriage for Mary and agreed that she should be sent to France to be educated there.[1]

Henry II placed great value on this marriage because Mary had a strong claim to the throne of England through her grandmother Margaret Tudor, sister of Henry VIII and wife of James IV. Indeed, when Mary arrived at St

---

[1] This summary is taken from Dawson, *Scotland Reformed*, 162–73 and Marcus Merriman, *The Rough Wooings: Mary Queen of Scots, 1542–1551* (East Linton, 2000), 224–5, 245, 260–3, 295–6.

Germain-en-Laye outside Paris on 16 October, Henry wanted her to be given precedence over his own children since she was already a queen. Her companions there were Francis, the dauphin (1544–60), Élisabeth (1545–68), who married Philip II of Spain in 1559, and Claude (1547–75), who became duchess of Lorraine, and it was with these older children that Mary learned about hawking and hunting.[2] They were brought up in a variety of royal palaces, such as Villers-Cotterêts and Fontainebleau, which had been embellished and extended by Francis I and which were attached to either a forest, a park, or both. Henry II favoured St Germain-en-Laye, Fontainebleau, Blois, Villers Cotterêts, and Compiègnes. He also visited Amboise and frequented the chateau of his mistress Diane de Poitiers at Anet.

In the sixteenth century the palace at Blois was surrounded by three forests, Blois immediately to the west of the palace, Russy across the Loire from the palace, and Boulogne also on the south side of the Loire where Francis I had built Chambord (Map 1). In 1528 the Venetian ambassador described the forest of Blois as 11 leagues (44km) long by 4 leagues (16km) wide, full of deer, and containing several smaller lodges or pleasure houses which were used when hunting in the forest.[3] To the west of the chateau lay the gardens and an alley of four rows of elms about 2km in length through which hunting parties rode in the shade to reach the hunt.[4] Farther west, the forest of Amboise was well maintained by Francis and Henry, who had both organised *reformations* there (see Map 2). Chenonceau, which was held by Diane de Poitiers from 1547 to 1559 lay on the north bank of the river Cher and its park lay to the north of the palace.[5] In Mary's time the forest of Amboise was the main hunting ground in the vicinity of both Amboise and Chenonceau.

Villers Cotterêts had reputedly been in the centre of a royal hunting ground since the time of the Merovingians in the seventh century, and in the sixteenth century it was surrounded by the forests of Retz, Laigue, and Compiègne.[6] They formed a large expanse of woodland where those areas which were important for hunting were placed in defence and protected. At a rough estimate, out of the three forests four-fifths were kept for hunting, a total of around 25,000ha, and only one fifth of the forest area was open to various rights of use by local villages and farms.[7] *Maîtres des eaux et forêts* managed the whole area from the thirteenth to the sixteenth century until Francis I set up a *capitainerie* at Villers Cotterêts. He cut the first ride through the forest of Retz, including the Allée Royale, to improve access through the

---

[2]   Gobry, *François II*, 24; Guy, *My Heart is My Own*, 45–6.

[3]   Chatenet, 'Un portrait du "père des veneurs "', 53.

[4]   Jacques Androuet Du Cerceau, *Les Plus Excellents Bastiments de France*, 2 vols (Paris, 1579), ii, fo. 3r.

[5]   Du Cerceau, *Bastiments de France*, ii, fo. 9r; *Les Triomphes Faictz a L'Entrée du Roy a Chenonceau Le Dymanche Dernier Jour de Mars* (Tours, 1559), 8, printed in *Inventaires de Meubles Bijoux et Livres estant a Chenonceau le huit Janvier MCCIII* (Paris, 1856).

[6]   Anne-Marie Bocquillon, 'Au Moyen Âge, vénerie royale et administrations forestières', in Corvol (ed.), *Forêt et Chasse Xe–XXe siècle*, 113–26, at 115.

[7]   Bocquillon, 'Au moyen âge, vénerie royale', 115–16.

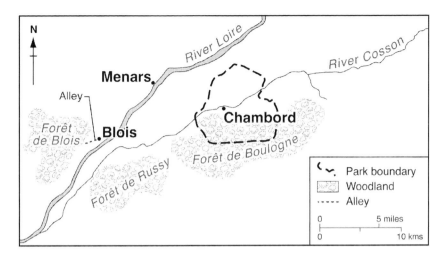

Map 1 Blois and Chambord.

forest for both hunters and spectators.[8] In the sixteenth century gardens lay close to the palace on its north and west sides and beyond them lay the park and the forest.[9]

The designed landscapes around royal chateaux were not identical, but parks and forests emphasised the hunting environment of these palaces. In the early sixteenth century, while the design of the forest, such as it was, could have been influenced by the requirements of maintaining high forest and protecting coppices and thickets, more advanced design was beginning to appear with the creation of long, straight alleys or rides. These were the palaces and parks where Mary was being raised and where she learned to hunt. She did not often accompany the court before she acquired her own household, but she still spent much of her time in the royal chateaux at St Germain, Villers Cotterêts, and, especially, Blois, though Amboise and Anet also figured in her itinerary.[10] Over the next ten years, Mary not only learned to hunt but observed the roles which elite women could fulfil when hunting.

Education at the French court

Mary's education was based on the liberal education of the humanists, which focussed on the *bonae litterae* (good letters/literature) of classical and other writers but was mixed with elements of the traditional training of princes which centred on activities such as hunting and military exercises. The prac-

[8] Collery, 'Evolution de la Forêt de Retz', 153.
[9] Du Cerceau, *Bastiments de France*, ii, fo. 4r, Illustrations 18 and 19.
[10] Ruble, *La Première Jeunesse*, 253–7.

ticalities of rulership and governance do not seem to have been taught as such, but had to be extrapolated from the literature and garnered from conversations, advice, and observations.[11] The necessary focus of Mary's early education was on French language and literature and the protocols of the French court. By 1554 she had progressed to studying Latin, but it has been argued that she was never fluent in that language.[12] Nonetheless the prepared speech which she delivered to the court in Latin in 1555 argued that women should have a knowledge of the classics and good literature.[13] There is some dubiety about her ability to reason and argue convincingly off the cuff on political matters, but, given time to prepare, she could certainly give a convincing performance.[14] Overall, the evidence suggests that Mary preferred the hunting field to the classroom. It is hard to avoid the conclusion that her tutor was quoting Mary's own words when he asked her to translate into Latin, 'Je voi au parc pour un petit recréer mon entendement qui est cause que je fai ici fin'.[15] Mary seems to have been more interested in being active rather than spending time on hours of study. She was, as the English agent Nicholas Throckmorton put it in July 1559, a 'great doer'.[16]

Turning to the outdoor aspects of Mary's education, falconry, as one would expect, could be introduced to children at a younger age than hunting on horseback. From 1549 the royal children had a servant in charge of their birds, which two years later included falcons, gerfalcons, tercels (male falcons), and merlins.[17] Mary probably started to learn to hawk aged six or seven, but the evidence given below suggests that she was being introduced to hunts only in the early 1550s. The easiest way to learn was simply to follow a hunt in a park, to observe what happened, and to listen to the explanations of a companion. The park would ensure that game was available, provide a limit to how far the hunt might travel, and render a successful end to the hunt more likely. Learning to control the hounds and keeping pace with them were skills which the pupil would need time to acquire. The difficulties are illustrated by the late sixteenth-century Italian artist Antonio Tempesta. One of his prints shows a woman learning to hunt accompanied by another rider who is holding a hound on a leash. The print suggests that the woman is clearly not comfortable riding astride, since she is clutching the saddle bow, while an attendant is running beside her holding the horse's bridle, all of which serves to emphasise the importance of horsemanship.[18]

[11]   Pollnitz, *Princely Education*, 210.
[12]   *Ibid.*, 213–14.
[13]   *Ibid.*, 3, 213.
[14]   *Ibid.*, 214–16; John Durkan, 'The Library of Mary, Queen of Scots', in Lynch, *Mary Stewart*, 71–104, at 83.
[15]   'I am going to the park for a little to refresh my mind because I have finished with this'. Montaiglon, *Latin Themes*, no. xxx.
[16]   *CSPF*, no. 987 p. 329.
[17]   Ruble, *La Première Jeunesse*, 68, 271, 302.
[18]   William A. Baillie-Grohman, *Sport in Art, An Iconography of Sport* (London, 1913),

Much could also be learned from those hunting treatises which were written with a didactic purpose in mind, such as Ferrières's *Roy Modus* and Phoebus's *Livre de Chasse*, and Mary certainly added to her knowledge of hunting by reading such works.[19] In the inventory of her books in Edinburgh Castle compiled in 1574–75 and delivered to James VI (r. 1567–1625) in 1578, there are two volumes called 'The Buik of Hunting' and a 'Little Buik of the Chas'.[20] It is hard to identify these two books because, for the purposes of the inventory, some texts which were written in French were given English titles. For example, it has been suggested that the 'Little Buik of the Chas' was the *Livre de Chasse* of Gaston Phoebus, published in the first decade of the sixteenth century, but it could equally well have been De Brézé's poem *La Chasse* in which Diane de Poitiers's father-in-law described a chase led by a woman.[21] A more likely possibility is that it was the *Master of Game*, which was written in the early fifteenth century by Edward duke of York and was largely a translation into English of Phoebus's *Livre de Chasse*. The identification of this work as the 'Little Buik of the Chas' arises because the author refers to it as 'this little simple book' and as 'this little treatise'.[22]

'The Buik of Hunting' in Mary's library could have been the *Book of St Albans*, the hunting section of which may have been written by Dame Juliana Berners in the second half of the fifteenth century.[23] It was first printed in 1486 and several reprints appeared in the sixteenth century. The attribution of the section on hunting to a woman might have appealed to Mary, but the inclusion of material on hawking and heraldry does not sit neatly with the title, a 'Buik of Hunting'. John Durkan seems to suggest that it was the *Cynegetica* of Pietro Angelio of Barga, whose *Carmina* also appears on the list.[24] It could conceivably also have been *La Vénerie* of Jacques du Fouilloux. However, given the similarity of the names, it is Phoebus's *Livre de Chasse* which is the most likely candidate for the 'Buik of Hunting'. It is unknown when Mary acquired these texts, but their existence in her library shows that she was prepared to use written treatises to improve her knowledge of hunting and of the game.

When learning to ride children needed horses which were easy to control. In 1551 Mary and the dauphin both had hackneys, general-purpose horses which trotted and cantered well and which were ideal for them when they were learning to hunt.[25] In 1551 Mary's hackneys were called Bravane and Madame La Reale.[26] Bravane sounds very much like Scots for 'braw ane' or

---

163–4, 167, fig. 104.

[19] Almond, *Daughters of Artemis*, 57–64, 77.

[20] *Inventaires de la Royne d'Écosse*, ed. J. Robertson (Edinburgh, 1863), p. cxliii.

[21] Julian Sharman, *Library of Mary Queen of Scots* (London, 1889), 122.

[22] *The Master of Game*, 3, 4.

[23] Sharman, *Library of Mary Queen of Scots*, 45.

[24] John Durkan, 'The Library of Mary, Queen of Scots', in Lynch, *Mary Stewart*, 71–104, at 84.

[25] Lucien-Jean Bord and Jean-Pierre Mugg, *La Chasse au Moyen Âge* (Paris, 2008), 235.

[26] Ruble, *La Première Jeunesse*, 305.

good-looking one and Madame La Reale could have been a Spanish mare, the royal lady.[27] By this time the dauphin, aged eight, was learning to hunt, and in December 1552 he was taking part in a *chasse aux toiles* around Amboise.[28] Mary was also taking a more active role in hunting and they may well have hunted together, as Ruble suggests.[29] Mary also wrote from Amboise asking for a small hackney so that she could follow Catherine de Medici on horseback – presumably when she was hunting. There is some debate about the recipient of Mary's letter and the date, but it seems most likely to have been sent to the dauphin in August 1553.[30] How often Mary, aged eleven, was allowed to follow Catherine at a hunt is another question.

Further evidence that Mary was learning to hunt is found in some of her school exercises. In 1554–55, while Mary was in the process of learning Latin, she had to translate into Latin letters written in French by her tutor. These letters survive in a volume, rebound in the seventeenth century, which is in effect a school exercise book, or jotter. The tutor gave Mary individual letters and Mary wrote her translation on the right-hand pages.[31] Subsequently the original French letters were copied into the jotter. Some of the exercises ended quite informally. In one, already mentioned, she wanted to finish her work so that she could go hunting, and in another her tutor asked her to translate 'Le roi m'a donné congé de prendre un daim au parc, je voi le chasser avec ma dame de Castres dont je n'ai loisir faire plus longue lettre'.[32] Madame de Castres was the sixteen-year-old illegitimate daughter of Henry II, also known as Diane de France, who had been brought up by Diane de

---

[27]   Guy, *My Heart is My Own*, 80; *DOST* sub 'brave, brawe'.
[28]   Hector de la Ferrière, *Les Deux Cours de France et de l'Angleterre* (Paris, 1895), 134. In 1557 Henri de Lorraine, age seven, started to hunt with his young companions at the 'little court' of France: Marjorie Meiss-Even, 'Portrait des Guises en "Gentilz veneurs". La Chasse noble au XVIe siècle entre symbolique et realité', *Revue des Sociétés Rurales*, 38 (2012), 85–118, at 91.
[29]   Ruble, *La Première Jeunesse*, 94. It must be noted that Ruble gives what sounds like an accurate list of their actions together but gives no sources for them.
[30]   The recipient is simply addressed as *Monsieur*. Hector de la Ferrière identified him as Francis, the dauphin, while Alphonse de Ruble suggested the letter was sent to Henry II in 1557: Ferrière, *Les Chasses de François Premier*, 75; Ruble, *La Première Jeunesse*, 105. However, the content of the letter does give some help on determining the recipient. In her letter Mary explained that Catherine de Medici had written to her saying that she would see Mary soon and Mary wrote to the recipient to say that she hoped that '*ce ne sera pas sans vous de quoy je me resjouy grandement*' (this [visit]will not be without you [the recipient] because I greatly rejoice [to see you]). Her delight at seeing the recipient again could relate to 1553, when she was probably in Amboise in August: Ruble, *La Première Jeunesse*, 63. Francis had just left the royal children a few months previously to enter the royal court and Mary would no doubt have been delighted to see her childhood companion again, especially if he turned up with a hackney for her.
[31]   Montaiglon, *Latin Themes*, iv–ix, 10.
[32]   'The king has given me leave to take a fallow deer in the park. I am going to hunt it with Madame de Castres and so I have no time to write a longer letter'; Montaiglon, *Latin Themes*, nos xxx, xxxi; BnF, Ms Latin 8660 ('Mariae Stuart, Scotorum reginae et Gallae Delphinae, epistolae variae latine et gallice'), fos 43v–46r.

Poitiers. She was legitimised in 1547 and was contracted to marry the duke of Castro.[33] She was a keen huntswoman and was undoubtedly showing Mary how to hunt. Mary continued to keep in touch with her, and as queen she appointed her to her household.[34] The tutor gave a place and date at the end of each exercise, although Mary did not usually include it in her translation. Not every letter is so dated by the tutor and it appears that he inserted dates only when they had changed residence. According to these exercises, Mary was in Villers Cotterêts by 8 September, 1554, leaving sometime after the 23 September, and was in Paris by 12 October.[35] These dates match the itinerary Ruble has worked out for Mary and, given that the two hunting letters were dated 14 and 15 September, we can be fairly certain that Mary, aged eleven, was learning to hunt in the park at Villers Cotterêts with Diane de France.[36] Hunting was a skill which had to be learned by following others and by repeated practice and copying. Reading treatises might help, but it was 'doing' it that mattered. What this exploration of Mary's education and her subsequent love of hunting tells us is that her kinaesthetic learning abilities were strong.

Regrettably little is known about specific instances when Mary went hunting apart from the fact that she wanted to follow Catherine de Medici and that Catherine often accompanied Henry II at such events.[37] In Catherine's description of the daily routine followed by the courts of Francis I and Henry II, the ladies often watched the men at their sports, but in the afternoon they might go hunting instead.[38] Henry hunted in the afternoons about twice a week and was often accompanied by considerable numbers of nobles and ladies.[39] Hunting seemed to form a large part of the lives of the royal children and Marguerite, born in 1553, said that until she was fifteen she thought of nothing else but amusements, dancing, and hunting. One suspects that Mary's view of life at this time was somewhat similar.[40]

Attitudes towards hunting

The attitude that hunting in France in the sixteenth century was ideally perceived as a male activity is reflected in the passive portrayal of women as falconers or as spectators at hunts, but this is also confirmed in several written

[33]   Rosalind K. Marshall, *Queen Mary's Women* (Edinburgh, 2006), 74–6.
[34]   Noirmont, *Histoire de la Chasse*, i, 289; Louis Paris, *Négociations, Lettres et Pièces Diverses Relative à la Règne de François II* (Paris, 1841), 745.
[35]   Montaiglon, *Latin Themes*, nos xxv, xxxv, xxxvi; BnF, Ms Latin 8660, fos 33v, 52v, 54v.
[36]   Ruble, *La Première Jeunesse*, 254–5.
[37]   Leonie Frieda, *Catherine de Medici* (London, 2003), 50, 115; Brantôme, *Book of the Ladies*, 53.
[38]   Chatenet, *La Cour de France*, 113, 190.
[39]   H. Noel Williams, *Henry II: His Court and Times* (London, 1910), 303.
[40]   *Memoirs of Marguerite de Valois*, ed. Violet Fane (London, 1892), 75.

sources. Gace de la Buigne in the late fourteenth century wrote a poetic hunting treatise, the *Roman des Déduis* (Book of Pastimes), which takes the form of a debate between men about the rival merits of hunting and hawking. He considered that women should not damage their reputations by chasing game while riding astride and using spurs, but he happily described the part they could play in hawking with sparrowhawks.[41] On similar lines, Ferrières towards the end of his *Roy Modus* included a poem which described a debate about the rival merits of hawking and hunting between two women who call on the count of Tancarville to determine a winner.[42] He very tactfully makes no decision but declares on the one hand that falconry is more pleasing to watch and birds are easier and cleaner to handle. On the other, he concludes, even although dogs are more trouble to keep, hunting with hounds is enjoyable because of its sights and sounds. The implication is that falconry was more suited to women than chasing game on horseback, and Ferrières, like de la Buigne, took time to describe the enjoyment which women would derive from hawking.[43] As far as hunting was concerned it was considered acceptable for women to attend the death and *curée* at the end of the hunt, when they were often given gifts of venison or the foot of the deer.[44] In literature as well as in art, and presumably also in reality, the presence of women at this stage of a hunt led to associations with the romantic. This aspect of hunting was reinforced by the dual meaning of the word *vénerie* which could mean 'hunting', derived from the Latin *venari*, to hunt and related especially to the *par force* hunt, but might also mean 'relating to Venus' from the Latin *venerius*. As previously mentioned, this amatory element of hunting is portrayed in the early fifteenth-century Devonshire Hunting Tapestries and in the early sixteenth-century tapestries, Les Chasses de Maximilien.[45]

In reality, many noblewomen in France did hunt by chasing game on horseback. The sixteenth-century poet Ronsard referred to the *châtelaines*, the wives of the lords of the castle, wearing red boots with their skirts hitched above their knees, hunting no doubt on their gaily caparisoned hackneys.[46] Ferrières's debate between two women was rewritten by Guillaume Cretin in 1527, entitled *Le Débat des Dames sur Le Passetemps des Chiens et des Oiseaux*.[47] As in Ferrières's earlier version, two noble women have been out with their husbands: one couple had been hawking and the other hunting. After returning to their host's castle for supper they fell into discussion which

---

[41] Noirmont, *Histoire de la Chasse*, i, 94–5, 128; Cummins, *The Hound and the Hawk*, 215.
[42] Ferrières, *Roy Modus*, 233–65.
[43] Ferrières, *Roy Modus*, 228.
[44] Cummins, *The Hound and the Hawk*, 7, 180.
[45] Almond, *Medieval Hunting*, 153–4; Cummins, *The Hound and the Hawk*, 81.
[46] Ferrière, *Les Grandes Chasses au XVI Siècle*, 2.
[47] 'The debate of the ladies on the pastime of [hunting with] dogs and [hawking with] birds'; *Débat entre Deux Dames sur le Passetemps Des Chiens et Des Oiseaux*, ed. Paul Lacroix and Ernest Jullien (Paris, 1882), 26–31.

continued as a more formal debate the following day in the castle garden. Whether this poem described a particular event or not it would make little sense if aristocratic women did not both hunt and hawk. The woman who argued in favour of hunting enjoyed various aspects of this activity: the hunt assembly where men and women enjoyed the meal on the grass, the loyalty of the dogs, the sight of a pack of hounds chasing the deer, the challenge faced by male and female hunters when the deer tried to throw the dogs off the scent, and finally the achievement of the kill. Clearly, she was praising a *par force* hunt, though in this sixteenth-century version she also praised the *chasse aux toiles*. In that hunt she would not have been a full participant, but she enjoyed driving boar into the toils and then watching them being attacked by men and dogs, which she compared with the delights of a *mêlée*, a mock battle between two teams of knights. She watched this 'terrible tempeste' from outside the toils and cheered on the hunters while others blew their horns, all adding to the excitement. The praise of the *chasse aux toiles* does not occur in the fourteenth-century version of the debate because it had not been fully developed by that time. It was a distinctive feature of this form of the drive that women could watch the killing in safety. They could follow on horseback as boar were driven up to the *accourre*, but it was considered too dangerous for them to combat a boar in the kill zone.[48]

The attitude which Mary developed towards the role of women at the hunt was acquired from her family and from other female members of the court. As will be explained in Chapter 4, Mary's mother, Marie de Guise, hunted regularly in Scotland, but it is impossible to assess how far she influenced her daughter's attitude towards this activity.[49] However, François duke of Guise, Mary's uncle, was certainly in a position to do so. He became *Grand Veneur* (Grand Hunter) at the French court from 1550 to 1562, kept establishments for the *chasse aux toiles*, for *par force* hunting, and for hawking, enjoyed hunting on his lands around Joinville, and wrote letters which show his interest in dogs and in falconry.[50] The maintenance of their hunting reserves and their hunting expeditions around their lands helped the Guise family to establish their control of their estates and reinforce their position as lords of the domain.[51]

Catherine de Medici and Diane de Poitiers, both keen huntresses, were also in a position to influence Mary's attitudes, since they oversaw her education along with the cardinal of Lorraine.[52] Catherine learned to hunt in Italy and developed her own style of riding side-saddle. She was an experienced huntress and could shoot deer from horseback using an *arbalète à jalet*, a crossbow which fired small, round stones rather than a bolt. Despite several accidents, Catherine hunted regularly with Francis I and continued to do so

[48] Robert de Salnove, *La Vénerie Royale* (Paris, 1665), 307.
[49] See pp. 93–4.
[50] Noirmont, *Histoire de la Chasse*, i, 168–9.
[51] Meiss-Even, 'Portrait des Guises en "Gentilz veneurs"', 85–6, 90, 99, 102–5.
[52] Pollnitz, *Princely Education*, 210.

with her husband, Henry II.[53] When Mary observed Catherine and Henry II, she was watching a queen who was a skilled participant and definitely not a spectator who only stood and shot deer from a platform.

Diane de Poitiers seems to have taken a particular interest in Mary's upbringing, an interest which is noticeable in two of Mary's letters. In the first, completed just after Christmas, probably at Blois, in 1555, Mary wrote to her mother in Scotland on matters relating to her wardrobe and household and then asked her to thank her Guise relatives for taking care of her. She thought their concern for her was 'incroiable [unbelievable]' and she added that she could not say less of Diane de Poitiers. In another letter to her mother, written two years later, she repeated these sentiments and referred to the increasing affection which Diane de Poitiers was showing her.[54] This letter also serves to demonstrate that Mary, now fourteen, was growing up and becoming more aware of matters of state. She expressed concern that the extent of royal lands in Scotland remained static while her nobles were becoming more powerful. She mentioned the marriage of Diane de France to the son of constable Montmorency and gave her support to the idea of a marriage between the earl of Arran and Diane de Poitier's daughter Mlle de Bouillon. She asked her mother to try to further this marriage to repay the affection which Diane was increasingly showing her.

Because Diane de Poitiers was in a position to influence Mary's education and attitude we need to understand the major part which hunting played in her life. Born in 1500, she learned to hunt when she was young and reportedly wore a mask to protect her face as did other elite women.[55] On the death of her husband, Louis de Brézé, in 1531, she inherited various lands between Chartres and Evreux, including the chateau of Anet where she hunted in the neighbouring forest of Dreux.[56] In 1540, when she was Henry II's mistress, she purchased land to expand the small park at Anet into a much larger reserve. She paid servants and officials to manage the woods and to organise the dogs and equipment for hunting.[57] From 1547 to 1552 she turned the chateau of Anet into a hunter's paradise dedicated to *la vénerie* in which she could entertain Henry. Not only did the estate of Anet with its park, forest, kennels, and stables provide all the facilities of the hunt, but the whole palace was themed around the hunt and the image of Diana as the goddess of hunting. The gateway contained a bas-relief in bronze of a sleeping Diana and was surmounted

---

[53] Brantôme, *The Book of the Ladies*, 53; Bord and Mugg, *La Chasse*, 211; Ivan Cloulas, *Henri II* (Paris, 1985), 346; Ferrière, *Les Chasses de François 1er*, 30–1.

[54] Alexandre Labanoff, *Lettres, Instructions et Memoires de Marie Stuart*, 8 vols (London, 1844), i, 32 (1555), 39–42 (1557); Jane T. Stoddart, *The Girlhood of Mary Queen of Scots* (London, 1908), 123.

[55] Philippe Erlanger, *Diane de Poitiers* (Paris, 1955), 24 n. 2.

[56] Kathleen Wellman, 'Diane de Poitiers. An Idealized Mistress', in Kathleen Wellman (ed.), *Queens and Mistresses of Renaissance France* (Yale, 2013), 185–223, at 190; Ivan Cloulas, *Diane de Poitiers* (Paris, 1997), 3; Philippe Erlanger, *Diane de Poitiers* (Paris, 1955), 24 n. 2.

[57] Cloulas, *Henri II*, 246.

by a statue of a stag held at bay by two hounds. In a courtyard there was a fountain showing Diana reclining on a stag, and on the first floor there was a series of tapestries, probably commissioned by Henry II, which illustrated the history of the goddess Diana and whose borders carried the monogram of Diane de Poitiers.[58] The development of Anet was important to Diane for various reasons. Instead of being seen as the king's mistress it promoted her image as Diana the goddess of the hunt, an honest and pure deity, and so cast Henry as a figure of medieval romance courting an upright lady.[59] Diane's power and influence at court depended on the emotional attachment between Henry and herself, and so developing this haven for hunting for his enjoyment consolidated her position at court. Diane, in effect, was using hunting for political ends.

Mary is known to have visited Anet on at least three occasions between 1553 and 1555 and one suspects that she, like the dauphin, enjoyed her visits.[60] Portrayals of Diane as the goddess Diana were unmissable and one wonders if anyone saw the irony of portraying the king's mistress as an upright, honest, virgin deity. At Anet Mary was in an environment where noble women could manage the facilities for the sport themselves and play a leading part in individual hunts. A further demonstration of this lay in a poem, now called *La Chasse*, composed by Diane's father-in-law, Jacques de Brézé, which he dedicated to Anne de Beaujeu, the daughter of Louis XI (r. 1461–83).[61] By the sixteenth century Anne was renowned as a keen huntress who took an interest in the breeding of hunting dogs.[62]

At the start of the poem, which describes a *par force* hunt, Jacques de Brézé and other huntsmen are searching the area designated for the hunt to find a suitable stag. Having located various stags, they head back to the hunt assembly and present the *fumées* to Anne, who is seated at the table.[63] Having examined the *fumées*, she asks for the location of the stags and decides that the stag which de Brézé had found is the best one to hunt.[64] She then divides the hounds into those which would course the stag and those which would be despatched to act as relays.[65] During the hunt Anne, riding an ambling horse called a *hobin*, keeps up with the hunt, and when the hounds lose the scent she is in amongst them shouting to the dogs by name. When the deer try to trick the hunters, she spots what is happening and manages to put the hounds back on the scent.[66] Eventually the stag turns at bay and the dogs

[58] Wellman, 'Diane de Poitiers', 216–19.
[59] Wellman, 'Diane de Poitiers', 198, 214–16.
[60] Ruble, *La Première Jeunesse*, 254–6.
[61] Jacques de Brézé, *La Chasse, Les Dits Du Bon Chien Souillard et Les Louanges de Madame Anne de France*, ed. Gunnar Tilander (Lund, 1959), 26.
[62] *La Vénerie de Jacques du Fouilloux … et L'Adolescence de l'Autheur*, ed. Gunnar Tilander (Karlshamn, 1967), 6. He refers to Anne as Anne de Bourbon.
[63] Brézé, *La Chasse*, 30 verse 10.
[64] *Ibid.*, 31, verses 11 and 12.
[65] *Ibid.*, 32 verse 14.
[66] *Ibid.*, 36 verse 24, 37 verse 2, 39 verse 30.

harry it till it falls down dead.[67] Anne dismounts, takes the stag's head, speaks to the dogs, and then leads the blowing of horns to mark the death. She asks de Brézé to start the unmaking of the stag by giving her a foot, the customary gift for women who had kept up with the hunt.[68] The carcase is then loaded onto a cart since the unmaking and the *curée* to reward the dogs is to be held at the castle.[69]

As de Brézé says in the poem, Anne was well informed and well educated in the hunt, which meant that she was a skilled practitioner who knew the appropriate terminology. As chief hunter she took command of various situations, the assembly, the ruses of the stag, and the death as well as the location and timing of the *curée*. The only concession to her sex and strength was that she asked de Brézé to carry out the butchering of the stag. Whether Mary was familiar with this poem or not, the whole environment of Anet supported the view that women could assume the role of chief hunter.

There is no specific record at this time of how Mary hunted, but we can assume that she was learning to chase deer on horseback when she was following Catherine de Medici or Diane de France. Similarly, because Mary was brought up with the dauphin, who hunted at the toils, and with Élisabeth, his sister, who practised the *chasse aux toiles* when she married Philip II of Spain, it is very likely that Mary also hunted in this manner.[70] At Aranjuez on the river Tagus outside Madrid, Élisabeth joined in hunts at the toils both by driving or chasing the game on horseback into the *accourre* or by waiting to shoot the game from an arbour built in the middle of the kill zone.[71] She taught Philip's sister, Princess Joanna, how to ride side-saddle in the French style and fire a crossbow at fallow deer while riding at the gallop. Given their upbringing together, there is little reason to doubt that, since Mary was an accomplished archer, she could shoot deer and game from horseback and at the toils.

Equestrianism

It was not just Mary's attitude to hunting which was influenced by the French court but also her equestrian practices. As we have seen, there were three basic riding styles which women practised in the early modern period: on a side-facing saddle with a *planchette*, astride, and side-saddle.[72] It is known

[67] *Ibid.*, 43 verse 42.
[68] Cummins, *The Hound and The Hawk*, 180.
[69] Brézé, *La Chasse*, 43–5 verses 42–6.
[70] *Catalogue des Actes*, i, 68.
[71] Ferrière, *Les Chasses de François 1er*, 64; *Journal Privé de Élisabeth de Valois*, in Henri de la Ferrière, *Deux Années de Mission à St Petersbourg* (Paris, 1867). Available at: https://babel.hathitrust.org/cgi/pt?id=hvd.hnxh2f&view=1up&seq=254 [accessed 25 November 2019].
[72] See Appendix II for the evidence on which this discussion of riding styles is based.

that Mary rode using the side-facing saddle and a platform stirrup because in 1559 she ordered a saddle for a hackney with a *planchette* and four sets of buckles to hold the stirrup leathers of the *planchette*, which hung from the saddle.[73] It seems unlikely that Mary as queen would have hunted in this very slow style of riding when she was taking an active part in the chase. In her accounts for 1551 there is mention of *devants de cotte* with sleeves and pairs of *chausse* of Florentine serge and, given that she was learning to hunt or about to learn, these might have been *devantières* and breeches for riding astride or side-saddle, but it seems unlikely.[74] However, when Mary was queen she ordered cloaks and *devantières* of serge for horse-riding for herself and for thirteen women and girls of the court, thus demonstrating that she and other female courtiers rode astride or side-saddle.[75]

Riding side-saddle was fairly widespread in the French court at this time. Élisabeth, Henry II's daughter, as already mentioned, rode side-saddle in Spain and we can safely assume that Mary was taught to do likewise. In 1566 when the French ambassador in the Netherlands was quizzed by Marguerite de Parma about women's riding styles he described how Catherine de Medici had taught all the ladies of the French court to ride side-saddle.[76] This would undoubtedly have included Mary, who would have been able to ride in each of these three styles, no doubt varying her style of riding and her dress to suit the hunt, the company, and the weather.

It has been argued that when women rode astride or were wearing breeches of some sort they were adopting male behaviours and were trying to acquire male authority and standing.[77] Certainly, when Catherine de Medici wore breeches and rode side-saddle in order to keep up with the hunt and be part of Francis I's *petite bande* (little band) of huntresses she was matching the behaviours of his male courtiers. She was positioning herself in their circle while maintaining the femininity of the side-saddle.[78] When Diane de Poitiers rode astride or side-saddle to hunt with Henry II she was doing likewise. Mary was brought up in an environment where it was perfectly acceptable for aristocratic women to participate in and enjoy hunting. Riding astride or side-saddle wearing breeches and a *devantière* was the accepted practice both at court and in noble houses because it was the safest and most comfortable way to chase game through woods or across country. Mary, therefore, was exposed to the image of control and the elements of masculinity which these styles conveyed and thus to the political aspects and uses of the hunt.[79]

---

[73]   *Catalogue des Actes*, ii, 696.
[74]   Ruble, *La Première Jeunesse*, 283, 287, 292.
[75]   *Catalogue des Actes*, ii, 694, 696.
[76]   Ferrière, *Les Chasses de François 1er*, 49.
[77]   Zanetti, 'Breeched and Unbridled', 163–5, 166, 181; Peacock, 'Women at the Hunt', 826–7, 829–32.
[78]   Brantôme, *The Book of the Ladies*, 53–4.
[79]   Zanetti, 'Breeched and Unbridled', 166, 181.

Performance at the French court

Hunting away from the spotlight of the court was a valued part of the private life of the monarch as typified by Francis I, but it was also an essential and critical part of the monarch's public life.[80] Both Francis I and Henry II organised *grandes chasses* involving hundreds of hunters and servants which were very much occasions of image and display.[81] Catherine de Medici joined Henry II regularly for hunt assemblies and *par force* hunts just as she had done with Francis I. The *chasse aux toiles* was described by Ferrières as a royal pastime because it could be enjoyed only by the powerful and their friends, who alone held large forests of a suitable size well stocked with game and who alone could gather enough men to form the *défenses* and build the barriers.[82] On such occasions hunting was clearly not just a pastime but also an outdoor performance staged to impress the nobility taking part, the spectators observing the chase or the kill zone, and the tenants and servants manning the *défenses* or acting as *ameneurs*. When Francis I hunted with Charles V at Fontainebleau to cement an alliance in the winter of 1539–40, or when Henry II in 1551 tried to impress several German ambassadors by staging the end of a hunt in their path as they left Fontainebleau, the political message was clear for all to see.[83] The breadth of the audiences at court performances and entertainments did vary considerably both in number and in status. While a hunt on a royal progress, unlike a royal entry to a town, was not accessible to all, it would be attended not only by the royal court but also by members of the local nobility and the *défenses* and *ameneurs* drawn from the host's tenantry. In terms of publicising a particular view of the monarch, hunting was one of the royal performances which could reach a wide audience.

During the 1550s Mary participated in a variety of events and ceremonies which helped to familiarise her with the performance aspects of court life. Apart from the daily routine of the court, Henry II involved Mary in special occasions where certain protocols were followed. In Blois, for instance, on 5 January, 1550, at the feast of the Queen of the Fève, when Diane de Poitiers was the queen for a day, Mary was seated second or third on the right-hand side of the king for the meal. At the ensuing ball in the *grande salle* (large/grand room) she sat on a raised platform with Catherine de Medici, her daughter Marguerite and several cardinals.[84] Mary was also involved in watching and

---

[80] Chatenet, *La Cour de France*, 29; Brantôme, *The Book of the Ladies*, 53.

[81] Chatenet, 'Un Portrait du "Père des Veneurs"', 28–9.

[82] Ferrières, *Roy Modus*, i, 105; ii, 274, '*deduit roial*'; Cotgrave, *Dictionary*, 'deduit' can mean delectation, sport, pastime.

[83] Hugue Salel, *Chasse Royale*, in *Débat Entre Deux Dames*, 7–31; R. J. Knecht, 'Charles V's journey through France 1539–40', in J. R. Mulryne and Elizabeth Goldring (eds), *Court Festivals of the European Renaissance* (London, 2002), 153–70, at 153, 160; Noirmont, *Histoire de la Chasse*, i, 165.

[84] Chatenet, *La Cour de France*, 218, 236, 250–1. Her own wedding in 1558 and that of the duke of Savoy were other examples.

participating in court masques and entertainments such as the royal entry to Rouen in 1550 during her mother's visit to France. She participated in a masque praising Henry II and Catherine de Medici in 1554, and on another occasion, acting as the Delphic priestess, a soothsayer, she foretold in Latin that Henry would rule Scotland and England. After the capture of Calais the cardinal of Lorraine arranged a banquet in 1558 for Mary and Catherine de Medici where a musical performance implied that Mary had the power to subdue the wild inhabitants of forests and mountains – surely an indirect reference to Scotland.[85] Mary was being given the experience and opportunity to appreciate how performances and events, including hunts, could carry social and political significance. It was an honour and a privilege to hunt with the monarch, but conversely it was also an invaluable way for the monarch to keep in touch with his (or her) leading subjects or, as Catherine de Medici said, 'to hear and know all things'.[86] Likewise, in the royal circle that surrounded Mary, hunting was seen as an important element of statecraft which could be used to impress foreign rulers and their ambassadors to secure their friendship and support.

In 1559, when Mary was sixteen, her education was considered complete. It had included a training in hunting, elements of linguistic and literary study, and experience of court life with its ceremonials, protocols, and performance culture. Political matters had probably been brought to her attention by the cardinal of Lorraine and her mother, amongst others; but not, perhaps, to the extent that would have been expected had it been known that she would, within two years, become queen regnant of Scotland. Nonetheless, Mary had received a varied education that was not untypical for contemporary royal women.

[85] Crépin-Leblond, 'Marie Stuart', 37–42.
[86] Brantôme, *Book of the Ladies*, 53.

3

The hunting couple

The traditional view of the reign of Francis II is that he more or less surrendered his power in favour of Mary's uncles, François duke of Guise and Charles cardinal of Lorraine, with the result that neither he nor Mary took any part in dealing with the political and religious issues of the time.[1] After his coronation on 18 September, 1559 it seems at first sight that Francis was consumed with his passion for hunting at the expense of his duties as monarch. As a result of the military successes of Duke François in Italy and the capture of Calais in 1558 there is little doubt that the power of the Guises had grown dramatically during the reign of Henry II. This political prominence was bolstered by the strength of family bonds and their extensive affinity of friends and clients.[2] On Henry II's death after a jousting accident in 1559, the Guises seized major posts in the council, removed the Montmorency family from power, and planned to govern the country in the young king's name.

However, as a result of the publication in 1991 of Francis II's itinerary and a calendar of his acts by Marie-Thérèse Martel, the traditional view of Francis's role in government has been modified. This, in turn, affects our view of his relationship with Mary and what she was learning as queen of France.[3] Martel's work shows that Francis, who was no longer considered a minor, was well aware of his position as a sovereign ruler and tried to pursue his duties conscientiously.[4] At the start of his reign Francis, influenced by his late father and the Guises, probably wanted to destroy the Huguenots, the Protestants intent on reforming the Catholic Church. During his short reign, however, guided by Catherine de Medici and to some extent by Charles of Lorraine, he focussed on trying to keep the peace between the different political and religious factions. He was generous and courteous, showed concern for the poor, and at around 1.8m (6ft) tall before his death he was not an insignificant figure.[5] Even Regnier de La Planche, a Huguenot, considered that when he became king one could see him change, in front of one's eyes, from a child into the 'homme parfait [perfect man]'.[6] Though he suffered from a chronic

[1] Fraser, *Mary Queen of Scots*, 123–4.
[2] Janine Garrisson, *A History of Sixteenth-Century France* (Basingstoke, 1995), 168; Carroll, *Martyrs and Murderers*, 58–9.
[3] *Catalogue des Actes, passim.*
[4] Gobry, *François II*, 49.
[5] *Catalogue des Actes*, i, p. xi; Gobry, *François II*, 17, 49, 214–16; René Marquis de Belleval, *Les Derniers Valois François II Charles IX Henri III* (Paris, 1869), 51–2; Carroll, *Martyrs and Murderers*, 125.
[6] Louis Régnier de la Planche, *Histoire de L'Estat de la France sous la Regne de François II*,

THE HUNTING COUPLE

ear, nose, and throat condition, he was fit enough to hunt frequently; but his passion for the chase did not cause him to neglect business. He may not yet, aged fifteen, have been deciding his own policy or been strong enough politically to confront the Guise family or Catherine de Medici even if he had wanted to, but that did not stop him being involved in affairs of state. He evidently was not in constant attendance at the grand council, but his itinerary shows that he regularly overlapped with their meetings, for instance, at Blois in November and December 1559. Also, in 1560, he called two council meetings in Catherine de Medici's chamber, one at Amboise in February and the other at St Germain in October.[7] His *conseil des affaires*, which could be expanded into his privy council, travelled with him.[8] At Romorantin on 7 May, on his own initiative but in line with earlier discussions, he sealed the Edict of Romorantin, which took a slightly more moderate approach towards the Huguenots by transferring cases of heresy from the lay to the church courts.[9] He was involved in the follow-up to the conspiracy of Amboise in March 1560 and was present at an assembly of notables at Fontainebleau from 21 to 26 August. Francis chaired the assembly for its three-day duration and, in a clear statement of dynastic solidarity, Mary and Catherine de Medici sat on either side of him. He had to intervene on several occasions to keep the peace, and ultimately he called on the moderate privy councillor Jean de Montluc, bishop of Valence, to suggest calling an estates general to tackle the bankruptcy of the government and the reconciliation of Catholics and Protestants.[10] On 30 August, after the assembly, and in a further demonstration of his authority, he warned the king of Navarre, Antoine de Bourbon, that if he did not persuade his brother, the duke of Condé, to come to court to explain his involvement in the conspiracy of Amboise, then he knew very well, he said, how to make him understand that he was the king.[11] This is not the customary portrayal of Francis II as a sickly, immature child. By his death in 1560 he was, in fact, an active, tall, good-looking young man with some presence; and, given time, which in the event he did not have, he could have become an effective monarch.

---

ed. M. E. Mennechet, 2 vols (Paris, 1836), i, 74.

[7]   *Catalogue des Actes*, i, 512, 545. Francis's itinerary is based on the itineraries worked out by Ruble and Martel. There are numerous gaps in the itinerary but Martel gives more information about her sources than Ruble. Her 'B' entries taken from a variety of non-official sources are very helpful: Ruble: *La Première Jeunesse*, 258–266; *Catalogue des Actes*, i, 477–533.

[8]   Belleval, *Les Derniers Valois*, 94–6; *Catalogue des Actes*, i, 45 nos 164, 165, 55 no. 200.

[9]   Gobry, *François II*, 121.

[10]   Gobry, *François II*, 127–45, esp. 137–41; *CSPF*, i, no. 442 p. 245. Charles de Marillac also called for a national council of the Church. This more tolerant approach is also highlighted by Robert. J. Knecht, *The Rise and Fall of Renaissance France 1483–1610* (Oxford, 2001), 282–4.

[11]   *Catalogue des Actes*, 539.

Did Francis II hunt excessively?

To obtain a more accurate picture of Mary's experience as queen of France there are several other misconceptions relating to Mary and Francis which need to be corrected or modified: that the time which Francis spent hunting was excessive; that he abandoned Mary while he went hunting; and that he used hunting as an excuse to avoid the work of government.[12] Firstly, the amount of time which Francis spent hunting was fairly typical of the Valois kings of the sixteenth century. Francis I was referred to as the *père des veneurs* (father of hunters) and regularly hunted in winter as well as summer. When he was in France and not at war he spent less than 50% of his time *en sejour* (in residence) and the remainder *en villages* or *aux champs* (in the villages or in the fields), in other words on progresses.[13] The Tuscan ambassador complained that the court spent long enough in one place only to hawk for herons, chase stags once or twice *par force* and *aux toiles* before moving on.[14] Henry II spent around 36% of his time on his travels, but he was known for hunting twice per week for six or seven hours and then following that by games of *jeu de paume*. It is not surprising that the Valois court is described as nomadic, because they were always on the move looking for new hunting grounds. Francis II, from the time of Henry's death, spent just under half of his time in residences of six days or longer and so was following the practice of his predecessors. According to Chantonay, the Spanish ambassador, Francis was daily on horseback chasing after deer and hares, playing *jeu de paume*, and holding *grandes chasses* twice a week. The impression is that, while Francis may have hunted more frequently than Henry II, he was basically doing what his father and grandfather had done. On his accession Francis was considered a sickly youth and that may well have given him added motivation to go hunting to prove otherwise. Before he grew to his full height, he might not have matched the physical image expected of a Valois monarch, but when he was hunting and arranging *grandes chasses*, Francis was behaving no differently from other Valois monarchs. What *was*

---

[12] These views are expressed in several histories including Frieda, *Catherine de Medici*, 126, 129; Fraser, *Mary Queen of Scots*, 135; Robert Stedall, *The Challenge to the Crown*, 2 vols (Brighton, 2012), i, 99.

[13] Chatenet, *La Cour de France*, 19, 128, 320–2, 338 n. 15. Chatenet's figures are based on whether court regulations were those which applied *en séjour* or *aux champs*. Chatenet did not work out a figure for Francis II and neither Ruble nor Martel specifies whether *en-séjour* or *en-villages* regulations were being applied in Francis's reign. Chatenet's figures include stays of less than six days, even stays of one day, when the *en-séjour* regulations applied. The author's figure for Francis II is based on six days because sometimes when on a progress Francis would stop for three or four days and six days seemed to be a suitable borderline to distinguish a stationary court from a travelling court.

[14] Ferrière, *Les Chasses de Francois Ier*, 18 which quotes the report.

different was his health, and it is possible that the frequency of his hunts was more than his body could stand.

Did Francis II abandon Mary?

Examination of the second misconception, that Francis abandoned Mary when he went hunting, requires consideration of Mary's itinerary and of the regularity with which Mary and Francis hunted together. Regrettably, Mary's household and stable accounts do not survive; nor are there sufficient references in other sources to establish a complete itinerary for her. It is known that the various royal households in sixteenth-century France could travel either together or separately.[15] However, when Mary's location is recorded, usually by foreign ambassadors, it nearly always coincides with that of Francis, and on an occasion when they were separated comment was made.[16] Consequently, both Ruble and Martel base Mary's itinerary on that of Francis unless there are reasons to suggest otherwise.[17]

Therefore, as one would expect, there are several occasions recorded when Mary and Francis were both travelling and hunting together. On 23 November, 1559 the court entered Châtelherault, which had been granted to James Hamilton, earl of Arran, in 1551 as a reward for helping to secure Scottish agreement for the marriage of Mary and Francis.[18] On their arrival the royal couple were given a formal entry proclaiming Mary as monarch of France, England, and Scotland, after which Francis spent several days hunting deer *par force*.[19] The court then, en route to an official entry at Amboise, stopped at Loches on 28 November, where Mary also went hunting. The English *attachés*, Henry Killigrew and Robert Jones, reported that in the evening a gentleman praised English geldings to Mary.[20] Mary wanted to know if they were good to run up hill and down dale because she was determined to 'run the hart' the English phrase for *chasse à courre*. She wanted to acquire geldings but one of the masters of her household said that she could

---

[15]   Crépin-Leblond, *Marie Stuart*, 2 n. 1; Chatenet, *La Cour de France au XVI Siècle*, 21.

[16]   Their itineraries coincided (1) at Villers Cotterêts in September 1559: n. 69 below; (2) on the journey to Villers Cotterêts: *CSPF 1558–9*, no.1406 p. 587; and (3) at Maillebois in June 1560: *CSPV*, vii, no. 178 p. 234. Other examples will be given below. Separate itineraries after Maillebois are referred to in the Maillebois source above.

[17]   Ruble, *La Première Jeunesse*, 259 ff. bases Mary's itinerary on the household accounts of Francis. Martel also assumed that Mary as well as Catherine de Medici and the court travelled with Francis: *Catalogue des Actes*, i. 522 n. 2.

[18]   However, it had been confiscated after he joined the Lords of the Congregation and fought against Marie de Guise in August 1559. He had fled from Châtelherault sometime in July 1560: J. Stevenson, *Mary Stuart, A Narrative of the First Eighteen Years of her Life* (Edinburgh, 1886), 177–82; *Catalogue Des Actes*, i, 501.

[19]   *CSPF 1559–60*, no. 337 p. 145–6.

[20]   A gelding is a castrated stallion, which is easier to control when hunting.

not obtain any from England without a licence from the queen. Mary was not enthusiastic about approaching Elizabeth and proposed instead to obtain some from Scotland. Nonetheless, she was advised that if she did apply to Elizabeth she would probably obtain a licence and so that was what she decided to do. Catherine de Medici was present but 'said nothing all this while'.[21]

Leading up to Christmas, Francis spent most of December 1559 at Chambord hawking and hunting. Mary and Catherine de Medici were with him, but he also arranged for the chancellor, the ageing François Olivier, and the privy council to accompany him in order to work on the desperate state of the royal finances for the following year: business was to be mixed with pleasure.[22] The attraction of Chambord lay not only in the palace and the surrounding forest of Boulogne but also in the newly developed park. Chambord had been built by Francis I supposedly as a more private lodge in a relatively unattractive area of marsh and heath in the forest of Boulogne. It was built as a private chateau to accompany Blois, just as La Muette accompanied St Germain-en-Laye and Chaillau accompanied Fontainebleau. Mary *may* have visited Chambord while at Blois but it was not till her seven-day visit in December 1559 that it can definitely be said that she stayed there.[23] The park, which was enclosed by a wall, was the largest of the royal parks and was centred on the chateau. What is intriguing about Chambord is that Francis I created the park by enclosing a large part of the forest of Boulogne, some of which was not in royal hands. The area south of Chambord in the forest of Boulogne was subject to the rights of usage of the villages in the area, while the area to the north included only a few coppices in the middle of cultivated lands.[24] This was not ideal territory on which to create the largest of the royal parks and it was an uphill struggle trying to guard the park and control poaching. In 1547, when a *reformation* was held, it emerged that there were thirty small farmers in the park who were paying rent to the county of Blois. There were meadows, ploughed fields, orchards, gardens, vineyards, and numerous marshy ponds. With the abundance of game the tenants must have tried to protect their fields by building and maintaining banks and hedges just as tenants who lived in royal forests were encouraged to do.[25] Archaeological fieldwork is now locating many areas enclosed by banks with external ditches designed to keep wild animals out. These banks are very reminiscent of the banks which protected assarts, areas cleared of trees to make way for agriculture.[26] The park provided the ideal designed landscape setting for the chateau

[21] *CSPF 1559–60*, no. 337 p. 146–7.
[22] Jane T. Stoddart, *The Girlhood of Mary Queen of Scots* (London, 1908), 226; CSPV, vii, no. 118 p. 138.
[23] Ruble, *La Première Jeunesse*, 260; *Catalogue des Actes*, i, 504.
[24] Monique Chatenet, *Chambord* (Paris, 2001), 140, 147.
[25] Chatenet, *Chambord*, 135–42, Bocquillon, 'Au moyen âge, vénerie royale', 119.
[26] Louis Magiorani, 'Domaines avant le XIIIe siècle dans Boulogne et Chambord'. Available at: http://www.archeoforet.org/ouvre/pluloin/dmaines/domains.pdf [accessed 21 August 2019]. An assart is an area cleared of trees to make way for agriculture.

THE HUNTING COUPLE

and was admired by visitors such as the Venetian ambassador in 1550, who enjoyed seeing deer and boar hunts from his windows; while another in 1577 admired how the park set off the magnificence of the chateau.[27]

During this time at Chambord Mary suffered an accident on 19 December when she was hunting on a gelding which she had clearly managed to source in France. As she was riding, presumably in the park at Chambord or in the forest of Boulogne, following a stag 'of force', as Killigrew and Jones wrote, she hit the branch of a tree and was knocked off her horse. Having winded herself, she could not call for help when three or four other gentlemen and ladies of her chamber rode past her so close that their horses trampled on the hood of her cloak. When she was noticed, she was helped up and, not feeling any pain, she immediately started to 'set her hair and dress up her head'. She returned to Chambord and went to her chamber where she recovered well; but she was clearly shaken by the episode and 'determined to change this kind of exercise', in other words, to stop hunting *par force*, a decision to which she certainly did not adhere.[28]

On 3 February, 1560 Francis, Mary, Catherine de Medici, and the Guise brothers set off on a hunting progress to the north of Blois, visiting the chateaux of the local nobility.[29] Hunt assemblies were held at Marchenoir, the home of the duke of Longueville, the prospective son-in-law of the duke of Guise; at Morée, north-east of Vendôme; and at Montoire, before reaching Amboise on 22 February. On 10 March they were again hunting together at Chenonceau.[30]

In April and May, Francis was hunting around Chenonceau, Chinon, and Loches, presumably with Mary because they both made a point of riding together from Chenonceau to Amboise on 24 April to meet the former Spanish ambassador to the English court, count de Feria, on his return journey to Spain.[31] On 8 June Francis left Blois with Mary and Catherine de Medici and proceeded to hunt around various chateaux in Sologne, Beauce, and Perche, helped by guides who knew the country (Map 2).[32] These local guides who helped him to navigate the forests and hunting grounds feature regularly in the accounts throughout his reign.[33] On 24 June he was at Maillebois, the home of Francois d'O, the unpopular captain of the French king's Scottish

---

[27] Chatenet, *Chambord*, 140.

[28] *CSPF 1559–60*, no. 508 p. 243.

[29] *Catalogue des Actes*, i, nos 506, 510, 512; Stoddart, *Girlhood*, 233; M. Charles Paillard, 'L'Histoire de la Conjuration d'Amboise', *Revue Historique*, 14 (Paris, 1880), 61–108, at 66, 82 n. 2, 83. When Chantonay and others say that Francis was in the villages this does not mean that he was staying in small houses; rather, it refers to the distinction between being on *séjour* or in residence at a royal palace as opposed to being on progress, *aux villages*.

[30] Paillard, 'Conjuration d'Amboise', 87, which quotes the French and Spanish versions of Chantonay's despatches.

[31] *Catalogue des Actes*, i, no. 520; *CSPV*, vii, no.155 p. 199.

[32] *CSPF 1560–61*, no. 233 p. 143.

[33] *Catalogue des Actes*, i, e.g., 513, 517, 526, 529, 544.

Guard, and it was there that the news of her mother's death in Edinburgh was eventually broken to Mary.[34] Mary was consumed by grief on receiving this news and both she and Francis wore mourning clothes, but instead of entering a strict period of mourning she seems to have stayed with Francis, who continued to hunt and organise hunt assemblies and stay in the chateaux of the area.[35] No hunt assembly was held at Maillebois, but assemblies followed at Nogent, St Leger, Dampierre, Rambouillet, the abbey of Vaux de Cernay, and La Ferté-Alais before reaching Fontainebleau. The Venetian ambassador on 30 June understood that Mary and Francis planned to observe the first anniversary of Henry II's death, to be held on 10 July, in two separate monasteries 'nearest to the place where their majesties now are'.[36] The use of the singular 'place' shows that he believed they were still together, suggesting that Mary stayed with Francis and used hunting and hawking to console herself (as she was to do in Scotland in 1563 when she received the news of the death of the duke of Guise).[37] In this case they would have been at St Leger on 30 June and by 10 July they would have been around Dampierre.[38] Francis observed the commemoration of his father's death at the abbey of Vaux de Cernay, but there is no separate record of Mary's whereabouts at this time.[39] She next enters the record at Fontainebleau on 6 August and it is likely that she had been there since Francis arrived from Paris on 20 July.[40] The plan had been that Francis would arrive with the two queens on 12 July, which implies that they intended to travel together to Fontainebleau.[41]

If Francis was following in the footsteps of his predecessors, so too was Mary. Catherine de Medici had travelled with the *petite bande* of noble women who followed Francis I on his hunting trips and she frequently attended the assemblies and the hunts of her husband, Henry II. Marie de Guise had hunted with James V on several occasions in Scotland; but a better known royal hunting couple were Maximilian I and his wife, Marie of Burgundy, whose shared love of hunting formed a bond of affection between them.[42] In a literary context,

---

[34] *CSPF 1558–9*, no. 1242 item 5; and *CSPF 1560–1561*, no. 233 p. 143.

[35] *CSPF 1560–61*, no. 233 p. 143; no. 254 p. 156; *CSPV*, vii, no. 178 p. 234. Once again an ambassador refers to Francis staying in local villages using the phrasing relating to being on progress. Chantonay states that Francis stayed with Mary to help her deal with her grief: *Catalogue Des Actes*, i. 529.

[36] *CSPV*, no. 178 p. 234; *CSPF 1560–61*, no. 254 p. 156–7. *Catalogue des Actes*, i, map 5 after p. 553 at p. xxx

[37] *CSPS*, ii, no. 2. It has been suggested that she retired to a room and wept for a week: Guy, *My Heart is My Own*, 113; or that she left Francis and went with Catherine to Fontainebleau.

[38] *Catalogue des Actes*, i, 529–31; Ferrière, *Grandes Chasses*, 49.

[39] *Catalogues, des Actes*, i, 529.

[40] *Catalogues des Actes*, i, 532; *CSPF 1560–61*, no. 411 p. 222.

[41] *CSPV*, vii, no. 178, 234. Francis had been around Paris for five or six days with all the 'princes and officials'. When he left for Fontainebleau Catherine went to her house at Monceaux, north of Paris: *CSPV*, vii, no. 190 p. 243.

[42] Almond, *Daughters of Artemis*, 86. Marie de Guise's hunting is discussed in Chapter 4, pp. 93–4.

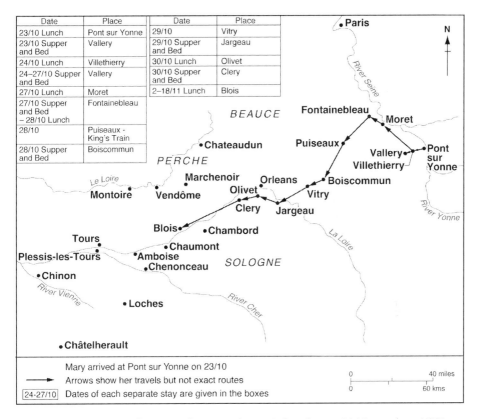

Map 2   Progress of Mary and Francis from 23 October to 18 November, 1559, and other places mentioned in the text.

too, the poem the *Debat des Dames*, suggests that while it may not have been common it was not unusual for couples to hunt together.[43] That Mary and Francis often hunted together on progresses and that they shared a love of hunting certainly provided the basis for a sound relationship between them.

Pictorial evidence

This mutual enjoyment of pastimes including hunting is occasionally represented pictorially and there is a possibility that such images of Francis and Mary were created. W. A. Baillie-Grohman, who had a thorough knowledge of medieval hunting and of early sporting art, argued that he had seen such an image of Mary and Francis hunting together with Mary riding pillion behind

---

[43] This poem is described in Chapter 2, pp. 48–9.

Francis. Mary, he wrote, had seen a series of twelve prints by the sixteenth-century engraver Virgil Solis which depicted sports for each month of the year.[44] Mary liked the plate for April, which portrayed a stag hunt, and requested that four panels should be woven to represent the four seasons for display in the Pavillion des Chasses (pavilion of hunts) at Fontainebleau. The designs, according to Baillie-Grohman, were still preserved in the Bibliothèque nationale de France in the early twentieth century, but only one of them was ever made into a tapestry and it used to hang in the Chambre de la Reine (Queen's Room) at Fontainebleau.[45] Regrettably Baillie-Grohman gave no sources for any of this and, while he was a reputable historian, there are several problems with his account: there is no series of twelve sporting prints by Virgil Solis; there was no Pavillion des Chasses at Fontainebleau in the sixteenth century; no designs for such tapestries have been found in the BnF; nor is there any such tapestry in Fontainebleau today.[46] There are several Solis hunting prints, two of single male riders and three which show women riding pillion behind a male rider which must closely resemble the scenes on the tapestry as described by Baillie-Grohman (Plate 1).[47]

There are other versions of this kind of sixteenth-century hunting scene which show a man and a woman hunting together.[48] The best known of these is the April tapestry of the *Chasses de Maximilien*, but the women there are hawking and not chasing deer and neither is in the pose described by Baillie-Grohman.[49] There is also a well-known enamel painted on bronze attributed to Leonard Limousin which shows a lord and lady hunting together with the lady riding pillion behind the lord. It had previously been thought to show Henry II and Diane de Poitiers hunting together.[50] It is now simply described as *Le Mois de Mai ou Le Printemps* (The month of May or the spring).[51] What is of interest here is that it was originally interpreted as

---

[44] Baillie-Grohman, *Sport in Art*, 98–9. Baillie-Grohman was a passionate big game hunter and a keen collector of sporting art. Historians know him best for the edition which he and his wife produced of the early fifteenth-century hunting treatise *The Master of Game* by Edward, duke of York.

[45] Baillie-Grohman, *Sport in Art*, 98–9.

[46] Two searches were generously conducted firstly by Severine Lapape and then by Caroline Vrand, Curators of the Department of Prints and Photography of the BnF. I am indebted to Jean Vittet, the Conservateur en Chef of Fontainebleau and Vincent Droguet, Directeur du Patrimoine et des Collections of the chateau for the information about Fontainebleau, April 2018.

[47] *Virgil Solis Single Sheet Prints II, Holstein's German Engravings, Etchings and Woodcuts 1400–1700*, vol 64, ed. D. Beaujean and G. Bartrum (Rotterdam, 2004). Prints nos 517 and 523 show single male riders. Prints nos 525, 526 and 527 show couples.

[48] C. F. G. R. Schwerdt, *Hawking, Hunting and Shooting. Illustrated in a Catalogue of Books Manuscripts Prints and Drawings*, 4 vols (London, 1927), iii, plate 173 after p. 22.

[49] Baillie-Grohman, *Sport in Art*, 76–84.

[50] M de Laborde, *Notice des émaux, bijoux et objets divers exposés dans les galeries de Musée du Louvre* (Paris, 1853), part i, 179.

[51] The url of the page on the Louvre website is https://collections.louvre.fr/en/ark:/53355/cl010117234 [accessed 25 November, 2023].

Plate 1　A sixteenth-century print by Virgil Solis showing a lord and lady hunting, with the lady riding pillion behind the lord. This is a *par force* hunt with a relay, represented by the huntsman and a hound hiding behind a tree waiting to join the hunt.

symbolising Diane de Poitiers's entrance to power on the accession of Henri II in 1547. If a similar tapestry or cartoon of Mary and Francis did exist, and given that riding on a side-facing saddle was considered to be the appropriate way for women to make a major entrance, an image of Mary and Francis could be interpreted in a similar manner. By 1556 spectacles and festivities were starting to promote the future marriage of Mary and Francis and such a hunting scene could have symbolised the entrance of Mary into the French royal family or, alternatively, if it was linked to Francis' coronation, it could be interpreted as representing Mary's entrance into royal power in France.[52] It has been commented that Mary had relatively little time as queen in which to produce such a tapestry, and at a time when French finances were virtually bankrupt it seems unlikely that large sums would have been spent on tapestries.[53] There were, of course, others who could have benefitted from commissioning such a tapestry. Catherine de Medici and Henry II would have been keen to promote Mary and Francis as the next royal couple in order to ensure their acceptance as monarchs and the continuation of the Valois dynasty. The Guises could also have commissioned a hunting tapestry of the pair to promote their family's own link to the future royal couple. The fact that only one of the four tapestries was ever completed, according to Baillie-Grohman, would certainly fit with the possibility that tapestries were commissioned, but that by the time of Francis's death only one had been completed. Despite the problems with this tapestry, it would seem that Baillie-Grohman had seen something which clearly convinced him that Mary was portrayed riding pillion behind Francis. This, however, was not the only occasion when Mary and Francis may have been portrayed together in a hunting context.

[52] Crépin-Leblond, *Marie Stuart*, 37. At this point I would like to thank various other people who have assisted me in the search for this tapestry: Jeremy Howard, Annie Renonciat, and especially Agnès Bos of the school of Art History in St Andrews University, and Thierry Crépin-Leblond, Director of the Musée Nationale de la Renaissance in Écouen.
[53] I am indebted to Rosalind Marshall for pointing this out to me and also for her help in trying to trace the tapestry.

Shortly after the death of Francis, Jacques du Fouilloux published a hunting treatise called, rather suggestively, *La Venerie … et L'Adolescence de L'Autheur* (Venery and the Youth of the Author) which was dedicated to Charles IX.[54] Du Fouilloux had been working on it for some time and had clearly written it for Francis II, in the light of which he had prepared plates and illustrations for the book. Licence to print was granted only on 23 December, shortly after Francis's death, and the engraving forming the frontispiece to the book supposedly showed Jacques du Fouilloux presenting his work to Charles IX (r. 1560–74). In 1561, however, Charles was only ten and the figure receiving the volume, who is as tall as the other courtiers, but also young and beardless, has been identified as Francis II (Plate 2).[55]

There has, however, been some debate about this, and it is worth considering in more detail why a portrayal of Francis II was included in the book when Charles IX was on the throne at the time of publication early in 1561. It has been suggested that the king was portrayed as an adult to flatter Charles IX, or alternatively that the figure is only meant to represent regal majesty in general, rather than any specific monarch in particular. Both explanations seem unlikely, especially when the author himself is accurately rather than symbolically portrayed.[56] Francis II's unexpected death was clearly part of the reason why his portrait was included rather than that of Charles IX, and the French book privilege system also helps to explain how this came about. Under this system a privilege granted by the royal chancery not only gave the book the royal seal of approval but also gave its printer a commercial monopoly over its printing. Because printers were very keen to obtain this privilege, they would usually submit a copy of the book along with the application for a privilege. Sometimes they even had the book printed and delayed its sale and distribution till they had received the privilege.[57] In such circumstances it is easy to see how Francis II appeared on the frontispiece. The privilege for this book was granted on 23 December and the application may well have been submitted before Francis's death along with copies showing Du Fouilloux presenting the book to the king. The woodcut, therefore, was not showing an actual event but it would have been flattering to show Francis II

---

[54] Fouilloux, *Vénerie*, fo. 1r Title Page.
[55] Fouilloux, *Vénerie*, fo. 2r. Available at: https://gallica.bnf.fr/ark:/12148/bpt6k15131176 ?rk=150215;2 [accessed 26 June 2020]; Noirmont, *Histoire de la Chasse*, i, 170; Marcelle Thiebaux, 'Review of *La Vénerie et l'Adolescence de Jacques du Fouilloux*, ed. Gunnar Tilander', *Speculum*, 4 (1971), 511–14, at 514.
[56] François Remigerau, *Jacques du Fouilloux et son Traité de la Vénerie* (Paris, 1952), 61,155–6. It is not known who carved this woodcut. Remigerau points out that Du Fouillux carved several of the hunting prints in the book but makes no comment on the frontispiece. Whoever engraved the plate knew Du Fouilloux's appearance and must have had some knowledge of the appearance of Francis II. The similarity of Du Fouilloux's portrait with that in *La Vénerie de Jacques du Fouilloux*, ed. Robin and L. Faure (Paris, 1864), suggests it is accurate.
[57] Elizabeth Armstrong, *Before Copyright: The French Book Privilege System 1498–1526* (Cambridge, 1990), 66, 70, 75.

Au treschrestien Roy
ET MONARQVE DE France, par son humble serf, du Foüilloux.

IL EST CERTAIN, Sire, que les hommes de tout temps se sont addonnez a plusieurs sciences hautes et occultes: les vns a la Philosophie, pour contenter leurs espritz, les autres aux artz mechaniques,

* ij

Plate 2   Frontispiece of *La Vénerie* by Jacques du Fouilloux, printed in 1561. Jacques du Fouilloux presents a copy of his hunting treatise to the king, Francis II, while the ladies of the court watch, presumably with Mary, his queen, at the front.

on the frontispiece and to dedicate the book to him. After Francis's death the text of the title page was altered to include Charles IX, but the woodcut on the frontispiece was so like Francis II that no one would have been fooled into thinking it was Charles. The text above the print translates as 'the very Christian king and monarch of France', and whether that was the original version or an updated version excluding Francis's name, the print would have been seen, no doubt, as a tribute to the late king.[58]

What has not yet been mentioned is that in this plate Francis, as well as being accompanied by the men of the court, is being observed by the ladies of the court and the woman at the front must presumably be his queen, Mary. She is the only one who is shown full length and she is also portrayed as a young woman. Her hands are placed in a modest pose which resembles classical statues of Aphrodite/Venus and of Botticelli's *Birth of Venus*, appropriately enough in a book called *La Vénerie*.[59] She is, therefore, given the prominence and flattering treatment befitting a queen. It would be going too far to call this a portrait of Mary – the unknown engraver may never have seen her – but it could more aptly be described as a representation of the queen. That Mary should be shown as an observer of the presentation of a hunting treatise to her husband is entirely in accord with the picture of them as a couple with a passionate interest in hunting.

Did Francis neglect the work of government?

The third misconception, that Francis was packed off hunting so that the Guise brothers could control the government of the country, requires modification rather than rejection. It is not the intention here to provide a total rehabilitation of Francis II nor to question that the Guises and Catherine de Medici were the political heavyweights of the reign. Rather, the aim is to show that Francis was not totally removed from the day-to-day work of government. It was the Spanish ambassador in his reports to Marguerite de Parma who first suggested that the Guises pushed Francis to go hunting; the idea has been current ever since.[60] Ambassadors certainly wanted to discuss matters with the cardinal of Lorraine and Catherine de Medici before they wanted to speak to Francis or Mary. Nonetheless, they still wished to have access to Francis and complained bitterly when they did not know where he was. Nicholas Throckmorton, the English ambassador, was certainly upset by the impossibility of locating Francis when he was travelling from Bar-le-Duc to Blois in October 1559, and again in June 1560 when he was hunting

[58] M. de Pressac, 'La Bibliographie Raisonné de Cet Ouvrage', in *La Vénerie de Jacques du Fouilloux*, ed. Robin and L. Faure (Niort 1864), 34–117 at 34.
[59] Kenneth Clark, *The Nude a Study in Ideal Form* (Princeton, 1953), 81–6.
[60] Ferrière, *Les Grandes Chasses*, 61 which quotes Chantonay.

around Chateaudun and Maillebois.[61] The Tuscan ambassador considered that he never knew where the court was headed or what it would be doing because hunting stags, he wrote, was its main business, thus implying that Francis found hunting to be a good excuse to avoid the work of government.[62] There was some truth in this in February 1560, when Francis, after spending a month at Blois, departed to hunt deer because he was tiring of court life and the constant stream of supplicants with whom he had to deal.[63]

Francis, however, was never excluded from government, nor did he lose touch with his council officials when he was on a progress. In 1559, when he stayed at Villers Cotterêts from 26 August to 11 September on his way to his coronation in Reims on 18 September, he combined the work of government with a hunt at Vivières which Mary probably attended.[64] But during this stay Francis was also party to discussions concerning the use of Savoy as a barrier against the Spanish in Italy, the election of a new pope, and an expedition to support the French position in Scotland. When Nicholas Throckmorton arrived to secure Francis's confirmation of the treaty of Cateau Cambrésis, he met Mary with the cardinal of Lorraine and the duke of Guise.[65] During this stay the cardinal of Lorraine persuaded Francis to reduce the number of judicial and military officials on his payroll and to accelerate Henry II's policy of persecuting the Huguenots.[66]

It has to be remembered that progresses were in themselves a valuable exercise in presenting the monarch to the people. They could establish working relationships with the elites of the neighbourhoods which they visited and they showed Francis and Mary fulfilling one aspect of their role as monarchs. The frequency of these progresses suggests that Francis was well aware of their importance, an impression supported by his conversations with Throckmorton at Fontainebleau in August 1560. On 19 August, in response to Francis's enquiry, Throckmorton confirmed that Elizabeth I also hunted during her progresses and planned to do so more often.[67] To discuss this with a foreign ambassador and for Throckmorton to report the conversation shows

---

[61] *CSPF 1559–60*, no. 233 p. 143; no. 234 p. 144.
[62] *Négociations Diplomatiques de la France avec la Toscane*, ed. Abel Desjardins, 6 vols (Paris, 1865), iii, 421.
[63] *Catalogue des Actes*, i, 506, 509.
[64] *Catalogue des Actes*, i, 488, and map 1 after p. 553; *CSPF 1558–9*, no. 1316 p. 539–40.
[65] Eric Thierry, 'Un sèjour de la cour de François II à Villers Cotterêts en 1559', *Histoire Aisne Memoires*, 39 (1994), 197–206, at 202–3. Available at: http://cfranquelin.free.fr/shrvc/production/francois_2_1994.pdf [accessed 27 August 2020].
[66] *Catalogue des Actes*, i, nos 104, 108, 110, 112–14.
[67] *CSPF 1560–61*, nos 411 p. 222, 444 p. 249–50. By 1564 it was noted by Robert Dudley, earl of Leicester, that Elizabeth was hunting more frequently on her progresses: Adams, 'The Queenes Majestie', 143. On 27 February, also, Francis had asked Throckmorton about Elizabeth's hunting and hawking: *CSPF 1559–6*, no. 777 p. 409. D. Neighbors considers that these enquiries show that Francis was making attempts to establish good relations with Elizabeth, given the threat of the Conspiracy of Amboise: Neighbors, 'Elizabeth I Huntress', 72.

that the matter of hunting on progresses was of some importance not only in the domestic presentation of the monarch but also in the creation of good relations with other monarchs. Highlighting that Francis and Elizabeth were monarchs engaged in similar activities helped to create an atmosphere of mutual respect between them which could be furthered, if they wished, by gifts of hawks, hounds, and hunting equipment.

The general pattern of a royal progress can be observed in the important initial journey which Francis and Mary conducted after his coronation. At Reims on 15 September Francis decided that he wanted to go hunting on horseback on his way to Blois. The Spanish ambassador, Chantonay, reported that Catherine de Medici had tried to dissuade Francis from this course of action and that Mary had been in tears pleading with him to alter his plans. Whatever their concerns, conducting a progress early in the reign was a sensible move for a young and relatively unknown king, one of whose valuable skills was the ability to hunt. Mary, whose health had been good since Villers Cotterêts, accompanied him on this progress, as one would expect, although she did feel unwell at Bar-le-Duc, purportedly as a result of hearing about her mother's difficulties in Scotland.[68] Also present were Catherine de Medici, Élisabeth, now queen of Spain, and Claude, duchess of Lorraine. At Bar-le-Duc, their first halt, they were met by their host, the duke of Lorraine and his aunt Anna de Lorraine. Christine, dowager duchess of Lorraine, later joined them for part of the trip.[69] Leaving Bar-le-Duc on 1 October they rode from one Guise chateau to another, hunting as they went, until they arrived at Fontainebleau on 27 October (see Map 2).[70] On a typical day the mid-morning meal, *diner*, was not eaten where they had stayed overnight but was taken at another chateau, probably as a kind of hunt breakfast wherever the hunt was being organised that day. In the evening the party would either return to the chateau where they were staying or move on to their next overnight stop for *souper*. Catherine de Medici commented that she had never seen so many hunts take place on a progress, but with Francis and three keen huntresses in the party that is hardly surprising.[71]

Nonetheless, Francis was meeting both Guise relations and local nobility – he visited around thirty chateaux during this progress – and continued with the day-to-day business of government. He signed a variety of acts relating to grants, confirmations of privileges, judicial matters, and appointments of officers while he was at Eclaron between 10 and 16 October and worked with his privy council on 22 October at Vauluisant and on 26 October at Vallery, the home of marshall Saint-André.[72] It was important politically for Francis

---

[68] *CSPF 1588–9*, no. 1406 p. 587.
[69] Ferrière, *Les Grandes Chasses*, 63, based on Chantonay; *CSPF 1588–9*, no. 1406 p. 586; Gobry, *François II*, 74; *Catalogue des Actes*, i, 495.
[70] *CSPF 1559–60*, no. 50 p. 26.
[71] *Lettres de Catherine de Médicis*, ed. Hector de la Ferrière, 12 vols (Paris, 1888–1943), i, 126, 127.
[72] *Catalogues des Actes*, i, nos 160–70, 172, 181, 183.

THE HUNTING COUPLE

to meet Saint-André and to win the support of someone with connections to both sides of the religious dispute. Apart from being friendly with the Guises, Saint André was a friend of Montmorency and had links with the reforming Bourbon princes, Antoine, king of Navarre, and his brother Louis, prince of Condé.[73] Their journey continued via Fontainebleau and the Loire valley, arriving at Blois on 2 November, almost six weeks after leaving Reims (see Map 2). On the one hand, the strong Guise/Lorraine bias to the first part of this progress benefitted the Guises because it stressed their connection, through Mary, to the royal family and enabled them to keep control of the king. On the other hand, Francis and Mary gained because it provided them with a supportive environment in which to start their first royal progress. Chantonay may have considered that the Guises sent Francis off to hunt to remove him from the work of government, but it was his youth and lack of experience as well as the influence of the Guises which minimised his role in the government at the start of his reign, not the amount of time spent hunting. His absences from court were no more frequent than those of his predecessors.

In 1560 Francis applied hunting as an instrument of royal policy in more specific ways both during the Conspiracy of Amboise in March 1560 and during the run-up to the estates general at Orleans in November 1560. During the hunting trip from Blois to Amboise between 3 and 22 February Francis heard news of a conspiracy against the Guises.[74] The plot, designed to attack the court at Blois and remove the Guises from power, was backed by the Huguenots, probably by Montmorency's nephew, Coligny, and by the prince of Condé. On 6 March, unaware that the court had planned to be at Amboise in March, the plotters had started gathering at Blois. Just four days later, despite the rumours of this revolt, Francis, Mary, and Catherine de Medici, rode through the forest of Amboise to go hunting at Chenonceau, which was now held by Catherine.[75] Francis accompanied by the queen and queen mother went hunting and hawking together with the rest of the court, which suggests that they were either relatively unconcerned or were in fact foolhardy, as the plotters were still at large in the area.[76] However, there is evidence that this hunting party on 10 March had something of a military flavour because many courtiers rode heavy horses and were allowed to carry guns.[77] Following their safe return to Amboise the normal activities of the court were only briefly interrupted when a party of rebel horsemen rode up to the chateau on 17 March. They were driven off by the duke of Guise and shortly afterwards the leader of the rebels, La Renaudie, was killed near Amboise.[78] The following day Francis, as if to celebrate, organised a *grande*

[73] Belleval, *Les Derniers Valois*, 400, 550–1.
[74] Paillard, 'Conjuration d'Amboise', 66, 82 n. 2, 83; *Catalogue des Actes*, i, 510–12.
[75] Ruble, *Première Jeunesse*, 246–7; Paillard, 'Conjuration d'Amboise', 87.
[76] Paillard, 'Conjuration d'Amboise', 87; Stoddart, *Girlhood*, 246–7.
[77] Paillard, 'Conjuration d'Amboise', 87–8.
[78] Carrol, *Martyrs and Murderers*, 117.

71

partie de chasse in the company of the Spanish ambassador and Henry, duke of Lorraine, the nine-year-old son of the duke of Guise.[79] Two days later, while Francis was hawking at La Heronnerie, Catherine and Mary rode to hawk and hunt at Chenonceau, where they no doubt took the opportunity to discuss arrangements for the forthcoming royal entry to that chateau.[80] Although the immediate threat of the conspirators had been removed from Amboise there was still Huguenot unrest in many areas of France, and in several provinces, especially in the south and east, order collapsed completely.[81] Nonetheless, a policy of moderation prevailed and no mass persecutions followed.[82] The hunting activities of Francis at this time are usually criticised as being foolhardy, but the use of heavy horses on the hunt on 10 March suggests that the court was not quite so naive as has been thought.[83] It argues that Francis and the Guises were aware of the danger but wished to convey that they were still in control, quite unaffected by the conspiracy.

This positive message was continued when Francis and Mary made their formal entry to Chenonceau on 31 March. Organised crowds cheered them through the gates of the chateau and the royal couple proceeded past two hastily erected triumphal arches and several other monuments on their way to supper in the chateau. In the evening they were entertained by the thunder of artillery, burning columns, and various other fireworks. The next day as they walked round the small park they read poems on panels attached to trees, one of which celebrated the park and its environment, another inviting Mary to take her time to admire the park.[84] Mary's arms, including those of France and Scotland, were displayed on the first triumphal arch; interestingly, according to Throckmorton, they included those of 'the Queen', presumably the queen of England.[85] This triumph promoted the idea that Francis had defeated the conspirators at Amboise, portrayed Catherine de Medici as a new political force in the country, and suggested that together they could unite the country behind the Valois monarchy.[86] It would be going too far to suggest that the hunts and the royal entry to Chenonceau were planned as a single programme, but they were obviously intended to help the court recover from the shock of Amboise and restore faith in the Valois dynasty.

---

[79]   Paillard, 'Conjuration d'Amboise', 103; *Catalogue des Actes*, i, 514 for 18 March. Henry started to learn to hunt at age seven: Chapter 2, n. 28.

[80]   *CSPV*, vii, 163; Stoddart, *Girlhood*, 250–2.

[81]   Carroll, *Martyrs and Murderers*, 122.

[82]   Knecht, *The Rise and Fall of Renaissance France*, 283.

[83]   Stoddart, *Girlhood*, 246–7.

[84]   *Les Triomphes Faictz à L'Entrée du Roy a Chenonceau Le Dymanche Dernier Jour de Mars 1559* (Tours, 1559), written by Le Plessis. Now printed in *Inventaires de Meubles Bijoux et Livres estant a Chenonceau le huit Janvier MDCIII* (Paris, 1856), 5, 15–16.

[85]   *CSPF 1559–60*, no. 952 p. 506; *Les Triomphes Faictz ... a Chenonceau*, 4. Throckmorton refers to Elizabeth as 'the Queen' and to Mary as the 'French queen'.

[86]   Benoit Bolduc, 'In fumo dare lucem. Les Triomphes faictz a l'Entrée du roy a Chenonceau (1559/60)', in Hélène Visentin and Nicolas Russel (eds), *French Ceremonial entries in the Sixteenth century: Events, Image, Test* (Toronto, 2007), 163–87, at 163, 184.

In November, when Francis was preparing for the estates general at Orléans, he again put his passion for hunting to good use. He needed to determine how much support Navarre and the duke of Condé could muster before charging Condé with complicity in the Amboise conspiracy. Francis knew that the ageing constable Montmorency was close to the Bourbon faction, so he invited him to a hunt at Vincennes to ascertain if he would stand in his way or not; in the event, he caused no problems. When Navarre and Condé arrived at Orléans on 30 October, Francis met them, told Condé he would be put on trial, and had him arrested.[87] In an attempt to divide and rule, he allowed Navarre freedom during the trial to hunt in the area. Almost every morning Francis invited him to attend his privy council and then hunted 'familiarly' with him thereafter.[88] Francis's charm offensive may have had some effect in limiting support for Condé, but it did not win over the king of Navarre. On 13 November Francis announced that he and Mary together with Catherine de Medici would lead a grand hunt at Chambord and Chenonceau which would last for the rest of the month, and nobles flocked to join them. Antoine, however, refused to take part because he feared that he would be assassinated under cover of a hunting accident.[89] Francis was putting hunting to sound use in an effort to consolidate his position prior to the estates general. This gathering, however, never happened because on 16 November Francis went hunting and returned with a recurrence of a severe ear infection, leading to his death on 5 December. He was succeeded by his brother Charles IX, aged ten, and, with Catherine's subsequent seizure of the regency, the era of Guise power had passed.

Because Francis loved hunting and regarded it as his chief exercise throughout his brief reign, he paid attention to the maintenance of his hunting establishment and hunting grounds. He took steps to ensure that his falconers, hunters and archers, and, if necessary, their widows were all suitably recompensed.[90] He continued to order *reformations* of the rights of use in his forests, and in an effort to help the royal finances he worked on a system for determining the value of these forests, much of which came from the carefully managed sale of wood and timber.[91] The Guises certainly realised the value of coppices of younger wood, but it is hard to evaluate how far Mary was aware of this.[92] She would certainly have seen aspects of forest management such as *coupes*, areas marked off for felling, and enclosed farms and grazing when

---

[87]   Gobry, *François II*, 178; CSPV, vii, no. 202 p. 263.
[88]   *CSPF 1560–1*, p. 394 Item 18; CSPV, vii, no. 206 p. 266.
[89]   CSPV, vii, no. 270 (rectius 207) p. 268; Regnier de la Planche, *La Regne de François II*, ii, 102, 115; CSPF, *1560–1*, no. 716 Item 27 p. 395.
[90]   *Catalogue des Actes*, i, no. 257.
[91]   Devèze, *La Vie de la Forêt*, 199.
[92]   Regnier de la Planche, *La Regne de François II*, ii, 252–6. His comments need to be tempered by remembering that he was a Huguenot opposed to the Guises.

hunting in the park at Chambord, which was still being reconditioned by Henry II. In the forest of Retz she would also have encountered areas which were earmarked to satisfy the local inhabitants' rights of use and were not reserved for hunting. More direct involvement in managing woodland was implied by the terms of her marriage contract in 1558, which stated that she could appoint officers on her dower lands in the duchy of Touraine and the county of Poitou. After Francis's death it was confirmed that this included the appointment of foresters, and no time was lost in starting to make arrangements for Mary's income from the rents of these dower lands.[93] An ordinance which was issued on 20 December stated that Mary would be allowed to take revenue from the woods and stands of high forest on these lands, but only in the form of tolls for grazing pigs and other animals and a variety of fines and forfeitures. Her servants were not to be allowed to cut the timber trees, but on advice of the royal officers they could take wood to maintain the houses, mills, and buildings on these lands. When she was resident in the area her servants were also permitted to collect dead wood, the wood from trees that did not fruit, to use as fuel.[94] In this context it is relevant that Mary possessed a copy of *De Arboribus* (About Trees) by the classical author Columella, which was becoming popular in the sixteenth century, a French edition of which had appeared in 1551. It dealt with the nurture of vines and described how rods and poles to support the vines had to be grown by coppicing willow and chestnut. Whether Mary acquired a copy at this time or later, the volume appears in the list of books in Mary's library, compiled in 1575, as *Columell of Historeis*, a mistranscription of *Columell of Treis*.[95]

Therefore, by the time that Mary left France on 14 August 1561, she had observed how hunting had helped Francis to establish his position as a monarch. While some of Francis's hunts were conducted familiarly with small groups, he had also organised large hunting parties at royal chateaux. Mary often accompanied Francis at these *grandes chasses* when they entertained the nobility by providing hunting for them in royal forests, identifying them as part of the ruling elite, and trying to establish a working relationship with them. While she had witnessed that hunting could not be allowed to result in neglect of government, she had also seen that it could be used to provide a break from the court and to control the access of ambassadors and supplicants to the monarch. Mary had observed how hunting could be employed for specific purposes when she had taken part in hunts to display the supposedly

---

[93] Devèze, *La Vie de la Forêt*, 152, 199; *Relations politiques de la France et de l'Espagne avec l'Écosse au XVIe siècle*, ed. A. Teulet (Paris, 1862), ii, 155–6; Greengrass, M., 'Mary Dowager Queen of France', in Lynch, *Mary Stewart*, 171–94, at 173.

[94] *Relations Politique de la France*, ed. Teulet, 155; Devèze, *La Vie de la Forêt*, i, 83. This referred to trees such as willow, thorn bushes, elderberry, broom, and alder.

[95] *Inventaires de la Royne*, p. cxliv; Sharman, *The Library of Mary Queen of Scots*, 60–2; Columella, *De Re Rustica*, trans. H. Bash, Loeb Library (London, 1948), 455–7, bk. iv, chaps xxx–xxxii.

THE HUNTING COUPLE

undisturbed authority of the Crown, both during and after the conspiracy of Amboise; and she had seen how Francis used hunting to prepare for the estates general.

The progress which Mary had made can be seen in Throckmorton's despatches. He saw her grow into her role as the queen to the point where, on 19 August 1560 at Fontainebleau, he had an audience with her during which she was seated under her cloth of state, unaccompanied by either her uncles or Catherine de Medici, and discussed the ratification of the Treaty of Edinburgh and an exchange of portraits with Elizabeth.[96] In December, after Francis's death, Throckmorton felt able to praise her ability 'in the wise handling herself and her matters' and her appreciation of 'good counsel and wise men (which is a great virtue in a prince or princess)'.[97] Mary had acquired the political sense to co-operate with Catherine de Medici and, when necessary, to argue with the Guises while still remaining on friendly terms with them.[98] During the summer of 1561, while she was preparing to leave France, she was already considering the style of her government in Scotland and had started to plan for the holding of her council.[99]

In May 1561, before departing for Scotland, she visited her Guise relatives in Lorraine, where she was awarded a 'gret triumphe' by Claude, duchess of Lorraine. The nobles of the area entertained her to various activities including 'hunting on the feildis'.[100] When the Scots who had arrived to escort Mary on her return to Scotland saw her being feted in this way as the widowed queen of France, they would have realised then, if they had not already done so, that they would be accompanying an experienced monarch to Scotland and not an inexperienced princess.

[96] *CSPF 1558–9*, no. 987 p. 379; *CSPF 1560–61*, no. 444, pp. 249–50.
[97] *CSPF 1560–61*, no. 833 p. 472–3.
[98] *CSPV*, vii, no. 155 p. 198; *CSPF 1559–60*, no. 1082 p. 597 Item 12; Guy, *My Heart is My Own*, *112*.
[99] Alexandra Nancy Johnson, 'Mary Stuart and her Rebels Turned Privy-Councillors: Performance of the Ritual Council', in Helen Matheson-Pollock, Joanne Paul, and Catherine Fletcher (eds), *Queenship and Counsel in Early Modern Europe* (London, 2018), 161–86, at 163–4, 172–3.
[100] Lesley, *History* (1570), 295. This is a copy of Lesley's original Scots version of his *History* presented to Mary around 1570. Leslie *Historie* (1596), ii, 456 only gives 'hunting'. Hunting in the fields contains the idea of hunting in a park.

4

Hunting at the Scottish renaissance court

Only by establishing the part played by hunting in the public role of the monarch in renaissance Scotland is it possible to assess how effectively Mary used hunting as an instrument of policy and to judge how far she fulfilled the expectations of her in a hunting context. It will be shown that the basic tasks expected of the monarch were to maintain suitable hunting grounds, to organise hunts, to invite nobles and lairds to attend, to provide accommodation for the royal party, and to arrange hospitality for the chief hunters. The public functions of hunting could then come into operation: creating ties between the monarch and nobility, demonstrating royal authority in the localities, impressing visitors and ambassadors, and establishing the authority and image of the monarch.

In the fourteenth century the main areas where the Stewart kings hunted had been established by Robert II (r. 1371–90) more by accident than by design. Influenced by the alienations of royal forests such as Ettrick and Jedburgh to the Douglas family in the reign of Robert I (r. 1306–29) and by the more plentiful supply of game in the Highlands, Robert II tended to hunt on lands held by his sons in Strathbraan, Strathearn, and Menteith, although he did also hunt in Kindrochit, which was held by the earl of Mar (Map 3). These hunting grounds, apart from Kindrochit, were specifically linked to the Stewarts and continued to be used by Stewart monarchs throughout the fifteenth and sixteenth centuries. James IV and James V hunted in the forest of Glenfinglas in Menteith, in the forest of Glenartney in Strathearn, and in the royal park attached to Falkland Palace in Fife. They also hunted further north in Balquhidder, Strathfillan, and in the forest of Ben More.[1] Royal hunts were held on the estates of the nobility in Glen Tilt in Atholl and on the hills between the Megget valley and Eskdale on lands held by Melrose abbey, the Hays of Yester, and the Maxwells.[2] This area, which the household accounts describe as 'Meggatland' was one of James V's favoured hunting grounds to which he made at least eleven hunting trips between 1525 and 1535.[3]

---

[1] Gilbert, *Hunting and Hunting Reserves*, 44–5; *TA*, i, p. lxxiv ff.; *TA*, ii, p. xvii ff.

[2] *Liber Sancte Marie de Melros*, Bannatyne Club (Edinburgh, 1837), no. 563; A. M. T. Maxwell-Irving, 'Cramalt Tower: historical survey and excavations', *PSAS*, 111 (1981), 401–29, at 402–5; Jamie Cameron, *James V* (Edinburgh, 2011), 8–5; *RMS*, iii, no. 1199; Pitscottie, *Historie*, i, 304; Andrea Thomas, 'Renaissance Culture at the Court of James V', unpublished PhD thesis (University of Edinburgh, 1997), 387–423 for James V's itinerary; NRS, E31/3, fo. 9v; E32/5 fos 10r, 10v, 98r; *Excerpta e Libris Domicilii*, 3.

[3] *Excerpta e Libris Domicilii*, 3, 156, 185, 194, 216; NRS, E31/3, fos 9v, 88r; Cameron, *James V* (Edinburgh, 2011), 78–80; *TA*, v, 422; vi, 27, 192–3, 215, 259, 263; James V's

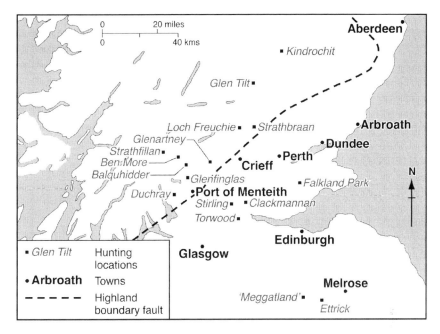

Map 3 Royal hunting grounds in Scotland from the fourteenth to the sixteenth century. These hunting grounds lie on the southern edge of the Highlands, which is more easily accessible from royal residences such as Stirling Palace and Doune Castle.

The size and composition of hunting parties

When a large drive was being organised, it was essential not only to secure the manpower for the tinchell or stable but also to ensure that there were sufficient deer in the area to support a drive rather than a chase. The tinchell summoned by the earl of Mar to hunt in 1618 was reckoned to comprise between five and six hundred men.[4] In Glenartney in 1506, James IV paid a tinchell of 306 men for their services, but when James V hunted with his army in 1530 he clearly had an ample supply of men to form a stable.[5] Normally it must have been the sheriff's or forester's responsibility to raise the necessary manpower. The size of the herds of deer in the area would also be of concern. Large hunts depleted herd numbers, especially when two or three hunts were held over different hills in the same area. In August 1533, when James planned to hunt in Megget for a fifth time in as many years, he ordered

---

itinerary in Thomas, 'Renaissance Culture', 387–408.
[4] Peter Hume Brown, *Early Travellers in Scotland* (Edinburgh, 1891), 122.
[5] TA, iv, 137. The 1530 expedition is discussed below.

that a proclamation be read out at Selkirk, Peebles, and Moffat to the effect that no one was to hunt in 'Meggatland', Eskdalemuir, or Tweedsmuir until he arrived.[6] He did not in fact appear in Megget until June 1534, which theoretically gave deer herds in the area almost two years to recover from his previous expedition there in 1532.

The extent to which these hunts fulfilled a wider political and social role whereby the king won the trust and loyalty of his subjects depended, of course, on the numbers of the nobility who attended. While there are no specific records of these numbers, it is possible to make sensible deductions about the size of the hunting parties. When a force was raised to pursue thieves and traitors in the Borders in 1530, it was raised from men aged between sixteen and sixty from various parts of Scotland from Kincardine and Forfar in the north-east to Kirkcudbright and Wigtown in the south-west. This army was estimated between eight and twelve thousand and, allowing for exaggeration, it is safe to say that the numbers were in the thousands rather than the hundreds. Pitscottie, whose tales can sometimes wander from the truth, linked this expedition to hunting, and on this occasion he was being accurate.[7] At the time, no one could have been in any doubt that this was a judicial raid into the Borders, but it gives an idea of how large these hunts could be that they could serve as cover for an expedition of this size.

While these figures may not be typical, James V's household accounts are helpful in gauging the size of hunting parties because they specify the supplies of bread and ale which were sent to the hunts, always bearing in mind that one loaf need not equal one person.[8] In 1530, 1532, and 1534 the average number of loaves supplied to Glenartney for a three-day hunt varied between 100 and 135 per day, whereas at Glenfinglas in 1530 and 1534 the average for hunts of the same length was between 175 and 220 per day.[9] Over the same periods the average amount of ale provided at Glenartney was 16 to 39 gallons (*laguinae*) per day and in the Glenfinglas area 40 to 50 gallons, indicating that the hunts at Glenfinglas tended to be larger affairs than those in Glenartney. The royal hunting party made up of courtiers, lords, and

[6] *TA*, vi, 137. James appears to have hunted in Argyll instead (*Excerpta e Libris Domicilii*, 44).

[7] Pitscottie, *Historie*, i, 334; Cameron, *James V*, 80; *Acts of the Lords of Council in Public Affairs 1501–54: Selections from Acta Dominorum Concilii*, ed. R. K. Hannay (Edinburgh, 1932), 328–9.

[8] John G. Harrison, '"The Bread Book" and the Court and Household of Marie de Guise in 1549', *Scottish Archives*, 15 (2009), 29–41, at 36. Christopher Dyer's study of nobles' and bishops' accounts in England in the thirteenth and fourteenth centuries suggests that the lord would provide a gallon of ale and two to three pounds of wheat bread per head for their households: C. Dyer, 'English diet in the later Middle Ages', in T. H. Aston *et al.* (eds), *Social Relations and Ideas: Essays in Honour of R. H. Hilton*, 191–216, at 193.

[9] Glenartney – NRS, E31/3 fos 87v–88v (1530); E 31/4, fo. 12r (1532); E 31/5 fo. 52v (1534). Glenfinglas – E31/3, fo. 95r (1530); E31/5, fos 67v, 68r (1534). These figures are based on *panes* (loaves) and exclude *pastilli* (pasties), which are not always itemised. These figures are only a guide because it is not always clear when items listed were not sent to the hunts. Some items were bought at or near to the hunts.

lairds can, therefore, be reckoned in the hundreds rather than the thousands. There would of course have been others in attendance who were not fed and watered by the king. At the hunt held in Mar in 1618, where no royalty were present, it was estimated that 1,400 to 1,500 persons were in attendance.[10] If such numbers were involved in royal hunts, then, based on the above figures, many hunters would have had to provide for themselves, bringing some of their own households to set up pavilions, supply fuel, tend fires, and cook and prepare food. In addition, the tinchell, perhaps comprising several hundred local tenants who knew the hills and the habits of the deer, would be expected to attend for a day or two with their own supplies, just as happened in Kildrummy and in Atholl.[11] Therefore, an overall total of between five hundred and a thousand persons of all ranks attending a royal hunt does not sound implausible.

Presumably the royal hunting party comprised those invited from the local nobility and gentry, from those holding royal office, from privy councillors, and from those nobles who were a regular presence at court. Although the tinchell allowed poorer tenants to be a part of the event and to share the feasting which followed, these hunts were focussed mainly on impressing the king's noble subjects and winning and retaining their support. The king presumably took some care over his choice of hunting companions and he seems to have invited men from different areas or sheriffdoms of Scotland to attend different hunts, very much resembling the muster for an army. In this way he extended his hospitality around the country, maintaining contact with different regions. In 1531 it was the gentlemen of Menteith and Lothian who were mustered for the hunting in Megget, but specific invitations went out to an East Lothian group, James Hamilton of Innerwick, George Hume of Spott, Lord Hay of Yester, and, interestingly, Elizabeth Hepburn, prioress of Haddington, who was a nun.[12] By entertaining the court and the nobility to hunt in his reserves the king reinforced his role as their lord giving the gift of hunting and, in return, expecting his followers to feel greater loyalty to himself. At a time when the king still depended on the support of the nobility to govern the country, personal ties between the monarch and his subjects were the foundation of good government, and hunting expeditions were an ideal opportunity to establish such ties.[13]

---

[10] Hume Brown, *Early Travellers in Scotland*, 122.
[11] *Illustrations of the Topography and Antiquities of the Shires of Aberdeen and Banff*, Spalding Club (Aberdeen, 1847–69), iv, 312; Charles Ferguson, 'Sketches of the early history and legends and traditions of Strathardle and its glens', *Transactions of the Gaelic Society of Inverness*, 23 (1898–99), 154–78, at 177.
[12] *TA*, v, 445; Cameron, *James V*, 91.
[13] Michael Brown, *The Wars of Scotland 1214–1371* (Edinburgh, 2005, repr. 2015), 32.

Accommodation at royal hunts

Accommodation at royal hunts has seldom been examined in any detail, and yet it was just as important in creating a particular image of the monarchy as a royal palace. These hunts were held in fairly remote areas, and so a variety of temporary accommodations were used for the royal party. The use of hunt halls is well known, but the use of more humble dwellings has not so far been fully appreciated. Whether it was seen as part of the adventure of hunting in the wild or as a way of escaping the grandeur and formality of royal palaces, the use of poorer accommodation when hunting was relatively common in Scotland. Sometimes these humbler buildings were purpose built, but sometimes whatever was available in the area of the hunt had to serve. In Strathfillan in 1501 James IV stayed in the church and in the dwelling of a man to whom he paid 14s.[14] In 1506 he stayed with the vicar in Balquhidder in what was, presumably, a fairly humble dwelling.[15] On the other hand, the lodges mentioned at 'Kinbrichtor' in Fife in the early thirteenth century and the hunting houses, *certae domus venationibus* (certain houses for hunting), in Duchray in Menteith, repaired by James III, support the idea that there was a tradition, when hunting, of using small, purpose-built dwellings for accommodation.[16] In the tales of Fionn hunting booths are frequently mentioned, though the Gaelic word used for them was *fianboth* rather than the alternative, *longphort*.[17] On the island of Rum *The New Statistical Account of Scotland* records that the place-name Tigh'n Sealg, hunting houses, was associated with the dykes which were used to funnel deer towards the kill zone. While the *NSAS* suggested these might have been houses into which the deer were driven to be killed, it seems more likely that they were the dwellings where the hunters stayed while they were hunting there.[18] W. J. Watson has also recorded the place-name 'Luchairt na Feinne', the encampment of the Fian, near Finlarig on Loch Tay.[19]

James II (r. 1437–60) is the first monarch on record to build hunt halls, and his building programme in 1458–59 included three of them, one in Glenfinglas, one at Loch Freuchie in Strathbraan, and one at Newark Castle. The Loch Freuchie hunt hall, which cost £24 to build, comprised a hall, a chamber, a kitchen, and four outbuildings, while the Glenfinglas lodge contained only a hall and two chambers at a cost of £5 6s.[20] James had a hall and two chambers built and some rooms (*domus*) repaired at Newark Castle, at

[14] *TA*, ii, 119–20.
[15] *TA*, iii, 337.
[16] *ER*, vi, 579; vii, 614; *RRS*, ii, no. 471.
[17] Watson, 'Deer and Boar', 86. This word will be discussed more fully in Chapter 6, pp. 129–31.
[18] *NSAS*, xiv, 152, 'Parish of Small Isles'.
[19] Watson, *Celtic Place-Names of Scotland*, 494.
[20] *ER*, vi 579.

a cost of £22, in preparation for his arrival there, presumably to attend the impending forest court.[21] Assuming that Newark already possessed a hall, this must have been a structure built outside the castle along the lines of his other hunt halls. The Loch Freuchie lodge does not appear to have been used after James II's reign, but the Glenfinglas lodge, where Mary later stayed, was used by James III (r. 1460–88), IV, and V. The exact location of the Glenfinglas hunt hall is not known, partly because the glen is now a reservoir. However, the 1946 aerial photographs suggest a possible site, a mound called Tom Buidhe, the yellow or pleasing mound, which is approximately 60m by 88m in size and is now marked as an island on the Ordnance Survey [OS] map (NN52310881).[22] The presence of hunting parties in the area is also suggested by the mound called Tom na Feilidh, which probably means the mound of the banquet. Before the glen was flooded it lay just below Tom Buidhe, between the Finglas Water and the Allt Gleann Casaig.[23] However, there are no visible remains of any structures on Tom Buidhe where one might have expected the remains of stone footings to survive, and so it is possible that the hunt hall lay lower down, nearer the valley floor, and has been flooded.

Given the costs of building these hunt halls it would seem likely that they were timber constructions, but it is hard to determine their size. They may have been quite substantial structures, resembling the internal dimensions of the hall of the stone castle at Kindrochit which was probably used by Robert II when hunting in Mar. This type of hall castle is well known from the thirteenth century onwards, although it is reckoned that many have not survived.[24] The earliest phase of Kindrochit used by Robert II was based on a hall measuring 30.5m by 9.1m.[25] Mackay Mackenzie considered that this was the standard size for these halls, but the size could vary as in, for example, the hall in Rait Castle, which was only 20m long but was still 10m wide.[26] A possible hunting lodge of thirteenth-century date with a clay-bonded base for the walls has been excavated by Derek Hall and Kevin Malloy and is located beside Buzzart Dykes park in the royal forest of Clunie (NO13054817). Its internal dimensions are approximately 32m by 5m and it seemingly has no internal divisions, which would certainly correspond with the idea of a

[21] *ER*, vi, 545. For comparative prices for purely internal work at Newark in 1472–3 see *ER*, viii 143.
[22] National Collection of Aerial Photography B0122/CPE/SCOT/UK/0194 nos 4315–17. Translations of Gaelic names are from Peter E. McNiven, 'Gaelic place-names and the social history of Gaelic speakers in Medieval Menteith', unpublished PhD thesis (University of Glasgow, 2011), 95, 268. This hillock has been planted with a few fir trees whose roots, it is to be hoped, have not destroyed any archaeological remains.
[23] OS 6-inch map, Sheet 94, First Edition, surveyed 1862.
[24] Chris Tabraham, *Scotland's Castles* (London, 1997), 37, 55.
[25] W. Douglas Simpson, 'The Excavation of Kindrochit Castle', *Antiquaries Journal*, 8 (1928), 69–75.
[26] W. Mackay Mackenzie, *The Medieval Castle in Scotland* (London, 1927), 160; Tabraham, *Scotland's Castles*, 55.

hall.[27] Whether the halls at Glenfinglas and Loch Freuchie were of this size is unknown, and while it may not be wrong to imagine them as halls with similar dimensions, other interpretations are possible.

In Strathdon in Banffshire in the late sixteenth century certain houses with fires, referred to as fire-houses, were also called halls. On the basis of the number of couples (frames) needed to support the roof of the principal dwelling of the settlement, it can be calculated that this house was between 12m and 21m in length.[28] Given the tendency for quite humble dwellings to be used for hunting accommodation, it is possible that some hunt halls were smaller vernacular structures, but still large enough to contain a fire and to be kitted out for feasting for a reduced number of people. In this scenario these structures are clearly hall houses, which consisted of a public hall with private living accommodation attached, as in the hall houses of fifteenth-century England. There are several examples in Scotland, such as the long hall house in Perth, which dates to the thirteenth century and which measured 15m by *c.* 6m, or the larger hall houses of the thirteenth and fourteenth centuries at Rattray Castle. The hall house at Glencairn in south-west Scotland, measuring 13.7m by 4.8m, sounds similar, although there are no details of its internal structure.[29] One has, therefore, to consider that the hunt halls in Glenfinglas and Loch Freuchie were structures of this type which followed a plan well known in both humble and higher-status buildings. The structure beside Newark Castle could also fall into the hall-house style of building. Continuing with the model of a hall house, one can envisage the Glenfinglas hunt hall as a central hall with a chamber at each end and the Loch Freuchie hunt hall as a similar structure with the chamber at one end of the hall and the kitchen at the other end. The four outbuildings at this lodge could then have been constructed around a courtyard. Whatever the size of the hunt hall, the accommodation for the royal party had to be supplemented by pavilions, which were in the care of the 'pavilion man', who was responsible for transporting and setting them up.[30] James V used them regularly at Megget and Glenartney and had his coat of arms painted on one.[31]

---

[27] Kevin Malloy and Derek Hall, 'Medieval hunting and wood management in the Buzzart Dykes landscape', *Environment History*, 25 (2019), 365–90, at 367. Canmore Id 28835 Middleton Muir.

[28] Alasdair Ross, 'Two Surveys of Vernacular Buildings and Tree Usage in the Lordship of Strathdon, Banffshire 1585–1612', SHS *Miscellany XIV* (Edinburgh, 2013), 1–60 at 8. This measurement is based on a house with five couples and two tail forks and a gap of 2.0m to 3.5m between the couples: Piers Dixon, 'Cruck Buildings in Scotland: A Review', in *Cruck Building: A Survey* (eds), N. Alcock, P. S. Barnwell and M. Cherry (Donington, 2019), 300–22. This would create six sections of between 2m and 3.5m in length each.

[29] Colin Platt, *Medieval England*, 202–4 and illustration no. 134; David Perry, Hilary Murray and Nicholas Q. Bogdan (eds), *Perth High Street Archaeological Excavations 1975–7, the Excavations at 75–95 High Street and 5 – 10 Mill Street Perth* (Perth, 2010), i, 131, 176–7; Peter Yeoman, *Medieval Scotland* (London, 1995), 93–4; Canmore Id 75337 at Glenesslin in Nithsdale. It was replaced by a tower.

[30] *TA*, iii, 156, 334.

[31] *TA*, v, 363, 423; vi, 215, 264, 433; vii, 87, 204.

The hunt hall in Glenartney, which was used by James IV in 1508 and which James V may also have used, was probably built between 1493 and 1508.[32] When James V hunted in Glenartney in September 1532 he stayed at 'Collybrothane', now called Cultybraggan (NN76821977), which may have been the site of the hunt hall, although that building could have been further up the glen. Certainly, when David Lord Drummond was granted Cultybraggan in 1536, it would have been part of his duties as forester of Strathearn to maintain any hunt hall in the area.[33] Pont, however, marks a substantial dwelling of two or three storeys which might have been a tower house or castle surrounded by a small enclosed wood or park on the edge of the nearby wood of 'Cultyuragan'.[34] If there was such a structure, one would expect it to render unnecessary the building and maintenance of a temporary hunting lodge. However, when the lands were granted to David Lord Drummond, no castle was mentioned, only orchards and a mill. Whether James IV's hunt hall was at Cultybraggan or not, James V definitely stayed somewhere in that area.

The best-known temporary hunting lodge in the sixteenth century, but also the least typical, was the remarkable structure erected by John Stewart, the third earl of Atholl, to entertain James V in 1532. Not only does it throw a surprising light on what was possible in the upper reaches of Glen Tilt, but its destruction was probably referenced in the celebrations of the baptism of Mary's son, James VI, discussed in Chapter 7.[35] Pitscottie somewhat excitedly described it as a 'curieous palice', meaning a palace which was beautiful and skilfully built, and where the royal party was 'honourabill ludgit as they had ben in Ingland France Itallie and Spaine ffor their hunting and pastyme'.[36] This 'faire palice' had three storeys, was built with young timbers bound with young birch branches, and had four sides or quarters with a round tower in each corner like a block house. There were two towers on either side of the entrance, which was filled with 'ane greit portcullis of trie [a wooden portcullis]'. Charles McKean considered that this structure was modelled on the tradition of the renaissance chateau. Its plan was identical to the chateau of Bury on the Loire and it was to be copied twenty years later at the castle of Boyne near Portsoy. It also resembled the plan for the new royal lodging which was built between 1528 and 1532 on the north-west corner of Holyrood Palace.[37] James was probably pleasantly surprised to find

---

[32] *TA*, iv, 137. It was not mentioned in the place-dates of charters issued in Glenartney in 1467 and 1493, when one would have expected it to be mentioned. The hunt hall of Glenfinglas was specified in the place-dates of charters of James IV in 1494: *RMS*, ii, nos 922, 923, 2185, 2198.

[33] *RMS*, iii, no. 1560; NLS, Adv. Ms. 70.2.9, Pont 21 ('Lower Glenalmond; Strathearn').

[34] This wood probably lay in the vicinity of the modern Cowden Wood and Drumchork Wood to the east and south of Cultybraggan.

[35] See below, p. 154–5.

[36] *DOST*, 'curious', meaning 2; Pitscottie, *Historie*, i, 335–8.

[37] Charles McKean, 'Finnart's Platt', *Journal of the Architectural Heritage Society of Scotland*, 11 (1991), 3–17, at 8; John G Dunbar, *Scottish Royal Palaces* (East Linton, 1999), 60–1.

a replica of his new Holyrood lodgings created for him in Glen Tilt. This may not have been a renaissance palace as such, but it was no rough shack. It was, according to Pitscottie, well carpeted with fresh turf, rushes, meadow sweet, and flowers. The walls of the rooms were covered with tapestries and silk hangings from Arras and the rooms, according to Pitscottie, were lit by glazed windows. James V had his bed transported there along with 'gear' from his wardrobe, including presumably not only clothes but also tapestries and hangings as well as crossbows.[38]

Remarkably, the whole structure was set on fire as the king departed. James V explained to the papal nuncio who accompanied him that this was the 'wse of our hielandmen [custom of our highlanders]' when they left a dwelling, no matter how good the accommodation there had been. W. J. Watson considered that it was not unusual for humble shelters of poles and branches to be burned after a hunt, but such bivouacs were on a different scale altogether from the 'palice' at Glen Tilt.[39] Other examples of similar practices in Gaelic culture can be found in pre-Norman Ireland, where there are many references to the construction of temporary halls for feasting on major Christian festivals, but the construction of these halls could also carry a political significance. Such halls were not necessarily burned, but they were temporary. If one king entered the hall of another king it was a sign of submission, but at the same time the act of constructing a hall for a superior king was seen as recognition of his higher status.[40] By the fifteenth century the custom could take on a rather different significance. In an early fifteenth-century poem, Sir Colin Campbell of Lochawe invited the O'Neill chief to hunt in Cowal and at the end of the hunting he burned the lodge where they had been staying. In the poem, the ostensible reason for the burning was Colin's embarrassment that his lodge did not match the splendour of O'Neill's home in Ireland. Burning the lodge was an attempt to impress the visitor with one's wealth and liberality, and this is exactly what happened at Glen Tilt.[41] The papal envoy was amazed when the lodge was burned. He said to James: 'I merwell that ze sould tholl zone fair palice to be brunt that zour grace hes ben so weill ludgit into.'[42] However, it was not James who had built the lodge but the earl of Atholl and, as will be discussed below, it is likely that he had good reason to try to impress James and to flatter him.

Pitscottie reported that the hunt took place in Atholl twenty miles from the nearest town. Charles McKean suggested that this lodge could have been sited near Moulin because Timothy Pont's map shows an outline plan of a

---

[38]   *TA*, v, 436; vi, 103.

[39]   Watson, 'Deer and Boar', 92.

[40]   Marie Thérèse Flanagan, *Anglo-Norman Settlers, Angevin Kingship, Interactions in Ireland in late 12th Century* (Oxford, 1989), 173, 180–9, 202–6; Sally Mapstone, 'Introduction', in Houwen, *A Palace in the Wild*, vii–viii.

[41]   Wiseman, 'Chasing the Deer', 109.

[42]   'I marvel that you should allow that fair palace in which your grace has been so well lodged to be burnt', Pitscottie, *Historie*, i, 338.

castle there which resembles the plan of the lodge described by Pitscottie.[43]
However, it is doubtful if Moulin could be described as twenty miles from the nearest settlement, and so it is more likely that what Pont was showing was the ruins of the thirteenth-century castle of Moulin and not the lodge of James V.[44] In 1792 the *Old Statistical Account of Scotland* for the parish of Blair Atholl recorded that the remains of the hunting lodge could still be seen on the river An Lochain, which flows from Loch Loch to Glen Tilt.[45] Pitscottie also wrote that the 'palice' was built in the midst of a fair meadow with a large ditch and a stretch of water 16ft (4.8m) deep and 30ft (9.1m) wide around the lodge. The local historian, John Kerr, located an area of flat ground near the junction of the An Lochain with the River Tilt which fits this description almost exactly apart from the depth of the water in the river, which could, of course, have been dammed to form pools for fish (Plate 3, and see Map 7).[46] The An Lochain flows around both sides of the site when the water is high and the site is marked as an island on the OS map (NN98267804.). The site is oval in shape and is about 38m by 53m, with enough room for a wooden lodge. The proximity of Mary's accommodation during her visit to Glen Tilt, examined in Chapter 6, confirms that this is indeed the site in question.[47]

At their own expense Stewart kings did provide a touch of sixteenth-century luxury for themselves when they were hunting, but not always to the extent of the Glen Tilt experience. The beds which James IV and V had sent to the hunts at Glenartney and Glenfinglas were unlikely to have been the state beds, but more probably the *lits de camp* which cost about £7 to make and were intended to be transported easily.[48] Wall hangings were sent to Glen Tilt and also to Glenfinglas, Douglas, and probably to Balquhidder.[49] Boards for setting up as tables were also sent to the hunts; but perhaps the ultimate in home comfort was the transport to the hunting of the royal stool of ease, the king's commode.[50]

---

[43]   Charles McKean, 'Timothy Pont's Building Drawings', in Ian C. Cunningham (ed.), *The Nation Survey'd: essays in late sixteenth-century Scotland as depicted by Timothy Pont* (Edinburgh, 2006), 111–24, at 122; NLS, Adv. Ms. 70.2.9, Pont 20 ('Garry, Tummel and Upper Tay, Dunkeld to Blairgowrie'). Pitscottie has the papal envoy say that the lodge was twenty miles from the nearest 'toune': Pitscottie, *Historie*, i, 337. In the sixteenth century there were settlements at Blair, Logierait, and Grandtully, all of which are shown by Pont. In addition, a settlement at Moulin was presumably at the site of the church at the centre of that parish: Ian B. Cowan (ed.), *The Parishes of Medieval Scotland* (Edinburgh, 1967), 152.

[44]   Canmore Id 26274. Nowadays beside Pirlochry.

[45]   OSAS, ii, 475 'Blair Atholl'.

[46]   John Kerr, *Life in the Atholl Glens* (Perth, 1993), 75; A. K. Bell Library (Perth) Local History Archive, MS249/2/47, *The Atholl Experience, being the Atholl papers of John Kerr,* 306; Canmore Id 373286.

[47]   The 'Lunkartis', Canmore Id 370113; NN98267804.

[48]   *TA*, iii, 157; vi, 48, 214; v, 370; vii, 252.

[49]   *TA*, v, 436 which explains that the king's gear, his 'graith', included hangings such as Arras work; vi, 215; vii, 252.

[50]   *TA*, vii, 87–8.

Plate 3 Site of James V's hunting lodge or 'palice' in Glen Tilt. The 'island' in the foreground fits Lesley's description of the site of James V's 'palice' in 1532. Mary's lunkarts lie in a bend of the river in the middle distance on the flat promontory lying to the right of the river.

Setting aside the unique Glen Tilt 'palice', the usual styles of royal hunting lodges conveyed an image of the king as the approachable ruler at ease amongst his people. Small hunting houses, chambers, pavilions, and hunt halls created an informal atmosphere in contrast to royal palaces. At Falkland and Stirling, for instance, the king had to be approached through a series of chambers which stressed the increasing remoteness of royalty. Hunt halls had no defensive pretensions but, rather, continued the tradition of timber halls in Scotland which had been built in the post-Roman period as displays of wealth and as locations for feasting and entertaining.[51] This informality, of course, must not be overstated. The king could live in a pavilion surrounded by his nobles while on a military campaign and the setting would not have been thought of as informal. While the size of the hunt halls varied and, while it would be wrong to imagine hundreds of courtiers feasting within them, the king entertained selected courtiers and

---

[51] Richard Oram, 'Royal and lordly residences in Scotland c.1050 to c. 1250 – an historiographical review and critical revision', *The Antiquaries Journal*, 88 (2008), 165–89, at 171. For evidence for these earlier halls see Sally M. Foster, *Picts, Gaels and Scots* (Edinburgh, 2014), 55–6; Chris Lowe, *Angels, Fools and Tyrants* (Edinburgh, 1999), 34–6. There is another site at Lathrisk in Fife: Canmore Id 297793.

local nobility in his hunt hall in an atmosphere which was less formal than that of the castle or the palace.

Provisions

The provisioning of these hunting parties also helped to create the image of the generous monarch who could indulge in liberal hospitality. The size of James V's hunting parties varied, but food and drink had always to be provided. While supplies fluctuate, they nearly always equalled or exceeded the amounts provided at court. Hundreds of loaves were sent to the hunts along with three or four marts (carcasses of beef), tens of sheep carcasses, capons (castrated cockerels), chickens, vast quantities of fish, as well as eggs, butter, and on one occasion in Glenfinglas 400 apples and pears.[52] These supplies were augmented by large quantities of alcohol as at Glenfinglas and Glenartney or, for example, at Megget in 1529, when 172 gallons of ale and 16 gallons of claret were sent to the hunt.[53] The king may not have stinted his provisions, but by far the most extravagant provision of food at a hunt was at Glen Tilt in 1532, when the earl of Atholl, according to Pitscottie, produced all kinds of drinks, meat, and delicacies. There was beer, white wine, claret, malmsey, muscatel, alicante, hippocras (a spiced wine), and whisky. Top-quality bread and gingerbread were provided along with beef, mutton, lamb, rabbit, herons, swans, wild geese, partridge, plovers, ducks, peacock, grouse, and capercailzie. One would have expected venison to be mentioned in this list, but perhaps the most likely explanation for its absence is that, as in Mar in 1618, some of the hunters ate venison but much of it was taken off to the lord's castle and to homes twenty to thirty miles away.[54] Since it was, in effect, provided free, Pitscottie probably took its consumption for granted, and if James and his party were not eating the venison – and it is hard to believe that they were not – then many others would have been.[55] The pools around the lodge were full of fish such as salmon, trout, perch, pike, and eels. To prepare the dishes for the banquets there were 'excellent cuikis', while 'cuning baxteris [bakers]' and pastry cooks provided sweet-

---

[52] *Excerpta e Libris Domicilii*, 156 for Cramalt, 230 for Cultybraggan; NRS, E32/2, fos 10r, 95r for Glenfinglas; E31/3, fo. 88r for Glenartney.

[53] *Excerpta e Libris Domicilii*, 156, 194.

[54] Fittis, *Sports and Pastimes*, 60.

[55] There is no evidence relating to Scotland, but the preference in Europe was to eat venison fresh from the chase, cooked on a spit, despite the presence of lactic acid in the meat – which does not taste well to the modern palate. In the medieval period the nobility did eat what they hunted, but it amounted to only 5% or 6% of the meat eaten and deer were about 30% of that: Lucien-Jean Bord and Jean-Pierre Mugg, *La Chasse au Moyen Age* (Paris, 2008), 293; Jean-Robert Pitte, 'Géographie culinaire des produits de la chasse et de la forêt en France', in Corvol (ed.), *Forêt et Chasse Xe–XXe siècle*, 127–34, at 127.

meats and desserts. Finally, to present the banquets there was tableware and table linen fit for a king, or so Pitscottie tells us.

Considerable effort and organisation were required to transport such large quantities of food and drink to Megget, Glenartney, and Glenfinglas, which were some way off the beaten track. Pack horses were the main form of transport for taking the king's pavilions, wardrobe gear, and food to his hunts; when wine was transported it would be carried on pack horses or carts, depending on the state of the track.[56] There were several routes for wheeled traffic from Peebles to Cramalt, the most direct of which left Peebles, ascended the Manor valley, and after crossing the hills descended directly into Cramalt from the north. This last came to be known as 'The King's Road' because it was used by James V on his numerous journeys to Megget from Peebles.[57] The difficulties of laying on supplies for hunting in Falkland and in Glenfinglas led to the creation of the burghs of Falkland in 1458 and of the Port of Menteith in 1467.[58] Turning these settlements into burghs meant that they could monopolise trade in their hinterlands and so they would have found it easier to supply royal hunting parties. Such details of provisioning and its related transport serve to emphasise the effort that went into the organisation of these hunts and the generous nature of the provision, given the remoteness of the sites.

Influence of Gaelic culture

Another striking aspect of life at these royal hunts was the influence of Gaelic culture not only on the hunting methods which were employed but also on the evening entertainments. When James IV was hunting in Glenartney, Glenfinglas, Balquhidder, or Strathfillan his entertainment could have included a clarsach player (player of the Gaelic harp), a fiddler, taborers or drummers, and highland bards.[59] Many Gaelic poems, including the tales of Fionn, could be sung to the clarsach and it was presumably such tales to which James IV listened.[60] While there is no record of the entertainment provided for James V after his hunts, he, like his father, was still hunting in the Gaelic-speaking Highlands. He copied highland dress, and in 1538 he had a short 'heland cot' made for himself along with 'heland tartane' hose and 'heland sarks'.[61] Although the month when these were made is not clear,

[56] *TA*, vi, 214, 215, 433; vii, 87; *Excerpta e Libris Domicilii*, 185, 194.
[57] *Peebleshire, An Inventory of Ancient Monuments*, RCAHMS (Edinburgh, 1967), ii, 351; Maxwell-Irving, 'Cramalt Tower', 403, 427.
[58] *RMS*, ii, 902; Fraser W. (ed.), *The Red Book of Menteith* (Edinburgh, 1880), ii, 297 no. 59.
[59] *TA*, ii, 119, 339, 137.
[60] *Heroic Poetry from the Book of the Dean of Lismore*, ed. N. Ross (Edinburgh, 1939), 16, 18.
[61] *TA*, vi, 436.

we can assume it was for his trip to Dunkeld, Atholl, and Badenoch for hunting in September and October of that year.[62] Tartan and highland dress were becoming prominent in the sixteenth century and a local style involving plaid wearing was probably emerging.[63] It is worth stressing that James did not look down on the highlanders but respected them. He did not mock 'our hielandmen' for carrying out what might have seemed to be a primitive custom, the burning of the lodge, but explained it.[64] This attitude would suggest that when he wore highland garb he did so out of respect for the highlanders and their customs and to be part of their hunting society. He was not wearing it as fancy dress or a masking costume, a point that should be borne in mind when considering Mary's attitude towards the wearing of highland garb in similar circumstances.[65]

The political role of hunting

Hunting could also support a more directly political role in sixteenth-century Scotland, both by demonstrating royal authority in the localities and through its use as a quasi-international language in diplomatic relations. James V's visits to 'Meggatland' were combined with the assertion of royal authority in a relatively lawless area. The idea of the judicial raid/hunt was a practical solution to the problem of conducting a judicial raid in areas of the Borders in order to enforce law and order without initiating open warfare. A hunting party, at least initially, would have seemed less threatening than an invading army. James V's visit to 'Meggatland' in June 1529, for example, was preceded by visits to justice ayres in Jedburgh and Peebles, and the lords of council who attended the ayres may well have joined him in Megget.[66] As already mentioned, when a force was raised to pursue thieves and traitors in the Borders in 1530, Pitscottie explained that lords and barons were summoned to deal with the thieves of Annandale and Liddesdale, but he immediately added that all gentlemen with good dogs had to bring them along so that James could hunt when he pleased. Consequently, when James left Edinburgh, according to Pitscottie, he 'passit out of Edinburgh to "Meggatland" to the hunting'.[67] It is worth briefly describing this raid because the impression is sometimes given that the hunting could not have acted as a cover for the raid and that it really formed no significant part of the progress. On this occasion, after hanging thieves at Douglas Burn they hunted at the Loch of the Lowes, Paper Hill

---

[62] Thomas, 'Renaissance Culture', 411.
[63] *Oxford Companion to Scottish History*, ed. Michael Lynch (Oxford, 2001), 179; David Caldwell, 'The Origins of Plaid Wearing', *SHR*, 254 (2021), 437–54, at 453–4.
[64] Pitscottie, *Historie*, i, 338; Mapstone, 'Introduction', vii.
[65] See Chapter 5, pp. 113–14.
[66] Cameron, *James V*, 73–4 and notes 35 and 37; *Excerpta e Libris Domicilii*, 156.
[67] Cameron, *James V*, 73–4, 78–80; Pitscottie, *Historie*, i, 334–5.

(NT213177 'Paiplaw'), and moving south of Hawick they reached Carlenrigg (NT396047), where Johnnie Armstrong was hanged. Pitscottie writes that they also hunted at Ewesdoors (NY372986) and Langholm (NT387007) and during this time he notes that they killed 360 harts, suggesting that various successful drives had been held.[68] This was not just a raid with a hunt thrown in. Hunting was a major part of the expedition and concluded with two days hunting at Cramalt from 15 to 17 June. Combining hunting with these raids encouraged nobles and lairds to attend, making the whole expedition appear less threatening. This *chevauchée* serves as a perfect example of how hunting could assist the demonstration of the king's power in the localities.

Royal hunting was not only about asserting royal authority on unruly areas. It was also about impressing foreign monarchs and their ambassadors. When Georg von Ehingen, an Austrian knight and diplomat, visited the court of James II, probably between June 1458 and July 1459, he felt it worth recording that honour had been shown to him in hunting.[69] Among the gifts which he received were two tents, which were presumably pavilions to be used as accommodation at hunting lodges. Gift giving was also part of the hunting repertoire when it came to impressing fellow monarchs and their ambassadors. At a very practical level guests were honoured to have venison served, as it was considered to be royal food. In 1498–99 James IV ordered Archibald Edmonstone, forester of Menteith, to send game and venison to him four times per year when he was south of the Mounth and whenever ambassadors and foreign visitors were entertained at court. Deliveries are recorded regularly between 1501 and 1507.[70] James IV took part in an exchange of horses in order to establish good relations with Louis XII of France in 1509 and with Ferdinand of Aragon in 1510.[71] Felicity Heal has shown how James V, Francis I, and Henry VIII conducted various exchanges of hawks or falcons, which were often delivered by ambassadors with letters of praise for their recipients, thus helping to open up diplomatic channels by establishing this bond between them.[72] They are a reminder once again that the monarchs of the time saw hunting as much more than a popular pastime.

This role of hunting is well illustrated when James V visited France in 1536 to arrange a French marriage for himself. He was invited to hunt with Francis I, which both honoured James and recognised him as a fellow monarch. From 23 October to 19 November Francis took James on a hunting progress around the Loire valley, visiting Amboise, Châtelherault, and Blois. At Loches

---

[68] Pitscottie, *Historie*, i, 334; Cameron, *James V*, 78–9. Pitscottie's 'Langoupe' is probably Langholm. In the royal accounts Heusdale in *Excerpta e Libris Domicilii*, 31 is Ewesdale and not Hensdale as in Thomas 'Renaissance Culture' 396.

[69] Christine McGladdery, *James II* (Edinburgh, 2015), 221–2.

[70] *ER*, xi, 159; *TA*, ii, 130, 142, 191, 397; *TA*, iii, 412.

[71] *Letters of James IV 1510–1513*, ed. R. L. Mackie (Edinburgh, 1953), nos 219 p. 135, 338 p. 184, 340 p. 185.

[72] Heal, 'Royal gifts and gift exchange in Anglo-Scottish politics', 290–1.

they hunted along with the dauphin, the future Henry II, and Antoine de Bourbon, the king of Navarre.[73] On this hunt hounds were chasing a large boar which turned and charged at Henry who was saved only when the king of Navarre wounded the boar.[74] It was not till after they returned to Blois that a marriage contract with Francis's daughter, Madeleine, was drawn up on 26 November, and one suspects that, despite there also being political reasons for the match, what we have here is the sixteenth-century equivalent of the groom seeking the approval of the father of the bride.[75] James also spent time before the wedding hunting in and around Paris in December along with Henry and Charles, duke of Orléans, another son of Francis I.[76]

The Glen Tilt hunt of 1532 also illustrates how hunting could further political ends, in this case to the satisfaction of both James V and the earl of Atholl. James invited his mother to the hunt along with Silvester Darius, the papal nuncio, who was visiting Scotland to assist with the collection of taxation agreed by the pope. Darius was keen to leave Scotland, but James wanted him to stay and continue his tax-collecting efforts.[77] Darius did seem to be impressed with his Glen Tilt experience, as Pitscottie reported that

> This ambassador of the paipis seand this great bancat and treumph being maid in ane wilderness, quhair thair was not toune near be xx myle, thocht it ane great merwell that sic ane thing sould be in Scottland considerand that it was bot the erse of the warld by wther contries, thair sould be sic honestie and polliecie in it and spetiall in the hieland quhair there is bot wode and wildernes.[78]

This was a rather back-handed compliment, but it was probably as much as James could expect in the circumstances. James continued to find the nuncio's presence helpful and did not let him depart till the spring of the following year.[79]

Atholl was also keen that the hunt should be a success. Along with others, he had been tasked with maintaining good order in Perthshire, especially

---

[73]   Edmond Bapst, *Les Mariages de Jacques V* (Paris, 1889), 302.

[74]   Mary Hollingsworth, *The Cardinal's Hat* (London, 2014), 117.

[75]   Cameron, *James V*, 133.

[76]   Bapst, *Les Mariages*, 304–5.

[77]   W. Stanford Reid, 'Clerical Taxation: The Scottish Alternative to Dissolution of the Monasteries 1530–1560', *Catholic Historical Review*, 32 (1948), 129–53, at 141; J. Wilson Ferguson, 'James V and the Scottish Church, 1528–1542', in T. K. Rabb and J. E. Seigel (eds), *Action and Conviction in Early Modern Europe: Essays in Honor of E. H. Harbison* (Princeton, 1969), 52–76, at 58.

[78]   'The pope's ambassador seeing this great banquet and triumph being held in a wilderness where there was no town within 20 miles, thought it was a great marvel that such a thing could exist in Scotland – considering that other countries [thought] it was but the arse of the world – that there should be such good quality and amenity in it especially in the Highlands where there is nothing but wood and wilderness.' Pitscottie, *Historie*, i, 337–8.

[79]   *The Letters of James V*, ed. R. K. Hannay and D. Hay (Edinburgh, 1954), 203, 223, 229, 237–8.

among the MacGregors. Robert Menzies, the holder of Apnadull, complained that Atholl was overzealous in his actions, resulting in Atholl's loss of his commission, but after its restoration in 1530 Atholl was keen to retain the support of James. This helps to explain Atholl's determined efforts to impress the king with his hospitality, spending, it was said, a total of £3,000 on the Glen Tilt hunt. The provision of a 'faire palice', good hunting, and plentiful feasting for James would not only honour James, but in Gaelic custom would highlight Atholl's acknowledgement of James's superior position. What was organised in Glen Tilt in 1532 was described as a great banquet and a triumph. It was in effect a staged performance focussing on the king and turning the hunt into an expression of his royal authority and magnificence.[80]

In Scotland, hunting was very much part of the life of the court. It was seen as part of the king's role to organise hunts, to invite nobles and lairds to take part, to provide lavishly for the event, and to promote the image of the generous and approachable monarch. The essence of this is found in a late fifteenth- or early sixteenth-century poem which encourages the king to pursue honest sports and realises that 'all trew … liegis [true lieges]' will get to know the king through honourable pastimes such as hawking, hunting, and archery.[81] The king, therefore, was expected to use the hunt to encourage the loyalty of his nobles, to impress ambassadors, and to demonstrate his authority in the localities. Maintaining his hunting reserves and dealing with issues which affected the area where he was hunting, especially issues relating to law and order and good governance, certainly impacted on local communities. Whether a queen regnant was also expected to perform these roles is an important question.

Scottish huntswomen

The evidence that elite women in Scotland did hunt is not abundant, but it is worth rehearsing since it helps to contextualise Mary's hunting activities. Apart from the dubious evidence of the Hilton of Cadboll Pictish stone, where a woman is portrayed on a side-facing saddle seemingly taking part in a hunt, the earliest evidence that females were involved in hunting is the Fionn poem, *The Enchanted Stag*. It survives in an early twelfth-century version which describes a hunt by 120 men of the Fian attended by another 100 women and men who presumably were part of the tinchell.[82] When William I's mother, Ada de Warenne, was present at St Mary's Loch in Ettrick Forest

---

[80] However, the commission was withdrawn again in 1533 and James had Atholl imprisoned for a spell in 1534: Cameron, *James V*, 2, 146.
[81] *Bannatyne Ms*, ed. W. Tod Ritchie (Edinburgh, 1928–34), ii, 256.
[82] Fraser, *The Pictish Symbol Stones of Scotland*, no. 123 Hilton of Cadboll; *Duanaire Finn*, i, 132.

HUNTING AT THE SCOTTISH RENAISSANCE COURT

in 1166x71 she may have been joining in hunts, but one cannot be certain.[83]
John of Fordun in his chronicle records that around 1272 Marjorie, countess
of Carrick, was hunting on horseback where she pleased, '*quo sibi placuerit*',
presumably chasing game rather than hawking, along with her squires and
handmaidens, when she met Robert Bruce, father of the future king.[84] The
allegorical poem, *King Hart*, written *c.* 1500, describes how Dame Pleasance
and her ladies set out to 'disport and to play' on the way to the castle of
King Hart. The poem mentions this episode in a very matter-of-fact manner, which does suggest that women hunting on horseback were not simply a piece of poetic imagination.[85] As already mentioned, Margaret Tudor
had probably taken part in a drive in Torwood Forest in 1504, while later, as queen mother, she was invited to the Glen Tilt drive in 1532. When
Elizabeth Hepburn, prioress of Haddington, hunted with James V in Megget
in 1531, she showed that a woman in holy orders was prepared to counter
accepted standards of behaviour for religious personnel and go hunting.[86] It
is clear that, as in France, women in Scotland did hunt, but the paucity of the
evidence suggests that it was not common.

While this shows that huntswomen were not unknown in Scotland, it
does not provide any specific context for the role of Mary as queen regnant.
There had not been a previous queen regnant and the closest parallels in
Scotland are the royal widows, Marie de Gueldres and Marie de Guise, who
both exercised power on their own as regents for their heirs. After the death
of James II in 1460, Marie de Gueldres continued to take an interest in the
development of Falkland Park and Palace and hunted in the royal forests of
Glenfinglas in 1461, and probably in Ettrick in 1463, the year of her death.[87]
As queen, Marie de Guise had hunted with James V in June 1538 around
St Andrews during the celebration of the solemnisation of her wedding.
Shortly afterwards she and James went to Falkland and no doubt hunted
in the park.[88] In August of that year Marie de Guise, accompanied by six
of her ladies, spent two nights in Glenfinglas at the hunt hall with James.
They had their bedding sent there from Stirling along with a chair, a board
for a table in their chamber, and a cupboard for service and display.[89] In the
spring and summer of 1539 Marie and James stayed in Fife for four months,

[83]   *RRS*, ii, no. 75.
[84]   G. W. S. Barrow, *Robert Bruce* (Edinburgh, 1976), 36; Fordun, *Chronica Gentis
Scotorum*, i, 304 (Latin) and iv, 299, chapt. LX (translation).
[85]   *The Shorter Poems of Gavin Douglas*, ed. Priscilla Bawcutt (Edinburgh, 1967), lxxii–
lxxix, 145, lines 129–36.
[86]   Gilbert, *Hunting Reserves*, 72–3; *TA*, v, 445.
[87]   John M. Gilbert 'Falkland Park to c1603', *Tayside and Fife Archaeological Journal*,
19–20 (2013–14), 78–102, at 99; *ER*, vii, 68, 69, 181.
[88]   Pitscottie, *Historie*, i, 381.
[89]   *TA*, vi, 434, 435; NRS, E32/7, fos 141r–143r. I am indebted to Michael Pearce for this
reference.

93

from 26 April to 28 August, during which they spent a lot of time at Falkland and Pitlethie, where hunting would have been on the agenda. Marie did not accompany James on all of his trips, but in September she set off to hunt with him for a few days at Glenfinglas, Balquhidder, and Glenartney.[90] After James's death in 1542, Marie's continued interest in hunting and hawking is reflected in the amount of time she spent at Pitlethie and at Falkland.[91] Her arrangements to feed wild boar in Falkland Park during the winter of 1551–52 raise the possibility that she may actually have hunted the boar in the park, although it is also possible they were being kept there for the larder rather than for sport.[92] As queen mother and then as regent Marie de Guise worked to maintain Glenartney Forest as an effective hunting ground by ordering the seizure of unbroken mares which were grazing there without permission. Then, in 1555, she tried to prevent the killing of deer which had travelled east out of Glenartney in a severe winter in an attempt to find food.[93] She also continued to manage the woodland in Falkland Park by clear-felling an area of the park in order to aid the growth of young healthy wood.[94] Shortly after Marie de Guise became regent in April 1554, she organised a judicial raid/hunt on the eastern Scottish Borders. When she referred to pursuing her pastime on this progress it can be assumed that the pastime in question was hunting.[95] Despite the increasing issues caused by the Reformation and the French alliance, Marie de Guise did manage to spend time at Pitlethie and Falkland, but the evidence is lacking to determine whether she organised lavish hunting expeditions to royal forests such as Glenartney. When Marie de Gueldres and Marie de Guise were acting as regents, hunting and the maintenance of royal hunting reserves was part and parcel of their lives just as it had been for their husbands. Consequently, we can conclude that Mary would have been expected to behave in similar fashion.

This evidence from the Scottish renaissance court of the early sixteenth century has shown that, as in France, hunting was an important part of the public and private life of the monarch. It was employed in very similar ways to establish authority and win support, although it would appear that the idea of

---

[90]   *TA*, vii, 251–2. Glenartney is not given in Thomas's Itinerary but James did send pavilions to Glenartney in September 1539 and arranged for the transport of the queen's and her ladies' coffers and bedding to Glenartney and 'uthir partis quhare hir grace travelit the said moneth': *TA*, vii, 204, 251–2.

[91]   In 1550 she stayed at Falkland from 17 to 21 January: NRS, E33/4/1, fos 30r–40r; at Pitlethie from 21 January to 13 February: NRS, E33/4/1, fos 40r–56r; at Falkland from 16 to 23 February: NRS, E33/5/1, fos 56r–69v, and in 1559 at Pitlethie from 18 to 31 October: NRS, E33/5/1, fos 27r–44r.

[92]   NLS, Adv Ms.29.2.5, fo.162a. I am indebted to Michael Pearce for this reference.

[93]   *RSS*, iv, no. 2125; NRS, GD160/528/28.

[94]   *RPS*, A1555/6/24.

[95]   Pamela E. Ritchie, *Mary of Guise in Scotland 1548–60. A Political Career* (East Linton, 2002), 124, 152–4.

the raid/hunt was peculiar to Scotland. In both countries, larger hunts could contain an element of performance to highlight the role of the monarch, although this had not reached the point where hunting figured as an element in court fetes. If, on her arrival in Scotland, Mary had not used hunting to establish her authority and win support she would have placed herself, quite unnecessarily, at a considerable disadvantage.

5

Diana the huntress

On 26 May, 1563, when Mary opened her first parliament in Scotland, she was preceded by James Hamilton, duke of Châtelherault, who 'bore the regall Crowne', Archibald Campbell, earl of Argyll, with the sceptre, and James Stewart, earl of Moray, with the sword of state. With seventy-eight members present, parliament was well attended and Mary was accompanied by around thirty noble women. When she finished her opening address members called out in approval 'Vox Dianae [the voice of Diana]'. What merits comment here is that of all the available goddesses of the classical pantheon, Mary was being compared not to Venus, Minerva, Juno, or Ceres, but to Diana, the goddess of hunting.[1] Evidently, within two years of landing in Scotland Mary was well known as a huntress and admired as such. By studying Mary's equestrianism and her hunting progresses in Scotland from 1561 to 1563, this chapter will explore how that came about and what it signified. In these years, since Mary stayed regularly at Falkland Palace in Fife, a case study will give a brief history of the palace, consider the development and use of the park and show how Mary hunted there.

On her return to Scotland, Mary was confronted by a variety of issues. The Reformation Parliament, which had been called by the Lords of the Congregation in August 1560, had established Protestantism as the only legal form of worship. Although its decisions had not been ratified by the queen in France, the Protestant settlement could not be ignored. At the start of Mary's reign, the nobility tended to favour one side or the other, but with varying degrees of commitment. The most important of the Catholic lords was George Gordon, fourth earl of Huntly, while Lord James Stewart, Mary's half-brother, Archibald Campbell, the fifth earl of Argyll, and James Douglas, fourth earl of Morton, were the leading Protestants. There were those such as John Stewart, fourth earl of Atholl, who were moderate Catholics and who accepted the Protestant settlement. Mary began her reign in a strong position, supported by Lord James, Argyll, Atholl, Huntly, James Hamilton, duke of Châtelherault and former regent, and his son, James, third earl of Arran. Since these lords had considerable power in different parts of Scotland and could support Mary's government in the localities, it was important for her to retain their loyalty. Managing their conflicting demands and expectations held the key to Mary's success or failure as queen regnant. The attempts of both France and England to control Scotland directly were terminated by the

---

[1] *CSPS*, ii, no. 9 p. 10; John Knox, *History of the Reformation in Scotland*, ed. W. C. Dickinson, 2 vols (London 1949), ii, 77–8.

Treaty of Edinburgh in July 1560, which stipulated that French and English troops should withdraw from Scotland and that Mary should lay aside her own claim to the English throne and recognise Elizabeth (r. 1558–1603) as queen of England.[2] Mary never gave the royal seal of approval to this treaty, but she did in effect downgrade the 'Auld Alliance' with France in favour of a policy of greater amity with England, a policy aimed at gaining recognition from Elizabeth of her right to the English throne.[3]

It was against this background that Mary had to establish her personal authority in Scotland, and hunting helped her to do so. The similarities of the hunting cultures of France and Scotland and Mary's training were such that hunting in Scotland did not, in most circumstances, present her with too many difficulties. The main challenges for her were the absence of relays in a chase and the dangerous nature of the drive as opposed to the *chasse aux toiles*. Mary, however, was by no means the first to transfer her cynegetic skills from one country to the other. Her father, James V, had hunted in France in 1537 and his companions presumably had done likewise.[4] Marie de Guise, her mother, had hunted in both countries and numerous nobles had visited France in 1550 and did so again in 1561.[5] Nobles regularly travelled between Scotland and the French court and several had French wives. Therefore, it can be assumed that many of the nobility of each country were familiar with the other's hunting styles.

It is important to determine whether the attitude that hunting was a male activity which was current in France also existed in Scotland and, if so, to what extent it affected Mary. Strikingly, Mary had to rule a country where, on the one hand, her accession to the throne in person after an interregnum of twenty years was not seriously challenged but, on the other hand, John Knox produced severe criticisms of Mary as a monarch because, *inter alia*, she was a woman and, in his view, women could not be allowed to rule over men.[6] While expressed in extreme terms, Knox's view was a sixteenth-century commonplace and historians have quite legitimately asked whether being a woman limited Mary's freedom of action as a ruler and whether she was forced to act differently from male rulers because of her sex.[7]

As we saw in the previous chapter, there is evidence that women hunted in Scotland, but its scarcity suggests that it was not an everyday activity and that hunting was perceived primarily as a male preserve. While there is no direct statement in the sources to that effect, there is strong indirect evidence

[2]   Gordon Donaldson, *James V – VII* (Edinburgh, 1965), 99–100; Dawson, *Scotland Reformed*, 212.
[3]   Warnicke, *Mary Queen of Scots*, 96–109; Simon Adams, 'The Release of Lord Darnley and the Failure of the Amity', in Lynch, *Mary Stewart*, 123–53; Walton, *Catholic Queen*, 89–96; *CSPS*, i, no. 1017 p. 551.
[4]   Cameron, *James V* (Edinburgh, 1998), 131.
[5]   Donaldson, *All the Queen's Men*, 160; Lesley, *History* (1570), 295.
[6]   Walton, *Catholic Queen*, 9–13, 35–8; Warnicke, *Mary Queen of Scots*, 9–13.
[7]   Groundwater, 'Afterword', 211ff; Broomhall, *Women and Power*, 11–15, 20–7; Walton, *Catholic Queen*, 15, 47, 90, 99.

to support the idea. Pitscottie considered that hunting and hawking were gentlemen's pastimes.[8] Bellenden and Lesley make no general reference to women hunting, and Bellenden, like Pitscottie, refers to hunting as an honourable game for kings, nobles, and gentlemen.[9] Lesley, when describing a drive which was similar to Mary's hunt in Glen Tilt in 1564, makes no mention of women even though he knew that Mary hunted.[10] That hunting was seen as a male activity is clearly conveyed by the two acts of parliament, including one from Mary's reign, which specified that it was the noble men of the realm – women are not mentioned – whose hunting and hawking were suffering from poachers with guns.[11] Even during Mary's reign there are only two references to other women taking part in hunting. In 1562 Thomas Randolph, the English ambassador, mentioned that the laird of Ormiston was hunting with his wife and son, and in 1563 Randolph referred to 'ladies' hunting with Mary at Pitlethie on 12 March. Mary Beaton, who was present at the 'dyninge place' after the hunt, may have been one of these 'ladies'.[12] Nonetheless, Mary did hunt in Scotland as both Margaret Tudor and Marie de Guise had done before her, so whatever the impact on Scottish noble women of the perception that hunting was a male pastime, it clearly posed no restrictions on Scottish queens in the sixteenth century.

Equestrianism

In Scotland the common styles of riding for women were either astride or on a side-facing saddle. When escaping from Holyrood after the murder of Riccio in 1566, Mary, who was pregnant, rode pillion on a side-facing saddle behind her equerry, and again when she surrendered at Carberry Hill in 1567 she was led away on a side-facing saddle. On the latter occasion the symbolism of this style of riding with its associated loss of control would not have been missed by the assembled troops (Plate 4).[13]

Although there has been some disagreement among historians whether or not Mary rode astride while in Scotland there is no doubt that she did so.[14] In September 1564 she ordered '*ung harnoy de chasse fect à la ristre*', a hunting saddle made in the style of the ritter, a pistol-carrying German cavalryman of

---

[8] Pitscottie, *Historie*, i, 163, 335.
[9] Bellenden, *History* (1821), i, 186; Boece, *Historiae* (1527), bk 5, fo. 35r line 37 .
[10] Leslie, *Historie* (1596), ii, 456. This hunt is described on pp. 132–7.
[11] *RPS*, A1551/5/3; 1563/6/15.
[12] *CSPS*, i, no. 1089 p. 612; ii, no. 2, p. 2.
[13] National Archives, MPF 1/366/2 Available at: https://www.nationalarchives.gov.uk/education/resources/uniting-kingdoms/ [accessed 11 November 2016]; Claude Nau, *History of the Reign of Mary Stewart from the murder of Riccio until her flight into England* (ed.), J. Stevenson (Edinburgh, 1883), xcvi, 228. Full discussion of riding styles and dress can be found in Appendix II.
[14] Guy, *My Heart is My Own*, 80; Adams, 'The Queenes Majestie', 151–2 and n. 51.

Plate 4   The surrender of Mary, Queen of Scots, at Carberry Hill on 15 June, 1567. Mary and Mary Seton appear to be riding on side-facing saddles. The lords of Grange and Hume and their troops await her arrival.

the sixteenth and seventeenth centuries who rode astride.[15] The pistols were normally carried in front of the saddle but could also be carried behind it.[16] In 1565 Mary ordered another saddle *à la ristre* and was reported as leaving Edinburgh in August during the Chaseabout Raid with a 'dagg', a pistol, on her saddle.[17] In the crisis of June 1567 Mary was well able to ride from Borthwick to Dunbar in a man's clothes 'booted and spurred' in order to escape from the Confederate Lords who had risen against her.[18]

In France, Mary rode astride wearing a *devantière* and she continued to do so in Scotland. Her treasurer's accounts contain orders for 'dewanters',

---

[15]   *Inventaires de la Royne*, 50; NRS, E35/3/5B, p. 90 and in microfilm MFiLPE35/3. *DOST*, 'reister'; Randal Cotgrave, *A French and English Dictionary* (London, 1673), 'reister'. *Ristre* is a version of *reistre*, a German rider or ritter, or in Scots a 'reister'.

[16]   Wikipedia 'reiter'; Jean Jacques Wallhausen, *Art Militaire à Cheval. Instruction et Fondements de la Cavallerie* (Frankfurt, 1616), 33, figure 8 after p. 26; Charles Oman, *A History of the Art of War in the Sixteenth Century* (London, 1937), 139–41; James B. Wood, *The king's army: warfare, soldiers and society during the wars of religion in France 1562–76* (Cambridge, 2002), 137.

[17]   *Inventaires de la Royne*, 157; CSPS, ii, no. 280 p. 323.

[18]   R. Keith, *History of the Affairs of Church and State in Scotland from the Beginning of the Reformation to the Year 1568* (Edinburgh, 1845), ii, 617; Guy, *My Heart is my Own*, 342, which quotes from the despatches of Sir William Drury, deputy governor of Berwick, to Elzabeth's secretary, William Cecil.

the Scots version of *devantières*, made of serge of Florence. Some of Mary's regular supply of *chausse* made of a coarse linen like *Hollande*, or taffeta, or woollen stemming, a thin worsted cloth, must have been upper hose more like breeches or riding hose.[19] Certainly the six pairs of hose stuffed or padded with crimson velvet, purchased for the queen in June 1565, had to be breeches like those worn by young boys at this time.[20]

Although both these riding styles, astride and on a side-facing saddle, were common in Scotland, definite evidence of side-saddles does not appear till after Mary's arrival in 1561.[21] Within a month of landing in Scotland, Mary ordered a variety of harnesses and saddles for herself and her female attendants, including six small black cushions 'ilk cussinat haifand ane stirrope girth stuffit witht downis'.[22] Because there is only one stirrup girth per cushion this has to be part of the equipment for side-saddles. Mary, therefore, continued to hunt and ride astride wearing breeches in Scotland, just as she presumably did in France.

Mary's wish to adopt the male role of ruler comes across clearly in her comments to Randolph during the campaign against Huntly in 1562, when she told him that she regretted that she was not a man to know what it was like to be all night in the fields or to walk the causeway wearing a jack (quilted tunic) and a knapscall (helmet) and carrying a Glasgow buckler (shield) and broadsword.[23] That Mary was able to hunt and ride astride inevitably led to comparisons, usually complimentary, with male capabilities. On the above occasion Randolph was impressed with Mary's good spirits, courage, and determination. Knox's continuator gave grudging respect to the way her courage increased 'man-like' during a journey in adverse weather conditions from Glasgow to Edinburgh during the Chaseabout Raid in 1565.[24] When Mary was reputedly at Seton House shortly after Riccio's murder, George Buchanan, poet, scholar, tutor, and eventual critic of Mary, said that she went into the countryside for her customary sports, which in his opinion were clearly unsuitable for women. However, these unsuitable activities appear to have been pall-mall and golf, not hunting.[25] John Knox may have criticised Mary for feasting, dancing, and enjoying music, but he simply noted when

---

[19] E.g., *TA*, xi, 349 (1565); *Inventaires de la Royne*, 147 (1564); *TA*, xii, 42, 351, 398 (1566); xi, 367, 454; Cotgrave, *A French and English Dictionary*, 'chausse'.

[20] *TA*, xi, 367; Melanie Schuessler Bond, *Dressing the Scottish Court, 1543–1553: Clothing in the Accounts of the Lord High Treasurer of Scotland* (Woodbridge, 2019), 59; Jane Ashelford, *A Visual History of Costume, The Sixteenth Century* (London, 1993), 15.

[21] 'each little cushion pad having a stirrup girth stuffed with feathers'; The earlier evidence for both side-saddle and side-facing riding is given in Appendix II

[22] *TA*, xi, 65–6.

[23] *CSPS*, i, no. 1138 p. 651.

[24] Knox, *History of the Reformation*, ii, 162.

[25] Geddes, Olive M, *A Swing through Time* (Edinburgh, 2007) 15–16; W. A. Gatherer (ed. and trans.), *The Tyrannous Reign of Mary Stewart George Buchanan's Account* (Edinburgh, 1958), 120, being part of Buchanan's *Rerum Scoticarum Historia*. *Consuetus* (customary) is not in Gatherer's version but is in Ruddiman's Latin edition of Buchanan's work – *Georgii Buchanani Opera Omnia*, ed. Thomas Ruddiman (Leyden, 1725), 633, bk xviii, chapt. xix.

Mary was hunting and offered no adverse comments. Either he accepted it as normal or, as is more likely, he realised that it was universally admired and there was no point in criticising it.

Consequently, when Mary was hunting in Scotland she was not pushing boundaries in any unsettling way. On the other hand, wearing men's clothes has been described as 'playing on the edges of rank and gender' on those occasions when there was no need to adopt male behaviours, such as the banquet for the French ambassador in February 1566 or walking the streets of Edinburgh with Darnley prior to their marriage in 1565.[26] However, this was not the case on the hunting field, where adopting male behaviours was essential for safety and success. As in France and England, so in Scotland such behaviour by elite women was considered to be perfectly respectable.[27] Furthermore, because she rode side-saddle or astride, and so presented herself as being in control, she signalled to her nobles that the queen riding to meet them was not adopting the role of the passive and submissive female, but of a queen ready and keen to rule on her own merits. It is hard to believe that this image did not carry over to some extent into other aspects of her rule.

Falkland Park and Palace

The hunting landscapes which Mary encountered in Scotland were in some ways vastly different from those she had experienced in France. The hills of Glenfinglas, Glen Tilt, Glenartney, and the Megget area bore little resemblance to the flatter terrain of the Loire valley. In other respects, the landscapes of the royal parks at Holyrood, Stirling, and Falkland would have been much more familiar to Mary. Falkland was the royal hunting park par excellence and it persuaded Mary to make regular visits to Fife and to Falkland Palace. At this time Fife was in many ways the Loire valley of Scotland, with its royal residences, nobles' houses, prosperous burghs, as well as facilities for hawking and hunting.[78]

It is worth looking at Falkland Park and Palace in some detail not only because of their well-known links with Mary but also because it allows us to understand the interrelationship of park and palace and obtain an idea of the nature of hunting in a park. Falkland Palace was unique among Scottish royal palaces because its attached park was regularly used for hunting.[29] When historians examine the palace, they tend to concentrate on the buildings and their history, but the park and its attached sporting facilities are of equal

---

[26] Parkinson, 'A Lamentable Storie', 149.

[27] Neighbors, 'Elizabeth I Huntress', 54, 55.

[28] Pitscottie, *Historie*, 161; Furgol, 'Itinerary', 219–32 Fiche 1 C1-D6. Future references to Mary's itinerary are taken from this article. Teulet, *Relations Politiques*, i, 117. For Marie de Guise's visits to Falkland and Pitlethie see p. 94, n. 91.

[29] For the evidence on which this section is based see Gilbert, 'Falkland Park to *c.* 1603', 78–102.

importance. Mary had come from a court where *jeu de paume*, *jeu de maille*, and hunting were practised regularly by women, and the facilities at Falkland allowed her to do likewise.[30] It is one of the few parks, alongside Chambord, Villers Cotterêts, and Stirling, where she is known to have hunted and it is possible to build a picture of the parallel development of the park and the palace in the fifteenth and sixteenth centuries.

During her reign Mary spent a total of fifty-one nights in Falkland Palace. She visited most frequently in 1562 and 1563, and up until 1564 she always managed one stay of a week or longer per year. Her mother may well have mentioned Falkland Palace to her and it would have looked like familiar territory because of its sporting facilities, its hunting park, and the renaissance facade of the inner courtyard which carried her mother and father's initials. It was also smaller than the other royal palaces at Linlithgow, Stirling, and Holyrood and perhaps more welcoming and relaxing to a young queen who loved hunting. By the time of Mary's personal reign, the design of the park and palace resembled the European pattern where one progressed from the castle or palace to the domesticated space of a garden and then to the park with its meadows, wilder woods, and watery features.

The palace had developed out of the late thirteenth-century castle of the earls of Fife, who had probably located it there because of the hunting (Map 4). Prior to the twelfth century, the surrounding area had been a royal thanage, an area of royal land managed by a thane, and it was probably, even at that early date, a hunting ground linked to neighbouring royal thanages. Although it is not recorded as a forest till 1371 there is every likelihood that it had been a hunting reserve well before then. The gate of the earls' castle faced north, towards the park, which suggests that the building of the castle and the park were linked, pointing to a similar thirteenth-century date for the park.[31] This date is supported by a variety of other evidence. Two pieces of thirteenth-century pottery have been found in the park pale and in an associated ditch. The manner in which the parish boundary turns at right angles to go round the park suggests that the park preceded the formation of the parish boundary, making a thirteenth-century date a possibility. The existence within the park of labour services to cut hay were the sort of services usually created only before the decline of serfdom in the fourteenth century.[32] The extension of the castle into a palace probably began in the reign of James II with the building of what is now called the east range, which may have been a long gallery leading to royal apartments in a south range.[33]

[30] Chatenet, *La cour de France*, 113–14, 123–7, 190.
[31] *RMS*, vi, no. 1746; NRS, C2/44/349; Grant, A., 'Thanes and Thanages from Eleventh Century to the Fourteenth Centuries, in A. Grant and K. Stringer (eds), *Medieval Scotland, Crown, Lordship and Community* (Edinburgh, 1993), 39–81, at 46, 63–6.
[32] Oliver O'Grady, 'Cash Wood – Discover the Ancient Lomonds', *Discovery and Excavation*, 17 (2016), 82.
[33] Clark, 'Falkland Palace', 86.

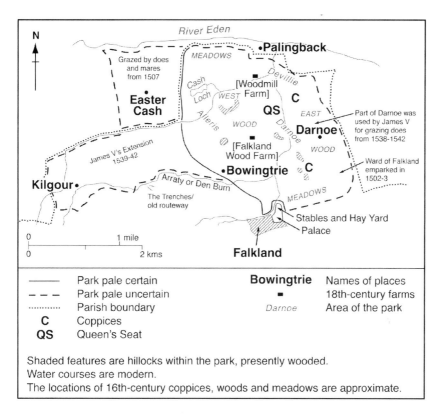

Map 4   Falkland Park in the sixteenth century.

The role of James II in the development of the palace has been confirmed in research by John Harrison. It was already well known that James II turned Falkland into a royal burgh in order to increase accommodation for courtiers and the royal household and to facilitate the provisioning of the palace. Harrison points out that this development necessitated a reorientation of the castle towards the burgh on the south rather than towards the park on the north, with the consequent need for a new gatehouse on the south side.[34] James IV finished the quadrangle of the new palace, completing the hall, the east range with its royal apartments, and the chapel royal in the south wing. James V then adapted this work to give the whole internal courtyard a renaissance flavour. Marie de Guise had written to her mother, the duchess of Guise, seeking her assistance to find a suitable candidate for the work. In the spring of 1539 this resulted in the appointment of Nicholas Roy as master mason. Several French buildings have been suggested as the

[34]   Harrison, *Falkland Palace*, 4.

inspiration for the inner courtyard at Falkland, including Villers Cotterêts and Fontainebleau, with both of which Mary was familiar.[35]

Like other royal palaces, Falkland was well equipped with sports facilities and it was James V, probably influenced by what he had seen in France, who developed what can be called a sports complex around the palace. There were butts for archery in a flat area to the east of the palace, and between 1539 and 1541 he built a 'caichpule' for playing 'caiche' or royal tennis.[36] To this tennis court he attached a long, narrow building which was roofed with beams made from trees felled when he had extended the hunting park in 1539. It used to be thought that this building was added onto the tennis court at a later date, but dendrochronology has shown that it was built at the same time. Based on the layout of other tennis courts in Europe, this building was most likely a kind of games hall for playing bowls or *jeu de maille*, a game played with balls and mallets, and it may even have included changing rooms.[37] There are no jousting lists mentioned in the sources, but James V did joust at Falkland in 1539, presumably in the area of the archery butts to the east of the palace.[38] What this shows is that, apart from jousting, the sports for which facilities were provided at Falkland, namely archery, 'caiche', *jeu de maille*, hunting, and hawking, could all be practised by women. While there is no specific record of Mary playing tennis or *jeu de maille* in Falkland, one can assume that she did so.

The park was, of course, the main sporting facility of the palace and its history closely matches that of the palace. Those kings who developed the palace, James II, IV, and V, also made major changes to the park. The palace and the park were not seen as separate entities but as part of a single property displaying the wealth and power of the monarch. While the park was prob-ably constructed along with the castle in the late thirteenth century, it does not enter the written record till 1451, when the earldom of Fife was in royal hands. James II and Marie de Gueldres started the compartmentalisation of the park, which enabled various activities to be pursued more efficiently within it. Marie de Gueldres had seen parks like this in France and may well have tried to develop Falkland Park along similar lines. When first built, the park had been constructed on fairly poor ground covered with heath and bog as well as woods of alder, hazel, hawthorn, and oak. The whole ecology of the area was altered dramatically because it was managed for a specific purpose, the preservation of deer for hunting, and it was isolated from the surrounding environment by a substantial pale. Excavation of the park pale in 2016 has

---

[35] J. G. Dunbar, *Scottish Royal Palaces* (Edinburgh, 1999), 34–6.

[36] H. M. Paton, *Accounts of the Master of Works* (Edinburgh, 1957), i, 112.

[37] Crone, *Falkland Palace: a dendrochronological study*, 23, 27–8; Addyman, *Falkland Palace*, 5–7; D. Bell, *The Tennis Court and Stables, Falkland Palace, Statement of Cultural Significance*, Report for National Trust of Scotland (Dunbar, 2010); Dunbar, *Scottish Palaces*, 208; Lance St J. Butler and Peter J. Wordie, *The Royal Game*, Falkland Palace Real Tennis Club (1989), 39–40.

[38] 492 *TA*, *vii*, 168.

shown that the bank was surmounted by a fence and accompanied by a shallow internal ditch which must have presented a reasonable obstacle to the semi-tame fallow deer held inside. The height from the bottom of the ditch to the top of the fence could have been about 2.5m to 3m.[39] What appears to be a larger external ditch does survive in Cash Wood, but archaeology has tentatively suggested that it was not associated with the pale.[40] This was a fairly large park which enclosed an area of approximately 485ha and was, therefore, large enough to stage chases or small drives.

During James II's reign the process of compartmentalisation involved the enclosure of woods and meadows within the park. The creation of smaller enclosed woods points to the use of coppicing to manage these woodlands, but there were also two stands of oaks called the East and West Woods. The meadows which existed at the northern and southern edges of the park were enclosed to exclude deer and other livestock till after the hay had been cut. Cattle were regularly grazed in the park along with some horses, but the main livestock were the fallow deer, although there are occasional references to red deer, roe deer, and even boar. It is hard to tell how many deer were kept there, but by estimating the demands made on pasture by the livestock and the available amount of grazing it is possible to produce a 'guesstimate' of around three hundred fallow deer in the park in the fifteenth century.

In the early sixteenth century James IV developed the park by extending it to around 650ha. One of the areas which he added was used specifically for grazing does and mares, presumably in order to remove them from the main park when hunts were in progress. This would enable hunting to take place at any time of year with no break for a 'fence' month in July when the deer were fawning. A deer fold was constructed in 1503 into which deer were driven and held either to be killed, to be transported live to other parks and palaces, or to be released to be hunted. It is worth stressing here that there is no evidence for the oft-repeated tale that deer had to be transported into Falkland Park for royal hunts.[41] The park was adequately stocked to meet the requirements of any royal hunts held when the king was in residence. James IV also had a loch built in the park which he stocked with pike, and it would have been there that swans were fed in 1503–4.[42]

Major developments also occurred in James V's reign, influenced by his visit to France where he had seen the large parks which surrounded the chateaux where he stayed. In 1539 he authorised a 160ha westward extension to Falkland Park, allowing him to increase the size of the deer herd and hunt

---

[39]   O'Grady, 'Cash Wood', 82.

[40]   I am indebted to Oliver O'Grady for this suggestion.

[41]   Iain Moncrieffe of that Ilk, *The Royal Palace of Falkland*, National Trust for Scotland (1968), 38; Fraser, *Mary Queen of Scots*, 218; Stedall, *The Challenge to the Crown*, i, 147. Deer were transported from Falkland by James IV to restock parks where they could be hunted, killed for the larder, or used to regenerate a herd as at Stirling from 1503 to 1506: Gilbert, 'Falkland Park to *c*. 1603', 93–5.

[42]   *ER*, xii, 197.

more frequently without adversely affecting the herd. In a further move which may also reflect his French visit he instructed his forester to cut all the young trees and scrub in the new extension so that an even crop of new young trees could grow in their place. However, when James died, Marie de Guise had to return the land to the owner from whom James had seized it. In 1555 she in turn took action so that more young wood would grow in the main park. This coppicing was probably aimed at producing both tall timber trees and younger wood for use, for instance, in making wattle fencing to enclose the woods and meadows. Just as happened elsewhere, the development of the park and the palace went hand in hand because they were seen to complement each other.

When Mary arrived in Falkland, the park, which had been expanded since the fourteenth century, probably held around four hundred fallow deer and still contained meadows, coppices, and woodland. It could have reminded her of a pocket-sized Chambord or Villers Cotterêts. The western area of the park was called 'Alleris' after the alder trees growing there, and today the woodland round Cash Loch gives an impression of the appearance of that part of the park in the sixteenth century. The construction of this loch can probably be associated with eighteenth-century drainage schemes and powering the mill at Woodmill Farm. The woodland still contains some very old alder stools which may go back as far as the pre-improvement woodland of the eighteenth century. They, in turn, may be descended from the alder trees which once grew in the park and gave 'Alleris' its name.[43]

Although it is known that Mary hunted in the park, it is a lot harder to work out how she hunted, but there are some clues. When she was riding 'a huntynge' in the park she was chasing deer rather than having them driven to her.[44] On some days she may also have been hawking, but it is not mentioned as such in the sources. Not long after Mary arrived in Scotland, she obtained a licence from Elizabeth to buy geldings, just as she had talked about at Loches, and so she was prepared to hunt by chasing game.[45] While the confines of a park could have made a chase easier, it must be remembered that deer could probably jump out of the park when in full flight. In the spring, when Mary tended to visit, the meadows would still have been enclosed, as would young coppices. Furthermore, the East and West Woods would obscure the view, necessitating the use of scenting hounds. The chase could have been even more confused if cattle, horses, and does in fawn had not previously been removed.

We are fortunate that there are other examples of chases taking place in the park. Pitscottie's version of James V's escape from the control of Archibald Douglas, sixth earl of Angus, after Easter 1527, shows that James V also hunted in the park by chasing deer. Pitscottie, who wrote in the 1570s, had

[43]   Mills and Quelch, *Falkland Park: Historic Woodland Assessment*, 17.
[44]   *CSPS*, i, no. 1089 p. 613.
[45]   *CSPS*, i, no. 1051 p. 580.

probably heard the story from the late Andrew Fernie, the hereditary forester at Falkland, whom he names as one of the sources for his history.[46] According to this story James plotted with Andrew Fernie to summon neighbouring lairds with their fastest dogs to come to Falkland early in the morning to slay 'ane fatt buke or tua [a fat buck or two]'. The fact that they were going to kill only a few bucks using their fastest dogs suggests a chase rather than a drive. However, James slipped away during the night and was not there in the morning for the hunt.[47] There is some dubiety about this tale, since Jamie Cameron dates James's assumption of power to June 1528, when the great seal was transferred from Edinburgh to Stirling.[48] Whether Pitscottie got his dates wrong or whether James was not always with the great seal, the tale would have made no sense if James V had not used fast dogs to chase game in Falkland Park.

The best picture of how a chase operated in the park comes from James VI's own description of a hunt he held there on 5 August, 1600 in the events leading to the Gowrie Conspiracy. James walked down from the palace, past the ruins of the old castle, to join the assembly at the green beside the stables. The hunt servants were already in the field, having located a suitable buck to hunt. After mounting up James then rode through the gate into the park and proceeded to one of the hillocks, probably one to the east of the present Dunshelt Road. From there he watched the deer being unharboured in a coppice below the hillock and then rode to join the chase. The whole event lasted from 7.00am to 11.00am and the *curée* was held where the buck was killed, within two bow shots of the stables.[49]

There are also indications that drives were conducted in the park, but, of necessity, these would need to have been small drives because large drives to kill tens or hundreds of deer would have wiped out the herd. With a customary cropping rate of 10% at this time and a herd of four hundred fallow deer, up to forty deer per year could be taken from the park, whether as the quarry of leisure hunting, as the venison caught for the larder, or as deer for transportation to restock other parks.[50] Anything higher would require some restocking of the park as James IV conducted in 1505, or some extension of the park such as James V created in 1539.

Further possible evidence of drives is found in the name *Bowingtrie* or bending tree which is recorded in 1602 beside the park pale on the western side of the park. It is the only specific tree ever mentioned in the park and perhaps

---

[46] *Sheriff Court Book of Fife 1515–1522*, ed. William C. Dickinson (Edinburgh, 1928), 324; Pitscottie, *Historie*, i, pp. xlviii, xliii, 2. The park is referred to as Falkland wood: *RMS*, iii, no. 549.

[47] Pitscottie, *Historie*, i, 324.

[48] Cameron, *James V*, 17–19.

[49] D. Calderwood, *History of the Kirk of Scotland*, ed. Rev. Thomas Thomson, Woodrow Society, 8 vols (Edinburgh, 1842–49), ii, 210.

[50] Birrel, 'Deer Framing in Medieval England', *Agricultural History Review* (1992), 112–26, at 124; S. A. Mileson, *Parks in Medieval England* (Oxford, 2009), 27.

possessed special significance, such as the tree where the king had awaited the drive.[51] The name Queen's Seat also survives in the first edition of the OS six-inch map in 1854.[52] Although there are other historical-sounding names in the area which are nineteenth-century inventions, such as Pillars of Hercules and Guelderland Walk, the Queen's Seat does not seem to be one of those.[53] The relevant entry in the *Ordnance Survey Name Book* in 1853–55 described the Queen's Seat as a small knowe on the west side of the Dunshelt Road 'on which it is said Queen Mary sat she being fatigued while walking'. It explains that the farmer had 'partially levelled' the knowe or hillock but the name had survived.[54] Two aspects of this entry are striking. Firstly, this was a relatively small knowe and if somebody had been trying to create names of historical interest there are far larger and more noticeable mounds to the east of the road to which a name could have been attached. Therefore, there had to be a reason for naming a smaller mound to the west of the road. Secondly, the explanation in the *Ordnance Survey Name Book* is unlikely, as the usual explanation of the name King's or Queen's Seat is to mark the spot where the king or queen organised, watched, or awaited a drive or a course, not where they rested when out for a walk. It is likely that when an explanation of the name was sought in the mid-nineteenth century the reason for the name had long been forgotten, thus highlighting its antiquity. It might be stretching the evidence too far to suggest that it was an anglicisation of the Gaelic *Tom nan ban Righ*, but it could have been a name formed when a queen was hunting in the park in the fifteenth or sixteenth centuries although it cannot now be attributed to any particular queen.

This hillock could have been used in the kind of drive often referred to as bow and stable hunting, which Edward, duke of York, described in his *Master of Game*, a book which Mary probably possessed.[55] This version of the drive could be adapted to ensure that only a few bucks were killed. The place of the king's stand would be decided – the Queen's Seat or the *Bowingtrie* would have been possibilities – and the stable would then be set out around the park ready to drive the required game to the king. When all was set, the forester would bring the king or queen to the stand where their bow or greyhounds would be ready for them. At this point, according to the duke of York, hounds called harriers were led into the area of the hunt to remove any unwanted deer. This kind of procedure would obviously have made sense at Falkland if cattle, fallow does, young bucks, and horses had not previously been removed. Only a few selected fallow bucks would be allowed to remain.

---

[51] *RMS*, vi, no. 1349; Simon Taylor and Gilbert Márkus, *The Place-Names of Fife*, 5 vols (Donington, 2007), ii, 146.

[52] It is also recorded in 1909 as a field name to the east of the Dunshelt road: NRAS, 3663/17/153, *Cropping Book, Falkland Estates with Farms and Field Plans indexed 1909–1932*.

[53] Taylor and Márkus, *Place-Names of Fife*, ii, 178.

[54] *Ordnance Survey Name Book 27 Fife and Kinross-shire* OSI/13/21/53.

[55] See Chapter 2, p. 45.

The stable then released their hounds, which were trained to hunt the bucks, and they would drive them up to the king's stand.[56]

Perhaps a more likely method of driving deer in Falkland would have been a version of hunting at the toils with which Mary had been acquainted in France and which Elizabeth I used in parks in England. There are several references from 1568 onwards which tell how Elizabeth went to a wooden stand where she would use a crossbow to shoot at game already driven into toils or an enclosure.[57] In September 1584 the French ambassador watched Elizabeth hunt at Windsor where sixty to eighty stags had been driven into the toils. They passed back and forth in front of a stand from which Elizabeth shot several with a crossbow before dogs were then set on those which had only been wounded. Elizabeth watched from a little hillock as deer were released at intervals into flat open country in the middle of the wood. On occasions she watched from a bower constructed at the exit from the toils as stags were let loose in ones, twos, and threes throughout the day. They were then coursed by greyhounds for two or three miles and were eventually pulled down by the dogs.[58] There was no gladiatorial combat in this method of hunting, as in the French *chasse aux toiles*. James V probably saw boar being hunted at the toils in France and may have tried something similar in Falkland. James III, IV, and V, and Marie de Guise all kept boar in Falkland Park at one time or another, and James V had a special enclosure constructed to hold boar which had been imported from France.[59] Mary was certainly a skilled archer and it is quite possible that she used the deer fold at Falkland as a kill zone in which to shoot deer or as a pen from which to release deer which she would then watch from the Queen's Seat as they were being coursed.[60]

Hunts and progresses 1562 to summer 1563

In the early years of her reign, Mary realised the importance of making progresses around her kingdom. Michael Lynch considered that such progresses formed part of Mary's political education because they enabled her to learn about the attitudes and characters of the nobility, but they were also, crucially, 'a ritual demonstration of royal power and accessibility'.[61] They were an essential part of establishing her personal authority in a country she barely

---

[56] Cummins, *The Hound and the Hawk*, 63–6; *Master of Game*, 188–200.
[57] Adams, 'The Queenes Majestie', 146–7, 160–3.
[58] Ferrière, *Chasses de François 1er*, 55–6.
[59] *ER*, v, 271; xii, 189; vii, 472; xvii, 20; NLS, Adv Ms 29.2.5, fo. 162a, 12 January 1552. I am indebted to Michael Pearce for this last reference. *TA*, vii, 461, 472 for the boar enclosure.
[60] *TA*, iii, 362; iv, 134. For Mary's archery see *CSPS*, no.1095 p. 620; *CSPF 1566–8*, no. 977 p. 182.
[61] Lynch, *Mary Stewart*, 12; Neighbors, 'Elizabeth I Huntress', 54.

ELITE HUNTING CULTURE AND MARY, QUEEN OF SCOTS

knew. She had of course taken part in royal progresses in France and was aware of their importance and the part hunting could play in them. Unlike Francis II, Mary spent a much larger portion of her time in residence, mainly at Holyrood, Edinburgh Castle, Stirling, and St Andrews. Consequently, between January 1563 and December 1566 she spent only about a quarter of her time on progress.[62] In October 1564 Randolph may have complained about having to kick his heels in Edinburgh till Mary returned from hunting, but, unlike the French court in the sixteenth century, her court could in no way be described as nomadic.[63] The smaller number of royal palaces and the exigencies of the climate no doubt played their part in limiting her travels. Mary was presumably also aware of the necessity of being in touch with foreign ambassadors and government officers after the criticisms which ambassadors levelled at Francis II. Nonetheless, Mary used her progresses very efficiently and, despite the shorter progressing season, it has been estimated that between August 1562 and September 1563 she covered an impressive 1,200 miles.[64]

In her travels in Scotland Mary took part in both small hunts with a few companions and larger, more formal show hunts. While few details of the methods of hunting used on these occasions are known, the records of her captivity in England make it clear that she was a skilled horsewoman who practised her archery, shot deer using her crossbow, galloped after hounds, enjoyed chasing both deer and hares, and could kill a deer at the end of a hunt – presumably all feats which she had practised in Scotland during her personal reign.[65] It is recorded that Mary often travelled with her hawks and dogs, and so there is no doubt that she did hawk and hunt on her travels.[66] In 1563, for example, when Mary was in St Andrews she received news on 15 March of the death of her uncle François, duke of Guise. Thomas Randolph saw this as the beginning of the queen's sorrows and wrote that she consoled herself by riding up and down, hawking and hunting from place to place.[67] He did not specify where exactly she went, but her itinerary shows that during the rest of the month she progressed to Cupar, Falkland Palace, Monimail, which was held by John Hamilton, archbishop of St Andrews, to the earl of Rothes at Ballinbreich, to William Crichton at Naughton, and finally to Moray's house at Pitlethie, where Randolph records, as noted above, she was

---

[62] This is based on calculating stays of over six nights in length as being in residence. Stays in St Andrews of thirty nights, Aberdeen of thirty-nine nights and Perth of eighteen nights may have occurred on a progress, but the court on these occasions can hardly be regarded as being on the move.

[63] *CSPS*, ii, no. 110 p. 84.

[64] Goodare, 'Mary [Mary Stewart]', 7.

[65] *CSPS*, ii, nos 703 p. 436, 873 p. 541; iii, no. 232 p. 171; viii, nos 116 p. 100, 624 p. 552, 667 p. 585; Samuel Cowan, *The Last Days of Mary Stuart and the Journal of Bourgoyne her Physician* (London, 1907), 161.

[66] *TA*, xi, 154, 159, 176, 199.

[67] *CSPS*, ii, no. 2 p. 2.

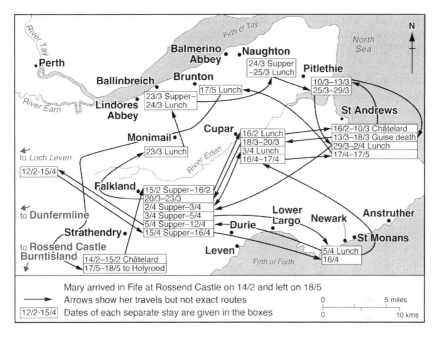

Map 5 Mary, Queen of Scots, in Fife from 14 February to 18 May, 1563. St Andrews and Falkland acted as the hubs from which Mary's journeys radiated and Cupar acted as a stopping-off point between them. Newark Castle was the only place visited on the south coast.

hunting with several female companions (Map 5).[68] Mary made similar visits to Fife in 1562, 1564, and 1565 although on these occasions she did not cover as much ground as in 1563.

Mary also planned to use the gathering of men for a hunting trip as cover for a judicial raid very much on the pattern employed by her parents. In 1566 she organised a hunt at Megget to precede a justice ayre at Jedburgh where she wanted to appear in force for her first visit to the Borders accompanied by her new husband, King Henry (Darnley). However, the justice ayre had to be postponed to avoid a clash with harvest time. This association of justice and hunting can also be seen earlier in her reign in her dealings with the earl of Huntly. In 1562 Mary had decided to progress to Inverness to confront the Catholic earl of Huntly, who had stopped attending council because he objected to the pursuit of amity with England and to her plans to meet with Elizabeth I. Huntly was also unhappy because Mary had decided to grant the earldoms of Mar and Moray to Lord James even though he had

[68] CSPS, ii, no. 2 p. 2.

been administering them for the Crown for several years.[69] At the same time Huntly was involved in a legal dispute because his third son, John Gordon of Findlater, who had been imprisoned for an attack on Lord Ogilvie of Airlie, had escaped and was refusing to attend court in Aberdeen.[70] Therefore, in well-honoured Stewart tradition, Mary ordered a progress to the north-east to demonstrate royal justice. She progressed there slowly, enjoying hunting and other pastimes on her way north, arriving in Aberdeen on 27 September, in time for the justice ayre which lasted till 18 October.[71] In Randolph's opinion, this trip was 'rather devised' by Mary 'than greatly approved by her council', and Mary seemed to thrive on the experience and cope well with the challenges presented.[72] According to Randolph, she was accompanied by most of her nobility. While they did not yet constitute an army, they would certainly have formed an imposing gathering.[73] Nonetheless, the elements of the judicial raid/hunt were all there, the justice ayre, the window-dressing of hunting to cover the gathering of a sizeable force of armed men, and a royal progress.[74] The outcome of the expedition was that Huntly and the Gordons were defeated and Lord James continued to hold the earldom of Moray.

Mary's journey to Argyll and the west in July and August 1563 was a much less formal event, since the progress had no specific judicial function. Her host, Archibald Campbell, earl of Argyll, was one of her three chief advisers together with Moray and William Maitland of Lethington. Lesley reported that Mary spent the whole summer enjoying hunting and other diversions, whereas Knox simply recorded that she 'passed in Argyll to the hunting'.[75] Although Mary must have taken advice on the matter of her progresses, she seems to have had considerable influence on the destination of these summer trips. Randolph certainly considered that she was instrumental in the progress to the north-east and her personal wishes in the choice of Argyll seem to have carried considerable weight. She found the earl of Argyll easier to relate to than Lord James because he was only four years her senior and his wife Jean was her half-sister and one of her trusted companions.[76] Mary had other personal reasons for wishing to visit the earl of Argyll and his wife: his marriage to Jean was in difficulties and Mary, who had even enlisted the support of John Knox, hoped to reconcile them during her visit.[77] However,

---

[69]   Donaldson, *All the Queen's Men*, 52–3; Dawson, *Scotland Reformed*, 247; Allan White, 'Queen Mary's Northern Province', in Lynch, *Mary Stewart*, 53–70, at 58–9.

[70]   Warnicke, *Mary Queen of Scots*, 82.

[71]   Knox, *History of the Reformation*, ii, 58.

[72]   *CSPS*, i, no. 1132 p. 645, no. 1138 p. 651.

[73]   *CSPS*, i, nos 1136 p. 649, 1138 p. 651, 1139 p. 653, 1141 p. 654.

[74]   White, 'Queen Mary's Northern Province', 61; Jane E. A. Dawson, *The Politics of Religion in the Reign of Mary Queen of Scots* (Cambridge, 2002), 117; Dawson, *Scotland Reformed*, 247–8.

[75]   William Forbes-Leith (ed.), *Narratives of Scottish Catholics under Mary Stuart and James VI* (London, 1889), 92; Knox, *History of the Reformation*, ii, 85.

[76]   Dawson, *Politics of Religion*, 28, 36; Donaldson, *All the Queen's Men*, 57–8, 60–1, 72–3.

[77]   Jane E. A. Dawson, *John Knox* (Yale, 2015), 235.

it was also politically advantageous for Mary to visit the earl of Argyll on two counts. Firstly, if Mary was not already aware of the intense feuding between the MacGregors of Glenstrae and Argyll's allies, the Campbells of Glenorchy, Argyll would certainly have enlightened her. This problem was solved temporarily in spring 1564, when Argyll sent Gregor MacGregor and his followers to Ireland to help the Dublin government of Elizabeth to fight the O'Neills. In 1560 Argyll had signed a contract to help Elizabeth, which would certainly have been in line with Mary's policy of amity with England.[78] Secondly, as Gordon Donaldson has pointed out, Mary did not have family links or ties with nobles in the top rank of the aristocracy, men with power in their own right based on their lands and followers.[79] She had been part of such a family group in France, the Guises, but the royal Stewarts such as Moray were not in that category, whereas Archibald Campbell, fifth earl of Argyll, certainly was. He had a large 'affinity', a group of supporters, kin, allies, dependents, and tenants, based on the Campbells and their extensive lands in the west Highlands and Argyll. Mary presumably hoped to consolidate his support by honouring him with her presence, thus demonstrating that she held him in high regard. How Mary hunted in Argyll is not recorded but, given the geography of the area around Inverary and Cowal, it would seem likely that this would have been her first encounter with the Scottish version of the drive.[80] That being the case, it is likely that Argyll would have organised this as a large show hunt to emphasise the importance of a royal visit to the area.

An interesting facet of this progress was the adoption of 'hieland apparell' by Mary and many of her retinue.[81] Historians have sometimes treated this as an extension of Mary's penchant for masques and fancy dress, but there is more to it than that. In Ireland, Gaelic chiefs and earls could change their dress to mark that they were moving from one culture to another.[82] J. Robertson in 1863 spotted examples of royalty and nobles in the sixteenth century adopting highland garb when they were going to hunt in the Highlands.[83] They were doing so not only because they were moving from lowland Scotland to the Gaelic culture of the Highlands but also, as John Taylor explained in 1618, because they wanted their hunting to be successful. Taylor, known as the Water Poet, conducted what he called a 'Pennyless Pilgrimage' from London to the Highlands of Scotland. He travelled without

---

[78] Jane E. A. Dawson, *Campbell Letters*, SHS, 10 (Edinburgh, 1997), 55; Martin D. W. MacGregor, 'A Political History of the MacGregors before 1571', unpublished PhD thesis (Edinburgh University, 1989), 334–5.
[79] Donaldson, *All the Queen's Men*, 61.
[80] Mary stayed in Inverary from 22 to 26 July and then travelled through Cowal, where Campbell hunted in the summer: *CSPS*, i, no.1068 p. 594; Dawson, *The Politics of Religion*, 77.
[81] *CSPS*, ii, no. 13 p. 13.
[82] Dawson, *Politics of Religion*, 119 n. 35.
[83] *Inventaires de la Royne*, lxvii.

money and joined Sir William Murray of Abercairny, his Scottish contact, and the earl of Mar to hunt with them in Braemar.[84] It struck Taylor that everyone at the hunt wore the 'habite of the High-land men'. During August and early September, he said, it was the custom for the nobility and gentry of the kingdom to go to the 'high-land countries' to hunt, and if they dressed like the highlanders their sport, according to Taylor, would be plentiful. This makes perfect sense, because not only did it show respect for the highlanders but on a practical level highland garb and tartan would undoubtedly have helped the hunters to conceal themselves as they lay awaiting the deer. This account also dispels the myth that it was not till the nineteenth century that gentlemen seeking sport went to the Highlands and adopted highland dress.

Mary obtained her highland apparel from Agnes Campbell of Dunyvaig on Islay and her accounts for August record the purchase of three cloaks, '*sayes*', three pairs of hose, '*chausses*', and other clothes in the highland style or, as her household accounts said, '*à la façon de sauvage* [in the style of the savage]'.[85] According to Taylor, such hose were made of 'warme stuffe of divers colours which they call tartane'.[86] This was not modern tartan, but simply cloth woven in checks with a variety of colours. Lesley describes female attire as a cloak decorated and gathered in folds like a plaid and made of *polymitas*, which in this context probably translates best as tartan. These cloaks were probably a version of the arisaid, the female version of the plaid.[87] In 1578 an inventory of Mary's clothes included highland mantles of black, blue, and white and it is possible that these were the three bought in 1563.[88] It may also have been on this trip that Mary paid a '*cornemusier*', a bagpipe player, 25s for his services.[89]

As a child at the French court Mary had been introduced to the idea of the highlanders as 'wild others' who attacked honour and virtue in their masques and fetes.[90] In Scotland, however, by the sixteenth century the idea that Gaeldom was the home of a society distinct from that of Lowland Scotland was just starting to break down. Some chiefs such as the earl of Argyll were both highland chiefs and Lowland magnates who were prepared to work with the king's government. The regular visits to royal hunting grounds in Glenfinglas and Glenartney by the Stewart monarchs since the fourteenth

---

[84] P. Hume Brown, *Early Travellers in Scotland* (Edinburgh, 1891), 118–23.

[85] *CSPS*, ii, no. 13, NRS E34/28/2, fo. 8v.

[86] Hume Brown, *Early Travellers*, 121.

[87] The Latin is quoted in *Inventaires de la Royne*, lxviii n. 1; Lesley, *De Origine* (1578), 94. *Polymitas* can mean damask but it can also mean 'motley, variously inlaid: *Revised Medieval Latin Word-List* ed., R. E. Latham (London, 1965), '*polymitus*'. It can also mean woven with threads of many colours: ΛΟΓΕΙΟΝ on-line dictionary '*polymitus*' and '*polymitare*': https://logeion.uchicago.edu/polymitare [accessed 22 June 2022]; Anita Quye and Hugh Cheape, 'Rediscovering the arisaid', *Costume*, 42 (2008), 1–20, at 5–7.

[88] *Inventaires de la Royne*, lxviii n. 2.

[89] NRS, E34/28/2, fo. 7v.

[90] Brantôme, *The Book of the Ladies*, 91–2; Giovanni Guidicini, *Triumphal Entries and Festivals in Early Modern Scotland: Performing Spaces* (Turnhout, 2020), 55–7.

century may have exemplified royal authority over those areas, but in turn they also introduced these monarchs to Gaelic culture, including Gaelic hunting techniques.[91] Mary's visit to the west Highlands on a hunting trip and the wearing of highland dress is symptomatic of this changing approach to the world of the highlander.

This examination of two of Mary's progresses shows how she used these hunting expeditions to establish her authority and win support, but she also used other hunts to her advantage. Mary could travel and hunt with her lairds and nobles on their hunting grounds, but she also invited courtiers to enjoy the privilege of coming to hunt with her on her terrain. In 1563 Randolph had visited Mary when she was hunting around Moray's estate at Pitlethie near Leuchars, but, more interestingly, on 30 March, 1562 Randolph was hunting with Mary in Falkland Park along with Lord James and Maitland of Lethington.[92] All were strong advocates of the policy of friendship with England and the fact that Randolph was invited to join this small hunting party suggests that the promotion of this policy was under discussion. In October 1561 Randolph had raised the possibility of a meeting between Elizabeth and Mary, but such a meeting was by no means assured.[93] It may have been on this occasion that it was decided that Lethington should lead a mission to the English court to discuss the meeting of the queens and related issues. Whatever was discussed, Lethington set off on 25 May to try to secure Elizabeth's recognition of Mary's claim to the English succession before considering a meeting of the two monarchs.[94] While this Falkland hunt demonstrated the diplomatic possibilities of a small hunting party, it also highlighted its dangers.

While they were in the park Mary learned that James Hepburn, earl of Bothwell, and James Hamilton, earl of Arran, had been plotting to capture her while she was hunting there.[95] When George Buchanan recounted these events he wrote that the alleged plan to kidnap Mary rested on the fact that she was in Falkland Park or nearby almost daily, accompanied by only a small retinue and, therefore, easier to kidnap.[96] This is a very likely scenario because the queen's household accounts for the following year show that when Mary was at Falkland the main part of her retinue stayed in St Andrews.[97] It would

---

[91]   Alison Cathcart, *Kinship and Clientage: Highland Clanship 1451–1609* (Leiden, 2006), 2, 5, 37–8, 48, 50.
[92]   *CSPS*, i, no. 1089 p. 613. Mary was riding 'in the fields a huntynge'. While 'in the fields' could mean 'in the countryside' it referred to the park when linked to Falkland Palace. When James VI hunted in Falkland Park on 5 August 1600 the huntsmen were referred to as 'staying in the fields: *RPS*, 1600/11/9 – testimony of Ludovic Stewart; Robert Pitcairn (ed.), *Criminal Trials in Scotland from 1488 to 1624*, 3 vols. (Edinburgh, 1933), ii, 215.
[93]   Simon Adams, 'The Release of Lord Darnley', 135.
[94]   Mark Loughlin, 'The Career of Maitland of Lethington c. 1526–1573', unpublished PhD thesis (University of Edinburgh, 1991), 140.
[95]   Robert K. Hannay, 'The earl of Arran and Queen Mary', *SHR*, 18 (1921), 274.
[96]   Gatherer, *The Tyrannous Reign of Mary Stewart*, 67.
[97]   *NRS*, E33/7/3, fos 20r, 21r for 1563. On occasions the whole train did stay at Falkland,

be quite normal for her to hunt in the park with only a few people, since it would have been considered, perhaps mistakenly, to be safer than hunting in open country.

In these early years it is also apparent that Mary appreciated the provision of facilities for good-quality falconry. She continued to source hawks and falcons from Orkney as had her predecessors and she realised the diplomatic significance of gifts related to hawking. Indeed on 25 August, 1562 she sent a gift of hawks to Elizabeth to support of her goal of reaching agreement with her about the succession to the English throne.[98] In February she presented the marquis of Elboeuf, her uncle, with hawks, hounds, greyhounds, and horses as a parting gift to thank him for accompanying her on the voyage from France. But more to the point Mary was hoping that Elbouef would pass on good reports of herself both to Elizabeth and to her uncles in France.[99]

Mary's progresses and hunts proved effective, as they established her position as ruler of her kingdom and, combined with a cautious religious policy, neutralised the more extreme opposition to her rule.[100] She visited Catholics, Protestants, lords, lairds, burgesses, and bishops. In Fife, where the lairds and burgesses mattered more than the lords, it can be argued that the impact of her frequent progresses is most notable. In 1562 she covered approximately 115 miles, and in 1563 when she stayed in Fife for almost three months she covered 285 miles, leaving only on 18 May to prepare for her parliament in Edinburgh on 26 May. The Reformation had received strong support in Fife from landholders such as Andrew Leslie, fifth earl of Rothes, and Patrick Lindsay of the Byres, and especially from St Andrews and the coastal burghs. However, Fife produced relatively little opposition to Mary's rule, and in 1565 during the Chaseabout Raid more Fife lairds supported Mary than opposed her.[101]

It was on her progresses that Mary established relationships with her lords and lairds and won their support, but she also worked with her Protestant advisers and adopted policies which made herself acceptable to both religions.[102] While her charm was undoubtedly instrumental in winning over the nobility, her skill as a huntress and her enthusiasm for hunting and hawking also played a part because they could share this pastime with her just as they would with a male monarch. Mary was behaving as people expected a monarch to behave, and they saw nothing wrong with her pastimes of hunting, hawking, and archery.[103] Other than by hunting regularly, Mary did not pro-

---

as from 3 to 19 April, 1563, but Mary was travelling around Fife at that time: NRS, E33/7/4, fos 4r–13r. The accounts for 1562 do not survive.

[98]   *TA*, xi, 190.

[99]   *CSPS*, i, no. 1083 p. 607,

[100]   Julian Goodare, 'The First Parliament of Mary Queen of Scots', *Sixteenth Century Journal*, 36 (2005), 55–75, at 60, 62, 63, 74 for examples of a more cautious policy.

[101]   Donaldson, *All the Queen's Men*, 73, 75.

[102]   Donaldson, *All the Queen's Men*, 56.

[103]   This point is also made in Donaldson, *All the Queen's Men*, 68.

mote the image of herself as the goddess Diana in either literature, masques, or painting. When parliament in 1563 greeted Mary's address with shouts of 'Vox Dianae' this was not the result of some carefully orchestrated campaign such as that organised in France by Henry II and Diane de Poitiers.[104] Rather, it reflected parliament's approval of her cynegetic skills and it marked the creation of her image as the huntress and ruler in charge. She was clearly established as the monarch and, in terms of hunting, this was marked by the progression from predominantly smaller hunts held on her nobles' parks and forests to larger show hunts organised for Mary and held in royal forests.

---

[104] Wellman, 'Diane de Poitiers', 214, 223.

6

Royal huntings

The years 1562–64 were arguably the most successful period of Mary's reign. Her parliament in 1563 accepted the Protestant rebellion, implied recognition of the reformed church, and passed a variety of acts which covered, amongst other matters, adultery, witchcraft, the registration of notaries, and economic issues relating to coinage, bullion, salt manufacture, burgh markets, and coal exports.[1] Because Mary had obtained Protestant acceptance of her government, this was a working parliament not wracked by religious division and argument. Mary continued to act on her concerns over the removal of tenants from, and the ownership of, church lands and commenced the establishment of new commissary courts to replace the Catholic Church's consistory courts, which had ceased to function effectively. This reflected her interest in improving the justice system, as did her appearance at the court of session in Edinburgh's Tolbooth in March 1564, when she urged that steps be taken to allow faster treatment of the cases of the poor.[2] This more assertive mood is reflected in her consideration of a proposed marriage with Don Carlos, heir to Philip II of Spain, in order, it seems, to pressure Elizabeth I into nominating her preferred candidate to be Mary's husband.[3]

Perhaps a sign that Mary had an ambition to provide good governance for the whole country lay in her adoption of the title of 'the queen's majesty'. This title was usually associated with the Holy Roman Emperor and Mary's use of it implied that she viewed her kingdom as an empire. She had always been referred to in this way in the privy council record, but she was now given this imperial title in her acts of parliament.[4] Since the reign of James III, the idea was being developed that the Scottish king ruled over an *imperium*, an empire. This did not mean that the king had conquered other countries, but that he had full territorial and jurisdictional authority over his kingdom with which no external authority could interfere. In Scotland this implied that the monarch could exercise sovereign authority over all his subjects and provided a theory on the basis of which the king could eliminate rival jurisdictions such as those of the Church or powerful magnates.[5] In practice, Mary already reigned over the whole of her kingdom – Orkney and Shetland and

---

[1]   Donaldson, *All the Queen's Men*, 54–5; Goodare, 'The First Parliament of Mary, Queen of Scots', 55–75, at 68–75; Loughlin, 'Maitland of Lethington', 152–3.
[2]   *CSPS*, ii, nos 64 p. 51, 135 p. 115.
[3]   Goodare, Mary [Mary Stewart] 8; Loughlin, 'Maitland of Lethington', 149, 167.
[4]   Goodare, 'First Parliament of Mary, Queen of Scots', 72.
[5]   Roger A. Mason, *Kingship and Commonweal* (East Linton, 1998), 126–30.

the Western Isles had been acquired in the later fifteenth century – but her jurisdictional authority was limited. Her legislation and orders to improve the life of the people were of little value if they carried no weight in some parts of the kingdom, hence the perceived need to focus on law and order in the Borders and the Highlands, a focus in which James V had shown hunting had a part to play.

This increasing confidence in her position and her ability to take the initiative are reflected in two large hunts in which she participated during these years. The first, in September 1563, was organised by herself in Glenfinglas, and the second, in August the following year, by the earl of Atholl in Glen Tilt. In Scotland these larger hunts were called solemn or royal huntings. When Lesley, in his *Historie of Scotland*, refers to such events as 'a solemne hunting', he is describing them as impressive occasions which were renowned throughout the country.[6] According to William Barclay, a Catholic exile and Marian apologist, people described these larger hunts in the presence of the monarch as '*regia venatio*', a royal hunting, which was characterised not only by the presence of the monarch but also by the amount of effort needed to organise the hunt and the considerable expense involved.[7]

Mary was aware that a particular image of a monarch could be presented through the medium of court entertainments and the performance of masques, but it is less well appreciated by historians that hunting served a similar purpose. It enabled Mary to present herself as the accepted ruler in a medium which was convincing to a predominantly male audience. The audience at these performances were members of the court, local elites, members of the tinchell, and the numerous other servants who were present. The action involved the hunt itself, while the stage was the forest or the hunting ground. The maintenance of the forest was fundamental because the whole performance was predicated on the sound management of the *vert* and *venison* within its bounds. The evidence of Mary's role in this regard is very slim. In Glenfinglas and Glenartney, for instance, royal input amounted to occasional reminders to the foresters to prevent poaching and illegal grazing. The work was left in the hands of the local noble appointed as royal forester. In those areas such as Megget and Glen Tilt which were not royal forests, their management lay in the hands of their landholders.

Managing deer and wood

Mary took no specific actions relating to woodland management in royal forests, but she was not unaware that there were shortages of wood and timber elsewhere. Outside royal forests there was some attempt during her reign to

---

[6]   Leslie, *Historie* (1596), i, 19.

[7]   Fittis, *Sports and Pastimes*, 54; Latin from William Barclay, *De Regno et Regali Potestate Adversus Buchannanum, Brutum, Boucherium, et Reliquos Monarchamochos* (Paris, 1600), 81.

preserve woodland and encourage planting. The chancery continued to issue a few free forest grants which applied only to woods or to areas where woods could be grown.[8] Feu charters issued in Mary's reign continued to require that improvements be made to the land by sowing broom, planting oak, ash, planes, and elms and by enclosing woods and shaws (coppices) with protective dykes of some sort.[9] The conversion of run-rig farmland into woodland by the Erskine family at Balgownie in Fife, which probably happened in the 1560s, does suggest that new woods were being planted, but it still seems to have been a fairly rare occurrence.[10] During Mary's reign there was no legislation relating to woodland management in the country as a whole, nor is there any evidence that inquisitions were held to ensure that landlords were planting trees as James V's legislation required. It would appear, therefore, that the policy of trying to encourage better standards of woodland management on private estates continued, but the extent of Mary's involvement in this was minimal. On a couple of occasions she did have to turn her attention to this issue in the north of Scotland. After hunting in Glen Tilt in 1564, Mary travelled through Badenoch to Inverness and, as a result of what she saw and heard about woods in the area, the privy council in Inverness expressed concern about bark-peeling and the intense and destructive cutting and selling of woods and timber in the region. The queen, therefore, authorised letters to go to sheriffs and burghs between Inverness and Aberdeen ordering that timber great or small should be traded only in burgh markets and that bark should be sold only on the tree. The aim was obviously to stop excessive felling and bark-stripping driven by easy and unsupervised sales. Justices were commissioned to inquire into illegal sales and two justice courts were to be held each year to deal with offenders.[11] The success of such proclamations was, as ever, limited, and by 1566 Hugh Rose of Kilravock was complaining that his woods in Nairn were suffering. Local inhabitants were cutting trees, peeling bark, and grazing animals in his woodlands, and yet another proclamation was issued, this time under Mary's signet seal.[12] Despite such efforts in the localities, illegal cutting did not cease, and timber generally continued to be in short supply and had to be imported.

---

[8] *RMS*, iv, nos 299, 640, 695, 1554; 1595 also at NRS, C2/32/2 no. 412; 1609 also at NRS, C2.32/2 no. 420; 1733. See the originals in NRS for the relevant section, which is not given in the printed calendar.

[9] E.g., *RMS*, iv, nos 1516, 1784. For meaning of shaws see John M. Gilbert, 'Place-Names and Managed Woods in Medieval Scotland', *The Journal of Scottish Name Studies*, 5 (2011), 35–56, at 45, 50–3.

[10] *Historic woodland survey at Balgownie Wood* in *Historic Environment Conservation Management*, Forestry Commission Scotland (2013), 3–4.

[11] *RPC*, i, 179–80.

[12] *A Genealogical Deduction of the Family of Rose of Kilravock* (eds), H. Rose, L. Shaw, and C. Innes (Aberdeen, 1848), 248–9.

Nonetheless, the situation was not hopeless. In 1565, in order to repair the royal artillery, the comptroller of artillery was sent to survey woods, gardens, and yards in the central belt of Scotland to locate suitable timber, preferably elm, ash, or oak.[13] Mary wrote to noblemen who had such timbers in their woods and felling was carried out 'with discretion' at Kincardine and Aberruthven, both near Auchterarder, Aberargie, west of Abernethy, and Moncrieffe, south of Perth. The timbers were then transported down the rivers Earn and Tay and by boat to Leith and so to Edinburgh.[14] Discretion, as requested by the privy council, does seem to have been applied because the wood of Kincardine, for example, continued to be managed successfully and was still a commercial proposition in the seventeenth century.[15]

Mary seems not to have been unduly concerned about the shortages of wood and timber, but she was exercised by the declining numbers of deer caused by both the climate and the use of guns. The early sixteenth century saw an improvement in the climate, but by the second half of the century cold winters and poor summers returned.[16] The growing season suffered, causing poor harvests and a reduction in the length of time each year when good grazing was available.[17] In the severe winter of 1555 Marie de Guise had to deal with the migration of deer which were searching for food. The signet letter ordering that these deer should not be killed, which she sent out in Mary's name, stated that Mary had been informed of the problem.[18] This may only be a form of words and the detail passed on to Mary, aged twelve, would have been limited, but it does suggest there could have been some communication about such issues. The hunt which Mary held in Megget in 1566, to be discussed in the following chapter, failed, and that could well reflect a decline in deer numbers in the area following the severe winter of 1564–65.[19]

By the mid-sixteenth century, however, the increasing impact of poaching due to the appearance of easily portable hand-held guns such as half hags, culverings, or pistolets was seen to be the main cause of the problem. On 25 August, 1561 the importance of this issue was highlighted in privy council letters read out at market crosses in the Borders and the south-west. Mary's contribution to this initiative would have been limited, since she had only arrived in the country six days previously. These letters included a repetition of Arran's ban on shooting wild fowl with guns, but which excluded shooting at deer. Two years later, when Mary attended its sittings, parliament repeated Arran's ban but extended it to shooting deer or any other game,

[13] *RPC*, i, 403.
[14] *RPC*, i, 446.
[15] J. M. Lindsay, 'The History of Oak Coppice in Scotland', *Scottish Forestry*, 29 (1975), 87–93, at 88, 91–2.
[16] *CSPS*, ii, nos 128 p. 110, 135 p. 115.
[17] Dawson, *Scotland Reformed*, 11; Ian Morrison, 'Climate', in Lynch (ed.), *The Oxford Companion to Scottish History*, 100.
[18] NRS, GD160/528/28.
[19] *RPC*, i, 477. See pp. 141–2.

under penalty of death.[20] Any offenders were to be brought to the sheriff for trial and punishment and whoever brought them in was to receive half of the offender's goods. Shortly after this, on 22 June, Mary, in conjunction with the privy council, sent a letter under her signet seal to David Lord Drummond, the keeper of Glenartney Forest, to have this act announced at all parish churches and market crosses in the stewartry of Strathearn. In 1563 the building of a hunting house in Glenartney had been ordered by Mary, and so it is likely that she planned to hunt there on her way from Drummond Castle to Glenfinglas on 14 September.[21] Consequently, she asked Drummond to add crossbows and hand bows to the ban and to extend its application beyond the forest, to a strip of land two miles wide around the forest, thus recreating the medieval idea of the *purlieu*, an area outside the forest or reserve but subject to some of the same regulations.[22] The death penalty was a sign of the government's inability to execute these laws and its willingness to collect revenue by way of compositions. Unsurprisingly, poaching with guns continued. In 1567 some poachers in the royal forests of Glenfinglas, Glenartney, and Glenshervie were identified, outlawed, and their goods confiscated.[23] Once again this showed a disconnect, but perhaps a sensible disconnect, between the enacted death penalty and the punishments imposed.

Glenfinglas, August 1563

After returning from her western progress at the end of August 1563, Mary rounded off her progressing season by hunting in Glenfinglas from 14 to 16 September. This was her first and only visit to the royal forest frequented by James IV and James V, and that may be partly attributable to the ravages of the MacGregors and the feud over the tenure of the offices of hereditary forester of Glenfinglas, keeper of Doune Castle, and steward of Menteith. In 1528, after a lengthy dispute, the Edmonstones, who had been foresters for many years, argued with James V and his mother and were replaced by their rivals the Stewarts of Beith. William Edmonstone did not accept this displacement and the feud rumbled on for another thirty-five years until he finally lost his case in the court of session in December 1563. Mary's presence in Glenfinglas in September that year no doubt helped to focus minds on this debate, and the offices were regranted by her to James Stewart of Beith early in 1564.[24]

---

[20]   *RPS*, A1563/6/15.
[21]   The hunting house is discussed in Chapter 7, pp. 144–5 and in Appendix I, pp. 174–7.
[22]   NRS, GD160/129/2.
[23]   *RSS*, v (part ii), no. 3324.
[24]   Mary had confirmed his tenure in 1561 and repeated it in 1564: *RMS*, iv, nos 1392, 1513; W. Fraser, *The Red Book of Menteith* (Edinburgh, 1880), i, 481–5.

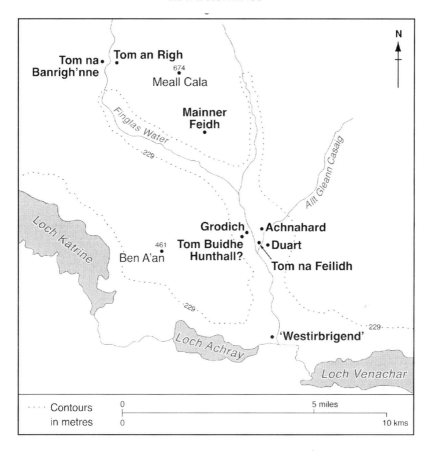

Map 6   Glenfinglas Forest.

Glenfinglas was not an unoccupied, barren glen in the sixteenth century. Several settlements held by the forester still survived in Glenfinglas, but others had been reduced in size or cleared to free up more pasture for the deer (Map 6).[25] The main settlement in the glen appears to have been Grodich, which is the only settlement marked on Gordon's map of Glenfinglas c. 1636–52. It lay just to the north of Tom Buidhe, a possible site of the 'Hunthall'.[26] Pont's

---

[25]   Gilbert, *Hunting and Hunting Reserves*, 117. The settlements of Achnahard, Grodich, Glenmane, and Duart, which were still being worked, lay in the lower part of the glen where the valley flattens out. Prior to the flooding of the glen in 1956, there were 'lovely meadows down by the river', as described to the author in 1971 by Mr Matheson who had worked on the farm at Achnahard.

[26]   NLS, Adv. Ms. 70.2.10, Gordon 51 (*A Map of the basin of the river Forth*), which is probably based on Pont's map, now lost, of c. 1583–96. Although Gordon placed Grodich on the north-east of the river, Pont's text correctly locates it on the west side of the river where it is marked on the first edition of the OS 6-inch map: NLS, Adv. Ms. 34.2.8

ELITE HUNTING CULTURE AND MARY, QUEEN OF SCOTS

text, which may have been altered by Gordon in the 1640s, mentions that there was a wood, 'Kaille Newyrr', on the middle reaches of the south side of the glen, although Gordon marks it on the north side.[27] However, regardless of where exactly the wood was, Pont's text describes the glen as 'good forrest and wood for hunting', and so, despite the dispute between Edmonstone and Beith, the efforts being made in the sixteenth century to maintain Glenfinglas as an effective royal forest were successful. While we do not have details of all the work being carried out to manage the forest we do have some evidence of its management in the time of Mary's grandfather. James IV had been hunting there in August and September 1507 and no doubt had deplored the reduced size of the deer herds in the area caused by illegal grazing and poaching.[28] In March 1508, therefore, he ordered William Edmonstone, William's father, to have proclamations made immediately at all the parish churches around Glenfinglas to the effect that within the forest no one should stalk with bows or rauchs, no one should travel through the forest, and, finally, no one should graze their animals in the forest. Edmonstone was authorised to seize all goods found with stalkers or herdsmen and to keep what could have amounted to a valuable collection of cattle, horses, sheep, and goats as well as bows, greyhounds, and rauchs.[29]

When Mary arrived in Glenfinglas she presumably stayed in one of the chambers in the hunt hall, while pavilions and more temporary accommodation would have been set up for the rest of the party. Evidence for a sizeable group being present comes from the queen's household accounts which survive for the time of this visit.[30] The provision of bread and wine continued to run at around four hundred loaves and nineteen gallons of wine per day, but the amount of ale increased from the usual seventeen gallons or so to forty-two gallons, which was necessary to meet the demands of a sizeable party. Mary was demonstrating that she too could make ample provision for a royal hunting party. Just as in James V's reign, the food supplies closely resembled the normal provision for the court, with bread, wine, ale, mutton, chicken, capons, a side of beef, and game birds as well as butter, fat, candle wax, candle holders, coal, and even the customary chamber lamp or night light.[31]

('Pont's Texts'), fo. 131v.

[27] The use of *coille* carries some idea of woodland management: Gilbert, 'Place-names and managed woods', 46–7.

[28] *TA*, iii, 337–8; iv, 75.

[29] *RSS*, i, no. 1637. For details of hunting dogs in Scotland, see Gilbert *Hunting and Hunting Reserves*, 64–5.

[30] NRS, E33/8/3, fos 59r–61r. Unfortunately, Mary's accounts do not specify the items which were sent to the hunts as clearly as James V's accounts do. Fortunately, at Glenfinglas the account of the *fourrière* (quartermaster) specifies four loads of coal for 'ce train' (this train). The account, therefore, is for only one part of the train and it would be very odd if that was for the group at Stirling rather than for those at Glenfinglas with the queen. Indeed, the fact that the accountant did not try to explain this in any way implies that the rest of the account was for the same train and so the whole account relates to Mary's train at Glenfinglas.

[31] 'dechet d'un mortier'. Thomas A. Small, 'Queen Mary in the Counties of Dumbarton

In a striking link to the legends of Fionn, there are two mounds in the upper reaches of Glenfinglas called Tom na Banrigh'nne and Tom an Righ (NN488127, NN491128), the mounds of the queen and king.[32] While these Gaelic names cannot be dated, they are presumably linked to a king or queen waiting with their dogs for the driven deer. Other Gaelic names in Glenfinglas confirm that drives were held in the area: Elrig (NS473983), Glac nan Sealg (NN434024), defile of the hunts, and Creag na Comh-Sheilg (NN580124), rock of the joint hunting. Mainner Feidh (NN518110), the fold of the deer, on the shoulder of Meall Cala, suggests that deer were driven over the ridge into a fold to be killed as in an elrick.[33] Remarkably, it is almost certain that Mary's seat where she awaited the drive was on the queen's hillock, the Tom na Banrigh'nne, in the upper reaches of the glen where Gordon also marked some woodland. The itinerary of the area compiled by Pont mentions the 'Tom na ban rie' in the upper part of the glen but makes no mention of the king's hillock, Tom an Righ.[34] Therefore, when Pont visited Glenfinglas in the 1580s or 1590s it was the queen's hillock which was mentioned to him, presumably because it was fresh in people's minds, suggesting it had been used by Mary when she was hunting there in 1563.

Deer could not have been driven up the glen to the queen's hillock because the hunters' camp lay in the lower part of the glen. The tinchell must have been sent out into neighbouring valleys down wind of the deer to drive them into the wind and over into the glen where the hunters would be waiting out of sight. The deer would not have been driven at speed as they were gathered and coaxed up and over into Glenfinglas, but as the sight or scent of the hunters began to cause alarm amongst the herd, the tinchell would have closed in.[35] As the deer approached, Mary with several others to protect her would have been concealed under cover of the hillock and whatever vegetation or woodland there was in the upper glen.

Feasting and entertainment followed and, as in the time of Fionn, the success of the hunt was judged by the number of kills. This sort of hunt, where the hunters waited to kill large numbers of game, has been interpreted as a sign of the growing decadence of absolute monarchy in seventeenth- and eighteenth-century Europe. Noble hunters were taking fewer risks and spending less effort to kill an ever larger number of game.[36] In Scotland, however,

---

and Argyll', *Scottish Historical Review*, 25 (1927), 13–19, at 17, n. 7; Cotgrave, *A French and English Dictionary*, 'dechet' means oil, 'mortier' a chamberlamp, therefore, oil for a chamber lamp.

[32] Peter E. McNiven, 'Gaelic place-names and the social history of Gaelic speakers in Medieval Menteith', unpublished PhD thesis (University of Glasgow, 2011), 100–1. There are many hillocks at the top of the glen, none of which is particularly outstanding.

[33] McNiven, 'Medieval Menteith', 95, 268.

[34] NLS, Adv. Ms. 34.2.8 ('Pont's Texts'), fo. 157v.

[35] Scrope, *Art of Deer Stalking*, 17–18, 133–5. Further discussion of how driven deer were controlled and how drives ended is examined below when looking at the hunt in Glen Tilt.

[36] Michael Brander, *Hunting & shooting from the earliest times to the present day* (London,

in the sixteenth century these large kills were not new. The traditional forms of these hunts continued, but they still required courage and some skill with weapons. These Scottish drives were more dangerous than the *chasse aux toiles* but less skilful than *par force* hunting. By ordering this hunt in a royal forest and by acting as chief hunter and host, Mary was expanding the sphere of her activities and meeting the expectation of the nobility that they should be provided with opportunities for hunting in royal forests.

This hunt in Glenfinglas gave Mary the opportunity to further the settlement of the feud between the Edmonstones of Duntreith and the Stewarts of Beith, but her visit to this area was also valuable because the MacGregors were still a cause for concern on the southern edge of the Highlands. As we have seen, in order to establish law and order in the Highlands and Borders, Scottish monarchs had to work through local magnates acting on their behalf or else launch judicial raids as James V had done in the Borders. These problems were aggravated in the Highlands as elsewhere by regional rivalries and internal feuding, and a royal hunt to this area served to bring a royal presence and royal authority to the locality. In this case, between 1437 and 1550 the MacGregors had assisted the Campbells of Glenorchy to expand their sphere of influence into Strathgartney, Menteith, Balquhidder, and Rannoch, but they had become too powerful and Colin Campbell of Glenorchy was keen to reassert his lordship over them.[37] This development worried the earls of Atholl, as the Campbells of Glenorchy seemed to be advancing into his territory and he perceived them as agents of the earl of Argyll. The MacGregors, however, fought against Campbell's attempts to control them in the 1550s and committed offences which enabled Colin Campbell to obtain government help to bring them to order. If these events were not managed carefully they had the potential to aggravate the rivalry between Atholl and Argyll.

It is likely that the effects of the illegal grazing and poaching carried out by the MacGregors in Glenfinglas came up for discussion in 1563, as they did in 1566, when they led to the non-payment of rents by the tenants of Glenfinglas.[38] Not only had members of Mary's council been present in 1563 – they had met at Stirling on 13 September – but local lords and lairds had probably informed her about the crimes of those perceived as broken men and outlaws. On 22 September, shortly after this hunt, the council met again at Stirling and decided to bring the broken men of the MacGregors to justice by pursuing them with 'fire and suerd [fire and sword]'.[39] Various lords were given a twenty-day commission which empowered them to take

---

1971), 58; Gunnar Brausewitz, *Hunting* (London, 1962), 115; *Master of Game*, 201. Fletcher gives a good description of these 'holding hunts' in Germany and reflects on the attitudes of sixteenth-century hunters towards them: Fletcher, *Gardens of Earthly Delight*, 210–20, 225.

[37] Dawson, *Scotland Reformed*, 57–8; Cameron, *James V*, 146–8; MacGregor, 'A Political History of the MacGregors before 1571', vii–viii, 315–45.

[38] Fraser, *Menteith*, 485.

[39] *RPC*, i, 246, 248–9. Mary is not recorded in the *sederunt* but she was in Stirling on 22 September and the letter of fire and sword was clearly issued in her name.

the necessary action over a series of geographical areas which coincided with their respective lordships. They were the earls of Argyll, Atholl, and Errol, David Lord Drummond, Colin Campbell of Glenorchy, James Lord Ogilvy, and Patrick Lord Ruthven, some or all of whom may have been present at Glenfinglas. The letter of fire and sword, however, did not settle matters and the issue of the MacGregors arose again when Mary was hunting in Glen Tilt the following year.

Glen Tilt, August 1564

Mary arrived at Glen Tilt on 2 or 3 August, 1564 accompanied by her privy council and left on 5 August to head north to Inverness.[40] Although she was once again dealing with the problem of the MacGregors, the main aim of her visit was to hunt. An invitation to hunt in Atholl from John Stewart, fourth earl of Atholl, would have suited Mary, since Glen Tilt formed a suitable staging post on her way north. As noted earlier, an eye-witness description of the hunt by William Barclay has survived and he considered that the earl of Atholl, like his predecessor, had gone to immense trouble and expense to prepare for this hunt. Although the arrangements had not been made by Mary or a royal forester, Barclay certainly thought of it as a 'royal hunting' because Mary was present and the hunt was being held in her honour.[41] Atholl, a privy councillor, held sway over part of the central Highlands and, as a powerful earl, he was exactly the sort of ally and confidante on whom Mary depended. This hunt also offered Atholl the opportunity to provide a valuable service to his queen at a point when, as a result of the impending return in September 1564 of Matthew Stewart, fourth earl of Lennox, from his exile in England, he was about to lose his position as the leader of the Stewarts.

Glen Tilt in the mid-sixteenth century, unlike today, was a well-occupied glen with settlements in the lower part and shielings in its upper reaches. Royal connections with the area go back to the twelfth century, when Glen Tilt was a royal thanage, a royal estate run by a thane. By the sixteenth century most royal thanages had disappeared, but Glen Tilt survived as a recognisable area within the earldom of Atholl, perhaps because it provided

---

[40]   NRS, GD112/1/149. Furgol, in his 'Itinerary' considered that her location on 1 and 2 August was unknown but he suggested that she may have been at Blair Castle, although Castle Menzies at Weem has also been proposed: D. P. Menzies, *The 'Red and White' Book of Menzies* (Glasgow, 1894), 193, 195, 197. She was in fact at Dunkeld on 1 August and her whereabouts are unknown only on 2 August, when she could have been at either of the above places or somewhere else en route to Glen Tilt: NRS, GD112/1/149. The privy council met in Inverness when Mary was there and so it is assumed that they travelled with her: *RPC*, i, 279. Maitland, her secretary, was certainly at Glen Tilt, since she used her signet seal which he kept: W. Fraser (ed.), *The Lennox* (Edinburgh, 1874), ii, 428; NRS, GD112/1/3/150.

[41]   Fittis, *Sports and Pastimes*, 54–5.

good hunting. It contained Bencrumby forest, and in the mid-fourteenth century the thane had to supply the earl of Atholl with four horses to hunt there.[42] It was this forest, centred on Loch Loch and Fealar where James V and then Mary hunted in the sixteenth century (Map 7). The hill Elrig 'ic an Toiseach (NN866788), the elrick of the thane, is one of several elrick names in the area which reveal the type of hunting which was conducted there.[43] In this mountainous terrain it was hard for hunters to chase deer on horseback or on foot, and so the drive was more effective.

The best-known example of a large drive in James V's reign is the hunt which took place in Glen Tilt in 1532 when James hunted there for four days accompanied by the queen mother, Margaret Tudor, and the papal envoy.[44] As we have seen, Pitscottie's description concentrated on the temporary accommodation provided in Glen Tilt, but he also tells us that they slew six hundred harts, hinds, roe deer, wolves, foxes, and wild cats.[45] Their hunts ranged over Beinn a'Ghlo, Beinn Iutharn Mhor, and a third mountain called 'Bencruine'.[46] The size of the kill, even allowing for exaggeration, was considerable, but it is worth remembering that in the early nineteenth century a drive of several hours on the hills around Glen Tilt could bring in five hundred to six hundred deer. Presumably, different areas were hunted on different days, depending on the location of the deer and the direction of the wind.[47]

When Mary was hunting in Glen Tilt she said in her letters that she stayed at the 'Lunkartis', a previously unknown site.[48] Timothy Pont marks several Luncarty place-names in Atholl: 'Loncartis' beside the River Tarff,[49] 'Lonkartis' west of the River Bruar,[50] and 'Lhontartis' on the banks of the An Lochain in Glen Tilt.[51] At the first two sites there is insufficient room

[42]   Stephen Boardman, *The Early Stewart Kings* (Phantassie, 1996), 28 n. 31; RMS, ii, no. 2655; A. Grant, 'Thanes and Thanages', 63–4, 79.
[43]   John Kerr, *The Living Wilderness* (Perth, 1996), 16, 21.
[44]   Thomas, 'Renaissance Culture', 393–5. This hunt was described by Robert Lindsay of Pitscottie, who dated it to 1529, but James's household accounts show that it actually occurred between 9 and 12 September 1532.
[45]   Pitscottie, *Historie*, 338.
[46]   This is probably Carn a' Chlamain (NN917758), the hill at the head of Gleann Craoinidh. This glen is referred to as Glen Croine in the nineteenth century and so the hill at its head could be Pitscottie's 'Bencrwine (Map 7): William Scrope, *The Art of Deer Stalking* (London, 1838), 210.
[47]   By this time the area was managed primarily for deer and the removal of sheep from the north side of Glen Tilt in the late eighteenth century had greatly increased deer numbers, with about seven thousand recorded in the Atholl estates in the 1820s: Scrope, *Art of Deer Stalking*, 165. Numbers of deer were not always so plentiful. In 1884–85 only 411 deer were shot in Atholl Forests: Kerr, *The Living Wilderness*, 32.
[48]   *Red and White Book of Menzies*, 196, 197; William Fraser (ed.), *The Lennox* (Edinburgh, 1874), ii, 428.
[49]   NLS, Adv. Ms, 70.2.9, Pont 20 ('Glen Tilt'). NN96018027 Canmore Id 131849.
[50]   NLS, Adv. Ms 70.2.9, Pont 19 ('The Forest of Atholl'). NN74877273. Canmore Id 25193.
[51]   NLS, Adv. Ms, 70.2.9, Pont 20 ('Glen Tilt'). NN98367780. Canmore Id 370113.

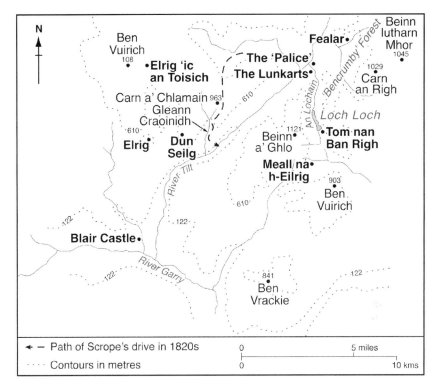

Map 7   The Glen Tilt area.

for an encampment of a party numbering in the hundreds, whereas there is sufficient space at the third site, which Pont marks with a circle on the west side of the An Lochain only a short distance upstream from the likely site of James V's lodge of 1532 (Plate 5). Pont also distinguishes this site from the others because he does not call it simply 'Lhontartis' but qualifies the name by adding 'Rederis', thus making the complete name 'Rederis Lhontartis', the lunkarts associated with red deer (see Plate 6).[52] This qualifying name, along with the proximity of this site to the likely site of James V's 'palice', combined with the fieldwork described in Appendix I, argues that this was the site where Mary stayed in 1564.[53] The earl of Atholl was clearly using his knowledge of the previous visit of James to arrange accommodation for the queen at a site which had already worked successfully as a base for a royal hunting expedition.

The nature of this accommodation is revealed by the name 'Lhontartis', which is given as 'Lunkartis' in two of the letters which Mary signed while

---

[52] The reading of the first word is problematical and is discussed more fully in Appendix I.
[53] Canmore Id 370113. For fuller discusion of this site and its discovery see Appendix I.

Plate 5   The Lunkarts in Glen Tilt, looking east. The remains of the huts and houses can be seen in the centre of the picture. The An Lochain river beyond flows from right to left.

she was there.[54] Henceforth lunkart will be used as the name for an individual building and lunkarts will mean a collection of such buildings. The word developed from the Gaelic *longphort* and came to mean an encampment, a palace, a shieling, or a hunting booth, and it survives in Scotland as the place-name Luncarty.[55] Theoretically, any of these meanings could have applied to Mary's lodgings in Glen Tilt: an encampment of pavilions and other shelters, a more substantial structure like the 'palice' of James V, or more humble hunting booths or shielings. That such lunkarts were fairly common is suggested by the way in which this site is referred to as the 'lunkartis in Glentilth', implying that there were other lunkarts – which, of course, there were.[56] Since several of these lunkarts would have been inhabited when grazing cattle or sheep, Pont had to explain that the lunkarts in Glen Tilt were those used when hunting red deer. Further light is shed on the use of lunkarts in Taylor's description of the hunt in Mar in 1618.[57] On the

---

[54] Because the letters 't' and 'c' were interchangeable 'Lhontartis' is the same as 'Lhoncartis'. Mary's letters – *The Red and White Book of Menzies*, 195–6 and NRS, GD50/186/11/vii/4; Fraser, *Lennox*, ii, 427 and NRS, GD112/1/150 – are discussed below.

[55] Watson, 'Deer and Boar', 97; Simon Taylor, *Place-Names of Fife*, 5 vols (Donington, 2012), v, 431; *DOST*, 'lunkart'.

[56] Menzies, *Red and White Book of Menzies*, 196, 197; Fraser (ed.), *Lennox* i, 428.

[57] Hume Brown, *Early Travellers in Scotland*, 121.

first day of his visit Taylor wrote that he travelled to 'where there were small cottages built on purpose to lodge in which they call Lonquhards'. When the earl of Mar called a hunt, he arranged that certain tenants who held lands by feu ferme would

> big and putt wp lunkardis for the said hunting and sall mak and putt furth tinschellis at the same according to wse and wont and sall caus them carie furth the necessaris requyrit for the said hunting to the lunkardis and sall carie the same back againe and tak up the slaine deir and raes to the lunkardis or to our house in Mar … as they have beine in use to doe in tyme bygaine.[58]

The obligation on tenants to provide for the lord's hunt had existed in various parts of Britain, and the Highlands were no different.[59] The earl of Atholl's tenants would be required to build the lunkarts for the royal hunt and presumably, with some supervision, they would build what they knew in the vernacular style. It is also relevant here to note that this custom of living in small shielings or bothies when hunting continued into the early nineteenth century, before more elaborate lodges were built.[60] The view here is that Mary and her companions were living in small, temporary cottages like shielings with walls of stone and turf or perhaps of wood and a thatch or turf roof.

One assumes that, like Marie de Guise when she hunted in Glenfinglas, Mary was accompanied by several women, and the possibility must be considered that Mary and her female companions were accommodated in a pavilion. These pavilions were substantial structures, to judge by those paid for in 1565 which were made of canvas from Brittany and supplied along with cords, supports, iron work, and pegs to secure the structure. At the same time Mary also paid for canvas wardrobes and a canvas stable for twelve horses.[61] However, based on the example of the hunt in Mar in 1610, where the lunkarts were built specifically for the hunt and where the chief hunters stayed in the lunkarts, the conclusion must be that Mary and her companions stayed in one or more of these buildings which had been prepared for them with bedding and wardrobes sent there in advance, while Mary's guard and other hunters were encamped nearby.

In some ways, living in lunkarts can be seen as an expression of the desire by the nobility, however transient, to live like the ordinary people, free of the responsibilities of power. For Mary, living in lunkarts in Glen Tilt was the equivalent, in a hunting context, of living like a merchant's wife in a

---

[58] 'build and put up lunkarts for the said hunting and shall collect and put out tinchells there according to use and wont and they shall carry the necessaries for the hunting to the lunkarts and carry them back again and bring the slain deer and roe to the lunkarts or to our house in Mar as they have been used to do since time bygone', *RMS*, ix, no. 99 (date 1634). There is a very similar feu charter in 1632 for Camusnakist in the Braes of Mar: *Fourth Report of the Historical Manuscripts Commission* (London, 1874), Part I, App 533/2.
[59] Rollason, *Power of Place*, 142; Jones, 'A Common of Hunting', 47.
[60] Kerr, *Living Wilderness*, 29.
[61] *TA*, xi, 407–8.

merchant's house in St Andrews.[62] Although, as we will see, the work of government and local affairs did not leave Mary behind in Glen Tilt, there is an element of escapism about this. It also illustrates an acceptance of the tradition, going back to the time of Fionn, of staying in humble dwellings when hunting.

The probable site of the 'Lunkartis' has now been located on the ground and lies to the west of the An Lochain, exactly as marked by Pont (Plate 6 and Map 7).[63] The site, which displays more than one stage of occupation, comprises ten buildings of various sizes, including six larger buildings as well as four smaller huts. Some of the slightly wider and longer rectangular buildings with stone-based walls, such as numbers 1, 4, and 9 on the plan, could have served as accommodation for Mary or as the equivalent of a hall (Plan 1). It is not possible to say if any of these structures followed the hall-house layout because the internal partitions of the buildings, if any, are undetectable on the ground. One can picture the scene much as John Taylor found it in Mar in 1618: a camp of several hundred men and horses with tents and pavilions spread around the lunkarts along the valley floor of the An Lochain; fires and camp kitchens to roast beef and venison as well as wild fowl and fish; and the earl of Atholl's tenants bringing in supplies of food, fuel, wine, and ale. Supplies and equipment were brought in by pack horse either up Glen Tilt or by the track called locally Rathad nam ban Righ, the Queen's road, which led from Blair Atholl around the south of Beinn a Ghlo.[64]

The hunt as described by William Barclay must have made a considerable impression on him as a teenager, since he still remembered it vividly in 1600 when he published his work supporting monarchy.[65] His purpose was not primarily to describe the hunt or Mary's role in it, but to stress a particular episode in the hunt which illustrated that, as a herd of deer had a leader, so a country also required a monarch whose lead it could follow.[66] While his account is neither flawless nor complete, by comparing it with other and later drives in the Highlands one can obtain a good idea of what was involved when conducting this drive. According to Barclay, the chief hunters, namely the queen and the nobility, waited for the deer to be driven to them. Barclay simply says that they waited in a valley, but local tradition records a queen's mound, Tom nan Ban Righ, at the south end of Loch Loch (NN989737).[67]

---

[62] *CSPS*, ii, no. 142 p. 120.

[63] Canmore Id 370113; NN98367781. As explained in Appendix I, I am indebted to the help of Piers Dixon in the analysis and identification of this site on the ground.

[64] *Chronicles of The Atholl and Tullibardine Families*, ed. John Stewart-Murray, 7th duke of Atholl, 5 vols (Edinburgh, 1908), i, 38.

[65] David Baird Smith, 'William Barclay', *SHR*, 11 (1914), 136–63, at 136.

[66] Barclay, *Contra Monarchomachos*, 81; Fittis, *Sports and Pastimes*, 54–5 gives the English translation of Thomas Pennant from his 1769 *Tour in Scotland and Voyage to the Hebrides* (London, 1772), part ii, 64–5.

[67] Another tradition places this hillock on the face of the hill on the east side of the loch, but both William Fraser in 1875 and John Kerr in 1982 heard that it lay close to the south end of the loch, where there are three or four very recognisable hillocks. Influenced

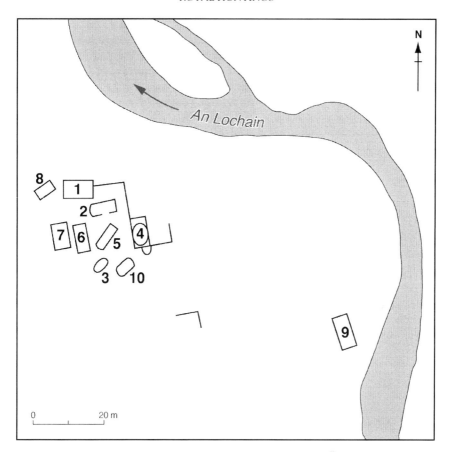

Plan 1   Sketch plan of the Lunkarts in Glen Tilt. Based on the sketch plan drawn by Piers Dixon. The numbers refer to the descriptions of the site in Chapter 6 and Appendix I.

Barclay informs us that two thousand highlanders were sent out for around two months to round up two thousand red, roe, and fallow deer from Atholl, Badenoch, Mar, and Moray. Clearly these figures are exaggerated. Regardless of the problems of feeding and organising two thousand highlanders as a tinchell, the task of driving deer over such a wide area with a line of men many miles in length was clearly problematic. Moreover, one has to consider the possible effects of the weather and the wind and how the collected deer

---

by eighteenth-century descriptions of elricks, Kerr thought it was an observation point for the queen away from danger, but it seems to have been fairly close to the action: *Chronicles of Atholl*, ed. Atholl, i, 38; Kerr, *Life in the Atholl Glens*, 82; *Sixth Report of Royal Commission on Historical Manuscripts*, Part 1 (London, 1877), 689b, 709a, in which Menzies Manuscripts are edited by W. W. Fraser in 1875 as dated on p. 709.

herd could have been kept together at night. The hunting roll call for the earl of Atholl's hunt in September 1667 amounted to just over three hundred men gathered from the whole estate from Balquhidder to Strathardle, nowhere near two thousand.[68] Normal practice as in Mar in 1618 and Atholl in 1710 and 1711 was to collect several hundred men the previous day so that they could be despatched early in the morning.[69] It is possible that a scarcity of game in 1564 could have resulted in a much longer drive, but a drive of several hours would seem to have been normal in the area.

It is often forgotten that driving deer was a skilful business full of pitfalls. Lesley believed that if the leading stag was killed or in danger the other deer would all follow in a stampede.[70] Edward VII's drives in 1905 in Glen Quoich Forest in Lochaber suffered for a variety of reasons: unexpected mist or heavy rain reducing visibility, change of wind direction, and a waiting hunter showing himself and turning the herd back towards the tinchell.[71] An eye-witness account of driving in Atholl comes from William Scrope, who was one of a small number of drivers taking part in a hunt in the Glen Tilt area in the 1820s (see Map 7). The striking points of his description include the skill and patience needed by the drivers to steer the deer in the desired direction. When the deer were moved gently, Scrope states, they followed each other in a line. It was then a question of the drivers staying down wind of the deer and showing themselves just enough to move the deer along into the wind. The deer were driven in from the valley of the Tarff Water to the west of Glen Tilt, then south into Gleinn Craoinidh, which lies immediately to the west of Glen Tilt. At this point they were driven over the ridge and thus into Glen Tilt. As they moved the deer, the drivers allowed hinds to escape if they attempted to do so, but escaping stags might be shot by one or two of the hunters who were with the tinchell. As the deer were driven up the ridge between the glens the tinchell closed in and formed a semicircle. As this happened the herd cautiously started to pick their way down into Glen Tilt towards the hunters who lay concealed at various places in the glen. Seeing no danger ahead of them, the deer picked up speed and when their course was decided the hidden hunters broke cover and the deer then dashed across the meadow and through the River Tilt.[72]

It is surprising that Barclay's account does not mention Loch Loch beside the Queen's hillock, and so it is possible that he was describing a drive

---

[68] *Chronicles of Atholl*, ed. Atholl, i, Appendix, xxi; Scrope, *Art of Deer Stalking*, 36. Scrope calculated on one hundred men per mile, 17.6 yards apart, making a line twenty miles long.

[69] Hume Brown, *Early Travellers in Scotland*, 121; *Chronicles of Atholl*, ed. Atholl, ii, 123–4, 133–4.

[70] Leslie, *Historie* (1596), i, 19–20.

[71] Iain Thornber, 'Morvern Lines with Highland Historian Iain Thornber', *Oban Times*, 24 April 2016 and pers. comm. This is information which he gleaned from local newspapers, and stalkers now passed away.

[72] Scrope, *Art of Deer Stalking*, 214–18 describes the drive and 17–18 and 133–6 describe the importance of the wind direction.

elsewhere during Mary's visit. However, it does seem likely that the hunt occurred in this area because of the place-names Tom nan ban Righ and the hill called Meall na h'Elrig which lies to the south-west of Loch Loch, both of which lay in Bencrumby Forest. While the queen's hillock could have been named after any other queen who hunted in this area, for instance, Margaret Tudor, it would be surprising if a queen's hillock and a major drive held by a Scottish queen which was worthy of entering the written record were not connected. Indeed, it may well have been the exciting and dangerous nature of this hunt which led to the naming of the mound where the queen was positioned.

One has the impression from the eighteenth-century description of an elrick that deer in a drive were usually driven along a narrow valley and into a trap formed either by a body of men or by an artificial construction of some sort, but here, just as Scrope described, the deer appeared on top of the ridge above the valley. Presumably the hunters were lying hidden, like those at Mar in 1618 and Scrope's companions in Glen Tilt in the early nineteenth century. The approaching deer, Barclay says, formed an impressive sight. The earl of Atholl, who was with Mary, pointed out the leading stag to her as it stood on the ridge of the hill. He told her that if fear or rage moved the stag from the ridge the situation would become dangerous.[73] If it ran down the hill towards the hunters, they would all be in danger as the rest of the herd would follow, trampling the hunters underfoot in their attempt to break through to the hill beyond them. When Mary first saw the deer Barclay said she was delighted, but after Atholl's warning 'she soon had cause to fear'.[74] This is the kind of scenario which Scrope described where the hunters waited in Glen Tilt and then showed themselves as the deer picked up speed going down the slope. The hunters shot the deer as they passed by on their flight to safety.

According to Barclay, when Mary had a hound unleashed prematurely to chase a wolf, she broke cover, frightening the leading stag, which turned back towards the tinchell. This was all the more dangerous because it was followed by the rest of the herd. Although the tinchell threw themselves on the ground, several were wounded and two or three were killed. The highlanders, however, managed to stop many of the deer escaping and they were still able to drive the deer down to the waiting hunters under some sort of control. When the deer reached the bottom of the valley, Barclay reports that the queen and the nobility released their dogs to chase and bring down the deer. This is reminiscent of the description of the hunt in Mar in 1618. The deer on that occasion also appeared on the hills around the hunters before the tinchell chased them down into the valley where the hunters lay. The deer were then attacked on both sides of the valley with two hundred strong Irish

---

[73]   Some have questioned whether a stag would lead a herd in this situation, but in similar circumstances the lead of a herd can be taken either by hinds or stags: Duff Hart-Davis, *Monarchs of the Glen* (London, 1978), 26; pers. comm. John Fletcher; Scrope, *Art of Deer Stalking*, 18.

[74]   Fittis, *Sports and Pastimes*, 54–5.

greyhounds 'as the occasion serves'. The slaughter in Mar continued with guns, dirks, daggers, and arrows killing eighty deer in two hours. At Glen Tilt, Barclay mentions no weapons other than dogs, perhaps because, with Mary present, it was safer not to be shooting deer with arrows, but presumably clubs, axes, and spears were used in the slaughter. Nor would guns have been used because, apart from reasons of safety, Mary's parliament had banned their use against deer and, while the law may have been flouted elsewhere, it could hardly have been ignored in Mary's presence. It is quite clear that the success of the hunt was, as usual, measured by the size of the kill. Barclay carefully reports that 360 deer, the same number as James V killed in Megget, were killed, along with five wolves and some roe deer. The similarity in numbers seems too good to be true and that number must have symbolised a successful hunt.

Mary's excitement may explain why she ill-advisedly ordered that a hound be released at a wolf, almost ruining the drive. This was probably only the second or third time Mary had participated in a large drive and her lack of experience was evident. She was not just a spectator who simply viewed the action from a prominence above the kill zone. The earl of Atholl's warning that the herd could be a danger to them, her feelings of fear, and her involvement in releasing dogs, all argue that she was beside the action. She was there on her hunting hillock with the earl of Atholl and perhaps others to protect her. This traditional Gaelic drive was a far cry from Mary's experience at the French renaissance court.

A recurring theme of this book has been the importance of the informal contacts between monarch and nobles which hunting could provide. It is possible to see glimpses of this in operation at Glen Tilt when the problem of the MacGregors resurfaced. Glenfinglas, Atholl, and Glenartney lay on the edges of the territory where the MacGregors roamed, and so it is little wonder that when Mary was hunting in these areas the MacGregor problem was brought before her. Colin Campbell had been overstepping the mark in the pursuit of his commission and, as a result, his powers had been limited to pursuing only those who offered hospitality to the MacGregors. When Mary arrived at Dunkeld on 1 August on her way to Glen Tilt she heard from the earl of Atholl that a Duncan MacGregor had been wrongly detained by Duncan Campbell of Glen Lyon. She promptly issued a royal warrant ordering Glen Lyon to deliver Duncan MacGregor within forty-eight hours 'to the Lunkartis at our present hunting in Atholl'.[75]

After Mary arrived at the Lunkarts on 2 or 3 August, James Menzies of Weem brought a different complaint to her, namely, that Colin Campbell had leased Menzies's lands in Rannoch to the Camerons and the Macdonalds of Keppoch and they had started to fortify an island in Loch Tay.[76] As Colin

[75] NRS GD112/1/149.
[76] *Sixth Report of the Royal Commission on Historical Manuscripts* (London, 1877), 707, no. 204. This is an order dated in 1566 but refers to Menzies's visit to 'Lunkartis' in 1564. The

Campbell of Glenorchy moved into Breadalbane, a long-running dispute over these lands started with Menzies of Weem.[77] Mary, having no doubt taken advice from members of her council who were present, such as Atholl, Maitland of Lethington, and Argyll, responded immediately by sending a letter on 3 August to Colin Campbell telling him to stop bringing in strangers and thieves and to desist from fortifying the island.[78] Since Mary did not have the time when hunting to deal with the problem in any more detail he was also asked to report to the council at Perth on Mary's return from the Highlands. On the following day she issued another order relating to the MacGregors. Partly to escape the pressure from Campbell, Argyll, and Atholl, a group of MacGregors, as we have seen, had gone to Ireland as mercenaries in the spring of 1564.[79] By the summer they were intending to return, but it suited both Mary and the Campbells to keep them in Ireland. Consequently, Mary issued an order under her signet seal to her sheriffs on the west coast to stop the MacGregors returning to Scotland. The order reveals that Campbell was present at Glen Tilt because it explains that the issue about the MacGregors returning from Ireland was 'humlie menit and schewin to ws by oure louit Coline Campbell of Glenvrquhay'.[80] Colin Campbell, having received his reprimand over his behaviour in Rannoch, no doubt brought forward his own concerns about the MacGregors, and Mary saw the opportunity to balance her criticisms of his behaviour in Rannoch with support of his efforts to stop the MacGregors returning from Ireland.

Therefore, while Mary was at Glen Tilt she was hearing at first hand about regional issues which had the potential to cause wider disagreements. What seemed a minor issue could quickly have developed into a crisis, given the relationships and groupings of those involved. Mary's handling of the situation kept the matter under control and prevented any trouble arising between Argyll and Atholl at this time.

Such large royal hunts were not a normal part of the daily life of the court. At a symbolic level they were special events and must be considered as performances of royalty, while at a personal level they illustrate Mary's courage and political awareness. She was not familiar with this type of drive, but

---

island had been the subject of a similar dispute in the time of James V: Cameron, *James V*, 146.

[77] Dawson, *Campbell Letters*, 36.

[78] Menzies, *The Red and White Book of Menzies*, 195–6; NRS, GD50/186/11/vii/4. Original is in BnF, Ms Anglais 166 referred to in Susan Dwight Bliss, *Collections des Manuscrits Livres, Estampes et Objets D'Art Relatifs à Marie Stuart Reine de France et D'Écosse en Bibliothèque Nationale* (Paris, 1931), 22.

[79] MacGregor, 'A Political History of the MacGregors', 333–5.

[80] 'humbly presented as a complaint and shown to us by our beloved Colin Campbell of Glenorchy', Fraser, *Lennox*, ii, 427; NRS, GD112/1/150.

there was no question of her refusing to order, or take part in, such hunts. She adapted to the local custom of sleeping in a lunkart and to the more dangerous practice of taking up her position on a hunting mound. There was also considerable political mileage to be gained by doing so, because it showed her recognising and accepting Gaelic hunting culture.

Mary was well aware of the power of performance and, although the full details of these hunts are absent, it is possible to detect the nature of the performance at these drives. The key features which would have presented an image of her monarchy were the initial gathering, the first sighting of the monarch, the size of the hunting party, the queen's accommodation, the procession to the kill zone, the allocation of hunting seats and of the queen's hunting mound, the provision of food and refreshment nearby, releasing the dogs at the on-rushing game, the laying out and counting of the game at the hunters' camp, the size of the kill, the queen's choice of deer to be gifted to various nobles and officials, and, finally, the organisation of feasting and the selection of a smaller group to eat with the queen.[81] This performance created an image of Mary as a monarch with authority and broad support – a 'credible figure of legitimate power' at ease with her nobility.[82] However, the relative calm and stability of the early years of her reign did not last.

[81] The laying out of the game and the choice of gifts are assumed in these hunts in Scotland but are mentioned by the duke of York in his *Master of Game*, 195–7.
[82] Groundwater, 'Afterword', 227.

7

Hunting for reconciliation

Mary organised three royal hunts in 1566, more than in any previous year of her reign: one in Meggetland and Traquair, one in the royal forest of Glenartney, and a third in Stirling Park which formed part of the celebrations of the baptism of her son, the future James VI. Although the royal household accounts for these hunts do not survive, they were all, as will be explained in this chapter, large events. If one royal hunt per year had sufficed for Mary in 1563 and 1564, one has to ask why three were required in 1566.[1] Basically, Mary wanted to use any means at her disposal to heal the divisions in her realm which she had created, mainly through her marriage in July 1565 to Henry Stewart, Lord Darnley. Alongside royal pardons, threats of trials in parliament, imposition of exile, and policy changes, these royal hunts played an important role in reconciling the various noble factions.

The divisions amongst the nobility in 1566 arose largely from two major episodes that resulted from Mary's marriage to Darnley: the Chaseabout Raid in the summer of 1565 and the murder of Riccio in March 1566. Mary's preference for Lennox and the Stewarts over Châtelherault and the Hamiltons, her marriage to Darnley, and a more assertive policy towards Catholicism in 1565 alienated Châtelherault and the earls of Moray, Argyll, Rothes, and Glencairn.[2] They rebelled in July 1565 in what is called the Chaseabout Raid but were decisively outmanoeuvred by Mary, who had widespread support led by Huntly, Atholl, and Lennox. Thereafter Mary began to realise how unsuitable Darnley was as a king and by Christmas their estrangement was well known.[3] By March 1566 many of the lesser rebels had received remissions and Châtelherault had been pardoned on condition that he went into exile.[4] However, the earls of Moray, Argyll, Glencairn, Rothes, and others were ordered to stand trial in parliament on 14 March 1566. These circumstances led to the second episode, which confirmed and widened the divisions amongst the elite. A *coup d'état* was planned by several of those

---

[1]   There is no specific record of any hunt in 1565. Pitscottie records that in April, when there were rumours of marriage to Darnley, Mary was 'at that tyme in Stirviling at the huntting'. She spent most of the month at Stirling apart from a total of seven days at Holyrood in the weeks prior to 22 April. There is no mention in her household accounts of any trips to Glenartney or Glenfinglas: Pitscottie, *Historie*, ii, 182. Therefore, it is most likely that she was hunting in Stirling Park.

[2]   Donaldson, *All the Queen's Men*, 72–3.

[3]   *CSPS*, ii, no. 319 p. 248; Dawson, *Scotland Reformed*, 256; Guy, *My Heart is My Own*, 241.

[4]   Donaldson, *All the Queen's Men*, 78.

due to stand trial and others who had been losing influence at court, such as Maitland of Lethington, James Douglas, earl of Morton, and Darnley, who was hoping to receive the crown matrimonial.[5] They picked on Mary's private secretary, Riccio, as their scapegoat and murdered him on 9 March 1566, ostensibly because he was Roman Catholic, Italian, and not of noble birth. Mary managed to detach Darnley from the plotters and escape from Holyrood to Dunbar. However, she was able to return to Edinburgh in force on 18 March because the earl of Bothwell, who had been recalled from banishment, together with the earls of Atholl, Mar, and Huntly, and John Lesley, remained loyal to her.[6]

Mary's determined attempts to unify the country in the wake of these events involved renewing the policy of amity with England and reassuring the Protestants that she was not going to attempt to reintroduce Catholicism on a nationwide basis.[7] By the end of March, she had pardoned Moray, Glencairn, and Rothes and they were sitting on the council with their former enemies, Bothwell, Huntly, and Atholl.[8] Unsurprisingly, all did not go smoothly. Bothwell and Moray's long-standing enmity dated back to 1559, when Bothwell had supported Marie de Guise and Moray had been a leading reformer.[9] Their differences now focussed on whether Maitland of Lethington should be pardoned and allowed to return to court.[10] To complicate matters, Atholl and Argyll were keen to restore Lethington, but their own rivalry had been aggravated by Argyll's attacks on Atholl's territory during the Chaseabout Raid.[11] Keeping the council together required considerable skill, and since the end of March Mary had let it be known that she wanted 'to quiet her country'.[12] She was losing patience with Moray and Bothwell, but around the end of April, according to Claude Nau, who was Mary's secretary after 1575 during her captivity in England, she believed that she had settled the disputes of Argyll and Moray with Atholl, Huntly, and Bothwell.[13] Although Mary had written to Lethington, no real progress had been made towards his return to the council.[14] The birth of Mary's son on 19 June rendered the need for unity all the more pressing, as unrest or worse might prevent the wholehearted acceptance of James as her heir.

The Lethington issue would not go away and may well have led to the rumoured split in the council prior to 24 June. Argyll, Moray, Mar, and Atholl, who were at court, were on one side, and Huntly and Bothwell – who

---

[5]   Loughlin, 'Maitland of Lethington', 215–16.
[6]   Donaldson, *All the Queen's Men*, 80
[7]   Dawson, *Scotland Re-formed*, 257.
[8]   *CSPS*, ii, nos 368 p. 273, 375 p. 278; Donaldson, *All the Queen's Men*, 77–80.
[9]   Guy, *My Heart is my Own*, 221–2.
[10]   *CSPS*, ii, nos 368 p. 273, 425 p. 299.
[11]   Dawson, *The Politics of Religion*, 125.
[12]   *CSPS*, ii, nos 368 p. 273, 375 p. 276.
[13]   Nau, *Memorials*, 23. Stevenson, who edited Nau's *Memorials*, considered that Nau based his history on what Mary told him during her captivity in England.
[14]   *CSPS*, ii, no. 375 p. 276.

was reluctant to come to court because of this dispute – were on the other.[15] Bothwell was a long-standing rival of Lethington in the Haddington area, and since he had received some of Lethington's forfeited estate he had no wish to see Lethington reinstated.[16] Bothwell was also reportedly threatening to seize Lethington if he tried to escape by sea to Flanders.[17] A series of remissions for several of the lesser Riccio murderers followed on 17 and 18 July and by 14 August matters appear to have been settling. Moray and Bothwell, however, were still at odds over Lethington and Mary, having witnessed their arguments, was determined to have the matter resolved.[18] It was at this point that she brought hunting into the equation and within days Moray and Bothwell were included in the royal hunting party going to 'Meggatland'.

Megget and Traquair, August 1566

This hunt should have been part of a judicial raid/hunt to the Borders which the privy council had proclaimed on 28 July. This 'rayd of Jeduard' was to start with a hunt at Megget from 13 to 16 August, followed by a justice ayre at Jedburgh on 17 August.[19] Following James V's practice, a force was to be mustered from the earls, lords, barons, freeholders, and landed men in the sheriffdoms of Fife, Kinross, Clackmannan, Stirling, Linlithgow, Haddington, Berwick, Peebles, Selkirk, and Lanark and they were requested to come geared for war to join the royal party at Peebles on 13 August.[20] Personal invitations were sent to seventy lords and lairds in Fife, Lanark, and the Borders.[21] However, the privy council had to change the date of the justice ayre to allow for the harvest and it was rescheduled for 19 October, but the hunt still went ahead.[22]

Mary travelled to Peebles around 13 August and went hunting in the Megget area until 17 August accompanied by Darnley and the earls of Moray, Mar, Bothwell, and Atholl. It is likely that Argyll and Huntly were also present, since, according to Nau, they too spent the summer with Mary. Bothwell, as sheriff of Selkirk, had perhaps been involved in some of the preparations and had probably received final instructions in a letter of 12 August.[23] The earl of Mar was one of the seventy who had received an individual letter and

[15] CSPS, ii, no. 400 p. 289.
[16] Loughlin, 'Maitland of Lethington', 221, 224; RSS, v (part 2), no. 2686.
[17] CSPS, ii, no. 400 p. 289.
[18] CSPS, ii, no. 425 p. 299.
[19] CSPS, ii, no. 425 p. 299. Referred to as the 'rayd of Jedward'.
[20] RPC, i, 475, 476.
[21] TA, xii, 14–16.
[22] RPC, i, 476.
[23] 663TA, xii, 20; Gatherer, The Tyrannous Reign of Mary Stewart, 106 n. 4, 167; Nau, Memorials, 23, 29–30.

we can assume that the other seventy lord and lairds were also permitted to attend the hunt if they wished.

The Megget valley was held by William Hay of Yester, sheriff of Peebles, and, although he was a staunch supporter of the Reformation, he had supported Mary at the time of the Chaseabout Raid.[24] He would have been involved in preparations for the visit and been aware of its significance. He would have prepared accommodation in the two towers at Cramalt for the main members of the hunting party and arranged space for pavilions as necessary.[25] Megget lay just outside Ettrick Forest and was renowned not only for its gold mine but also for its 'innumerable great harts'.[26] This was, therefore, a large hunt in a traditional hunting ground and all must have looked set for a successful hunting trip which would help to rebuild and maintain workman-like relationships.

Following the practice of James V, Mary no doubt had drives organised in the area and expected kills in the hundreds, but in the event the hunting was poor, probably because deer stocks had not recovered from the harsh winter of 1564–65. On 16 August the privy council at Rodono bemoaned the fact that the queen and king could get 'na pastyme of hunting' because the local population were shooting deer with culverins, half haggs, pistols, and bows.[27] An officer of arms was ordered to enforce the ban on these weapons but this action proved no more effective than its predecessors.[28]

Nonetheless, as far as Mary was concerned all was not lost, because there seems to have been some discussion about her son's baptism. Mary had already started to plan this event and in early August she had despatched letters inviting foreign representatives to James's baptism in October, although subsequently the baptism had to be postponed to December to allow these representatives time to travel.[29] Based on the surviving invitation sent to Lord Gray, signed at Cramalt on 16 August, further discussions of arrangements and of the guest list must have occurred there. A whole series of letters were sent out from Edinburgh on 17 August, including a letter to Lord Gray, presumably the one signed at Cramalt, which suggests that the other letters may also have been invitations to the baptism.[30] That arrangements for the baptism were being discussed while Mary was on this hunting trip adds to the impression that the political aim of the trip was reconciliation as well as the furthering of royal authority in the Borders.

---

[24]   Donaldson, *All the Queen's Men*, 74; *RPC*, i, 335, 347, 455.
[25]   Maxwell-Irving, 'Cramalt Tower', 404, 420–3.
[26]   Leslie, *Historie* (1596), i, 19.
[27]   *RPC*, i, 477. Although Henry is referred to as king he had not been awarded the crown matrimonial.
[28]   *RPC*, ii, 506.
[29]   *CSPS*, ii, no. 425 p. 299; Lynch, 'Queen Mary's Triumph', 4.
[30]   *Letters and Papers Relating to Patrick Master of Gray*, ed. Thomas Thomson (Edinburgh, 1835), Appendix, no. x; *TA*, xii, 20. These are described as 'clois writtingis of our soverains'. Gray's letter was signed by Mary. It is possible that letters signed at Cramalt by Mary or Darnley or both were taken to Edinburgh to be despatched on 17 August.

HUNTING FOR RECONCILIATION

On 18 or 19 August the party moved to Traquair House, owned by John Stewart, a moderate Protestant and supporter of Mary.[31] If Mary had managed to co-operate with Darnley at Cramalt to the extent of making arrangements for the baptism, the stay at Traquair showed how fragile that co-operation was. Nau reported a conversation which suggests that after the failures at Cramalt the royal party had switched to chasing deer with dogs.[32] Darnley, he said, asked Mary to attend a stag hunt, but she, knowing the hunt could involve galloping at pace, whispered to Darnley that she might be pregnant again. Darnley's response was insensitive, saying that if they lost this child they could make another; and, when challenged by Stewart of Traquair, he added insult to injury by saying that one must work a mare well when it is in foal. If little progress was being made with Darnley, it appears that participating in the hunting together had strengthened the settlements made between the other disputants. No accord, however, had been reached with Lethington, though his case must have been discussed and there may have been agreement to tackle the problem directly at Glenartney. By 14 August Mary was certainly on record as planning 'to end the mater' with him when she was at Stirling on 24 August.[33]

Glenartney, August 1566

After Traquair Mary returned to Edinburgh, and on 22 August escorted her son, James, to the greater security of Stirling, where she left him in the care of the earl of Mar and his wife. She then set off with Darnley to hunt in the royal forest of Glenartney from 25 to 29 August without having met Lethington.[34] Glenartney was still being actively maintained as a hunting forest in the sixteenth century despite the advances of farming, both pastoral and arable, in the preceding centuries. Settlements on the south side of the Ruchill had already entered the record in the fifteenth century at Auchnashelloch and Findhuglen, and the farms of Dalclathick and Blairhoorie appeared on

[31] Donaldson, *All the Queen's Men*, 134.
[32] Nau, *Memorials*, 30; Guy, *My Heart is My Own*, 293.
[33] *CSPS*, ii, no. 425 p. 299.
[34] Guy, *My Heart is My Own*, 271; Gatherer, *The Tyrannous Reign of Mary Stewart*, 106 n. 4, 167; George Chalmers, *The Life of Mary Queen of Scots* (London, 1822), i, 283. There is some uncertainly about the dates of this trip. Furgol in his 'Itinerary' suggests that the hunt in Glenartney lasted from 23 or 24 August till the 30th, when Mary went to Drummond Castle. Melville, however, expected Mary still to be in Stirling on the 24th: *CSPS*, ii, no. 425 p. 299. Forster, the warden of the English middle march, thought Mary was back in Stirling by 28 August. In fact she was signing privy seal letters at Drummond Castle on 30 and 31 August: *Sixth Report of Royal Commission on Historical Manuscripts*, Part 1, 692b; *RPC*, v part 2, no. 3044 p. 202. A hunting trip of six days would have been a long time, given the effect on deer stocks and the sanitary arrangements of the time. Three to four days was more usual, and so the dates of the Glenartney trip are more likely to have been from 25 to 29 August.

143

ELITE HUNTING CULTURE AND MARY, QUEEN OF SCOTS

the north side of the Ruchill in Pont's map c. 1583–1601.[35] As in Glenfinglas, this process must have limited the hunting forest to the hill ground, with the result that by the eighteenth century the forest of Glenartney had been reduced to a small area of the high ground between the Ruchill and Loch Earn (Map 8).[36] In 1518 James V or, rather, the governor, the duke of Albany, had concerns about illegal wood-cutting and hunting in Glenartney. The keeper of the forest was ordered to stop the use of bows by common stalkers and hunters and anyone caught was to have a finger on their right hand cut off at the joint and their dogs confiscated.[37] There were still problems in 1540, when James ordered Drummond to seize nine broken men who had been grazing stock and poaching deer without permission. Just as James IV had done at Glenfinglas in 1508, James V ordered Drummond to issue proc-lamations at parish churches outlawing those who poached, grazed cattle, cut young wood, or travelled through the forest without permission.[38] The Crown itself had grazed cattle and unbroken horses there at least since the reigns of James III and IV, but by 1553 tenants in Glenartney had also started to graze unbroken mares there and Marie de Guise ordered their horses to be seized. Henceforth, the right to graze horses was to be limited solely to the foresters.[39] As already mentioned, Mary also worked to maintain Glenartney Forest when, in 1563, she banned the use of guns, crossbows, and hand bows in and around Glenartney in an effort to protect the game from poachers.[40]

Preparations for Mary's visit seem to have begun on 11 August, when letters were sent to James Stewart, the steward of Menteith, and his deputies as well as to David Lord Drummond, the steward of Strathearn and forester of Glenartney. They received further letters on 20 and 21 August, no doubt confirming the date of arrival.[41] Both Drummond and Stewart, who was based in Doune, needed to be informed of the visit because hunting could have taken place both within Glenartney and over the hills in Menteith. A letter was also sent to Colin Campbell of Glenorchy and he too was invited to attend along with Archibald Campbell, earl of Argyll.[42]

James Stewart would have been particularly interested in this hunting trip because he had not been paid for the hunting house he had built for Mary in Glenartney.[43] For whatever reason, it appears that Mary was not happy with the hunt hall in Glenartney and ordered the building of a 'hunting hous', a '*domus venatorie*', which brings to mind the hunting houses in Duchray, the

---

[35] NRS, GD160/70; NLS, Adv. Ms, 70.2.9, Pont 21 ('Lower Genalmond; Strathearn').
[36] NRS, RHP3405, Plan of Grazings of Callander and Glenartney in annexed estate of Perth (1772).
[37] NRS, GD160/528/9.
[38] NRS, GD160/129/1.
[39] *ER*, ix, 119, 329; x, 566; xii, 186; *RSS*, iv, no. 2125.
[40] NRS, GD160/129/2.
[41] *TA*, ii, 20.
[42] Dawson, *Campbell Letters*, 141.
[43] *ER*, xxi, 549.

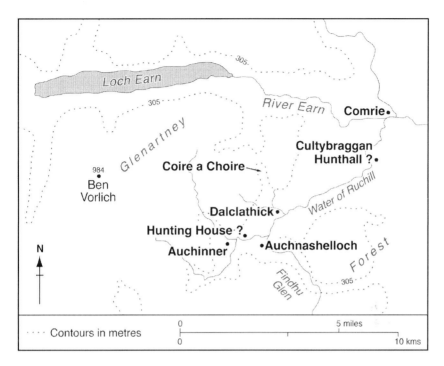

Map 8   Glenartney Forest.

lunkarts in Glen Tilt and Mar, and the hall-house style of hunting lodge. James Stewart built the hunting house in August 1563 'or thairby' within the bounds of Glenartney at a cost of 200 merks (£133 6s 8d). At first sight it seems surprising that Stewart from Menteith rather than Lord Drummond, the forester, was involved in the building of this dwelling, which was in Strathearn. In a hunting context, however, Glenartney was also considered to be in the ambit of Doune Castle, and when James II was described as hunting around Doune in 1456 or 1457 he was actually hunting in Glenartney.[44] Stewart, as the keeper of Doune Castle, would also have been well versed in managing construction work and repairs to royal property. Since he had not been paid, he appealed to the exchequer auditors in 1580 and settled for £32 as payment for the total sum.[45] At a possible cost of no more than 200 merks this was not a small shieling, but a more substantial dwelling.[46] A hunting

[44] ER, vi, 325, 'citra Down'.
[45] ER, xxi, 40, 549; NRS, E1/6 Books of Responde. The memorandum of the exchequer decision is now bound beside fo. 88r.
[46] By way of comparison, in 1531–32 the stables and avery house at Falkland Palace, which were built of stone and which had six large doors and a hay loft, cost £73 10s 1d to build, excluding the roof: Accounts of the Masters of Works, ed. Henry M. Paton, 2 vols (Edinburgh, 1957), i, 112–14. Building and repairing two houses at Holyrood Palace cost

house by definition cannot have been a sizeable building, but it was certainly larger and more substantial than a shieling, and so it may be thought of as a more comfortable version of the lunkarts Mary experienced in Glen Tilt. As such, it could have been built in the local vernacular style with stone and turf walls, and couples to hold up a thatch roof. Alternatively, it could have been a wooden construction, but, given the short-term use of the building, a stone and mortar structure is unlikely.

However it was constructed, the house must have focussed more on the chambers of the queen and her female attendants rather than on a hall. When Marie de Guise had hunted in Glenfinglas, she had travelled with six women and had stayed at the hunt hall, presumably in the two chambers which were attached to it. Mary may have had a similar arrangement in Glenartney, with two chambers along with a presence chamber which could also serve as a place in which to set up the boards and eat. This house has not yet been located, but it could have been built beside the older hunt hall, which, as suggested earlier, might have been at Cultybraggan. On the other hand, as explained in Appendix I, in later centuries the upper reaches of the glen were seen as a good base for those managing the reserve and for those intending to hunt in the forest, and the same could also have been true in the sixteenth century. If ruins which have been located near Dalclathick in the upper part of the glen are the remains of Mary's hunting house, they would belong to the only building which Mary is known to have commissioned during her reign.[47] If Stewart remembered the construction date correctly, Mary may have already visited it when riding from Drummond Castle to Glenfinglas on 14 September 1563. While no document states that she actually stayed in the hunting house in August 1566, it seems very likely that she did so, given that she had commissioned it.[48]

It is hard to know who accompanied Mary at Glenartney, but it is safe to assume that, as in the time of James V, it was a smaller group than attended at Glenfinglas or Megget. We know that Darnley, Campbell of Glenorchy, and Argyll were present, and it is almost certain that Drummond and Stewart of Doune were also there. Other privy councillors such as Moray, Huntly, and Atholl were presumably also invited. Whether or not Bothwell went to Glenartney is harder to determine, but it seems unlikely, given the problems on the Border. He may well have returned to fulfilling his duties as sheriff of Selkirk and warden of the Scottish middle march in preparation for the forthcoming ayre.[49] There is no record that Maitland of Lethington was present, but there is a strong possibility that he was. Moray, Argyll, and Atholl were pushing for his rehabilitation and the hunt in Glenartney provided an opportunity for personal contact to be made with Lethington. He had pre-

---

£273 15s in 1577: *TA*, xiii, 163.

[47] There is further discussion of this hunting house in Appendix I, pp. 174–7.

[48] NRS, E33/8/3, fo. 59r.

[49] *CSPF 1566–8*, nos 598 p. 110, 655 p. 119, 673 p. 122, 677 p. 124.

viously been given hospitality by Argyll and then by Atholl in Dunkeld and Callendar, but on 28 July he had been at Campbell of Glenorchy's stronghold of Balloch, now Taymouth Castle, near Kenmore.[50] Glenorchy and Argyll both attended the hunt at Glenartney and there would have been every opportunity to bring Lethington there from Balloch.[51] The rumours reported by Sir John Forster on 28 August at Berwick, that Atholl and his friends brought Lethington to meet Mary at Stirling, point to a meeting prior to that date. Mary was not in Stirling at that time and so the meeting could well have taken place in Glenartney.[52] Mary met Lethington on 5 September in a private house in Stirling, pardoned him, and invited him to attend court in Edinburgh on 11 September. The final step in his rehabilitation, a rapprochement with Bothwell, took place in Edinburgh before 20 September, again in a private house.[53]

Thereafter the various rivals succeeded in co-existing without major disagreements. The Jedburgh justice ayre was held successfully between 9 and 14 October with Moray, Argyll, and Maitland in attendance.[54] Bothwell could not attend because he had been wounded; on 15 October, after attending the ayre, Mary, Moray, and other courtiers visited him at Hermitage Castle. Lord Scrope reported that Bothwell held a continuation of the justice ayre at Hermitage the following day, which suggests that there was a business-like judicial reason for the visit.[55] In early November, after Mary had recovered from a near-fatal illness in Jedburgh, Bothwell joined her party for a progress through south-east Scotland and reached Craigmillar Castle outside Edinburgh by 20 November. There, Mary and several of her council stayed for some days and by this time it was clear that there was an irreparable breakdown in Mary's relationship with Darnley.[56] Whether the nobles at Craigmillar plotted Darnley's murder or merely planned how to limit the damage of the breakdown, it is noticeable that Moray, Argyll, Huntly, Bothwell, and Lethington were all co-operating peacefully.[57] As Lynch has pointed out, this Craigmillar Conference needs to be seen against the background of planning

[50] CSPS, ii, nos 375 p. 276, 400 p. 289, 419 p. 297; Loughlin, 'Maitland of Lethington', 226.
[51] Dawson, Campbell Letters, 141 no. 87.
[52] CSPF 1566–8, no. 677 p. 124.
[53] CSPF 1566–8, no. 706 p. 128; CSPS, ii, no. 428 p. 300.
[54] Guy, My Heart is My Own, 273.
[55] CSPF 1566–8, no. 764 p. 139. Scrope called it a court of oyer and terminer (hear and determine), which heard criminal cases and, as Guy suggested, that could have been a continuation of the justice ayre (Guy, My Heart is My Own, 125).
[56] Guy, My Heart is My Own, 275–6.
[57] Guy, My Heart is My Own, 282–3; Gordon Donaldson, The First Trial of Mary Queen of Scots (London, 1974), 30–1.

the baptism and discussing further proposed remissions for Riccio's murderers, including the earl of Morton.[58]

In the spring of 1566, the composition of these two hunting parties would have looked like a recipe for disaster, but the hunts served to consolidate agreements which had already been made and enabled further co-operation between the rivals to occur. The hunts, therefore, were one of the tactics which Mary employed to heal the divisions which she had created. Unlike the threat of exile, trial, or legal procedures, they focussed on building relationships on which reconciliation depended.

James VI's Baptism at Stirling, December 1566

The celebrations for James's baptism were held in Stirling Castle from Tuesday 17 to Thursday 19 December, 1566. The festivities for this event have been well studied and it has been noticed that hunting was part of the celebrations, although the significance of the hunt has been missed.[59] The sort of themes which historians have seen running through the celebrations are an attempt to heal divisions, the promise of a renewed Stewart monarchy, the affirmation of Mary as a great renaissance monarch, a pastoral theme expressing a delight in the countryside and hunting, the existence of countrywide support for Mary and James, and praise for highland culture. The festivities included the kind of triumphal entries, masques, and entertainments which Mary had experienced in France, for example, at Châtelherault in November 1559 and Chenonceau in March 1560.[60] Through a combination of a royal entry, a military or chivalric display, indoor entertainments, and lavish expenditure, these sixteenth-century festivals conveyed a message glorifying the monarch and his or her ability to create and lead a united and prosperous kingdom.[61] Although Mary was familiar with the various elements, the Stirling celebration was not a copy of any French event. It showed French influences, but it included elements which must have resulted from Mary's personal wishes.[62] She was involved in the overall organisation of the event, discussing it as early as her visit to Megget, and she seems to have taken personal oversight of the preparations.[63]

The celebrations began on 17 December with the formal entry of the queen and the ambassadors from France, England, and Savoy. The baptism

[58] Lynch, 'Queen Mary's triumph', 5.
[59] Lynch, 'Queen Mary's triumph', 11; Peter Davidson 'The entry of Mary Stewart into Edinburgh', *Renaissance Studies*, 9 (1995), 416–29; Carpenter, 'Performing diplomacies'; Mickel, 'From bourgeois wife', 48–61; Guidicini, *Triumphal Entries and Festivals*, 52–62.
[60] *Les Triomphes Faictz ... a Chenonceau.*
[61] Roy Strong, *Splendour and Renaissance Spectacle and Illusion* (London, 1973), 23.
[62] Lynch, 'Queen Mary's triumph', 8–9; Mickel, 'From bourgeois wife', 49–55.
[63] Carpenter, 'Performing diplomacies', 219, 222–3.

was followed by a formal supper with dancing and entertainment.[64] On 18 December a hunt was held in Stirling Park and on 19 December there was a round-table banquet, a musical entertainment with satyrs and nymphs, a fort-holding, and a fire display.[65]

Shortly before the festivities started Mary's spirits were low and James Melville of Halhill remembered that she took him by the hand and, leaving the castle, walked down through the park and back up through the town. During the walk, Mary talked about the business which she would need to discuss with Bedford, the English ambassador.[66] While this anecdote shows how the park was integral to the life of the palace, what is more relevant here is that during their walk Mary explained that she wanted to run her government in such a way that she might win over her future competitors and enemies 'as sche had done at her first hamecommyng'.

Hunting was not normally part of such festivities. Usually there would be a chivalric military display involving some variety of tournament, but, since Mary could not take part in a tournament, she substituted a hunt, which would support the policy of reconciliation more effectively.[67] Not only were there opportunities to conduct business during a hunting expedition, but the occasion also provided a chance to forget differences in a more informal setting where all had a common aim. The location of Stirling also played its part because the park was a major feature of the landscape when looking down from the castle. John Lesley was struck by the view, describing the 'fair and plesand sychte' over the fields, the river, and the park towards the mountains beyond.[68] The park was still used for hunting and Mary had hunted there in 1565.[69]

Significantly, the park was also thought to have a connection with the chivalric world of King Arthur. He was believed to be a historical king of both Scotland and England, whom Mary one day hoped to emulate. In the fourteenth century, in the reign of David II, it was claimed that Stirling was the site of the legendary Snowdon, the stronghold where Arthur placed his round table. As John Barbour's *Brus* makes clear, the supposed round table at Stirling was a physical feature which Edward II had to pass when escaping after the battle of Bannockburn.[70] In the 1530s, David Lindsay of the Mount, James V's chief herald, also mentioned the 'rounde tabill' in his *Testament of the Papingo*.[71] The site of the seventeenth-century King's Knot below and

---

[64] A *Diurnal of Remarkable Occurrents* (A Journal of Remarkable Events), 104.

[65] Lynch, 'Queen Mary's triumph', 11–13; Nau, *Memorials*, cxlix.

[66] Sir James Melville of Halhill, *Memorials of His Own Life 1549–1593* (Edinburgh, 1827), 168–70.

[67] Lynch, 'Queen Mary's triumph', 11; Mickel 'From bourgeois wife', 55–6.

[68] Leslie, *Historie* (1596), i, 28. In 1575 the regent Morton had 'good pastime' hunting in the park: CSPS, v, no. 202 p. 197.

[69] Footnote 1 above.

[70] Katie Stevenson, 'Chivalry, British sovereignty and dynastic politics: undercurrents of antagonism in Tudor Stewart relations c. 1490–1513', *Historical Research*, 85 (2013), 604–13, at 607 and 611.

[71] A mock-up of a parrot was often used for archery practice: DOST, 'papingo'. John

to the west of the castle corresponds neatly with Barbour's location of the round table, and recently a multivallate structure has been located beneath it.[72] This earthwork, which resembles an iron-age fort or enclosure and which may have been altered at a later date, appears to have been interpreted as Arthur's round table and was seen to provide Scottish kings with a direct link to the ancient British monarch. This claimed connection to Arthur would not have sat comfortably with the English representatives at the baptism, since English monarchs also claimed a connection to Arthur and possessed their own round table in Winchester. The use of an Arthurian-style round table for the celebration banquet on the Thursday would also have grated on the English representatives. Such an Arthurian heritage gave Scots monarchs a claim to rival that of their English counterparts and to rule over both kingdoms.

Another feature of the festivities was a short entertainment or masque composed by George Buchanan, Mary's tutor and adviser, who had a hereditary attachment to the Lennox family. After the murder of Darnley, Buchanan was extremely critical of Mary, accusing her of murder and adultery, though at this point he was still working with her. Because satyrs and fauns are mentioned in this short masque, it has been suggested that it was performed on the Thursday evening when players dressed as these mythical characters served the tables at the banquet. However, an early text of the masque, called *Pompae Deorum Rusticorum* (Processions of the Rural Gods), suggests otherwise.[73] The version of this masque in the edition of Buchanan's works published in Amsterdam in 1687 states quite simply that it was enacted on the occasion of the banquet which followed the baptism of the king. That must refer to the dinner held on the Tuesday which is mentioned by the *Diurnal of Remarkable Occurrents*, and not the banquet on the Thursday as Michael Lynch suggested.[74] The contention here is that this short masque was held on the Tuesday to serve as an introduction to the hunt on the Wednesday. This cannot be certain but, even if it were performed on the Thursday as a celebration of the hunt held the day before, the message contained within the masque would still have been appropriate.

The masque comprised five short verses in which a procession of rural deities presented gifts to Mary and to James and spoke Buchanan's verses. In classical mythology, satyrs of the woods are portrayed with small horns and the tails of horses or goats and dressed in the skins of animals with wreaths of vine, ivy, or fir. They were linked to the worship of Dionysus, hence their

---

Barbour, *The Bruce*, ed. A. A. M. Duncan (Edinburgh, 1997), 499; David Lindsay of the Mount, 'The Testament of the Papingo', in *The Works of Sir David Lindsay*, ed. Douglas Hamer (Edinburgh, 1931), i, 75.

[72] Stephen Digney and Richard Jones, 'Recent Investigations at the King's Knot Stirling', *The Forth Naturalist and Historian*, 36 (2013), 129–48 at 134, 143, 144. Canmore Id 46256.

[73] The 1687 text used here is printed by Davidson, 'The entry of Mary Stewart into Edinburgh', 426–9.

[74] Davidson, 'The entry of Mary Stewart into Edinburgh', 426; Lynch, 'Queen Mary's triumph', 11.

love of wine and their identification with the luxury and bounty of nature.[75] In this masque they speak to James and urge the infant to become a hunter and to enjoy the delights of the country before the town.

> But when strength comes with growing years
> You will take the roe deer[76]
> With the keen Molossian hounds.
> Take with nets the savage boar.
> Learn this from our hunting-cry:
> Prize the pleasures of our woods
> Before the pleasures of the town.

The nereids, the sea nymphs, praise the magnetic power of Mary's virtue which attracts people from far and wide, while the river nymphs, the naiads, tell James that they rejoice at his birth. Fauns – half man, half goat, with horns and bearing some similarity to the satyrs – congratulate Mary on the birth of her child. When Buchanan calls the final group, the Orcades who come from the mountains, he is combining the *oreades* or mountain nymphs with people from Orkney, the *Orcades*. They bring gifts from the Orkneys or from faraway mountains and, returning to the first message given by the satyrs, they tell James that when he is older he will chase the roe deer and drive the boar into nets, and, just like the satyrs, they conclude by advising James to prefer the wild corners of the woods to the proud towns.[77]

> And as your body stronger grows
> In time you'll chase the roe deer
> With the keen Molossian hounds
> Drive the boar into the nets.
> Through the labyrinth of trees
> Will you snare the flying birds,
> Or will you chase Napean goats.
> The shaggy mazes of the woods
> You will value over all,
> Over all the lofty towns.

There is some discussion about the political significance of this masque because, on the one hand, it has been suggested that it contained no statement of policy, had no allegorical or political meaning, and was merely a rural panegyric.[78] On the other hand, however, it has been argued that it aimed to present the picture of a kingdom united behind the Stewarts, because the

---

[75] William Smith, *Smaller Classical Dictionary* (London, 1858), 'satyri'.

[76] 'Mountain goats' in Davidson's translation. The translation of *caprea* could be either goats or roe deer. Roe deer seems more sensible, although goats may sound more classical.

[77] *Caprea* again translated here as roe deer.

[78] Davidson, 'The entry of Mary Stewart.' 424.

satyrs represent all areas of the country and all are praising Mary and James.[79] Given the political nature of many such masques, the latter view seems more likely. The verses are praising the countryside, the enjoyment of the hunt, and the baby James. The message here is not only that the whole of Scotland supports Mary and James, but also that by travelling around the country and hunting rather than spending time in the towns and palaces, James will see Scotland and bring its people together. While ostensibly addressing James, Buchanan is reflecting Mary's experience. Her travels and her progresses had helped her to be accepted as queen and enabled her to gain popularity and support from her people. The importance of this was not lost on Buchanan, who, as James's tutor in later years, seems to have drilled this message into his pupil. Certainly, James in his turn advised his son Henry that hunting was the most honourable and noble sport and ideal exercise for a monarch. It resembled warfare and would keep a king fit for travel, 'which is very necessarie for a King'. James also pointed out that some parts of the country would be visited only when the king was on a hunting trip.[80]

The hunt on the Wednesday is mentioned in an account of the christening, probably composed for the earl of Bedford. It states that on 'the 18th they had in the park the hunting of the wild bull at which the queen was present'.[81] This hunt is remarkable not only because it featured a wild bull but also because the cattle kept in the park were 'wilde quhite cullourit ky'.[82] Boece thought that these white cattle survived only in Cumbernauld, but in the 1560s Lesley said they also survived in the parks at Stirling, Cumbernauld, and Kincardine near Auchterarder.[83] Writing in the 1520s, Boece said that the white bulls with their crisp curly manes like a lion's were wild and fierce and avoided human contact.[84] Nineteenth-century accounts of similar animals describe them with dark noses and dark tips to their ears and horns, though by that time the fuller manes which Boece described had gone. The debate about whether they were direct descendants from the wild *urus* or ox or whether they were descendants of a domesticated race which was preserved on account of its colour has now been settled in favour of the latter view.[85] These animals were hunted for their meat, which Lesley describes as being 'of a trim taist', but how exactly they were hunted is not clear. Boece said they could be captured only with great skill and effort because they would rush on

[79]   Mickel, 'From bourgeois wife', 56–7.
[80]   Johann P. Somerville, *King James VI and his Political Writings* (Cambridge, 1994), 55, 56, 164.
[81]   Nau, *Memorials*, cxlix.
[82]   Harrison, *The Creation and Survival of some Scots Royal Landscapes*, 32, 36, 53, which quotes from Home of Polwarth in 1573.
[83]   Leslie, *Historie* (1596), i, 29–30.
[84]   Bellenden, *History* (1821), i, Discription of Albion, p. xxxix; Boece, *Historiae* (1527), *Descriptio*, fos 11r line 34–11v line 49.
[85]   James Ritchie, *The Influence of Man on Animal Life in Scotland* (Cambridge, 1920), 67; Harriet Ritvo, 'Race Breed and Myths of Origin: Chillingham Cattle as Ancient Britons', *Representations*, 39 (Summer 1992), 1–22, at 17–18.

the hunters and knock them to the ground when they were attacked. They showed no fear of spears or of hounds and, according to Lesley, they could overcome men on horseback and attack men and dogs with their hooves and horns.[86]

Stories of bull hunts survived from the time of the Frankish kings and of Charlemagne, when men on horseback armed with swords, bows, and spears seem to have hunted them with packs of running hounds.[87] By the early eleventh century, they were probably being hunted in England and they continued to be hunted there in the medieval and early modern periods, when it was considered to be a good pastime.[88] In Scotland, Boece told a tale of King Robert Bruce hunting a white bull, and in 1507 James IV ordered spears to slay a bull in Cumbernauld.[89] It is possible that when Mary visited Lord Fleming at Cumbernauld in January 1562 she joined the earl of Atholl and Lord Sempill when they went hunting in the park, but no specific details of the type of hunt survive.[90] Eighteenth- and nineteenth-century accounts state that when wild bulls were hunted in parks or were disturbed, they ran off in a herd and then turned to face their attackers. This could happen several times, but each time they stopped they halted closer to their attackers and were known to charge and injure them, just as Boece described.[91] Eighteenth-century bull hunts at Chillingham perhaps give a better idea of what happened at Stirling. Chillingham in Northumberland was famous for its white cattle, and when it was announced that a wild bull was to be killed, a hundred horsemen armed with guns and five hundred unmounted spectators would gather. Those on foot stood on walls or climbed on trees to try to view proceedings, while the horsemen separated the bull from the rest of the herd and chased it till it turned at bay. Sometimes twenty or thirty musket shots were needed to kill it.[92] The elements of Mary's show-hunt at Stirling could have been similar: horsemen separating a bull from the herd, chasing it with dogs till it turned at bay, and then spearing it or shooting it with bows or perhaps guns. Alternatively, it could have been driven into a fold at the end of the hunt and speared or shot where spectators could see it being killed.

The hunt was one of the unique elements introduced to the celebration of her son's baptism, presumably at Mary's request. Hunts had probably occurred before and after French fetes such as those at Chenonceau and Châtelherault, but they were not integral parts of the triumph. That Mary chose to make the hunt a central feature of the festivities shows that it carried a particular significance for her. She was casting herself in the role of the hunter in charge of the hunt and demonstrating that she was fulfilling the hunting image of

---

[86] Leslie, *Historie* (1596), i, 29–30.
[87] D. Rollason, *Power of Place*, 154; Noirmont, *Histoire de La Chasse*, i, 172–3.
[88] Jones, 'A Common of Hunting', 57.
[89] Bellenden, *History* (1821), i, Discription of Albion, p. xxxix; *TA*, iii, 400.
[90] *CSPS*, i, no. 1071 p. 598.
[91] Fittis, *Sports and Pastimes*, 24–6.
[92] W. Youatt, *Cattle Their Breeds, Management and Diseases* (London, 1834), 8.

the Stewart monarchy. At the same time, by taking part in the hunt, Mary was ensuring that the image of herself as Diana the huntress was also in the minds of her audience. The performance of Buchanan's *Pompae* the night before, with its satyrs and nymphs, helped set the scene because in classical mythology the goddess Diana was often accompanied by these deities.[93] The hunt in the park also exploited the legendary and Arthurian connections of Stirling, which would have added to the sheer enjoyment of the occasion for most of the hunters. As they rode into the park past Arthur's round table they were about to take part in a hunt just as the heroes of the past had done. Not only were there tales of Charlemagne and Bruce hunting bulls, but there was also the mystique attached to chasing a white bull.[94] This was a rare event in Scotland and would not soon be forgotten by those who took part.

On Thursday 19 December, the final day of the celebrations, a magnificent fire display was held which involved burning a wooden fort, throwing fire-balls, and firing cannons. Mock castle sieges or fort-holdings frequently formed part of European triumphs, where the fort could represent the stable power of the monarch against the forces of war and chaos or it could stand for a bastion of evil to be captured by the forces of good, commanded by the king. French parallels with the Stirling fort-burning are hard to make because the Stirling record does not identify the allegorical roles of the defenders and assailants, nor whether the fort held out or was taken. What is not in doubt is that the high point of the celebrations occurred to the accompaniment of fireworks when the fort was set on fire by players dressed as highlanders.

The destruction of the fort has been linked to the burning of James V's 'palice' in Glen Tilt in 1532 and to a Gaelic tradition of burning settlements which were no longer needed.[95] While this is in essence true it is perhaps rather overstated. Temporary halls were built and on occasions they might be burned, but the evidence, as has been shown, does not suggest it was a regular occurrence. If nothing else, shortage of wood would have mitigated against such a practice. Regardless of the ubiquity or otherwise of such a tradition, the parallel with the Glen Tilt lodge is instructive, since it would again reference the hunting theme. Pitscottie referred to that expedition as a great banquet and a triumph in which the extravagant burning of James V's 'palice' drew attention to the largesse of Atholl's efforts to honour the king. Mary, when hunting there in 1564 and staying beside the burned-out remains of the lodge, must have heard tales of that triumph. Consequently, it presented her with a model on which to base the spectacular finale of the baptismal celebrations. Perhaps, therefore, the burning was intended to symbolise how rich and prosperous her country was if she could afford to set fire to such a fort. The Glen Tilt burning may have provided not only a model

---

[93] Lynch, 'Queen Mary's triumph', 11. Diana also had a part in the verses which Buchanan composed for Mary's wedding in 1565: Carpenter, 'Performing diplomacies', 216.

[94] Fletcher, *Gardens of Earthly Delight*, 127–31.

[95] Mapstone, 'Introduction', vii; Mickel, 'From bourgeois wife', 59.

for the event but also an architectural model for the fort. It has been argued, on the basis of the materials used, that the Stirling fort was square in plan, so it is not inconceivable that it was designed to resemble the rectangular, chateau-like 'palice' in Glen Tilt.[96] It would have provided a neat conclusion to the hunting theme of the celebrations. The highlanders who torched the fort would have been recognisable as symbolising the tenants of Atholl, even if in rather fanciful goat-skin costumes to make them resemble satyrs or fauns. They were not despised, nor were they solely representing the 'wild others' of renaissance masques. In a hunting context they were the people with whom the Scottish nobility had to work when they hunted in the Highlands.[97]

While the political purpose of Mary's earlier hunts has to be inferred and was often of a more general nature, the political role of these hunts in 1566, to achieve co-operation among rivals, is much more apparent. This hunt was part of the overall performance designed to display the magnificence of the Stewart monarchy, the unity of the country behind the monarch, and hence the monarch's role as the reconciler of the kingdom, a role in which hunting played a part. These, however, were stage-managed performances. While hunting could help to win and keep support and demonstrate a particular image of monarchy, it had its limitations. After James VI's baptism there is no further evidence that Mary hunted in Scotland. It was a pastime which could be employed to political advantage, but it could not counteract the errors of policy, the loss of support, and the defeats which Mary suffered in 1567 and 1568.

[96] Philip Butterworth, 'The Baptisme of Hir darrest Sone in Stirviling', in *Medieval English Theatre*, 10 (1988) 26–55, at 42, 44.
[97] The view that the highlanders were being lauded rather than criticised as wild and uncivilised is also expressed by Mickel and Guidicini: Mickel, 'From bourgeois wife', 59; Guidicini, *Triumphal Entries and Festivals*, 61–2.

Envoi: Hunting for hope: captivity in England, 1568–87

While the time which Mary spent in captivity in England between 1568 and her death in 1587 does not relate to the ways in which a monarch could employ hunting to establish and develop their image and authority, the English sources tells us about her love of hunting more directly than either the French or Scottish sources. She did, after all, spend more time as a huntress in England than she ever did in Scotland or in France. In England, hunting was not only a source of enjoyment for Mary but a means of expressing liberty during her captivity.

The castles and houses where Mary was held in England were all well equipped for hunting, with hunting parks and deer forests nearby. Indeed, such facilities would seem to have played a part in the choice of residence for Mary on at least one occasion, when it was proposed to move her from Carlisle to Tutbury in July 1568 for safety, better air, and 'hunting as the season required'.[1] Although Tutbury had three deer parks close to the castle and lay within Needwood Forest, after some deliberation Mary was eventually sent to Bolton Castle in Wensleydale, which also had two or three deer parks to the north, one of which boasted a stone tower which served as a stand from which to shoot deer or to observe coursing.[2]

Hunting, hawking, riding, and exercise in the open air were crucial to Mary's health. She presented with various symptoms such as abdominal pain, vomiting, and pain in her legs which have drawn a variety of diagnoses such as porphyria, a gastric ulcer, and arthritis. Whatever the cause of her ailments she seemed to be able to recover quickly and progress fairly rapidly from being crippled to being able to ride and gallop on horseback. Mary had hunted regularly throughout her life, and being deprived of outdoor exercise had an adverse effect not only on her physical well-being but also on her state of mind. She recognised this, and in 1571 complained bitterly that she could not endure being deprived of the pleasure of riding in the countryside, hawking and hunting, for the rest of her life.[3] This must have struck a chord with Elizabeth, and it appears that her captors also realised the importance of exercise to Mary. As early as November 1568, Sir Francis Knollys was aware

---

[1] CSPS, ii, no. 734 p. 459.
[2] Evelyn Shirley, *Some Account of English Deer Parks* (London, 1867), 175; Stephen Moorhouse, 'The medieval parks of Yorkshire: function, contents and chronology', in Liddiard (ed.), *The Medieval Park*, 118.
[3] CSPS, iii, no. 730 p. 563.

that depriving Mary of horse-riding would 'be a deathe unto hyr disposition'.[4] What struck her various captors throughout her captivity was Mary's singular delight in hunting, hawking, and horse-riding.[5] Elizabeth herself, a keen huntress, realised that taking exercise and hunting were important for health, and on occasion she encouraged others to do likewise.[6] However, Mary's keepers were not always inclined to be so enlightened about her health and exercise, for they sometimes thought that she was play-acting in an attempt to manipulate the situation. Nonetheless, there was a basic appreciation that her health and exercise were interdependent, and whenever recreation was mentioned during the rest of her captivity it was nearly always linked to her health. Captivity, of course, added another dimension to Mary's delight in hunting. Whenever she wanted restrictions on her outdoor exercises to be eased, she always phrased it as a request for liberty to take the air or liberty to ride abroad.

In captivity, Mary did present a threat to Elizabeth and her government because of her desire to be restored to the Scottish throne, to succeed Elizabeth as queen of England, and to use military aid from any foreign power prepared to provide it, more specifically France and Spain. The greater the threat which Mary posed, the harsher her captivity was. Just as restrictions on her freedom to write letters or on the number of her servants and companions reflected the English government's perception of the seriousness of the threat which she posed, so the freedom given to her to hunt and hawk acted very much as a barometer of the government's suspicions or otherwise of her activities. Looked at from this point of view, Mary's captivity before her final move to Fotheringhay can be roughly divided into three periods.

1568–71

During the initial period, from 1568 to 1571, when Mary was more of an embarrassment than a threat, she received what can only be regarded as considerable freedom to pursue her pastime.[7] She hunted, hawked, and coursed hares almost daily at Bolton accompanied by her warder, Sir Francis Knollys. Her captors there were impressed by the speed at which she could gallop.[8] Even when there were fears of her escaping while hunting there was still no attempt to limit her outdoor activities.[9] In 1569, when Mary was moved to Tutbury Castle under the keepership of George Talbot, sixth earl of Shrewsbury, she arrived there with a stable of ten horses, which presumably implied

[4]   *CSPS*, ii, no. 880 p. 544.
[5]   *CSPS*, ii, no. 893 p. 551; vii, no. 580 p. 600.
[6]   Adams, 'The Queenes majestie', 43, 158.
[7]   *CSPS*, iii, no. 666 p. 506.
[8]   *CSPS*, ii, nos 703 p. 436, 873 p. 541.
[9]   *CSPS*, ii, nos 830 p. 514, 873 p. 541, 883 p. 545.

that she was planning to continue hunting.[10] She was, however, given less freedom than at Bolton and had to seek permission to hunt or hawk at times which suited Shrewsbury. Restrictions were also placed on local gentry coming to hunt with her, but she was allowed to practise with her longbow.[11] At Chatsworth in July 1570 those restrictions were continued and Elizabeth stressed to Shrewsbury that he must continue to stop local gentry visiting her because there seemed little point in restricting Mary's liberty to hawk and hunt if the gentry could visit her freely.[12] Nonetheless, in August, Mary was authorised to hunt 'at her pleasure' in Shrewsbury's company, despite rumours of plots to arrange her escape 'under colour of hunting'.[13] Around the grounds of the house Mary had to limit her riding and hunting to within two miles, but no such limits were placed on her when she was riding on the moors to the east of the house.[14] Considering that at this time Mary was involved with Ridolfi's schemes and with marriage plans with the duke of Norfolk, her basic freedom to hunt was generous. However, because there was an uprising of the pro-Catholic northern earls of Cumberland and Westmoreland in late 1569, matters were not to continue in this manner.[15]

1571–81

In the second period of her captivity, from 1571 to 1581, Mary's freedom of movement was considerably reduced as the seriousness of the threat she posed became more evident. In 1570 Mary had associated herself with Ridolfi's next but related scheme. Backed by the Spanish army from the Netherlands, he hoped to start a Roman Catholic uprising in England, secure Mary's escape, and install her as queen of England. When this came to light in the summer of 1571 commissioners were sent to visit Mary at Sheffield to lay charges before her.[16] Involvement in this plot naturally damaged Mary's reputation in England, where she became the hated Catholic enemy, and it resulted in a far stricter regime during her captivity there.

Mary was based in Sheffield from November 1570 to August 1584 and initially, in the early part of 1571, she was still riding and going abroad, presumably to Sheffield Park, although on occasions Shrewsbury did stop

---

[10] *CSPS*, ii, no. 987 p. 417.
[11] *CSPS*, iii, no. 232 p. 171; John D. Leader, *Mary Queen of Scots in Captivity* (Sheffield, 1880), 21 n. 1.
[12] Leader, *Mary Queen of Scots in Captivity*, 124 n. 1; *CSPS*, iii, nos 378 p. 281, 551 p. 417.
[13] Leader, *Mary Queen of Scots in Captivity*, 126 n. 1; *CSPS*, iii, no. 393 p. 289.
[14] Leader, *Mary Queen of Scots in Captivity*, 136.
[15] Fraser, *Mary Queen of Scots*, 501.
[16] Fraser, *Mary Queen of Scots*, 507.

ENVOI: HUNTING FOR HOPE: CAPTIVITY IN ENGLAND, 1568–87

her.[17] Sheffield Castle was attached to a very large and well-wooded deer park which was almost 996ha in size and held up to one thousand fallow deer.[18] Within the park, a lodge or manor had been built in the early sixteenth century and the sixth earl built a smaller stand or turret in the form of a three-storey tower which, it has been claimed, was used by Mary.[19] By May of that year, however, the situation had changed and Mary complained vociferously. While she could still practise with her longbow at the butts, her freedom to ride in the countryside and to hunt and hawk had been severely limited.[20] By October she was basically a prisoner under house arrest. The consequences for her of the Ridolfi Plot were not to her liking, because she was confined to her chamber and allowed only to walk on the leads, the roof, of Sheffield Castle.[21] By April 1572 matters had relaxed slightly as the danger was seen to have passed, but while she was allowed to walk and ride abroad with Shrewsbury there was no mention of hunting.[22] However, parliament was demanding Mary's execution and so she was again placed under house arrest, though in July 1572, in an attempt to evade parliament's demands, Elizabeth sent commissioners to lay various charges before Mary and to record her answers.[23] During this visit Shrewsbury did take her to a stand near the castle to watch deer being coursed in order to show the commissioners that she was not under such severe imprisonment as she was suggesting.[24] While this might seem rather disingenuous of Shrewsbury, one has to remember that he was walking a tightrope in an attempt to please all sides. There was some relaxation by October on the grounds of Mary's health, but only to the extent of allowing her to go out for a walk.[25] It was not till December that she was allowed to ride again, and sometimes even without Shrewsbury if his health was not good.[26]

Over the next eight years there is little mention of Mary's outdoor activities, and in February 1576, when Mary was in the process of sending dogs, including scenting hounds, to James Beaton, nominally the archbishop of Glasgow, her ambassador in Paris, she had to confess that she could not give him an assessment of their quality in the field because she was not, at that time, allowed out on horseback nor to go to the hunt.[27] It would appear from this that Mary had been banned from outside exercise and hunting

---

[17] *CSPS*, iii, no. 715 p. 552.
[18] Shirley, *Some Account of English Deer Parks*, 215.
[19] Leader, *Mary Queen of Scots in Captivity*, 156.
[20] *CSPS*, iii, no. 730 pp. 562–3.
[21] *CSPS*, iv, no. 40 p. 30.
[22] *CSPS*, iv, no. 225 p. 201.
[23] Leader, *Mary Queen of Scots in Captivity*, 263.
[24] Leader, *Mary Queen of Scots in Captivity*, 264.
[25] Leader, *Mary Queen of Scots in Captivity*, 275.
[26] Edmund Lodge, *Illustrations of British History, Biography and Manners in Reigns of Henry VIII, Edward VI, Mary, Elizabeth, James I Exhibited in a Series of Original Papers* (London, 1791), ii, 83.
[27] Labanoff, *Lettres* (London, 1844), iv, 283.

throughout this period. If this was an extensive period of house arrest it may have been related to the involvement of her Guise relatives in the massacre of Huguenots in Paris in August 1572 during the French Wars of Religion and to her continued plotting with Spain, France, and Scotland, which had led to arrests and investigations in 1575.[28] One might have expected that the collapse of her support in Scotland by May 1573 would have led to some alleviation of the terms of her imprisonment, but this does not appear to have been the case. Shrewsbury was always very conscious of the need to please Elizabeth, and she and her two secretaries, William Cecil, Lord Burghley, and Francis Walsingham, were not slow to call him to account when they heard tales that he was relaxing his grip. He also seemed to be wary of antagonising Mary unduly or unnecessarily because she, in her turn, would send in reports about her loss of liberty which could also lead to Shrewsbury being contacted by Elizabeth's secretaries.

During this period Mary was regularly moved for short spells in the summer months, occasionally to the spa at Buxton but more regularly to Chatsworth and the lodge in Sheffield Park to vacate Sheffield Castle while it was cleaned out and freshened up. One suspects that safe and secure hunting activities such as firing a crossbow at deer from a stand may have occurred at these times. Matters did not improve during 1580 and the first half of 1581, but illness may well have prevented Mary taking advantage of any increased liberty on offer. By October 1581 she was again complaining about new restrictions on her liberty, which led to signs of a growing relaxation in the third and final stage of her captivity from 1581 to 1586, prior to all outdoor activity being ended.[29]

1581–86

When Robert Beale, clerk of the privy council, was sent to meet Mary in November 1581 to discuss her dealings with James VI, she took the opportunity to complain about her lack of liberty, and she did so to good effect. Firstly, she was sent a coach to use to travel around when she could not walk or ride, and then, by April 1582, she had been given permission to exercise within the park for her health and recreation.[30] When Shrewsbury was given the authority to extend this concession as he thought fit as her health improved, Elizabeth and Burghley officially put hunting and hawking within his park back on Mary's agenda.[31]

Mary, ever the plotter and schemer, was her own worst enemy, and no sooner had she been granted these privileges than she planned to use them to

[28] Alexandre Teulet (ed.), *Correspondance Diplomatique de Bertrand de Salignac de La Mothe Fénélon* (London, 1840), vi, 427, 429.
[29] Labanoff, *Lettres*, v, 265.
[30] *CSPS*, vi, nos 84 p. 88, 89 p. 101, 90 p. 103, 102 p. 111; vii, no. 578 p. 598.
[31] *CSPS*, vi, no. 103 p. 112.

ENVOI: HUNTING FOR HOPE: CAPTIVITY IN ENGLAND, 1568–87

engineer her escape from Sheffield and join a proposed invasion by the duke of Guise. Unfortunately for Mary, her messenger, Du Ruisseau, who managed her estates in Vermandois, was arrested by Shrewsbury and the whole plot was exposed in early September 1582. As Elizabeth had said, Mary needed to stop blaming her close detention on others and start to look at herself as the cause. She should not, she said, do as the dog does 'that resorteth to the stone and forgetteth the caster'.[32] Her detention was tightened, but, again surprisingly, not for long, and by the end of October it was once again left to Shrewsbury's discretion to work out convenient times for her recreation, which of course included hawking and hunting.[33] Mary's health seemed to improve and it was probably around this time that she argued for permission to ride up to twelve miles from Sheffield Castle.[34]

There was a renewed setback when Mary's part in the Throckmorton Plot emerged in November 1583 and when her health, as usual, deteriorated over the winter. In 1584 she was limited to exercising near the castle on foot or in her coach and was not allowed to go out on horseback, but the importance of exercise for her health was recognised and the freedom to exercise on foot or in her coach for recreation was not to be withdrawn.[35] While hunting on horseback was ruled out, archery practice, shooting at deer from a stand, and hawking were still possibilities.

In January 1585 Mary was again moved to Tutbury and Sir Amyas Paulet became her warder. Although Mary did not like Tutbury Castle itself, it was, as had been recognised in 1568, well equipped for hunting. There was a small park attached to the castle which was about a mile in circumference and which probably held about thirty deer. A mile away and linked to the Castle Park lay Castle Hay, which in the early seventeenth century held 480 deer and was well wooded with timber. Paulet was instructed to cut these trees sparingly for fuel because the park was still used for herbage – grazing domestic livestock on grass – and for pannage – grazing pigs on beech and oak mast.[36] Slightly farther afield but still within two miles of the castle lay Stockley Park, which had a circumference of two and three-quarter miles and was still stocked with deer.[37] These were small parks, more suited to shooting deer from a stand rather than chasing deer, although a short chase might have been possible. Watching deer being chased or coursed as they were released from a pen or shooting deer held in a paddock would have been more likely and might have pleased Mary, because that was how Elizabeth often hunted at this time.[38] While Ralph Sadler was still acting as Mary's warder before Paulet's arrival, he took Mary hawking four or five times to

[32] CSPS, vi, no. 79 p. 76.
[33] CSPS, vi, no. 192 p. 189; Labanoff, Lettres, v, 313.
[34] CSPS, vi, no. 403 p. 397; vii, 123 p. 136.
[35] CSPS, vii, nos 41 p. 44, 44 p. 48.
[36] CSPS, vii, no. 560 p. 580.
[37] Shirley, Some Account of English Deer Parks, 175.
[38] Adams, 'The Queenes majestie', 146–8, 158–63.

ELITE HUNTING CULTURE AND MARY, QUEEN OF SCOTS

the moors and rivers between Tutbury and Burton as she recovered from her winter illness. He allowed her to ride on horseback because she could not go on foot, but they were always accompanied by his soldiers.[39]

In April Sir Amyas Paulet arrived at Tutbury and, although his regime within the castle was harsher, he was authorised to be more lenient with Mary's outdoor activities and he duly obliged.[40] He had been appointed as keeper in March along with his son-in-law, John Somer, and with assistance from Richard Bagot, a local magistrate and landholder. Paulet's instructions from Elizabeth allowed him, at his discretion, to take Mary on horseback under guard for health or recreation within two miles of the castle, which meant that they could go coursing and hawking in the nearby deer parks.[41] On 14 July, 1585 Mary was keen to watch one of her greyhounds course a deer there, and during the summer she coursed and hunted in Stockley Park on at least three occasions. She had to be carried there, but Paulet reported that 'she hath coursed and hunted every time of her being there'.[42] Given the growing international tension between England and Spain at this time relating to the revolt in the Netherlands against Spain, it is of note that Mary was not under strict house arrest as she had been at Sheffield. Perhaps the assessment of her threat was low, given that she was becoming more out of touch with her organisation abroad, especially in France, and her own contacts were being infiltrated by agents such as Thomas Morgan and Gilbert Gifford.[43] Consequently, Paulet, who is often seen as a much harsher warden than Shrewsbury, was in this context less so. Nonetheless, the strict internal regime within the castle continued to filter all of Mary's communication and correspondence.

In response to French complaints, Mary was moved in December 1585 to the more comfortable manor house of Chartley Hall, which had been built beside the earlier medieval castle.[44] She probably went hunting in Chartley Park around Christmas, when she and her servants had tried to work out whether Phelippes, another member of the hunting party at the time, was working for Walsingham, Elizabeth's secretary of state, or for Paulet. He was in fact Walsingham's chief deciphering agent.[45] Even so, Mary's health suffered over the winter and it did not start to recover till June. She had to be carried to watch duck-hunting on 3 June in the ponds around the house, but by 27 July she considered that she was able to hunt again.[46] In a letter to Thomas Morgan, the double-agent and secretary of James Beaton, the archbishop of Glasgow in Paris, Mary made it clear that she was fit enough to be

[39] *CSPS*, vii, nos 578 pp. 598–9, 580 p. 600.
[40] *Letter Books of Amias Paulet*, ed. John Morris (London, 1874), 108.
[41] *CSPS*, vii, no. 563 p. 585; viii, no. 101 p. 85.
[42] *Letter Books of Amias Paulet*, 60; *CSPS*, viii, nos 18 p. 21, 116 p. 100.
[43] Fraser, *Mary Queen of Scots*, 555.
[44] Guy, *My Heart is My Own*, 458.
[45] *CSPS*, viii, nos 595 p. 529, 624 p. 551; Guy, *My Heart is My Own*, 482.
[46] *Letter Books of Sir Amias Paulet*, 201; *CSPS*, viii, no. 624 p. 552; Labanoff, *Lettres*, vi, 426.

rescued on horseback. She wrote that she was planning to ride a horse, gallop after hounds, and handle a crossbow in Chartley Park in the afternoon and would have planned to go farther afield if she had been permitted to do so. There was certainly some truth in her claims, because her captors used this ability to hunt to their advantage.

Antony Babington had been plotting since May 1586 to start a Roman Catholic uprising in England, to assassinate Elizabeth, and to encourage a Spanish invasion of England, since Philip II of Spain was contemplating putting Mary on the English throne. Walsingham and his agents knew of the plot and hoped to let Mary incriminate herself. She had heard from Babington around 10 July, and on 17 July she replied endorsing his plot and suggesting, very conveniently for Paulet as it turned out, that she could easily be rescued while riding on the quiet moors between Chartley and Stafford.[47] This was the letter which was to lead to her execution at Fotheringhay on 8 February 1587.

By 3 August 1586 it was suggested to Paulet that, on the pretext of hunting, Mary should be removed from her rooms at Chartley so that her papers could be seized and sent to Walsingham to be searched.[48] Paulet immediately realised that Mary could easily be persuaded to go over the moors towards Stafford to kill a stag in the park at Tixall, which was now held by Sir William Aston. On 9 August he received his final instructions to set this up; in the afternoon, when walking with Mary, he asked her if she would like to go hunting a stag in Sir Walter Aston's park the following day.[49] Aston, he said, wanted her to kill the stag herself as she had done before in that park. Mary, unaware of what lay in store, readily agreed.[50]

They set out for the hunt on 11 August, and as they rode over to Tixall a group of horsemen approached her party. This, however, was not Mary's rescue party. It was in fact Sir Thomas Gorges, Elizabeth's emissary, who had been sent to take her into custody at Tixall. From there Mary was soon moved back to Chartley and then to Fortheringhay. Her love of hunting, which had always been one of her strengths, had finally turned out to be her Achilles heel.

---

[47]   CSPS, viii, no. 586 p. 521; no. 595 p. 529; Guy, My Heart is My Own, 481–2.
[48]   CSPS, viii, no. 667 p. 585.
[49]   CSPS, viii, no. 690 p. 607.
[50]   Cowan, Bourgoyne's Journal, 161.

Conclusion

In France and Scotland during the middle ages and the Renaissance, aspects of elite hunting relating to politics, hunting rights, land management, and the preservation of game and its habitat impacted on all levels of society and played a part in royal governance, the political power of the monarch and the image of monarchy.

In the sixteenth century the widening scope of legislation, combined with the expansion of personnel, whether tenant-foresters, royal officials, or commissioners of enquiry, contributed to the growth of royal authority in the localities as they worked to maintain herds of deer and to preserve their environment. Due to her enthusiasm for the hunt, Mary, in certain forests, urged the control of poaching, grazing, wood-cutting, and of the growth of feu-ferme tenure. Consequently, in 1621 parliament restricted the right to hunt to wealthy landholders, ensuring that it remained an exclusive activity. Hunting greater game carried political significance because it was an elite activity. Royal hunts proved to be a valuable strategy for what would now be called social networking because they brought together the monarch and a selection of the wealthy and powerful of the kingdom. Thus, the political significance of the hunt is evidenced from the extended impact of royal governance which it entailed and from the opportunities it afforded to a selected group to interact with the monarch in a more informal setting.

Mary's upbringing in France had a major impact on her life. During her education and her short time as the French queen she saw how hunting could help to establish royal power and authority. But perhaps more importantly, her royal upbringing freed her from some of the restrictions which many women faced in the sixteenth century. Although women were never depicted chasing deer on horseback because that was seen as a typically male behaviour, Mary learned to regard hunting as an enjoyable and acceptable activity. The political side of her education benefitted from accompanying Francis II on his progresses around central France, when she saw that the young king was conscientious and intent on becoming an effective monarch. Francis did not hunt excessively but continued the nomadic nature of the Valois court as in the reigns of Francis I and Henry II. He did not abandon Mary while he went off hunting and, although he had to defer to Catherine de Medici and the Guises, he did not ignore the work of government. Mary was present at several major events of the reign and witnessed the efforts made to find a compromise solution to the religious differences engulfing France. She may not have been expected to become the queen regnant of Scotland but, nonetheless, she had grown into the role of being a queen, as witnessed by the English ambassador, Throckmorton.

CONCLUSION

When Mary assumed her personal reign in Scotland in 1561, she made full use of her love of the hunt. While the evidence suggests that this activity was seen as a male preserve and was not a common activity for women in Scotland, Mary seems to have received no criticism for taking part in hunts. It formed part of her early progresses in Fife, Argyll, and Angus, where her ability to ride astride and side-saddle added to the image of the ruler in charge. It gave her the opportunities to develop relationships with, for instance, the English ambassador Randolph, her half-brother Lord James, and the earl of Argyll.

The uses to which Mary put hunting reflected what was happening during her reign. In the early years it was employed to establish her position as monarch, but as her confidence grew she started to host hunts on royal hunting grounds in Glenfinglas, Megget, and Glenartney. A similar 'royal hunting' held in Glen Tilt in 1564 on the lands of the earl of Atholl centred on Mary and was held in her honour. On these occasions the hunt reflected her position as the monarch, at the centre of the invited elite. She was organising and participating in hunts where she was on show to impress her nobles and other subjects as she adopted the traditional role of the monarch as hunter on a highland stage. These hunts also demonstrated her authority and position to the people of the localities away from the court and allowed her to tackle local issues. After the divisions caused by the Darnley match, hunting became one of her tactics to reconcile the various noble factions prior to the baptism of her son, James.

As the centrepiece of the celebrations of James's baptism at Stirling in 1566 Mary chose to provide a rare hunt of a white bull. Although the celebrations contained recognised elements of other such festivals, this was no copy of any French fete and shows signs of having been designed by Mary. This hunt was a key part of the triumph, marking the continuation of the Stewart line, which was presented as popular, powerful, and ready to rule the whole of Britain. Fittingly, in celebrations which focussed on a hunt, Mary referenced her father's triumph in Glen Tilt by using the burning of his 'palice' there by the men of Atholl as the model for the burning by 'hieland men' of the fort which featured at the end of the festival. Mary, in short, was suggesting that she had built her monarchy in the image of her predecessors.

Much has been made here of the hunting image of Stewart monarchs, and it is important to determine what that was. Most European monarchs and rulers were keen hunters who provided facilities for the hunt and hosted large hunts for their elites at considerable expense. One has to ask, therefore, whether there was anything unique about the hunting image that Stewart monarchs sought to project. In many respects the answer is that, with inevitable local variations, they conformed to European norms which were readily understood by foreign commentators. Georg von Ehingen, who visited James II's court, praised him for the excellent hunting he provided and portrayed him with a fallow deer at his side.[1] Since fallow deer were usually kept in

---

[1] Christine McGladdery, *James II* (Edinburgh, 2015), front cover and illustration opposite

parks, von Ehingen associated James with his hunting parks, such as that at Falkland where James had developed both the park and the palace. James IV is shown in a contemporary portrait holding a peregrine falcon, and Pedro de Ayala, the papal ambassador, described him as the archetypal king when he wrote that 'when not at war he hunts in the mountains'. He also made reference to the Scottish nobility who mainly resided on their estates, where they had great forests for hunting game.[2] Pitscottie referred to the royal hunt in Glen Tilt in 1532 as a triumph which clearly amazed the visiting papal ambassador.[3] Lesley referred to the abundance of stags in Scotland's high mountains where kings regularly hunted.[4] When the French ambassador wrote to Catherine de Medici in January 1565, he commented on the gracious and leisurely life which Mary led, spending every morning at the hunt and every evening at dances and masques.[5] The Stewart monarchs, therefore, were well known as hunters.

What were particular to the Stewart monarchy were those large drives which they organised in their summer hunting trips at Glenfinglas, Glenartney, Kindrochit, Balquhidder, and Glen Tilt.[6] From the time of Robert II in the fourteenth century these were the traditional hunting grounds of the Scottish monarchs, where at various times they held hunts which could feature humble accommodation, mobile tinchells, the assistance of the local population, the use of hunting hillocks, large kills, and, at least in the sixteenth century, the wearing of the highlanders' style of dress. To those outside the Highlands, and especially to those outside Scotland, hunting in the Highlands assisted by 'wild highlandmen' would have been a unique experience that formed a distinctive part of the image of the Stewart monarchy. In the sixteenth century it is not the chase on horseback in the Lowlands, but the drive in the Highlands which Lesley and Barclay describe as a royal or solemn hunting.

It was Mary's skill as a horsewoman, her courage and her tenacity that enabled her to successfully adopt this image of the Stewart monarch. She became used to chasing game without the use of relays and to facing up to large-scale drives. As a result of the location of royal lands, the decline of lowland woodland, and the availability of game these drives were, by the fifteenth and sixteenth centuries, concentrated on the edge of the Highlands. Consequently, this led to direct contact with Gaelic hunting culture, which

---

138, 221–2; Wurttemburgische Landesbibliothek Cod.hist.qt.141. fo. 97. Available at: https://digital.wlb-stuttgart.de/sammlungen/sammlungsliste/werksansicht?tx_dlf%5B double%5D=0&tx_dlf%5Bid%5D=17735&tx_dlf%5Border%5D=title&tx_dlf%5Bpage %5D=101&cHash=e129cbfcf032a13f71648f5be084b339 [accessed 18 April 2024].

[2]   Gilbert, *Hunting and Hunting Reserves*, fig. 13; Hume Brown, *Early Travellers in Scotland* (Edinburgh 1891), 41.

[3]   Pitscottie, *Historie*, ii, 337–8.

[4]   Lesley, *Historie* (1596), i, 19.

[5]   Alexandre Teulet (ed.), *Papiers d'Etat Relatifs à l'Histoire de l'Écosse au 16e Siècle*, 3 vols (Edinburgh, 1852–66), ii, 31.

[6]   Gilbert, *Hunting and Hunting Reserves*, 36, 40, 42, 44.

meant that Mary encountered the use of hunting mounds, the wearing of highland dress, the use of a lunkart or a hunting house as accommodation, and, no doubt, the recitation of Gaelic hunting tales which could be sung and accompanied by the clarsach. Mary seems to have wholeheartedly embraced this aspect of Scottish hunting culture, which shows her willingness to learn about and to adapt to customs which were markedly different from those she had experienced in France. Hunting, therefore, played a large part in Mary's ability to be accepted by a male-dominated society and in this she was by no means unique as a female ruler in sixteenth-century Europe.[7] Like many of these able and strong-willed women, Mary had to adopt what were traditionally seen as the male roles of ruler and hunter.

This study has also demonstrated how hunting can give an insight into the character and ability of a monarch which is not necessarily obtained from other, more frequently analysed evidence. It has revealed that Mary was adept at making the most of her abilities and her early upbringing. Her willingness to adapt to the Scottish hunting culture and her determination to emulate her Stewart predecessors show a confident and realistic approach to her role. Although she made many mistakes, suffered from illness, and fell prey to bouts of self-doubt, Mary has emerged from this study as active, energetic, and courageous, and thoroughly in tune with the idea of the monarch as huntress.

Hunting in the Scottish court in the sixteenth century was a regular and organised activity very much in line with the practices of the Tudor, Habsburg, and Valois courts of Europe. It could be a pastime, but it was much more than that. Mary's hunts on her progresses, her smaller hunts at Falkland and around Pitlethie, and her larger show hunts were not peripheral to the life of the court. We have caught glimpses of how Mary employed hunting to influence ambassadors, to discuss particular policies, and to form personal ties. Large hunts with privy councillors, nobility, and lairds or smaller hunts with select companions allowed Mary and other monarchs to network, to pursue dialogue, and to give and receive counsel in an informal environment away from the protocols and procedures of the royal palaces. That this should be the case in Scotland is not surprising. Hunting was a common interest among the aristocracy and was central to their culture, as evidenced by the effort they made to acquire and maintain their hunting rights and hunting reserves. Having the wealth, the territory, and the right to hunt game, especially deer, whether in open forest or enclosed park, was a mark of their identity and status. Chasing deer across country or awaiting the drive were seen as activities especially appropriate for a monarch, requiring the military qualities of skill with weapons, excellent horsemanship, and courage. Hunting was, therefore, central to the life of the royal court. Study a period or a reign and ignore the study of hunting, and one omits a major area

---

[7] Peacock, 'Women at the hunt', 829–32; Noirmont, *Histoire de la Chasse*, i, 129; Almond, *Daughters of Artemis*, 59, 86–7; Neighbors, 'Elizabeth I Huntress', *passim.*

of interaction between the monarch and his or her nobility; an important location outside the palace where monarch and nobles could pursue private political conversations; and, finally, one ignores a custom-built activity in a suitably managed environment ideal for the presentation and exercise of effective royal authority.

Appendix I: Fieldwork

The Lunkarts in Glen Tilt

Identifying this site presented several problems: finding the two letters signed at the 'Lunkartis' by Mary, Queen of Scots, which D. Hay Fleming did not identify when compiling his itinerary of Mary; reading the name, 'Rederis Lhontartis', on Pont's map; locating the site on the ground; and, finally, interpreting the surviving earthworks to determine whether they could be the remains of a hunting encampment rather than a shieling.[1]

The documents relating to the first issue have already been referenced and in fact four sources have been located which show that Mary was hunting at the 'Lunkartis' in Glen Tilt in 1564.[2] Turning to the second issue, Pont, as we saw, marks this site with a circle and named it 'Rederis Lhontartis' (Plate 6). The 't' and 'c' are interchangeable, and so the second word can be read as 'lhoncartis'. By comparing the letters of the first word with the letters in other words on the original map in the National Library of Scotland map room it is clear that the last four letters are 'deris'.[3] The fainter text in which this word is written is the secretary hand of Pont himself. Most of the darker text is written by Robert Gordon of Straloch, over-writing Pont's italic hand which he generally used for place-names.[4] The first point to note is that the stroke above the first word is not an abbreviation mark but Pont's initial drawing of the south bank of the An Lochain or the 'Avon Lochin' before Gordon drew over it and darkened it. The 'd' and the 'e' of 'deris' match the letters in Pont's version of the 'Dee' in the sentence at the top right corner of the

---

[1]   NN9836577808, Canmore Id 370113; Fleming, *Mary Queen of Scots*, 529.
[2]   a) NRS, GD112/1/149; b) Menzies, *The Red and White Book of Menzies*, 195–6 and NRS, GD50/186/11/vii/4; c) Fraser, *Lennox*, ii, 427 and NRS, GD112/1/150; d) *Sixth Report of the Royal Commission on Historical Manuscripts* (London, 1877) 707 and no. 204; Menzies, *The Red and White Book of Menzies*, 196–7.
[3]   I am indebted to several people for their help deciphering this place-name, Norman Reid, Rachel Hart, Simon Taylor, and Christopher Fleet. The interpretation given here is, the author hastens to add, his conclusion: NLS, Adv.Ms.70.2.9, Pont 20 ('Glen Tilt'). The following discussion on the reading of the place-name can be followed more easily on the Pont map on the NLS website. The whole map is too large to duplicate here in sufficient detail.
[4]   Christopher Fleet, 'Writing and Signs. Pont's Writing: Form and Content', in Cunningham (ed.), *The Nation Survey'd*, 35–48, at 36–9.

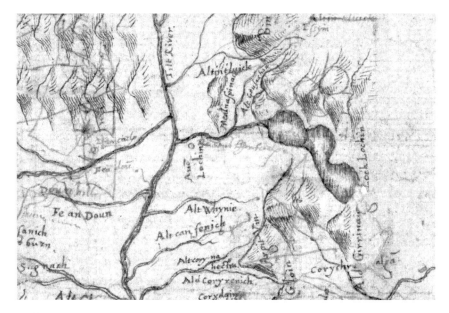

Plate 6   An extract from Pont's map of Glen Tilt, c. 1583–96. The circle in the centre of the picture with 'Rederis Lhontartis' written to the right of it represents the site of the lunkarts used by Mary. 'Loch Lochin' (Loch Loch) is on the right centre and the River 'Avon Lochin' (An Lochain) is named below the circle. Another 'Lhoncartis' is written on the left centre, just above a stream which flows into the 'Tilt River'.

original map. The 'r' matches the 'r' in 'nord east' in the same sentence. The 'is' ending is clear. The first letter is clearly a capital 'R', but the second letter is not so clear. However, on the original of his map one can see that Pont has overwritten the initial 'Re' in his italic hand but not finished converting the whole of the name. Unlike many other names on this map, it has not been overwritten in the darker hand of Gordon of Straloch. The italic form of the 'R' and the 'e' can be seen in 'Branches and River of Tilt' in the title of the map which was written by Pont and which has also not been overwritten by Gordon. The word, therefore, is 'Rederis', and has proved difficult to read because it is in both Pont's italic and his secretary hands. It is not surprising to find red deer referred to as such in the sixteenth century. Mary would be accustomed to regard them as one of the *bêtes rousses* in France. In Scotland, 'rede dere' is probably the more common form of the name, but 'redeir' is also found and it is a version of that form which Pont has written here.[5] Pont, therefore, was stressing that these were not normal 'lunkartis' or shielings but shielings used when hunting red deer.

[5]   *DOST*, 'rede dere'.

APPENDIX I: FIELDWORK

When it came to tackling the third problem, it emerged that many shielings survive in Atholl and some were recorded in this area as early as 1656 and 1669, but shielings in Perthshire can date to the fifteenth century or earlier.[6] The word 'shieling' can refer to an area of pasture used in the summer in the practice of transhumance or to the small dwellings or huts on that pasture. The area of pasture on the south-west side of the An Lochain is called Garbh Sron (Rough Promontory), the rough hillside between the Tilt and the An Lochain. There are three groups of buildings on this pasture, two of which, comprising twelve buildings in total, lie on the face of the hillside.[7] The third group, which comprises ten buildings lying beside the river (NN9836177810 centred), was spotted by Judith Harris for the National Monuments Register of Scotland and then visited by John Kerr, the local historian, although neither was aware of the site's hunting connection.[8]

Description of the site

The site lies on a broad haugh on the south bank of the An Lochain and comprises a close grouping of ten buildings and shieling huts with an outlier 50m to the south-east (9 on Plan 1).[9] As a *general* guide, in the following description, a 'building' is more than 3m in internal breadth and 6m in length internally and a 'hut' less than 3m in breadth. Three buildings (1, 4, and 7) are arranged around a yard open to the south and there is a terraced garden plot on the east of the eastern building (4 on plan). At this point, note that the hut inside building 4 will be referred to as building 4b although it is not marked as such on the plan. Within the yard there is another group of five structures (2, 4b, 10, 3, and 6) forming a roughly rectangular arrangement with hut 5 arranged diagonally across the square. Building 4 is part of both groups, as it comprises a round-ended turf shieling hut (4b) built inside a rectangular building (4). Thus it appears that the huts are secondary to the buildings.

<u>Building 1</u> is 5.6m from E to W by 3.2m within grass-covered banks containing stone footings spread to 1.5m along the sides and standing to 0.7m in height, especially at the E end, which is thicker than the rest, suggesting

[6]   John Kerr, 'East by Tilt', *Transactions of the Gaelic Society of Inverness*, 54 (1987), 30; *Chronicles of Atholl*, ed. Atholl, i, Addenda to Appendix, p. xxxiii; *Ben Lawers: An Archaeological Landscape in Time*, Scottish Archaeological Internet Reports, 62 (Edinburgh, 2016), 259; Albert Bil, *The Shieling*, 248–9.

[7]   Canmore Id 83333 and 83332.

[8]   A. K. Bell Library (Perth), MS249: John Kerr, *The Atholl Experience*, vol. 42(1), Working Map of Glen Tilt and Glen Loch; photograph in vol. 19/6, 309, photo no.19/245/1 where it is entitled as the remains of twelve shielings beside the An Lochain.

[9]   NN9836577808, Canmore Id 370113. The site was visited by the author and Piers Dixon on 12 July, 2020. The author is indebted to Piers Dixon for drawing the sketch plan and writing the description of the site on which the following description is almost entirely based. The author is also indebted to him for his realisation that the site does not resemble the normal layout of a summer shieling.

171

APPENDIX I: FIELDWORK

a collapsed gable. The presence of possible facings set back within the bank on the E by about 0.5m may also indicate that the building was longer than measured bank to bank. There may be an entrance on the S and a yard wall runs off from the NE corner.

Building 2 measures 6.75m from E to W by 2.5m within grass-covered stone footings 0.3m in height spread to 1.2m in thickness.

Hut 3 measures 2.35m from E to W by 1.5m within turf banks 1.3m in height spread to 1.7m in thickness.

Building 4 measures 5.8m from N to S by 3m within grass-covered stone footings 0.3m in height and 0.9m in thickness. Inside it there is a secondary turf-walled hut (4b) of oval plan 3.3m in length by 2.1m in breadth within banks standing to 0.6m in height and 1.1m in thickness with a gap suggesting an entrance on the W. An outshot has been added to the S end that is slightly offset to the E and a bank runs N from the NW corner to the edge of the terrace, while on the E there is a terraced garden plot.

Hut 5 measures 7m from NE to SW by 2m within grass-covered stone footings 0.3m in height and spread to 1.2m in thickness. An oblong bank aligned on the same axis occupies the SW end and it has a possible entrance on the NW. The bench feature is analogous to those recorded at the cattle fair site of Druim Tighe Mhic Gille Chattan on the Isle of Mull (Canmore Id 22043).

Hut 6 measures 5.5m from NNW to SSE by 2.2m within turf banks 0.3m in height and 1.7m in thickness.

Building 7 measures 8.2m from NNW to SSE by 2.4m within turf banks up to 0.4m in height that are spread to 1.1m in thickness. The banks are patchy and ill-preserved.

Hut 8 is rectangular and measures 4.7m from WSW to ENE by 2.7m within stone footings 0.3m in height spread to 1.2m in thickness.

Building 9 stands about 50m to the SE on the edge of the river terrace and extends about 9m from NNW to SSE by 3m transversely within stone footings about 1m in thickness with an entrance on the W.

Hut 10 is turf walled and measures 4.2m from E to W by 2.3m within banks standing 0.3m in height and spread to 1.3m in thickness.

APPENDIX I: FIELDWORK

Interpretation

This site is atypical of other shieling sites in the area in various ways. Other shielings in this area are located on the hillsides, often levelled into the hill-side and spread out in loose groupings.[10] This shieling is on the flood plain of the An Lochain and the buildings are in a tight group and not strung out, both of which suggest that this site was not constructed as a summer shieling. The buildings themselves, however, are not unique to the area. On the east side of the An Lochain in the Fealar estate Judith Harris found a greater variety of shieling structures than anywhere else in the estate, ranging from smaller huts to larger buildings up to 17m by 4.5m in size overall.[11] The usual form was a rectangular or sub-rectangular structure 9m by 4m on average. It is not surprising to find similar structures at this site because they would have been built by local tenants and they would have built what they knew. What is unusual is the predominance of larger rectangular buildings. It used to be thought that smaller oval huts were older than rectangular buildings, but it is now realised that rectangular buildings and smaller oval huts were co-eval and could date to the sixteenth century or earlier.[12] In a shieling context, rectangular buildings were probably meant to be more permanent structures and could also be intended for people of higher status.[13] Lairds might move to these summer towns, and in the late eighteenth century it was considered that the buildings and huts were constructed in proportion to the affluence and rank of their possessors.[14]

The buildings at the 'Lunkartis' could, therefore, be of sixteenth-century date and the rectangular buildings could be accommodation for the queen, her ladies, the earl of Atholl, and others of the nobility. The buildings whose ruins survive are, as mentioned above, not all of the same date, since a small turf-walled oval hut is built inside rectangular building 4. In view of the practice in Mar it seems likely that lunkarts would have been specially built for Mary. When they were no longer used for hunting, local tenants may have utilised them as shielings. The two different arrangements of buildings (1, 7, 4, and 2, 4b, 6, 3, 10) probably represent two different stages of use. The outer group (1, 7, 4), based on the evidence of building 4 and hut 4b, would be the earlier group and the inner group (2, 4b, 6, 3, 10) would represent later reuse of the site.

Therefore, it is possible to argue that the original rectangular arrangement of buildings, 1, 4, and 7, around a courtyard open to the south was built for Mary's visit. Buildings 1 and 4 are distinctive, since building 1 may have been

[10] Judith Kerr, *Fealar Estate, An Archaeological Survey*, National Monuments Record of Scotland (1999), 5.
[11] A. K. Bell Library (Perth), MS 249, *The Atholl Experience*, vol. 19 2/50 Barr 'n t-Iobairt p. 310; vol. 20 Fealar; Judith Kerr, *Fealar Estate*, p. 13, site FL14.
[12] *Ben Lawers*, 259; Bil, *The Shieling*, 248.
[13] Bil, *The Shieling*, 234, 235, 248; *Ben Lawers*, 259.
[14] Robertson, *General View of Agriculture of the County of Perth*, 336.

gable-ended; building 4 is the only building to have an attached yard; both are linked by a courtyard wall, and at present both appear to be slightly wider than building 7. They also have stone-based walls, suggesting more substantial structures, and so they could have served as accommodation for Mary and her ladies. The outlying building 9 is the largest building on the site and consequently can be considered as the most important. Like buildings 1 and 4, it is rectangular and has stone-based walls, tentatively suggesting it could belong to the earlier phase of the site. It could have served as accommodation but, given its size, it could also have been used as a hall.

The second and roughly rectangular arrangement of structures (building 2 and huts 4b, 10, 3, and 6 with hut 5 placed diagonally in the centre) could have been used either for a later hunting party or perhaps as shielings. In this group, hut 5 stands out from the others since it has a central position and seems to be protected by the other huts. It also has a possible bench at its south-west end, all of which make it distinctive. In a hunting context, some of the later smaller huts could have been used for storage or as accommodation for servants. In a shieling context, they could have acted as storage or accommodation for herds or dairymaids.[15]

These comments on the use of individual buildings can only be informed suggestions. Nonetheless, what is clear is that, while archaeology might be able to establish the stages and date of occupation, the outline of the structures, and the status of those who used the site, some of these buildings did accommodate the hunting party of Mary and the earl of Atholl in August 1564.

Glenartney

There are three documented sites relating to hunting in Glenartney: the hunt hall used by James IV, James V's accommodation at Cultybraggan, and Mary Queen of Scots' hunting house, all of which are as yet unlocated.[16] There are various problems in trying to find these sites and what is offered here is not a final solution to these problems but a contribution to what the author hopes will be the ongoing search them. Unfortunately, Pont's map of the area does not mark any of these sites although, as discussed in Chapter 4, it does raise the possibility that James V's accommodation at Cultybraggan was the two- or three-storey building marked by Pont, which, again, has not been located.[17] The major difficulty, however, in trying to identify a hunt hall or a hunting house is that we are still at an early stage of establishing the typology of these structures.[18] The specific problems which emerge as a result

---

[15] Bil, *The Shieling*, 234.
[16] *TA*, iv, 137; *Excerpta e Libris*, Appendix, p. 35 for 25 September; *ER*, xxi, 549.
[17] See p. 83; NLS, Adv. Ms. 70.2.9, Pont 21 ('Lower Glenalmond; Strathearn').
[18] See pp. 80–82, 128–32, 144–6.

APPENDIX I: FIELDWORK

Plate 7   The location of the ruined building near Dalclathick. The site lies on the small, lighter-coloured terrace in the centre of the picture. The track along the north side of Glenartney runs across the slope from the top of the wood on the centre left of the picture. The River Ruchill runs in the valley in the foreground. This could be Mary's hunting house rather than a hunt hall or a sheep or goat house. The Coire Choire lies over the ridge at the top right of the picture.

are well illustrated by a site at Dalclathick which has been suggested as the possible site of the Glenartney hunt hall (Plate 7).[19]

Description of site near Dalclathick

The site lies in the upper part of the glen on the north side of the river, the same side as the path of the Roman road from Comrie to Callander.[20] The site is located on a small terrace on sloping ground just above the Water of Ruchill, on what was once the farm of Dalclathick. This terrace appears to have been built up, with the result that it is much drier than the surrounding ground (Plan 2). There is flat land beside the meanders of the river at this point where tents and pavilions could have been pitched. It lies 2km from Dalclathick Farm and so is not an immediate part of that settlement and it

[19] I am indebted to both Richard Oram, who first located this as a possible site for the hunt hall in Glenartney, and Piers Dixon for sharing their views of the site with me. I would also like to thank John Harrison and Michael Pearce for answering my questions relating to this site in a most helpful manner.
[20] NN70081594; *Discovery and Excavation* (1985), 51.

175

APPENDIX I: FIELDWORK

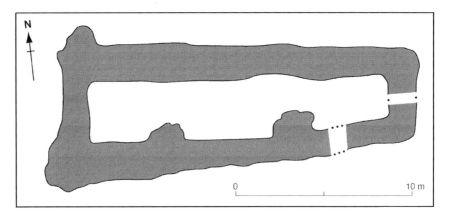

Plan 2   Sketch plan of the ruined building in Glenartney near Dalclathick.

lies below an area of the deer forest, Coire a Choire, which was and is well known as an area with good grass where deer can shelter.[21] The building measures 16.8m from WNW to ESE in internal length and varies in breadth from 3.1m in the W two-thirds to 2.3m at the E end within grass-covered stone footings. There is a very narrow doorway in the E end and there may possibly be a wider one on the S side 2.8m from the E end. The walls are about 0.4m in height, spread to anything between 0.9m and 1.8m at the E end, to 1.8m and 1.95m at the W end. There are two tumbles of stone in the S wall which intrude into the interior. They may be random or they could be the remains of internal features.

Interpretation

The first point to make is that this structure has been built in an appropriate area of the glen for a hunting-related building. It is accessible on horseback from Doune Castle and Drummond Castle and it is in the heart of the forest. Not only does it lie below Coire a Choire but in 1810 the earliest lodge in the area, Glenartney Lodge, was at Dalclathick.[22] In the late seventeenth century and in the eighteenth century there are records of foresters staying at Findoglen and Auchinner as well as Dalclathick.[23] This area, therefore, was seen in the eighteenth and nineteenth centuries as a good base for those

---

[21]   Scrope, *Art of Deer Stalking*, 416; pers. comm. Alasdair Work, retired deerstalker of Glenartney Forest.
[22]   Drummond Estate Office, [Maps of] *The Property of Mr and Mrs Drummond Birrell*, surveyed by James Knox (1810).
[23]   NRS, GD160/210/4/5; GD 160/254; GD E777/71, p. 5.

managing the reserve and for those intending to hunt in the forest, and the same could also have been true in the sixteenth century. It is therefore reasonable to interpret this site in the context of hunting.

Consequently, a first possible interpretation is that it was the hunting house of Mary, Queen of Scots. It is built in the vernacular style, just like Lunkarts in Glen Tilt, and while it is around the same width as most of these buildings it is double the length of most of them, 16.8m as opposed to 5m–7m, and so it could qualify as a more comfortable version of a lunkart. If the internal tumbles of stones do represent internal divisions, then the house would have been neatly divided into three, thus matching on a much-reduced scale the layout of royal apartments, progressing, in this case, from a private closet/bed chamber at the west end to a presence chamber and then to an outer chamber in the east which controlled entry and exit to the house. However, as far as it is possible to tell from the surviving remains, such a building would not have cost anything like the 200 merks (£133) which it cost James Stewart to build. For a building in the vernacular style, materials would have been available locally. Wood could have been obtained from the royal woodlands in Glenartney and Strathearn for which the forester was responsible and stone and turf were in plentiful local supply. Just as in Mar in the early seventeenth century, one would expect that local tenants would have provided all necessary labour and carriage and constructed any accommodation or lunkarts related to the lord's hunting as a condition of their lease.[24] Even if the wood for crucks or couples and for the construction of the rest of the roof had to be paid for it would not have amounted to anything like £133, since the wood for the house in Strathdon mentioned in Chapter 4, which was of a similar size, came to only £45 about twenty years later in an age of inflation.[25]

It is also possible to interpret this building as a hunt hall of the smaller type postulated in Chapter 4, based on a hall-house. In the light of the tradition of using smaller houses as hunting lodges, this could have been a smaller vernacular structure with a fire but without internal divisions, or it could have been more like a hall-house with chamber and kitchen attached at opposite ends of the structure.

However, this building in Glenartney also displays the characteristics of a sheep or goat house. It is a long, narrow building, has a door in one end of the building and it is built in an area where sheep and goats were kept in the mid-eighteenth century.[26] Sheep houses or sheep cotes were low-roofed buildings constructed to shelter sheep at night in wintertime because the sheep were not hardy enough to winter outside. They also protected sheep from wolves, foxes, birds of prey, and other predators. They had been in use since the medieval period and were still being recommended in the

[24] See p. 131; *RMS*, ix, no. 99.
[25] See p. 82; Ross, 'Two Surveys of Vernacular Buildings', 8.
[26] *In the Shadow of Bennachie*, RCAHMS and SAS (Edinburgh, 2008), 213–14.

APPENDIX I: FIELDWORK

seventeenth century in Scotland.[27] Sheep houses on this pattern of long, narrow buildings occurred across Scotland and surviving examples are often thought to belong to the improvement era in the eighteenth and nineteenth centuries. The presence of a second door would not preclude this from being a sheep house, nor would internal partitions, since a well-documented sheep house in Menstrie Glen dating to the mid-eighteenth century measured 12.2m by 3.1m internally with three compartments.[28]

It is unlikely that this structure within the royal forest of Glenartney would have been a medieval sheep house because sheep, which ate the same grass as the deer and damaged young trees, were positively discouraged in royal deer forests.[29] In 1701 the foresters of the Drummonds were still trying to control grazing in the forest to ensure that there was enough grass for the deer in winter. They were instructed to soume (calculate) the number of mares that the local tenants could graze in the forest. There is no mention in their instructions of either cattle or sheep and so they were still, presumably, officially excluded from the deer forest.[30] Nevertheless, sheep and goats were kept by the tenants of Dalclathick in the mid-eighteenth century and so the sheep house possibility cannot be discarded. After the 1745 uprising, the estate of the duke of Perth, which included Glenartney, was forfeited to the Crown and run by the Commissioners for the Annexed and Forfeited Estates. In 1755 their survey of Glenartney showed that the 6 tenants and 4 cottars of Dalclathick held 24 horses, 96 black cattle, 200 sheep, and 84 goats.[31] This first clear reference to sheep grazing in the area, along with the mention of goats, supports the possibility that the building in question was constructed as either a sheep or a goat house. A complication arises with this identification because in 1765 an inspection of all the Perth estates severely criticised the nightly housing of sheep in winter, a practice which was obviously still common.[32] Around this time in the 1760s, this area was one of the first regions of the Highlands into which blackface sheep were introduced from the south, and by 1764 the hills between Callander and Comrie were being grazed by blackface sheep.[33] However, because these sheep could over-winter outside, the practice of sheep housing in Highland Perthshire died out, becoming obsolete by 1799.[34] If this was a sheep house it is most likely that it was built in the mid-eighteenth century when the new tenant of Dalclathick, Colonel Graeme of Gorton who was also the forester, consolidated this holding into a

[27] J. A. Donaldson, *Husbandry Anatomized, An Enquiry into the present manner of teiling and manuring the Ground in Scotland* (Edinburgh 1697), 99.
[28] *In the Shadow of Bennachie*, 213–14; John Harrison, 'Well Shelterd and Well Waterd', *Menstrie Glen, a farming landscape near Stirling*, RCAHMS and NMRS (Edinburgh, 2001), 30, 46, 59.
[29] *RPS/1535/18; 1555/6/34; 1594/4/3.*
[30] NRS, GD160/210 no. 5.
[31] *Statistics of the Annexed and Forfeited Estates 1755–6*, HMSO (Edinburgh, 1973), 48–9.
[32] *Reports on Annexed Estates 1755–69*, ed. Virginia Wills (Edinburgh, 1973), 64–5.
[33] Bil, *The Shieling*, 320.
[34] Bil, *The Shieling*, 316–17; Robertson, *General View of the Agriculture of Perth*, 337.

178

APPENDIX I: FIELDWORK

sheep farm and in 1762 banned the keeping of goats.[35] Prior to that date the construction of a goat house could also make sense because the sale of goat's cheese and whey brought in valuable income to the tenants of Dalclathick prior to their goats being banned.[36] Whether the forty-seven men, women, and children of Dalclathick, including the six tenants and four cottars, would have considered it worthwhile constructing a goat house is debateable.[37]

The identification of this building as a sheep house cannot be certain because sheep houses usually lay either close to the township for whose sheep they were built or else were placed in the area where sheep were grazing in the hills, at some distance from the settlement. This structure is 2km from the settlement of Dalclathick, nor is it suitably located to shelter the sheep at night while grazing above the agricultural land on the hills in the forest. The structure is also quite small if it was meant to house all of Dalclathick's sheep, which numbered two hundred in 1755 and probably upwards of three hundred in 1770–75 after Colonel Graeme developed his sheep farm.[38] It is also noticeable that when Graeme listed buildings he had made in Dalclathick he did not mention a sheep house as a tenant in Strathgartney did.[39] Nor are there the usual pens and yards around it to assist in handling the sheep. It would also seem to be a fairly unique structure in Strathearn, since the Canmore website records only two sheep houses in Perthshire and they are at Dunning.[40] None of this is conclusive, but it does cast doubt on the interpretation of the structure as a sheep house.

This one simple building, therefore, illustrates the difficulties involved in trying to identify these hunting-related structures in Glenartney. With fragmentary remains of this sort it can be hard to distinguish between human habitation and housing for stock.[41] The crucial factor in categorising this building is the date of its construction. If it can be dated to the sixteenth century, then one can be fairly confident in identifying it as a building associated with hunting and, given its narrow width, it could be identified as Mary's hunting house, although the cost of 200 merks would still require explanation. If it was built in the eighteenth century the interpretation as a sheep or goat house would be appropriate. Whatever use it had, it appears to have fallen out of use by the 1770s because it does not appear in the plans of the Glenartney grazings in 1772, nor in the estate plan of Dalclathick in 1810. Nor does the building appear on the 1st edition of the OS 6-inch

[35] NRS, E777/111/2; E777/161 no. 355; Bil, *The Shieling*, 310, 328.
[36] NRS, E777/184; E777/161 no. 232.
[37] *Statistics of Annexed Estates* (Edinburgh, 1973), 49.
[38] NRS, E777/311, p. 15, which states that Graeme was allowed one hundred soumes on the pasture. If he allocated soumes to cattle, horses, and sheep he could have had over three hundred sheep. One soume could equal one cow, two mares, or six ewes: Annette M Smith, *Annexed and Forfeited Estates*, unpublished PhD thesis (St Andrews University 1975), 144.
[39] NRS, E777/111/5(2); *Reports on Annexed estates 1755–69*, 75.
[40] Canmore Id 292474, Id 320528.
[41] Harrison, *Menstrie Glen*, 60.

APPENDIX I: FIELDWORK

map of the area.[42] These omissions could simply mean that the building was not considered important enough to record, although estate plans tend to record such buildings. But another reason for its omission could be that it was already in ruins or disused by the 1770s, thus rendering its interpretation as hunting accommodation much more likely.

[42] NRS, RHP 3405, Glenartney Grazings; Drummond Estate Office, [Maps of] *The Property of Mr and Mrs Drummond Birrell*, 1810.

Appendix II: Equestrianism

This appendix discusses relevant aspects of the development of riding styles and dress in France and in Scotland which support the details and views given in Chapters 2 and 5.[1]

Astride

That women had been riding astride throughout the medieval period and probably earlier is shown by Philippe Contamine and others who have collected relevant examples from French sources dating from the twelfth to the fifteenth century.[2] From at least the fifteenth century, instead of wearing a loose-fitting skirt, women could wear a *devantière*, a kind of apron or split skirt to ride either astride or side-saddle. This kind of apron, usually open at the back because it was more comfortable not to be sitting on it, sounds very like the modern wrap-round apron which women wear over breeches when riding side-saddle and which is cut away between the legs, with leg straps to hold it in position.[3] It is Catherine de Medici who is credited with introducing the fashion of wearing drawers or breeches for the sake of modesty when dismounting her horse.[4] These bifurcated garments resembled the close-fitting breeches worn by men which stopped at the knee and were made of silk or velvet.[5] In the late sixteenth century, Fynes Moryson noted similar

---

[1]   See Chapter 2, pp. 52–3 and Chapter 5, pp. 98–100.

[2]   Contamine, 'Dames à Cheval', 209–15, which shows that an order for a pair of spurs for one lady is evidence of riding astride; Almond, 'The Way Ladies Ride', 38; Almond, *Daughters of Artemis*, 76; Veauvy, *Cavalières Amazones*, 53. Confusingly, riding as an Amazon is used to mean both riding astride and riding side-saddle. Contamine uses it in both senses. Almond employs the former and Veauvy *et al.* actually use it to mean a side-facing saddle. In terms of the classical allusion, astride is correct.

[3]   A. Hatzfeld, *Dictionnaire General de la Langue Française du XVIIe siècle jusqu'à nos jours* (Paris, 1890–1900), '*devantière*'; E. J. Lewandowski, *The Complete Costume Dictionary* (London, 2011), '*devantière*'; Ferrière, *Les Chasses de François Ier*, 47–9; R. S. Summerhays and V. Russel, *Encyclopedia for Horsemen* (Buckingham, 1993), 'apron'; De Noirmont, *Histoire de la Chasse*, i, 129.

[4]   Margaret Wade Labarge, *A Baronial Household of the Thirteenth Century* (London, 1965), 141; Frieda, *Catherine de Medici* (London, 2003), 311.

[5]   Robert J. Knecht, *The French Renaissance Court 1483–1589* (London, 2003), 313.

APPENDIX II: EQUESTRIANISM

styles being worn in Italy; they were also illustrated by Antonio Tempesta, an Italian painter and engraver.[6]

Riding astride was also perfectly common in Scotland at this time for both men and women. In 1503 and 1505 pairs of stirrups had been ordered for Margaret Tudor, wife of James IV, showing that she was riding astride with two stirrups long before Mary's arrival.[7] When Mary arrived at Leith in 1561, the horses sent to take her and her party to Edinburgh were saddled in the same way for both sexes, which presumably reflected accepted practice as well as a lack of time to prepare, rather than a calculated insult.[8]

Side-facing saddle

The second method in which ladies rode involved sitting on a saddle which faced sideways with a *planchette* or small piece of wood on one side of the horse as a footrest. Although this type of saddle was generally called a *sambue* it had a wide variety names, such as *selle à dossier, en croupe, en trousse, à la planchette, à la fermière*, which may all have represented slightly different variations in the saddle. They were fairly common and so, to avoid confusion, it is easiest to call it a side-facing saddle because that immediately gives a picture of the rider's position on the horse.[9] Confusion can also arise with the name *en croupe*. Veauvy considered that in the middle ages ladies rode astride when riding pillion, *en croupe*, but Contamine, is clear that *en croppe* and *en trousse* refer to a side-facing position behind another rider.[10] Certainly, when Mary and Darnley were escaping from Holyrood after the murder of Riccio and Mary rode *en croupe* she was definitely riding in the side-facing position. Darnley, according to Nau, urged her to ride faster, which would not have been necessary if she had been riding pillion and astride. Furthermore, Mary was almost six months pregnant and the side-facing saddle would have been safer and more comfortable.[11] Images of this type of riding are well known from the illustration for August in *Les Très Riches Heures du Duc de Berry*, in which a woman is riding pillion behind a male rider.[12] The earliest portrayal of a Scots woman riding in this manner is the illustration of the entrance of Margaret, the daughter of James I of Scotland, to Tours in 1436 for her wedding to the dauphin, the future Louis XI.[13]

[6]   Baillie-Grohman, *Sport in Art*, 98; Fynes Moryson, *Itinerary* (Glasgow, 1908), iv, 222.
[7]   *TA*, iii, 148; *CDS*, iv, no. 1715.
[8]   Brantôme, *Book of the* Ladies, 100.
[9]   Contamine, 'Les Dames à Cheval', 207, 212; Weiss, 'Backwards in High heels', 4; Noirmont, *Histoire de la Chasse*, i, 129.
[10]   Veauvy, *Cavalières Amazones*, 40; Contamine, 'Dames à cheval', 207.
[11]   Nau, *Memorials*, 17.
[12]   848 *Musée Condé*, MS 65 ('Les Très Riches Heures,'), fo. 8v.
[13]   BnF, Ms Français 2691 ('Jean Chartier, *Chronique de Charles VII*'), fo. 93r. Available at: https://gallica.bnf.fr/ark:/12148/btv1b10023823h/f217 [accessed 5 July 2023]; Contamine,

APPENDIX II: EQUESTRIANISM

Surprisingly, this type of saddle where the woman rode pillion seems to have been used successfully when hunting. *The Book of Hours of Marguerite d'Orléans*, which was compiled in the early fifteenth century, shows two noble women facing sideways riding pillion, clinging on to their male companion but clearly enjoying a *par force* hunt with a new relay of hounds about to join the chase.[14] The May illustration in *Les Très Riches Heures du Duc de Berry* shows women riding independently on a side-facing saddle. This seems to have required a saddle with a high rim for safety and a crupper strap to prevent the saddle sliding forward; while the rider may have been able to ride very slowly in this manner, she had absolutely no control of the horse with her legs.[15]

In Scotland the side-facing saddle is probably portrayed on the Hilton of Cadboll stone in the eighth century, which shows two hunters with shields and spears chasing a deer being attacked with two dogs.[16] At the top of the scene are two trumpeters and a woman who is riding on a side-facing saddle, with a companion on another horse beside her. This woman is not taking part in the hunt because, as has been explained, it was not possible to ride at speed while riding on a side-facing saddle without a groom to lead the horse or without another rider to hold on to. Margaret Tudor, on her arrival in Scotland in 1503 to marry James IV, rode pillion on her palfrey behind James on 7 September when they coursed a tame stag with a greyhound. On 1 June Margaret had been given a saddle and a pillion decorated with red roses by Henry VII, and it may have been this on which she was riding.[17] In 1507 other saddles of this type were made for Queen Margaret, one of which was described as a 'heich quhit sadil for the queen for ane pilzane'.[18] There are references to the high saddle riding before the woman, which sounds as though the pillion might be at the back of it.[19] The pillion itself could be made from three to four ells of velvet, buckram, or damask as well as ten pounds of feathers to stuff its cushion.[20] The women's saddles recorded in 1504 and 1505 were probably also side-facing saddles. The footstools of the saddles of the queen's ladies which were covered in 1540 and 1543 must have been platform stirrups for these saddles.[21]

It would appear that Mary preferred side-saddle of some sort for official occasions, because when she arrived at Leith she was upset to discover that

---

'Dames à Cheval', 216 n. 71 and illustration no. 14.

[14] Almond, *Medieval Hunting*, Illustration 46 after p. 152; BnF, Ms Latin 1156B ('*Book of Hours of Marguerite d'Orleans*'), f.163r. Available at: https://gallica.bnf.fr/ark:/12148/btv1b52502614h [accessed 28 August 2020].

[15] *Musée Condé* ('Les Très Riches Heures'), fo. 5v; Weiss, 'Backwards in High Heels', 4.

[16] Fraser, *Pictish Symbol Stones*, no. 123 Hilton of Cadboll.

[17] Leland, *De Rebus Britannicis Collecteana, Account of John Younge Somerset Herald* (London, 1770), iv, 286; *CDS*, iv, no.1721.

[18] *TA*, iii, 399.

[19] *TA*, iii, 270, 399. Veauvy, *Cavalières Amazones*, 57, considers that in Europe a little cushion could be attached to the saddle of the horseman to accommodate the lady.

[20] *TA*, iii, 44, 270.

[21] *TA*, vii, 327; viii, 182.

the horses were 'saddled and bridled' in the same manner for both men and women.[22] The only portrayal of Mary riding a horse is a watercolour sketch of her surrender at Carberry Hill in June 1567 (see Plate 4), and it shows her riding and facing sideways on a horse which was being led.[23] Illustrations of side-saddle riding where the woman faces forwards with her feet at different levels are clearly distinguishable from portrayals of women riding with a platform stirrup, because the rider's feet on a platform stirrup are both at the same level. In addition, the person riding side-saddle would also be holding the reins and controlling the horse. While it might be reading too much into this rough sketch, it would appear that Mary was not on a side-saddle as has been suggested, but on a side-facing saddle.[24] Her feet in the sketch are at the same level and not at different heights as they would have been on a side-saddle. Mary was still wearing a borrowed red skirt which reached half-way down her legs, which was probably not appropriate for riding side-saddle or astride, and so it would appear that in an attempt to maintain some sort of dignity in the situation she had chosen or been given the side-facing saddle, a recognised style for special occasions.[25] As pointed out in Chapter 5, it also demonstrated her loss of control.[26]

Side-saddle

Side-saddle riding had been current from at least the thirteenth century, but the earliest versions are best described as proto-side-saddle rather than true side-saddle. In proto-side-saddle riding there were no pommels on the saddle and the lady's legs, which were both on the same side of the horse, were supported in two stirrups, one on a longer stirrup leather than the other.[27]

Much of the evidence for the proto-side-saddle comes from contemporary illustrations. Contamine gives several thirteenth-century examples, the best of which is a painting on the vault of the chapel of St Julien in Petit Quevilly in Rouen where the Virgin Mary is shown riding side-saddle with two stirrups, with one leg bent more than the other.[28] The horse is, however, still being led by a servant, as Mary holds Jesus with both hands. There is also a rather confusing reference in the early thirteenth-century poem *Histoire de Guillaume le Maréchal* where events in 1141 are being described, which suggests the use of a side-saddle. When the empress Matilda was fleeing from

---

[22] Brantôme, *Book of the Ladies*, 100.
[23] The National Archives, MPF 1/366/2 extracted from SP52/13.
[24] H. Smailes and D. Thomson, *The Queen's Image* (Edinburgh, 1987), 36.
[25] *CSPF 1566–8*, no. 1313, p. 254; Teulet, *Relations Politiques*, ii, 303; Guy, *My Heart is My Own*, 343.
[26] See p. 98.
[27] Contamine, 'Dames à cheval', 210–11.
[28] For the church's website see http://www.petit-quevilly.fr/histoire/histoire/chapelle-saint-julien/ [accessed 27 August 2020].

APPENDIX II: EQUESTRIANISM

London, her companions told her that she was holding them up because she was riding '*en seant*', translated by the editors as side-saddle, and could not spur the horse. Her companions instructed her to separate her legs and ride over the saddle bow, which she duly did.[29] Riding '*en seant*', sitting, actually meant riding sitting on a side-facing saddle.[30] Matilda, therefore, could have changed from riding on a side-facing saddle to riding side-saddle with one leg over the saddle bow just as side-saddle riding was described in the sixteenth century, but it is more likely that she changed to riding astride, enabling her to use two spurs rather than one.[31]

When true side-saddle riding appeared, the woman's right leg was placed round the saddle bow and bent to a greater degree than in proto-side-saddle and in a higher position, which offered greater stability and more speed. There is an illustration, in the *Berlin Hours of Mary of Burgundy* compiled in *c.* 1480 which was copied into the *Book of Hours of Joanna I of Castile* around 1500, in which a woman is shown holding the reins and sitting with both legs on the left or far side of the horse from the viewer. She is facing forward and not in the kind of three-quarters forward position seen in the proto-side-saddle illustrations. This is one of the earliest illustrations of genuine side-saddle riding with the right leg over the saddle bow.[32]

Based on the reminiscences of Brantôme, it is often stated that Catherine de Medici introduced side-saddle riding into France. According to this court gossip, she did so to keep up with Francis I more easily when he was hunting and to show off her shapely legs. Despite Brantôme's claims, Catherine may not have been the first to put her leg round the saddle bow, but what she did was to introduce this style of riding to the French court and make it popular and acceptable. She rode side-saddle with one leg round the saddle or the pommel of the saddle and the other leg stretched into a stirrup.[33] Brantôme, however, also wrote that it was Christine, duchess of Lorraine, who was the first to ride side-saddle because, he said, she always rode with stirrup and pommel and not with the *planchette*. She had been taught how to ride in this manner by her aunt Marie, queen of Hungary and governor of the Netherlands from 1531 to 1555, who, he wrote, may also have taught Catherine de Medici.[34] Marie had visited France in 1538 and hunted with Francis I in the forest of Compiègne and it has been suggested that this would have been an opportunity for Catherine to have learned to ride side-saddle

[29] *History of William the Marshall*, ed. and trans. F. J. Holden and S. Gregory, with notes by D. Crouch, 2 vols (London, 2002), i, 13, lines 213–24.
[30] Contamine, 'Dames à cheval', 212.
[31] Veauvy, *Cavalières Amazones*, 42, considers that Matilda was riding on a side-facing saddle with a removable back and changed to riding astride.
[32] BL, Add Ms 35313 ('*Book of Hours of Joanna I of Castille*'), fo. 158v. Available at: http://www.bl.uk/manuscripts/FullDisplay.aspx?ref=Add_MS_3513 [accessed 27 August 2020].
[33] Ferrière, *Les Chasses de François 1er*, 47–9; Frieda, *Catherine de Medici*, 50, 311; Brantôme, *The Book of the Ladies*, 53.
[34] Adams, 'The Queenes Majestie', 151; Brantôme, *The Book of the Ladies*, 274.

APPENDIX II: EQUESTRIANISM

from Marie, assuming that Brantôme's gossip written down many years later is accurate.[35] Certainly the style was widespread by mid-century, when the French ambassador to the Netherlands in 1566 discussed its spread in the courts of France and the Netherlands with Marguerite de Parma.[36]

The first mention of the side-saddle proper in Scotland is in 1597, but there is evidence which suggests that this type of saddle may have been current in Scotland earlier in the sixteenth century.[37] The entries in the treasurer's accounts relating to 'saddilis of frans' in 1508, 'ane franche sadill', saddles 'of the frenche fassioun', and 'frenche ladyis saddilis' in 1537 and 1538 do sound like references to side-saddles in the French style, and certainly in Europe riding side-saddle could be referred to as riding *à la francaise*.[38] However, French-style saddles were also made for men and the style of the saddles made for French women is not specified.[39]

Chapter 5 has explained that the first clear evidence in Scotland of side-saddle riding proper occurs in September 1561, when Mary ordered several harnesses for her female attendants including saddle cushions with only one stirrup attached.[40] The appearance of side-saddle in Scotland at this time is supported by its contemporaneous arrival in England, where Elizabeth I, on the evidence of her great seal images, was also using a side-saddle in the 1560s. In 1567 an order of iron stirrups for some of her ladies and gentlewomen, at the rate of one per person, is evidence for the use of side-saddles.[41] Side-saddle riding, therefore, was being introduced into Scotland and England around the same time as its popularity was expanding in the courts of Europe.

Riding dress

It is also possible to obtain some idea of the clothes worn by women in Britain when hunting astride by comparing the wardrobes of Mary and Elizabeth I. In both countries the *devantière* seems to have initially been called a safeguard. In the 1560s Elizabeth had riding hoods and a black velvet riding outfit which included a kirtle (skirt and bodice), a gown, and a cloak. By the 1570s, however, she had changed to wearing an apron-like skirt like the *devantière*,

---

[35] Veauvy, *Cavalières Amazones*, 61–4; *Letters and Papers Foreign and Domestic of Henry VIII*, ed. James Gardner (London, 1893), 13:2, nos 680, 692; *Catalogue des Actes de François 1er* (Paris, 1989), iii, nos 10362–68, 10386.

[36] Ferrière, *Les Chasses de François 1er*, 49.

[37] *DOST*, 'side-saddle', where the reference is to *Charters and Documents Relating to Burgh of Paisley 1163–1665* (Edinburgh, 1902), 192.

[38] *TA*, ii, 206; vi, 434; vii, 98; Adams, 'The Queenes Majestie', 151; Ferrière, *Les Chasses de François 1er*, 65.

[39] *TA*, ii, 206; iii, 399; vi, 336, 434; vii, 98, 205, 400.

[40] See p. 100. *TA*, x, 65–6.

[41] Adams, 'The Queenes Majestie', 152–3.

APPENDIX II: EQUESTRIANISM

called a safeguard, which had strings to tie to feet or to the stirrups.[42] There are references to 'saifgards' in Scotland in the reign of James VI, but 'wardegard' was used with the same meaning in the 1550s.[43] They were made of buckram or fustian and were ordered for regent Arran's wife and daughter between 1551 and 1553, but there is no reference to them in the treasurer's accounts thereafter.[44] *DOST* interprets 'wardegards' as containers or bags to protect clothes, but they were also safeguards used when riding side-saddle or astride.[45] By Mary's reign the treasurer's accounts refer to 'dewanters', the Scots version of *devantières*. Dewanters, therefore, were not all stomachers or aprons as Antonia Fraser and *DOST* have suggested.[46] When dewanters were ordered along with riding cloaks and hoods as in France and were made of heavier material such as three to five ells of serge of Florence, they would have been *devantières* for riding.[47] When Mary ordered a riding cloak and skirt made of black serge of Florence for herself, along with fifteen cloaks and skirts of black stemming, a woollen worsted cloth, for her female companions, they were all, presumably, to be used for riding.[48] It has been suggested that the riding skirt in England may have been shorter than the usual ladies' gown, and that seems to have been the style worn by Catherine de Medici.[49] If Mary thought of copying this style, the Scottish weather may have given her other ideas.

The stories of Mary wearing breeches, which historians mention but for which they give no sources, presumably refer to the wearing of *chausses*, which can mean stockings, hose, or breeches.[50] Hose were like socks tied under the knee, but men also had upper hose which covered the thigh and were tied to the lower hose or stockings. For men, riding hose could be a combination of both of the above, while breeches usually went from the waist to just below the knee and were fuller and sometimes padded at the top.[51] In Scotland, as mentioned in Chapter 5, Mary had a regular supply of *chausses*, some of which, depending on the materials used, were stockings or upper hose, while others were more like breeches or riding hose.[52]

---

[42] Adams, 'The Queenes Majestie', 153–4; Janet Arnold, *Queen Elizabeth's Wardrobe Unlocked* (Leeds, 1988), 142.
[43] *DOST*, 'saifgard'.
[44] Schuessler-Bond, *Dressing the Scottish Court*, 104, 395, 399, 404, 431, 447, 449, 450.
[45] Schuessler-Bond, *Dressing the Scottish Court*, 104.
[46] Fraser, *Mary Queen of Scots*, 225; *DOST*, 'dewanter'.
[47] E.g., *TA*, xi, 349 (1562); *Inventaires de la Royne d'Écosse*, 147 (1564); *TA*, xii, 42, 351, 398 (1566).
[48] *TA*, xi, 66.
[49] Adams, 'The Queenes Majestie', 153.
[50] Cotgrave, *Dictionary*, 'chausse'. The Scottish sources for her *chausses* are given in Chapter 5, nn. 19, 20 on p. 100.
[51] Schuessler-Bond, *Dressing the Scottish Court*, 57–9, 109.
[52] *Inventaires de la Royne d'Écosse*, 133, 136, 137, 147.

Glossary

accourre	the kill zone at the end of a *chasse aux toiles*
affinity	the followers, kin, tenants, and allies of a lord
assart	an area cleared from a wood to make way for agriculture, usually surrounded by a bank and ditch to mark off the assart and to deter wild animals
avery	the place where provender for horses was kept
bêtes noires	bear, boar, fox, otter
bêtes rousses or *fauves*	red deer, roe deer, fallow deer, hare
bow and stable hunt	a hunt which could be held in a park where selected deer were driven to the waiting hunters, who would shoot the deer with arrows or release hounds to catch them
breuils	a closed area for animals, a reserve for game like a deer park
buisson	an area covered with bushes which was prepared for hunting by growing hedges to assist driving game into clearings where hunters waited to shoot it. Ferrières in his *Roy Modus* has a chapter entitled 'Comment tailler les buissons pour les bêtes noires de déduit royal' (How to arrange the *buissons* for black beasts for the king's pastime), which is about checking the area for game, arranging men for the *défenses*, and setting up extra nets or fences.
caiche	the Scots name for *jeu de paume* or royal tennis played with rackets
chasse aux toiles	hunting by driving game to waiting archers or into a kill zone with the help of screens or nets
chasse par force	hunting by chasing game with hounds
commissary court	courts which replaced the ecclesiastical consistory courts which collapsed after the Reformation in Scotland. They had a similar jurisdiction over matters such as marriage, divorces, and wills.

GLOSSARY

composition	a payment made to compensate the king and injured party which led to the end of legal proceedings. This was not a pardon.
consistory court	courts where bishops exercised jurisdiction over executry and matrimonial cases. They broke down after the Reformation in Scotland.
coppice	the practice of cutting wood and allowing new wood to grow from the stump or stool. Animals were prevented from grazing in a freshly cut coppice till the young shoots were strong enough to survive. When the wood was cut again depended on what type of wood was required. The coppice might be cut again in six or eight years for rods, twenty years for poles, or one hundred years for timber.
coupe	an area of a coppiced wood. A coppiced wood would have several coupes or sections all set to be cut at different times on different coppice cycles.
couple	an A-framed roof support made up of several pieces of wood
coursing	chasing game with the same pack hounds throughout the hunt without the help of relays. This could also mean setting one or two hounds to chase game when released from a fold or pen.
court of session	the principal judicial body of lay and ecclesiastical judges initiated by James V in 1532 to try civil cases
curée	the ceremonial rewarding of the dogs after the death of the game being hunted, usually combined with the butchering of the carcase
défenses	lines of men set out to stand still and ensure that the game did not leave the intended path along which they were being driven towards archers or into a kill zone
elrick	a trap to help to surround and kill deer. Such traps could be two converging walls or barriers, circular enclosures, or narrow valleys.
feu-ferme tenure	a tenure whereby the tenant in the sixteenth century paid a greatly increased rent for land in order to hold it heritably
fold	a small enclosure to hold a small number of animals
forest	in English this word can mean either a hunting reserve or a large wood

GLOSSARY

foresta	in Scotland the Latin version of this word usually referred to a hunting reserve. In France in the Carolingian era it meant a hunting reserve, but thereafter it more commonly meant a large wooded area.
forêt	originally a hunting reserve, but after the tenth century it meant a large wooded area
forrest	the Scots version of this word. In Scotland it could mean both a hunting reserve and a large area of wood. The arrival of French speakers in the eleventh and twelfth centuries who used *fôret* to mean wood no doubt influenced the use of the Scots forrest. In Scotland it was used more frequently than *foresta* to mean woodland.
fort-holding	the siege of a mock fort in which the king could either hold the fort and fend off the forces of war and chaos, or where the king representing the forces of good would capture the castle representing the forces of evil
fumées	the fumes or droppings of deer
garennes	French word for a hunting reserve often within a *forêt*. It was the French word for an unenclosed hunting reserve after the tenth century, when *forêt* came to mean a wooded area. By the thirteenth century it could also refer to an enclosed area to nurture rabbits.
gelding	a castrated male horse, which is easier to control
greater game	red deer, fallow deer, roe deer. Wolves were sometimes included as greater game.
greyhound	a hound which was fast, hunted by sight, and was often large enough to attack a deer
hackney	an ambling mare often ridden by women with a side-facing saddle
haie	a fence or hedge. It could also refer to the area enclosed by the hedge. In a hunting context this could resemble a park or a *buisson*.
herbage	grazing on summer grass
high forest	a forest comprising tall timber trees

GLOSSARY

hunting mound	a mound or hillock where several hunters awaited driven game and on which or behind which they could conceal themselves from the driven game. It could also refer to a hillock where the chief hunter organised the placing of the beaters in a drive. If it was a feature more like a hill rather than a hunting hillock, it could be the spot where the chief hunter watched the hunt.
italic hand	created in Italy, its use was an indicator of the Renaissance and a mark of education. It had clear and simple letter forms as compared with secretary hand.
jeu de maille	a game which resembled croquet, played outside or inside with a ball and a stick like a mallet
jeu de paume	real tennis, played with rackets in the sixteenth century but originally played with the hand
labour services	work which a lord demanded from his tenants, usually unfree serfs or neyfs, in return for their land, e.g., cutting hay, ploughing, carting, and carrying
lesser game	hare, rabbit, otter, badger, wildcat
letter of fire and sword	an order issued by Scottish monarchs in the sixteenth century to certain nobles authorising them to pursue certain offenders or rebels by burning their houses and killing them
lunkart	from the Gaelic 'longphort', which meant a shieling, an encampment, a palace, or a hunting booth. In the sixteenth-century maps of Timothy Pont it meant shielings where herdsmen stayed with their animals in the summer. In Glen Tilt it described the humble dwellings built for Mary's hunt there in 1564.
lymer	a scenting hound trained not to bark which was used to locate game
masque	a courtly entertainment with characters having allegorical roles who performed on a stage with words and music, usually to glorify the monarch
occupatio	the Roman law principle that game as *res nullius* belonged to whoever caught and killed it
pannage	grazing pigs on beech mast and acorns, for which permission was usually required from the lord
parc	a name for the kill zone at the end of the *chasse aux toiles*

GLOSSARY

park	an area enclosed by banks, ditches, and fences or walls in which deer and other game were held captive and nourished for hunting, killing for the larder, or transporting to restock other parks
purlieu	the area around a hunting forest where some forest restrictions applied, often relating to hunting
rauch	a hound which hunted by scent
relays	two or three couples of hounds placed along the expected route of a *par force* hunt to join the hunt when it reached them
remission	a form of royal pardon which required the accused to pay compensation within forty days
res nullius	the Roman law principle that game belonged to no one, and so anyone entitled to hunt could kill game anywhere
réserve	the area of wood or forest surrounded by ropes or screens in a *chasses aux toiles* to ensure the game did not escape the drive to the kill zone
rods and poles	smaller wood, as opposed to large timbers, which was divided into rods and poles: rods being thinner and more flexible than poles. Rods and poles were used for fences, wattles, agricultural implements, utensils and furniture. They were valuable commodities.
running hound	a hound which hunted by scent
seat	the place where hunters waited for the driven game and where or near where they could be entertained with food and drink before the hunt arrived
secretary hand	the joined-up writing of the sixteenth century which was meant to be written quickly and read everywhere without difficulty
shaws	a Scots word for woods that were coppiced
shieling	the humble huts and houses used by herdsmen when grazing their herds on the summer pastures in the hills. The pastures were also referred to as shielings.
soume	calculating how many animals could be grazed on pastures. For instance, depending on the quality of the pasture, one soume could equal 1 cow, 2 mares, or 6 ewes. The laird might give a tenant ten soumes; the tenant could then graze 10 cows, or 20 horses, or 60 sheep, perhaps with foals or lambs.

GLOSSARY

stable	the beaters who drove game towards archers waiting at a predetermined point. The stable in a bow and stable hunt in England was similar but could be stationary, like the *défenses* in France.
standing	the spot where the hunters awaited a drive in a bow and stable hunt
stools	the base from which shoots grow after a tree has been cut when being coppiced
summertowns	the collections of shielings/buildings to which people moved in the summer when they left their main settlements to take their herds to hill pastures
tail fork	the wooden frame for the gable end of a house
timber	the larger wood used in major construction for high-status buildings, artillery, ships, etc.
tinchell	the stable who drove game to the waiting archers. It is a Scots word derived from the Gaelic, timchoill.
toils	nets
tolbooth	the municipal building in a medieval Scottish burgh where the burgh court was held, where the town council met, and where prisoners were confined
triumph	a court festival designed to glorify the monarch which could include triumphal arches, tournaments, masques, fort-holdings, music, and ballet
tryst	the spot where archers awaited driven game or where relays awaited the *par force* hunt
unharbour	the process of starting a hunt by raising the deer from the shelter where it spent the night
vert and venison	the vert, the vegetation, and the venison, the game, which were reserved in hunting forests
wood	wood which was smaller than timber

Bibliography

Primary Sources

Unprinted

A. K. Bell Library (Perth)
MS249: *The Atholl Experience* being the papers of John Kerr

Bibliothèque nationale de France (Paris)
Fonds Français
Ms Français 616: Gaston Phoebus, *Livre de Chasse*
Ms Français 2691: Chartier, *Chronique de Charles VII, roi de France*
Ms Français 3133: *Recueil des lettres et des pièces originales*
Ms Français 5837: *Le Débats des Hérauts d'Armes de France et d'Angleterre*
Fonds Latin
Ms Latin 8660: *Mariae Stuart, Scotorum Reginae et Galliae Delphinae, epistolae variae, latinè et gallicè*
Ms Latin 1156B: *Book of Hours of Marguerite d'Orléans*, available at: https://gallica.bnf.fr/ark:/12148/btv1b52502614h

Drummond Estate Office (Muthill, Perthshire)
The Property of Mr and Mrs Drummond Birrell, surveyed by James Knox (1810).

British Library (London)
Add Ms 35313: (*'Book of Hours of Joanna I of Castille'*), available at: http://www.bl.uk/manuscripts/FullDisplay.aspx?ref=Add_MS_3513
Royal Ms 2 B vii: (*'Queen Mary's Psalter'*), available at: http://www.bl.uk/manuscripts/Viewer.aspx?ref=royal_ms_2_b_vii_f084r
Yates Thomson MS 13: (*'Taymouth Book of Hours'*), available at: http://www.bl.uk/manuscripts/Viewer.aspx?ref=yates_thompson_ms_13_fs001r

Museé Condé (Chantilly)
Ms 65: *Les Très Riches Heures du Duc de Berry*, available at: https://les-tres-riches-heures.chateaudechantilly.fr

National Collection of Air Photographs (Edinburgh)
B0122/CPE/SCOT/UK/0194: Air photographs of Glenfinglas 1946

BIBLIOGRAPHY

The National Archives (London)

MPF 1/366/: Three items extracted from SP 52/13 – a sketch of Mary's surrender at Carberry Hill, near Edinburgh, Scotland, available at: https://www.nationalarchives.gov.uk/education/resources/uniting-kingdoms/

National Library of Scotland (Edinburgh)

Adv. Ms. 34.2.8: ('Pont's Texts')
Adv. Ms. 70.2.9: Pont 20 ('Glen Tilt')
Adv. Ms 70.2.9: Pont 19 ('The Forest of Atholl')
Adv. Ms. 70.2.10: Gordon 51 ('A Map of the basin of the river Forth')
Adv. Ms. 70.2.9: Pont 21 ('Lower Glenalmond; Strathearn')
Adv. Ms 29.2.5: Balcarres Papers

National Record of Archives for Scotland (Edinburgh)

NRAS, 3663/17/153, *Cropping Book, Falkland Estates with Farms and Field Plans indexed 1909–1932*. Accessible in Falkland Estate Office, The Stables, Falkland.
NRAS, *Scone Palace*, MS 776 (Mansfield Papers). Accessible in Dundee University Library Archive Department.

National Records of Scotland (Edinburgh)

C2: *Registrum Magni Sigilli Regum Scottorum* (Register of the Great Seal of the Kings of Scots)
E1/6: Books of Responde
E31/3, 4, and 5: Libri Domicilii
E32/2, 3, and 5: Libri Emptorum
E33/3, 4, 5, 7, and 8: Despenses de la Maison Royale
E34/28/2: Mary Queen of Scots, Accounts of the Queen's Stable
E35/3: Accounts of silks and other items delivered from the wardrobe by Servais de Conde, valet de chambre
E777: Forfeited Estate Perth
GD50/186: Menzies Writs
GD112/1/149: Mounted Documents. Royal warrant from Mary Queen of Scots to Duncan Campbell of Glenlyon
GD160/129: Legal papers regarding heritable keepership of Glenartney Forest
GD160/528: Royal letters and charters in Drummond of Perth Archives
RH2/1/5–7: Transcripts of Justiciary Court Books (Old Series)
RHP 3405: Grazings of Callander and Glenartney in annexed estate of Perth 1772. A copy of this map is also available on Scotland's Places website, https://scotlandsplaces.gov.uk/record/nrs/RHP3405/plan-of-grazings-of-callander-and-glenartney-in-annexed-estate-of-perth [accessed 22 September 2023]

Wurttembergische Landesbibliothek (Stuttgart)

Cod.hist.qt.141: Ritter Georg von Ehingen Selbstbiographie, available at: https://digital.wlb-stuttgart.de/sammlungen/sammlungsliste/werksansicht?tx_dlf%5Bdouble%5D=0&tx_dlf%5Bid%5D=17735&tx_dlf%5Border%5D=title&tx_dlf%5Bpage%5D=101&cHash=e129cbfcf032a1 3f71648f5be084b339

BIBLIOGRAPHY

Printed

Accounts of the Lord High Treasurer of Scotland, ed. T. Dickson *et al.* 13 vols (Edinburgh, 1877–1970)

Accounts of the Masters of Works, ed. Henry M. Paton (Edinburgh, 1957)

Acts of the Lords of Council in Public Affairs 1501–1554: Selections from Acta Dominorum Concilii, ed. R. K. Hannay (Edinburgh, 1932)

Aelred of Rievaulx, *Epistola de Genealogia Regum Anglorum*, in *Patrologia Cursus Completus*, ed. J. P. Migne, 195 (Paris, 1855)

Bannatyne Ms, ed. W. Tod Ritchie, 4 vols (Edinburgh, 1928–34)

Barbour, John, *The Bruce*, ed. A. A. M. Duncan (Edinburgh, 1997)

Barclay, William, *De Regno et Regali Potestate Adversus Buchannanum, Brutum, Boucherium, et Reliquos Monarchamochos* (Paris, 1600)

Bellenden, John, *History and Chronicles of Scotland written in Latin by Hector Boece and translated by John Bellenden*, ed. T. Maitland, 3 vols (Edinburgh, 1821)

Boethius, Hector, *Scotorum Historiae* (Paris, 1527)

Bower, Walter, *Scotichronicon*, ed. D. E. R. Watt, 9 vols (Aberdeen, 1993–8)

Brantôme, Pierre de Bourdeille Abbé de, *Book of the Ladies* (*Illustrious Dames*), trans. Katherine D. Wormeley (Boston, 1899)

Brézé, Jacques de, *La Livre de Chasse du Grand Seneschal de Normandye*, ed. J. Pichon (Paris, 1858)

Buchanani, Georgii, Opera Omnia, ed. Thomas Ruddiman (Leyden, 1725)

Budé, Guillaume, *Traitté de la Venerie*, trans. into French from Latin by Louis Le Roy for Charles IX, ed. Henri Chevreul (Paris, 1861)

Calendar of Documents relating to Scotland, ed. J. Bain, 4 vols (Edinburgh, 1881–8)

Calendar of State Papers Foreign, Elizabeth, ed. Joseph Stevenson *et al.* 25 vols (London, 1865–1950)

Calendar of State Papers relating to Scotland and Mary Queen of Scots, ed. J. Bain *et al.* 12 vols (Edinburgh, 1898–1952)

Calendar of State Papers Venice and Northern Italy, ed. Raymond Brown and C. Cavendish Bentinck 37 vols (London, 1890)

Catalogue des Actes de François II, ed. Marie-Thérèse Martel, Centre Nationale de La Recherche Scientifique 2 vols (Paris, 1991)

Clancy, Thomas Owen (ed.), *The Triumph Tree, Scotland's Earliest Poetry 550–1350* (Edinburgh, 1998)

Coke, John, *Débats des Hérauts d'Armes de France et d'Angleterre*, ed. Leopold Pannier (Paris, 1877)

Columella, Lucius Junius Moderatus, *De Re Rustica*, trans. H Bash, Loeb Library (London, 1948)

Cooper, Charles Purton (ed.), *Correspondance Diplomatique de Bertrand de Salignac de La Mothe Fénélon* (Paris and London, 1840)

Cowan, Samuel (ed.), *The Last Days of Mary Stuart and the Journal of Bourgoyne her Physician* (London, 1907)

Débat entre Deux Dames sur le Passetemps Des Chiens et Des Oiseaux, ed. Paul Lacroix and Ernest Jullien (Paris, 1882)

Desjardins, Abel, *Négociations Diplomatiques de la France avec la Toscane*, 6 vols (Paris, 1865)

Diurnal of Remarkable Occurrents 1513–1575 (Edinburgh, 1833)

Donaldson, J. A., *Husbandry Anatomized, An Enquiry into the present manner of teiling and manuring the Ground in Scotland* (Edinburgh, 1697)

BIBLIOGRAPHY

Du Cerceau, Jacques Androuet, *Les Plus Excellents Bastiments de France*, 2 vols (Paris,1579). The url is https://gallica.bnf.fr/ark:/12148/bpt6k10411354/f7.item

Duanaire Finn, The Book of the Lays of Fionn, ed. Eoin McNeil (London, 1908)

Excerpta e Libris Domicilii Jacobi Quinti, Bannatyne Club (Edinburgh, 1836)

Exchequer Rolls of Scotland, ed. George Burnett *et al.* 23 vols (Edinburgh, 1878–1908)

Ferrières, Henri de, *Le Livre du Roy Modus et de la Royne Ratio*, ed. Gunnar Tilander (Paris, 1932)

Fordun, Johanis de, *Chronica Gentis Scotorum*, ed. and trans. W. F. Skene, 4 vols (Edinburgh, 1871–2)

Fouilloux, Jacques du, *La Vénerie de Jacques du Fouilloux ... et L'Adolescence de l'Autheur* (Poitiers, 1561). BnF, RES M-S-33. Available online, https://gallica.bnf.fr/ark:/12148/bpt6k15131176?rk=150215;2

Heroic Poetry from the Book of the Dean of Lismore, ed. N. Ross (Edinburgh, 1939)

Historical Manuscripts Commission, Fourth Report of the (London, 1874)

Historical Manuscripts Commission, Sixth Report of the (London, 1877)

Holyrood Ordinale, ed. Eeles, F. C., in *The Book of the Old Edinburgh Club*, 7 (Edinburgh,1914)

Illustrations of the Topography and Antiquities of the Shires of Aberdeen and Banff, 4 vols (Aberdeen, 1847–1869)

The Institutes of Justinian, ed. T. Abdy and B. Walker (Cambridge, 1876)

Inventaire des meubles bijoux et livres estant a Chenonceaux le huit Janvier MDCII (Paris 1857), Appendix, 'Les Triomphes Faictz a l'entrée de Francoys II et de Marye Stuart au Chasteau de Chenonceau 31 Mars 1559'

Inventaires de la Royne d'Écosse, ed. J. Robertson (Edinburgh, 1863)

Journal Privé de Élisabeth de Valois in Henri de la Ferrière, *Deux Années de Mission à St Petersbourg* (Paris, 1867), 236–241. The url is https://babel.hathitrust.org/cgi/pt?id=hvd.hnxh2f&view=1up&seq=254.

Knox, John, *History of the Reformation in Scotland*, ed. W. C. Dickinson, 2 vols (London, 1949)

Labanoff, Alexandre (ed.), *Lettres, Instructions et Mémoires de Marie Stuart* (London, 1844)

Leland, J., *De Rebus Britannicis Collecteana, Account of John Younge Somerset Herald* (London, 1770)

Lesley, John, *De Origine, moribus et rebus gestis Scotorum* (Amsterdam, 1675)

——, *History of Scotland from the death of King James I in 1436 to the year 1561*, ed. Thomas Thomson, Bannatyne Club (1830)

——, *Historie of Scotland by Jhone Leslie*, trans. Father J. Dalrymple in 1596, eds Father E. Cody and William Murison, 2 vols, Scottish Text Society (Edinburgh, 1888 and 1895)

Letter Books of Amias Paulet, ed. John Morris (London, 1874)

Letters and Papers Relating to Patrick Master of Gray, ed. Thomas Thomson (Edinburgh, 1835)

Letters from a Gentleman in the North of Scotland to his Friend in London ... Likewise an Account of the Highlands with the Customs and Manners of the Highlanders to which is added A Letter Relating to the Military Way among the Mountains begun in the Year 1726, ed. R. Jamieson, 2 vols (London, 1818)

Letters of James IV 1510–1513, ed. R. L. Mackie (Edinburgh, 1953)

Letters of James V, ed. R. K. Hannay and D. Hay (Edinburgh, 1954)

BIBLIOGRAPHY

Lettres de Catherine de Médicis, ed. Ferrière, Hector de la, 12 vols. (Paris, 1888–1943)

Liber Sancte Marie de Melros, Bannatyne Club (Edinburgh, 1837)

Lodge, Edmund (ed.), *Illustrations of British History, Biography and Manners in Reigns of Henry VIII, Edward VI, Mary, Elizabeth, James I. Exhibited in a Series of Original Papers* (London, 1791)

Master of Game by Edward second duke of York, ed. William A. and F. Baillie-Grohman (London, 1904)

Melville of Hallhill, Sir James, *Memorials of His Own Life 1549–1593* (Edinburgh, 1827)

Memoirs of Marguerite de Valois, Queen of Navarre, ed. Violet Fane (London, 1892)

Meyer, Kuno (ed.), *Fianaigecht* (Dublin, 1910)

Montaiglon, Anatole de (ed.), *The Latin Themes of Mary Stuart* (London, 1855)

Moryson, Fynes, *An Itinerary containing his ten yeeres travel through the twelve dominions of Germany, Bohmerland … Italy, Turky, France, England, Scotland & Ireland* (repr. Glasgow, 1908, orig. London, 1617)

Munro, R. W. (ed.), *Monro's Western Isles of Scotland and Genealogies of the Clans 1549* (Edinburgh, 1961)

Nau, Claude, *History of the Reign of Mary Stewart from the murder of Riccio until her flight into England*, ed. J. Stevenson (Edinburgh, 1883)

Négociations Diplomatiques de la France avec la Toscane, ed. Abel Desjardins, 6 vols (Paris, 1865)

New Statistical Account of Scotland, 15 vols (Edinburgh, 1834–45)

Old Statistical Account of Scotland, ed. John Sinclair, 21 vols (Edinburgh, 1791–99)

Oran na Comhachaig (The Song of the Owl), ed. and trans. P. Menzies (Edinburgh, 2012)

Ordnance Survey Name Book 27, Fife and Kinross-shire OSI/13/21/53

Ordonnances Des Rois de France; Regne de François 1er, Imprimière Nationale (Paris, 1902)

Paris, Louis, *Négociations, Lettres et Pièces Relative à la Règne de François II* (Paris, 1841)

Phoebus, Gaston, *Livre de Chasse*, ed. Gunnar Tilander (Karlshamn, 1971)

Pitcairn, Robert (ed.), *Criminal Trials in Scotland from 1488 to 1624*, 3 vols (Edinburgh, 1933)

Pitscottie, Robert Lindsay of, *The Historie and Cronicles of Scotland*, ed. A. J. G. Mackay, 3 vols (Edinburgh, 1899–1911)

Régnier de la Planche, Louis, *Histoire de L'Estat de la France sous la Regne de François II*, ed. M. E. Mennechet, 2 vols (Paris, 1836)

Quoniam Attachiamenta, ed. T. D. Fergus, Stair Society, vol. 44 (Edinburgh, 1996)

Recueil des Anciennes Lois Françaises, ed. Isambert (Paris, 1821–1833)

Regesta Regum Scottorum, ii, The Acts of William I, 1165–1214, ed. G. W. S. Barrow (Edinburgh, 1971)

Register of the Privy Council of Scotland, ed. J. H. Burton *et al*. First Series, 14 vols (Edinburgh, 1877–1933)

Registrum Magni Sigilli Regum Scottorum, Register of the Great Seal of the Kings of the Scots, ed. J. Thompson *et al*. 11 vols (Edinburgh, 1882–1914)

Registrum Secreti Sigilli, Register of the Privy Seal of the Kings of the Scots, ed. M. Livingstone *et al*. 8 vols (Edinburgh, 1908–1982)

BIBLIOGRAPHY

Relations politiques de la France et de l'Espagne avec l'Écosse au XVIe siècle, ed. A. Teulet (Paris, 1862)

Reports on Annexed Estates 1755–69, ed. Virginia Wills (Edinburgh, 1973)

Salel, Hugue, *Chasse Royale*, in *Le Debat Entre Deux Dames*, ed. Lacroix and Jullien, 59–81

Salnove, Robert de, *La Vénerie Royale* (Paris, 1665)

Scottish Annals from English Chroniclers AD500–1286, ed. Alan O. Anderson and David Nutt (London, 1908)

Scottish Verse from the Book of the Dean of Lismore, ed. W. J. Watson (Edinburgh, 1937)

Sheriff Court Book of Fife 1515–1522, ed. William C. Dickinson (Edinburgh, 1928)

Shorter Poems of Gavin Douglas, ed. Priscilla Bawcutt (Edinburgh, 1967)

Silva Gadelica, ed. S. H. O'Grady, 2 vols (London, 1892)

Statistics of the Annexed and Forfeited Estates 1755–6, HMSO (Edinburgh, 1973)

Teulet, Alexandre, *Relations Politiques de la France et d'Espagne avec l'Écosse au XVIe siècle*, 5 vols. (Paris 1862)

——, *Papiers d'État Relatifs à l'Histoire de l'Écosse au 16e Siècle*, Bannatyne Club, 3 vols (Edinburgh, 1852–1866)

Les Triomphes Faictz a L'Entrée du Roy a Chenonceau Le Dymanche Dernier Jour de Mars (Tours, 1559) in *Inventaires de Meubles Bijoux et Livres estant a Chenonceau le huit Janvier MCCIII* (Paris, 1856)

La Vénerie de Jacques du Fouilloux, ed. Robin and L. Faure (Paris, 1864)

La Vénerie de Jacques du Fouilloux … et L'Adolescence de l'Autheur, ed. Gunnar Tilander (Karlshamn, 1967)

Virgil Solis Single Sheet Prints II, Holstein's German Engravings, Etchings and Woodcuts 1400–1700, vol. 65, ed. D. Beaujean and G. Bartrum (Rotterdam, 2004)

Wallhausen, Jean Jacques, *Art Militaire à Cheval. Instruction et Fondements de la Cavallerie* (Frankfurt, 1616)

The Works of Sir David Lindsay, ed. Douglas Hamer (Edinburgh, 1931)

Wyntoun, Andrew, *The Original Chronicle of Andrew of Wyntoun*, ed. F. J. Amours (Edinburgh, 1903–14)

Websites relating to primary sources

Bibliothèque nationale de France, https://archivesetmanuscrits.bnf.fr (accessed between 2016 and 2023)

British Library, www.bl.uk (accessed between 2016 and 2022)

Chapel of St Julien, Petit-Quevilly, http://www.petit-quevilly.fr/histoire/histoire/chapelle-saint-julien/

Musée Condé, Chantilly, https://www.musee-conde.fr/fr/

The National Archives, London, https://www.nationalarchives.gov.uk

Records of the Parliaments of Scotland to 1707, ed. K. M. Brown *et al.* (St Andrews 2007–10), available at http://www.rps.ac.uk (accessed between 1916 and 1922)

BIBLIOGRAPHY

Secondary sources

Published

Adams, Simon, 'The Release of Lord Darnley and the Failure of the Amity', in Lynch *Mary Stewart*, 123–153

——, '"The Queenes Majestie … is now become a great huntress": Elizabeth I and the Chase', *The Court Historian*, 18 (2013), 143–164

Addyman, Tom, *Falkland Palace. Preliminary Analytical assessment of the roofs of the south range and stables*, Report for the National Trust for Scotland (2015)

Almond, Richard, *Medieval Hunting* (Stroud, 2003)

——, *Daughters of Artemis: the Huntress in the Middle Ages and Renaissance* (Woodbridge, 2009)

——, 'The Way the Ladies Ride', *History Today*, 62 (2012), 36–9

Ansell, Michael, 'Place-Name Evidence for Woodland and Hunting in Galloway and Carrick', *Scottish Woodland History Discussion Group Notes*, 11 (2006)

Anthenaise, Claude d' and Monique Chatenet (eds), *Chasses princières dans L'Europe de la Renaissance* (Arles, 2007)

Anthenaise, Claude d', 'Chasses aux toiles, chasses en parc', in Anthenaise, *Chasses princières*, 73–100

Armstrong, Elizabeth, *Before Copyright: The French Book Privilege System 1498–1526* (Cambridge, 1990)

Armstrong, W., 'The Justice Ayre in the Border Sheriffdoms 1493–1498' *SHR*, 92 (2013), 1–37

Arnold, Janet, *Queen Elizabeth's Wardrobe Unlocked* (Leeds, 1988)

——, 'Dashing Amazons: The Development of Women's Riding Dress c.500–1900', in Amy de la Haye and Elizabeth Wilson (eds), *Defining Dress: Dress as Object, Meaning and Identity* (Manchester and New York, 1999)

Baillie-Grohman, William A., *Sport in Art: An iconography of Sport covering the period from 1400–1900* (London, 1913)

Bapst, Edmond, *Les Mariages de Jacques V* (Paris, 1889)

Barrow, G. W. S., *Robert Bruce and the Community of the Realm of Scotland* (Edinburgh, 1976)

Bell, D., *The Tennis Court and Stables, Falkland Palace, Statement of Cultural Significance*, Report for National Trust for Scotland (2010)

Belleval, René Marquis de, *Les Derniers Valois François II Charles IX Henri III* (Paris, 1898)

Ben Lawers: An Archaeological Landscape in Time, Scottish Archaeological Internet Reports, 62 (Edinburgh, 2016)

Bil, Albert, *The Shieling 1600–1840: The Case of the Central Scottish Highlands* (Edinburgh, 2001)

Birrel, Jean, 'Deer and Deer Farming in Medieval England', *Agricultural History Review*, 40 (1992), 112–126

Blakeway, Amy, *Regency in Sixteenth-Century Scotland* (Woodbridge, 2015)

Bliss, Susan Dwight, *Collections des Manuscrits, Livres, Estampes et Objets d'Art Relatifs à Marie Stuart Reine de France et d'Écosse en Bibliothèque Nationale* (Paris, 1931)

Boardman, Steve, *The Early Stewart Kings: Robert II and Robert III* (East Linton, 1996)

201

BIBLIOGRAPHY

—— and Julian Goodare (eds), *Kings, Lords and Men in Scotland and Britain 1300–1625: Essays in Honour of Jenny Wormald* (Edinburgh, 2014)

Bocquillon, Ann-Marie, 'Au Moyen Âge, vénerie royale et administrations forestières', in Corvol (ed.), *Forêt et Chasse Xe–XXe siècle*, 113–126.

Bolduc, Benoit, 'In fumo dare lucem. Les Triomphes faictz a l'Entrée du roy a Chenonceau (1559/60)', in Hélène Visentin and Nicolas Russel (eds), *French Ceremonial entries in the Sixteenth century: Events, Image, Text* (Toronto, 2007), 163–87

Bord, Lucien-Jean, and Jean-Pierre Mugg, *La Chasse au Moyen Âge, Occident Latin, VIe–XVe siècle* (Paris, 2008)

Brander, Michael, *Hunting & shooting from the earliest times to the present day* (London, 1971)

Brausewitz, Gunnar, *Hunting: Hunters, game, weapons and hunting methods from the remote past to the present day* (London, 1962)

Broomhall, Susan (ed.), *Women and Power at the French Court 1483–1563* (Amsterdam, 2018)

Brown, Michael, *The Wars of Scotland 1214–1371* (Edinburgh, 2015)

Budé, Guillaume, *Traitté de la Venerie*, trans. into French from Latin by Louis Le Roy for Charles IX, ed. Henri Chevreul (Paris, 1861)

Buridant, Jérôme, 'La forêt et la chasse au XVIe siècle', in Anthenaise, *Chasses princières*, 159–78

Butler, Lance St J. and Peter J. Wordie, *The Royal Game*, Falkland Palace Real Tennis Club (1989)

Butterworth, Philip, 'The Baptisme of Hir darrest Sone in Stirviling', *Medieval English Theatre*, 10 (1988), 26–55

Calderwood, D., *History of the Kirk of Scotland*, ed. Rev. Thomas Thomson, Woodrow Society, 8 vols (Edinburgh, 1842)

Cameron, Jamie, *James V: The Personal rule, 1528–1542* (Edinburgh, 2011)

Carpenter, Sarah, 'Performing Diplomacies: The 1560s Court Entertainments of Mary Queen of Scots', *SHR*, 82 (2003), 194–225

Carradine, David and Simon Price (eds), *Rituals of Royalty: Power and Ceremonial in Traditional Societies* (New York, 1987)

Carroll, Stuart, *Martyrs and Murderers: The Guise Family and the Making of Europe* (Oxford, 2011)

Casset, Marie, *Les Évêques aux Champs: Châteaux et Manoirs des Évêques Normands au Moyen Âge (XIe – XVe siècles)* (Caen, 2007)

Cathcart, Alison, *Kinship and Clientage: Highland Clanship 1451–1609* (Leiden, 2006)

Chalmers, George, *The Life of Mary Queen of Scots* (London, 1822)

Chatenet, Monique, *Chambord* (Paris, 2001)

——, *La Cour de France au XVIe Siècle* (Paris, 2002)

——, 'Un Portrait du "père des veneurs" ', in Anthenaise, *Chasses princières*, 17–42

Chronicles of The Atholl and Tullibardine Families, ed. Atholl, John Seventh duke of, 5 vols (Edinburgh, 1908)

Clark, David, Alice Blackwell and Martin Goldberg, *Early Medieval Scotland: individuals, communities and ideas* (Edinburgh, 2012)

Clark, Kenneth, *The Nude: a Study in Ideal Form* (Princeton, 1953)

BIBLIOGRAPHY

Clarke, J., 'Falkland Palace', *Discovery and Excavation*, 14 (Tisbury, 2013)

Cloulas, Ivan, *Henry II* (Paris, 1985)

——, 'Review of *Catalogue des Actes de François II*, ed. Marie-Thérèse Martel (Paris, 1991)', *Bibliothèque d'Humanisme et Renaissance*, 55 (1993), 189–90

——, *Diane de Poitiers* (Paris, 1997)

Collery, René, 'Evolution de la Forêt de Retz à travers les Âges', *Société Historique Regionale De Villers Cotterêts*, 9 (1963), 151–175.

Contamine, P. and G. Contamine (eds), *Marguerite d'Écosse : reines, princesses, et dames du XVe siècle* (Paris, 1999) 201–217

——, 'Dames à Cheval', in P. and G. Contamine (eds), *Marguerite d'Écosse*, 201–217

Corvol Andrée (ed.), *Forêt et Chasse Xe–XXe siècles* (Paris, 2004)

——, *Histoire de la Chasse, Homme et la Bête* (Paris, 2010)

Cotgrave, Randal, *A French and English Dictionary* (London, 1673)

Cowan, I. B., 'The Roman Connection: Prospects for counter-Reformation during the personal Reign of Mary, Queen of Scots', in Lynch, *Mary Stewart*, 105–122

Cowan, Ian B. (ed.), *The Parishes of Medieval Scotland* (Edinburgh, 1967)

Crépin-Leblond, Thierry, 'Marie Stuart à la cour de France', in Crépin-Leblond *et al. Marie Stuart*, 33–52

——, *et al.*, *Marie Stuart, le destin français d'une reine d'Écosse* (Paris, 2008)

Crone, Anne, *Falkland Palace: a dendrochronological study*, Report for the National Trust of Scotland (2017)

Cummins, John, *The Hound and The Hawk, The Art of Medieval Hunting* (London, 1988)

Cunningham, Ian C. (ed.), *The Nation Survey'd: essays on late sixteenth-century Scotland as depicted by Timothy Pont* (Edinburgh, 2006)

Davidson, Peter, 'The Entry of Mary Stewart into Edinburgh', *Renaissance Studies*, 9 (1995), 416–429

Dawson, Jane E. A., *Campbell Letters*, SHS, 10 (Edinburgh, 1997)

——, *The Politics of Religion in the Age of Mary Queen of Scots: the Earl of Argyll and the struggle for Britain and Ireland* (Cambridge, 2002)

——, *Scotland Reformed 1488–1587* (Edinburgh, 2007)

Dalby, D., *Lexicon of the Medieval German hunt – Middle High German Terms (1059–1500)* (Berlin, 1965)

Derex, Jean-Michel, 'Les parcs de Vincennes et de Boulogne au XVIᵉ siècle', in Anthenaise *Chasses princières*, 251–268

Devèze, Michel, *La Vie de la Forêt Française au XVI Siècle* (Paris, 1961)

——, *Histoire des Forêts* (Paris, 1965)

Dictionary of the Older Scottish Tongue, ed. W. A. Craigie and A. J. Aitken (London 1937- 2001) accessible online at http://dsl.ac.uk which is the website of the Dictionary of the Scots Language/Dictionar o' the Scots Leid

Digney, Stephen, 'Recent Investigations at the King's Knot Stirling', *The Forth Naturalist and Historian*, 36 (2013), 129–148

Dixon, Piers, 'Medieval Rural Settlement in Marginal Landscapes', *Ruralia*, 7 (Turnhout, 2007)

——, 'Cruck Buildings in Scotland: A Review', in *Cruck Building: A Survey*, eds N. Alcock, P. S. Barnwell and M. Cherry (Donington, 2019), 300–322

BIBLIOGRAPHY

——, 'Settlement in the hunting forests of southern Scotland in the medieval and later periods', in G. De Boe and F. Verhaege (eds), *Rural Settlements in Medieval Europe*, Medieval Europe Brugge 1997 Conference (Zelik, 1997), vi, 345–354

Donaldson, Gordon, *Scotland James V to James VII* (Edinburgh, 1965)

——, *The First Trial of Mary Queen of Scots* (London, 1969)

——, *All the Queen's Men: Power and Politics in Mary Stewart's Scotland* (London, 1983)

Duceppe-Lamarre, François, *Chasse et Pâturage dans les forêts du Nord de la France: Pour une archéologie du paysage sylvestre (XIe–XVIe siècles)* (Paris, 2006)

Dunbar, John G., *The Historic Architecture of Scotland* (London, 1966)

——*Scottish Royal Palaces* (Edinburgh, 1999)

Duncan, A. A. M., *Scotland: The Making of the Kingdom* (Edinburgh, 1975)

Durkan, John, 'The Library of Mary, Queen of Scots', in Lynch, *Mary Stewart*, 71–104

Erlanger, Philippe, *Diane de Poitiers* (Paris, 1955)

Ferguson, Charles, 'Sketches of the Early History and Legends and Traditions of Strathardle and its glens', *Transactions of the Gaelic Society of Inverness*, 23 (1898–9), 154–178

Ferguson, J. Wilson, 'James V and the Scottish Church, 1528–1542', in T. K. Rabb and J. E. Seigel (eds), *Action and Conviction in Early Modern Europe: Essays in Honor of E. H. Harbison* (Princeton, 1969), 52–76

Ferrière, Hector de la, *Deux Années de Mission à St Petersbourg* (Paris, 1867)

——, *Les Grandes Chasses au XVI Siècle* (Paris, 1884)

——, *Les Chasses de François 1er* (Paris, 1886)

——, *Les Deux Cours de France et de l'Angleterre* (Paris, 1895)

Fittis, Robert S., *Sports and Pastimes of Scotland* (Paisley, 1891)

Fitzpatrick, Elizabeth, '*Formail na Fiann*: Hunting Reserves and Assembly Places in Gaelic Ireland', *Proceedings of the Harvard Celtic Colloquium*, 32 (2012)

Flanagan, Marie Thérèse, *Anglo-Norman Settlers, Angevin Kingship, Interactions in Ireland in late 12th Century* (Oxford, 1989)

Fleet, Christopher, 'Writing and Signs. Pont's Writing: Form and Content', in Cunningham (ed.), *The Nation Survey'd*, 35–48

Fleming, David Hay, *Mary Queen of Scots from her Birth to her Flight into England: A Brief Biography with Critical Notes, a few Documents hitherto unpublished and an Itinerary* (London, 1898)

Fletcher, John, *Gardens of Earthly Delight: The History of Deer Parks* (Oxford, 2011)

Forbes-Leith, William (ed.), *Narratives of Scottish Catholics under Mary Stuart and James VI* (London, 1889)

Foster, Sally M., *Picts, Gaels and Scots* (Edinburgh, 2014)

Fraser, Antonia, *Mary Queen of Scots* (London, 1970)

Fraser, I., *The Pictish Symbol Stones of Scotland* (Edinburgh, 2008)

Fraser, W., *The Lennox* (Edinburgh, 1874)

——, *The Red Book of Menteith* (Edinburgh, 1880)

Frieda, Leonie, *Catherine de Medici* (London, 2003)

Furgol, Edward M., 'The Scottish Itinerary of Mary Queen of Scots, 1542–8 and 1561–8', *PSAS*, 117 (1987), 219–32

Garrison, Janine, *A History of Sixteenth-Century France* (Basingstoke, 1995)

BIBLIOGRAPHY

Gatherer, W. A. (ed.), *The Tyrannous Reign of Mary Stewart, The Account of George Buchanan* (Edinburgh, 1958)

Geddes, Jane, *Hunting Picts, Medieval Sculpture at St Vigeans, Angus* (Edinburgh, 2017)

Geddes, Olive M., *A Swing through Time: Golf in Scotland 1457–1744* (Edinburgh, 2007)

Gilbert, John M., 'Crossbows on Pictish Stones', *PSAS*, 107 (1975–6)

——, *Hunting and Hunting Reserves in Medieval Scotland* (Edinburgh, 1979)

——, 'The Statutes of Ettrick Forest', Stair Society *Miscellany II* (Edinburgh, 1984)

——, 'Place-Names and Managed Woods in Medieval Scotland', *The Journal of Scottish Name Studies*, 5 (2011), 35–36

——, 'Falkland Park to c.1603' *Tayside and Fife Archaeological Journal*, 19 (2013–4), 78–102

——, 'Hunting with Mary Queen of Scots', *Review of Scottish Culture*, 28 (2016), 18–42.

——, 'Woodland Management in Medieval Scotland', *PSAS*, 146 (2016), 215–252

Gobry, Ivan, *François II 1559–60* (Paris, 2012)

Goldberg, Eric J., *In the Manner of the Franks: Hunting, Kingship and Masculinity in Early Medieval Europe* (Philadelphia, 2020)

Goodare, Julian, *State and Society in Early Modern Scotland* (Oxford, 1999)

——, *The Government of Scotland 1560–1625* (Oxford, 2004)

——, The First Parliament of Mary, Queen of Scots', *Sixteenth Century Journal*, 36 (2005), 55–75

——, 'Mary [Mary Stewart]', queen of Scots,' *Oxford Dictionary of National Biography* (Oxford, 2007) at www. Oxforddnb.com.

Grant, A. and K. Stringer (eds), *Medieval Scotland, Crown, Lordship and Community. Essays presented to G. W. S. Barrow* (Edinburgh, 1993)

Grant, A., 'Thanes and Thanages from Eleventh Century to the Fourteenth Centuries', in Grant and Stringer (eds), *Medieval Scotland, Crown, Lordship and Community*, 39–81

Green, Judith A., 'Forest Laws in England and Normandy in the Twelfth Century', *Historical Research*, 86 (2013)

Greengrass, M., 'Mary Dowager Queen of France', in Lynch, *Mary Stewart*, 171–94

Griffin, Emma, *Blood Sport, Hunting in Britain since 1066* (London, 2008)

Groundwater, Anna, 'Afterword: What Now?', in Wormald, *Mary Queen of Scots*, 207–238

Guidicini, Giovanni, *Triumphal Entries and Festivals in Early Modern Scotland: Performing Spaces* (Turnhout, 2020)

Guy, John, *My Heart is My Own: The Life of Mary Queen of Scots* (London, 2004)

Hall, Derek and Kevin Malloy, 'Always Chasing Deer – further excavations at Buzzart Dykes and Kincardine park and new excavations at Kincardine Castle in 2013', *Tayside and Fife Archaeological Journal*, 21–22 (2015–6), 25–34

Hamilton, David, *Golf, Scotland's Game* (Kilmacolm, 1998)

Hannay, Robert K., 'The earl of Arran and Queen Mary', *SHR*, 18 (1921)

Harrison, John G., *'Well Shelterd and Well Waterd', Menstrie Glen, a farming landscape near Stirling* (Edinburgh, 2001)

BIBLIOGRAPHY

——, '"The Bread Book" and the Court and Household of Marie de Guise in 1549', *Scottish Archives*, 15 (2009), 29–41

——, *Falkland Palace, Some documentary Evidence*, A Report for the National Trust for Scotland (2016)

Hart-Davis, Duff, *Monarchs of the Glen* (London, 1978)

Hatzfeld, A., *Dictionnaire General de la Langue Française du XVIIe siècle jusqu'à nos jours* (Paris, 1890–1900)

Heal, Felicity, 'Royal Gifts and Gift Exchange in Anglo-Scottish Politics', in Boardman and Goodare (eds), *Kings, Lords and Men in Scotland and Britain 1300–1625*, 283–293

Henderson, George and Isobel, *The Art of the Picts: sculpture and metalwork in early medieval Scotland* (London, 2004)

Hengel, Steven J. H. van, *Early Golf* (Liechtenstein, 1985)

Hennesy, Ronan and Elizabeth Fitzpatrick, 'Finn's Seat: topographies of power and royal marchlands of Gaelic polities in medieval Ireland', *Landscape History*, 38 (2017) 1–38

Historic woodland survey at Balgownie Wood, in *Historic Environment Conservation Management*, Forestry Commission Scotland (2013)

Hollingsworth, Mary, *The Cardinal's Hat* (London, 2014)

Hooke, Della, 'Royal forests and hunting and other forest uses in Medieval England', in D. Dauksta and E. Ritter (eds), *New Perspectives on People and Forests* (London, 2011) 41–59

Houwen, L. A. J. R., A. A. MaDonald and S. L. Mapstone (eds), *A Palace in the Wild: essays on vernacular culture and humanism in early Medieval and Renaissance Scotland* (Leuven, 2000)

Hume Brown, Peter, *Early Travellers in Scotland* (Edinburgh, 1891)

In the Shadow of Bennachie, RCAHMS and SAS (Edinburgh, 2008)

Jansen, Sharon L., *The Monstrous Regiment of Women: Female Rulers in Early Modern Europe* (Basingstoke, 2002)

Johnson, Alexandra Nancy, 'Mary Stuart and her Rebels Turned Privy-Councillors: Performance of the Ritual Council', in *Queenship and Counsel in Early Modern Europe*, ed. Helen Matheson-Pollock, Joanne Paul and Catherine Fletcher (London, 2018), 161–186

Jones, Graham, 'A Common of Hunting', in Langton, *Forests and Chases*, 36–67

Jullien, Ernest, *La Chasse, son Histoire et sa Legislation* (Paris, 1868)

Kamen, Henry, *Early Modern European Society* (London, 2006)

Keith, R., *History of the Affairs of Church and State in Scotland from the Beginning of the Reformation to the Year 1568* (Edinburgh, 1845)

Kelly, F., *Early Irish Farming: A Study Based Mainly on the Law Texts of the 7th and 8th Centuries AD* (Dublin, 1997)

Kerr, John, 'East by Tilt', *Transactions of the Gaelic Society of Inverness*, 54 (1987)

——, *Life in the Atholl Glens* (Perth, 1993)

——, *The Living Wilderness* (Perth, 1996)

Kerr, Judith, *Fealar Estate An Archaeological Survey*, NMRS (1999)

Knecht, Robert. J., *The Rise and Fall of Renaissance France 1483–1610* (Oxford, 2001)

——, 'Charles V's journey through France 1539–40', in Mulryne and Goldring (eds), *Court Festivals of the European Renaissance*, 153–170

BIBLIOGRAPHY

——, *The French Renaissance Court 1483–1589* (London, 2003)

Labarge, Margaret Wade, *A Baronial Household of the Thirteenth Century* (London, 1965)

Laborde, M de, *Notice des émaux, bijoux et objet divers exposés dans les galeries de Musée du Louvre* (Paris, 1853)

Laing, Henry, *Descriptive Catalogue of Impressions from Ancient Scottish Seals* (Edinburgh, 1850)

Langton, John, 'Medieval Forests and Chases: Another Realm?', in Langton and Jones (eds), *Forests and Chases*, 14–35

——, and Graham Jones (eds), *Forests and Chases of Medieval England and Wales c.1000–c.1500* (Oxford, 2010)

Leader, John D., *Mary Queen of Scots in Captivity* (Sheffield, 1880)

Lewandowski, E. J., *The Complete Costume Dictionary* (London, 2011)

Liddiard, Robert (ed.), *The Medieval Park: New Perspectives* (Macclesfield, 2007)

Lindner, K., *Die Jagd im Frühen Mittelalter*, trans. C. Montandon (Paris, 1950)

Lindsay, J. M., 'The history of oak coppice in Scotland', *Scottish Forestry* (1974), 87–93

Lowe, Chris, *Angels, Fools and Tyrants: Britons and Anglo-Saxons in southern Scotland* (Edinburgh, 1999)

Lynch, Michael (ed.), *Mary Stewart Queen in Three Kingdoms* (Oxford, 1988)

——, 'Queen Mary's Triumph: The Baptismal Celebrations at Stirling in December 1566' *SHR*, 69 (1990), 1–21

Mackenzie, W. Mackay, *The Medieval Castle in Scotland* (London, 1927)

Magiorani, Louis, 'Domaines avant le XIIIᵉ siècle dans Boulogne et Chambord', accessible at www.archaeoforet.org, http://www.archeoforet.org/ouvre/pluloin/dmaines/domains.pdf

Malloy, Kevin, and Derek Hall, 'Medieval hunting and wood management in the Buzzart Dykes landscape', *Environment History*, 25 (2019), 365–90

Mapstone, Sally, 'Introduction', in Houwen *et al.* (eds), *A Palace in the Wild*, vii–xviii.

Marcelle Thiebaux, *The Stag of Love: The Chase in Medieval Literature* (London and New York, 1974)

Marshall, Rosalind K., *Queen Mary's Women* (Edinburgh, 2006)

Marvin, William Perry, *Hunting Law and Ritual in Medieval English Literature* (Cambridge, 2006)

Mason, Roger A., *Kingship and Commonweal: Poitical thought in Renaissance and Reformation Scotland* (East Linton, 1998)

Maxwell-Irving, A. M. T., 'Cramalt Tower: historical survey and excavations', *PSAS*, 111 (1981), 401–429

McGladdery, C., *James II* (Edinburgh, 2015)

McKean, Charles, 'Finnart's Platt', *Journal of the Architectural Heritage Society of Scotland*, 11 (1991)

——, 'Timothy Pont's Building Drawings', in Cunningham (ed.), *The Nation Survey'd*, 111–24

Meiss-Even, Marjorie, 'Portrait des Guises en "gentilz veneurs" La chasse noble au XVIᵉ siècle entre symbolique et realité', *Histoire et Sociétés Rurales*, 38 (2012), 85–118

Menzies, D. P., *The 'Red and White' Book of Menzies: the history of clan Menzies and its chiefs* (Glasgow, 1894)

Merriman, Marcus, *The Rough Wooings: Mary Queen of Scots, 1542–1551* (East Linton, 2000)

Mickel, Lesley, 'From Bourgeois Wife to Renaissance Monarch: The royal Entertainment and Imperial Ambition of Mary Stewart (1561–66)', *Review of Scottish Culture*, 27 (2015), 48–61

Mignet, F. A., *The History of Mary Queen of Scots* (London, 1851)

Mileson, S. A., *Parks in Medieval England* (Oxford, 2014)

Millar, Neil S, *Early Golf. Royal Myths and Ancient Histories* (Edinburgh, 2022)

Mills, Coralie M. and Peter M. Quelch, *Falkland Park: Historic Woodland Assessment Survey, A report for the Living Lomonds Landscape Project* (2015), archived in Falkland Estate Office, The Stables, Falkland

Moncrieffe, Iain, *The Royal Palace of Falkland*, National Trust for Scotland (1968)

Morrison, Ian, 'Climate', in *The Oxford Companion to Scottish History*, 100

Moorhouse, Stephen, 'The Medieval parks of Yorkshire: Function, Contents and Chronology', in Liddiard (ed.), *The Medieval Park*, 99–127

Mulryne, J. R. and Elizabeth Goldring (eds), *Court Festivals of the European Renaissance: Art Politics and Performance* (London, 2002)

Murray, John, *Literature of the Gaelic Landscape* (Dunbeath, 2017)

Neighbors, Dustin, 'Elizabeth I "Huntress of England"', *The Court Historian* (2023), 49–79

Nelson, Janet L., 'The lord's anointed and the people's choice: Carolingian royal rituals', in David Carradine and Simon Price (eds), *Rituals of Royalty: Power and Ceremonial in Traditional Societies* (New York, 1987), 137–80

Noirmont, Dunoyer de, *Histoire de la Chasse en France depuis les temps les plus reculés jusqu'à la Révolution*, 3 vols (Paris, 1867)

O'Grady, Oliver, 'Cash Wood – Discover the Ancient Lomonds', *Discovery and Excavation*, 17 (Tisbury, 2016)

Oggins, Robin S., 'Review of Richard Almond, *Daughters of Artemis*', *The Medieval Review* (2010), review no. 10.06.40.

Oman, Charles, *A History of the Art of War in the Sixteenth Century* (London, 1937)

Oram, Richard, 'Royal and Lordly Residences in Scotland c.1050 to c.1250 – an historiographical review and critical revision', *The Antiquaries Journal*, 88 (2008), 165–189

——, 'Rural Society', in *The Oxford Companion to Scottish History*, 548–9

——, *Domination and Lordship: Scotland 1070–1230* (Edinburgh, 2011)

——, 'The worst disaster suffered by the people of Scotland in recorded history', *PSAS*, 144 (2014), 223–244

——, 'Public Policy and Private Practice: Production, Management and Development of Scotland's Woodland Resources from the 12th to 17th Centuries', NWDG *Scottish Woodland History Conference: Notes 21* for 2016 (2022), 1–7

Oxford Companion to Scottish History, ed. Michael Lynch (Oxford, 2001)

Paillard, Charles, 'L'Histoire de la Conjuration d'Amboise', *Revue Historique*, 14 (Paris, 1880)

Paris, Paulin, *Études sur François Premier*, 2 vols (Paris, 1885)

Parkinson, David, '"A Lamentable Storie": Mary Queen of Scots and the inescapable *querelle des femmes*', in Houwen *et al.* (eds), *A Palace in the Wild*, 141–160

Peacock, Martha Moffat, 'Women at the Hunt: developing a gendered logic of

BIBLIOGRAPHY

rural space in the Netherlandish visual tradition', in Albrecht Classen and Christopher R Classen (eds), *Rural Space in the Middle Ages* (Berlin, 2012), 819–864

Peebleshire, An Inventory of Ancient Monuments, RCAHMS (Edinburgh, 1967)

Richards, Penny, 'The Guise Women: Politics, War and Peace', in Jessica Munn and Penny Richards (eds), *Gender, Power and Privilege in Early Modern Europe* (London and New York), 2003

Perry, David, Hilary Murray and Nicholas Q. Bogdan (eds), *Perth High Street Archaeological Excavations 1975–1971, the Excavations at 75–95 High Street and 5–10 Mill Street Perth* (Perth, 2010)

Petit-Dutaillis, Charles, *Studies Supplementary to Stubbs' Constitutional History* (Manchester, 1908–29)

——, 'De la signification du mot forêt à l'Époque Franque', *Bibliothèque de l'École des Chartes*, 76 (1915) 97–152

Pitcairn, R. (ed.), *Criminal Trials in Scotland from 1488–1624*, Bannatyne Club, 3 vols (Edinburgh, 1833)

Pitte, Jean-Robert, 'Géographie culinaire des Produits de la Chasse et de la Forêt en France', in Corvol (ed.), *Forêt et Chasse Xe–XXe siècles*, 127–134

Platt, Colin, *Medieval England: A social history and archaeology from the conquest to 1600A.D.* (London, 1978)

Pollnitz, Aysha, *Princely Education in Early Modern Britain* (Cambridge, 2015)

Poole, Austin Lane, *From Domesday Book to Magna Carta 1087–1216* (Oxford, 1954)

Pressac, M. de, 'La Bibliographie Raisonné de Cet Ouvrage', in *La Vénerie de Jacques du Fouilloux*, ed. Robin and L. Faure (Niort, 1864), 34–117

Quye, Anita and Hugh Cheape, 'Rediscovering the arisaid', *Costume*, 42 (2008), 1–20

Rackham, Oliver, *Trees and Woodland in the British Landscape: The Complete History of Britain's Trees, Woods & Hedgerows* (London, 2001, orig. 1976)

——, *The History of the Countryside: The classic history of Britain's landscape, flora and fauna* (London, 2000, orig. 1986)

——, *The Last Forest: the story of Hatfield Forest* (London, 1993)

——, *Woodlands* (London, 2006)

Reed, John L., *Forests of France* (London, 1954)

Reid, W. Stanford, 'Clerical Taxation: The Scottish Alternative to Dissolution of the Monasteries 1530–1560', *Catholic Historical Review*, 32 (1948), 129–153

Remigerau, François, *Jacques du Fouilloux et son Traité de la Vénerie* (Paris, 1952)

Reports on Annexed Estates 1755–69, ed. Virginia Wills (Edinburgh, 1973)

Revised Medieval Latin Word-List, ed. R. E. Latham (London, 1965)

Richardson, Amanda, 'Putting the "royal" back into forests: kingship, largesse, patronage and management in a group of Wessex forests in the thirteenth and fourteenth centuries', in Langton and Jones (eds), *Forests and Chases*, 125–140

——, '"Riding like Alexander, Hunting like Diana": Gendered Aspects of the Medieval Hunt and its Landscape Settings in England and France', *Gender and History*, 24 (2012), 153–70

Richardson, Glenn, 'Hunting at the Courts of Francis I and Henry VIII', *The Court Historian*, 18 (2013), 127–141

Ritchie, James, *The Influence of Man on Animal Life in Scotland: A Study in Faunal Evolution* (Cambridge, 1920)

209

BIBLIOGRAPHY

Ritchie, Pamela E., *Mary of Guise in Scotland 1548–60. A Political Career* (East Linton, 2002)

Ritvo, Harriet, 'Race Breed and Myths of Origin: Chillingham Cattle as Ancient Britons', *Representations*, 39 (1992), 1–22

Rixson, Denis, *The Small Isles Canna, Rum, Eigg and Muck* (Edinburgh, 2001)

Robertson, James, *General View of the Agriculture of the County of Perth* (Perth, 1799)

Rollason, David, 'Forests, parks, palaces and the power of place in early medieval kingship', *Early Medieval Europe*, 20 (2012), 428–449

——, *The Power of Place: Rulers and their Palaces, Landscapes, Cities, and Holy Places* (Oxford, 2016)

Rose of Kilravock, A Genealogical Deduction of the Family of, ed. H. Rose, L. Shaw and C. Innes (Aberdeen, 1848)

Ross, Alasdair, *Two Surveys of Vernacular Buildings and Tree Usage in the Lordship of Strathdon, Banffshire 1585–1612*, SHS, *Miscellany XIV* (Edinburgh, 2013)

Ross, John, *The Book of the Red Deer* (London, 1925)

Ruble, Alphonse de, *La Première Jeunesse de Marie Stuart* (Paris, 1891)

Salvadori, Philippe, 'François 1ᵉʳ et le droit de chasse', in Anthenaise, *Chassse princières*, 43–60

Schroeder, Nicolas, '*In locis vaste solitudinis*: Représenter l'environnement au haut moyen âge : l'example de la Haut Ardenne (Belgique) au VIIᵉ siècle', *Le Moyen Âge*, 116 (2010)

Schuessler Bond, Melanie, *Dressing the Scottish Court, 1543–1553: Clothing in the Accounts of the Lord High Treasurer of Scotland* (Woodbridge, 2019)

Schwerdt, C. F. G. R., *Hawking, Hunting and Shoooting. Illustrated in a Catalogue of Books Manuscripts Prints and Drawings* (London, 1927)

Scrope, William, *The Art of Deer Stalking* (London, 1838)

Sekules, Veronica, 'Women and Art in England in the thirteenth and fourteenth centuries', in Jonathan Alexander and Paul Binski (eds), *Age of Chivalry. Art in Plantagenet England 1200–1400* (London, 1987), 41–8

Sharman, Julian, *The Library of Mary Queen of Scots* (London, 1889)

Shirley, Evelyn P., *Some Account of English Deer Parks: with notes on the management of deer* (London, 1867)

Simpson, W. Douglas, 'The Excavation of Kindrochit Castle', *Antiquaries Journal*, 8 (1928)

Smailes, H. and Thomson, D., *The Queen's Image: a celebration of Mary, Queen of Scots* (Edinburgh, 1987)

Small, Thomas A., 'Queen Mary in the Counties of Dumbarton and Argyll', *Scottish Historical Review*, 25 (1927), 13–19

Smith, David Baird, 'William Barclay', *SHR*, 11 (1914), 136–163

Smith, William, *Smaller Classical Dictionary, of Biography, Mythology and Geography* (London, 1858)

Smout, T. C., Alan R. Macdonald, and Fiona Watson, *A History of the Native Woodlands of Scotland* (Edinburgh, 2005)

Somerville, Johann P., *King James VI and His Political Writings* (Cambridge, 1994)

Statistics of the Annexed and Forfeited Estates 1755–6, HMSO (Edinburgh, 1973)

Stedall, Robert, *The Challenge to the Crown*, 2 vols (Brighton, 2012)

Steer, K. A. and J. W. M. Bannerman, *Late Medieval Monumental Sculpture in the West Highlands*, RCAHMS (Edinburgh, 1977)

BIBLIOGRAPHY

Stevenson, J., *Mary Stuart: A Narrative of the First Eighteen Years of her Life, Principally from Original Documents* (Edinburgh, 1886)

Stevenson, Katie, 'Chivalry, British Sovereignty and dynastic politics: undercurrents of antagonism in Tudor Stewart relations c.1490–1513', *Historical Research*, 85 (2013) 604–613

Stoddart, Jane T., *The Girlhood of Mary Queen of Scots: from Her Landing in France in August, 1548, to Her Departure from France in August, 1561* (London, 1908)

Strong, Roy, *Splendour at Court: Renaissance Spectacle and Illusion* (London, 1973)

——, *Art and Power: Renaissance Festivals 1450–1650* (Woodbridge, 1984)

Summerhays R. S. and V. Russel, *Encyclopedia for Horsemen* (Buckingham, 1993)

Sykes, Naomi, 'Animal Bones and Animal Parks', in Liddiard (ed.), *The Medieval Park*, 49–62

Tabraham, Chris, *Scotland's Castles* (London, 1997)

Taylor, A., *The Shape of the State in Medieval Scotland 1124–1290* (Oxford 2016)

Taylor, Simon and Gilbert Markus, *The Place-Names of Fife*, 5 vols (Donington, 2007 – 2012)

——, 'The Toponymic Landscape of the Gaelic Notes on the Book of Deer', in Katherine Forsyth (ed.), *Studies on the Book of Deer* (Dublin, 2008), 275–308

Thiebaux, Marcelle, 'Review of *La Vénerie et L'Adolescence de Jacques du Fouilloux*, ed. Gunnar Tilander, *Speculum*, 46 (1971), 511–14

Thierry, Eric, 'Un sèjour de la cour de François II à Villers Cotterêts en 1559', *Histoire Aisne Memoires*, 39 (1994), 197–206 at 201

Thomas, Andrea, *Princelie Majestie, The Court of James V of Scotland 1528–1542* (Edinburgh, 2005)

Thornber, Iain 'Morvern Lines with Highland Historian Iain Thornber', *Oban Times*, 24 April 2016

Turner, G. J., *Select Pleas of the Forest* (London, 1901)

Veauvy, Isabelle de, Adélaïde de Savray and Isabelle de Ponton d'Amecourt, *Cavalières Amazones: une histoire singulière* (Paris, 2016)

Walton, Kirsten P., *Catholic Queen Protestant Hierarchy: Mary, Queen of Scots, and the Politics of Gender and Religion* (Basingstoke, 2007)

Warde, Paul, '*Ecology, Economy and State Formation in Early Modern Germany* (Cambridge, 2006)

——, 'Fear of wood shortage and the reality of the woodland in Europe c. 1450–1850', *History Workshop Journal*, 92 (2006) 28–57

Warnicke, Retha M., *Mary Queen of Scots* (London, 2006)

Warren, W. L., *King John* (Harmondsworth, 1966)

——, *Henry II* (London, 2000, orig. 1973)

Watson, W. J., 'Aoibhinn an Obair an t-sealg', *Celtic Review*, 10 (1913–14)

——, 'Deer and Boar in Gaelic Literature (Aoibhinn an Obair an t-Sealg)', in John Ross, *The Book of the Red Deer*, 75–100

——, *The History of the Celtic Place-Names of Scotland* (Edinburgh, 2011, orig. 1926)

Weiss, Ulrike E., 'Backwards in high heels; a brief history of the sidesaddle', in Weiss and Pfeiffer, *Sidesaddle 1690–1935*, 1–18.

—— and Claudia P. Pfeiffer, *Side Saddle 1690–1935* (Middleburg, 2018)

Wellman, Kathleen, 'Diane de Poitiers. An Idealized Mistress', in Kathleen Wellman (ed.), *Queens and Mistresses of Renaissance France* (Yale, 2013), 185–223.

BIBLIOGRAPHY

White, Allan, 'Queen Mary's Northern Province', in Lynch, *Mary Stewart*, 53–70
Wiesner-Hanks, Merry E., *Women and Gender in Early Modern Europe* (Cambridge, 2019)
Williams, H. Noel, *Henry II: His Court and Times* (London, 1910)
Wood, James B., *The king's army: warfare, soldiers and society during the wars of religion in France 1562–76* (Cambridge, 2002)
Wormald, Jenny, *Mary Queen of Scots: A Study in Failure* (London, 2017)
Yeoman, Peter, *Medieval Scotland* (London, 1995)
Youatt, W, *Cattle Their Breeds, Management and Diseases* (London, 1834)
Young, Charles R., *The Royal Forests of Medieval England* (Leicester, 1979)
Zanetti, Valerio, 'Breeched and Unbridled. Bifurcated Garments for Women in Early Modern Europe', *Costume*, 55 (2021), 163–185

Unpublished

Jack, K. S., 'Decline and Fall: The earls and earldom of Mar *c*.1281–1513', PhD thesis (University of Stirling, 2016)
Loughlin, Mark, 'The Career of Maitland of Lethington *c*.1526–1573', PhD thesis (University of Edinburgh, 1991)
MacGregor, Martin D. W., 'A Political History of the MacGregors before 1571', PhD thesis (University of Edinburgh, 1989)
McNiven, Peter E., 'Gaelic place-names and the social history of Gaelic speakers in Medieval Menteith', PhD thesis (University of Glasgow, 2011)
Smith, Annette M., 'Annexed and Forfeited Estates', PhD thesis (University of St Andrews, 1975)
Thomas, Andrea, 'Renaissance Culture at the Court of James V', PhD thesis (University of Edinburgh, 1997)
Wiseman, Andrew E., 'Chasing the Deer: Hunting Iconography and Tradition of the Scottish Highlands', PhD thesis (University of Edinburgh, 2007–9)

Websites relating to secondary sources

Canmore, the National Record of the Historic Environment, part of HES, https://www.canmore.org.uk (accessed between 2016 and 2022)
Dictionary of the Scots Language/Dictionar o' the Scots Leid, http://dsl.ac.uk (accessed between 2016 and 2023)
Harrison, John G., *The Creation and Survival of Some Scots Royal Landscapes* (2012), www.johnscothist.com, Research and Reports (accessed between 2016 and 2017)
ΛΟΓΕΙΟΝ: https://logeion.uchicago.edu/polymitare (last consulted 10 October 2021)
NLS Pont Maps, https://maps.nls.uk/pont/index.html (accessed between 2016 and 2022)
Oxford Dictionary of National Biography (Oxford, 2007), www. oxforddnb.com
Scotland's Places, https://scotlandsplaces.gov.uk (last consulted 3 March 2023).
Scottish Archaeological Internet Reports, www.sair.org.uk and http://journals.socantscot.org/index.php/sair (accessed in 2019)
Scottish Woodland History Conference Notes, http://www.nwdg.org.uk/woodland-history/history-archive/ (last consulted 10 September 2021)

Index

Page numbers in bold relate to illustrations.

Aberargie Wood   121
Aberdeen   112
Aberuthven Wood   121
Accourre   20, 49
Acts of Scottish Parliament
  1401   30
  1474   30
  1504   39
  1535   35
  1551   39
  1563   121–2
Ailred of Rievaulx   25
Amboise   37, 42, 59, 61
  boar hunt in courtyard of   21
  conspiracy of   57, 71
Ameneurs   20
Anet, chateau of   42, 50, *see also*
  Diane de Poitiers
Anne de Beaujeu   51
Archery   104, 108
Argyll   112
Assembly of Notables   57
'Auld Alliance'   41
Ayala, Pedro de, papal
  ambassador   166

Babington, Antony   163
Bagot, Richard   162
Bagpipe player   114
Balgownie wood   120
Ballinbreich   110
Ballivi ad extra   37
Balquhidder   76, 80, 126

Barbour, John   149–50
Barclay, William   119, 127, 132, 135
Bar-le-Duc   68, 70
Beaton, David, archbishop of St
  Andrews   41
Beaton, James, archbishop of
  Glasgow   159, 162
Beaton, Mary, lady-in-waiting to
  Mary, Queen of Scots   98
Bedford, earl of, *see* Russel
Bellenden, John, chronicler   30 n.70
Bencrumby Forest   128, 135
Ben More Forest   24, 76
Berlin Book of Hours of Mary of
  Burgundy   185
Bêtes noires   14
Bêtes rousses   14, 170
Blois   42, 43, 60, 69ff, 90, 91
Boece, Hector, chronicler   25, 30,
  152, 153
Boar   13, 14, 16, 94, 109
Bolton Castle   156
Book of Hours of Marguerite
  d'Orléans   183
Book privilege system in France   66
Boulogne, Fôret de   42
Bourbon, Antoine de, king of
  Navarre   57, 71, 91
Bourbon, Louis de, prince of
  Condé   57, 71
Bow and stable hunt   24–5, 108–9
Brantôme, Pierre de Bourdeille, abbé
  de   185–6

INDEX

Breeches 53, 100, 181–2, 187
Brézé, Jacques de, author of *La
   Chasse* 45, 51–2
Brézé, Louis de 50
Buchanan, George 100, 115, 150–1
   and masque for baptism of James
   VI 150–2
Budé, Guillaume de, author of *Traitté
   de la Vénerie* 21
Buigne, Gace de la, author of *Roman
   de Déduis* 48
Buzzart Dykes 81

Caiche 1, 104
Campbell, Agnes, of Dunyvaig 114
Campbell, Archibald, fifth earl of
   Argyll 96, 112, 113, 127, 137,
   139ff, 146ff
Campbell, Colin, of Glenorchy 113,
   127, 136, 137, 144, 146
Campbell, Colin, of Lochawe 84
Campbell, Duncan, of Glen
   Lyon 136
Capitaineries des chasses 36, 42
Carberry Hill 98, 184
Carlenrigg 90
Carlisle Castle 156
Carrick, Marjorie, countess of 93
Catherine de Medici 8, 47, 49–50,
   53, 54, 56, 60, 68, 75, 181, 185
Cecil, William, Lord Burghley 160
Chambord 36
   park of 37, 60–1, 73, 102
Chantonay, ambassador 58, 70, 71,
   72
Charles V, Holy Roman Emperor 54
Chartley Hall 162
Chasing game 14–18, 106, 107
Chasse aux toiles **19**, 20–1, 48, 49,
   54, 58, 109
Châteaudun 69
Châtelherault 59, 148
Chatsworth House 158, 160
Chausses, *see* breeches
Chenonceau 42, 61, 71

entry of Mary and Francis to 72,
   148
Chillingham Castle 153
Chinon 37, 61
Christine, duchess of Lorraine 185
Claude, duchess of Lorraine 42, 70,
   75
Columella, author of *De
   Arboribus* 74
Commissioners of crown lands 37
Compiègne 42, *see also* Retz, Forêt de
Coppicing, *see under* woodland
   management
Coursing game 17–18, 30
Court ceremonies 5, 148
   audiences 54, 119
   entry to towns 5, 59, 148
   fêtes champêtres 5
   fort-holding 5, 154–5
   masques 55, 114, 150—2
   triumphs 72, 75, 91, 92, 148, 165
Cowal 84, 113
Craigmillar Castle 147
Crichton, William, of
   Naughton 110
Cramalt Towers 88, 90, 142
Cultybraggan 83, 146, 174
Cumbernauld 152, 153
Cunningham, Alexander, fifth earl of
   Glencairn 139, 140
Cupar 110

Dalclathick 143, 146, 175–6
Darius, Silvester, papal nuncio 84,
   91
David I, king of Scotland 21, 22
*Débat des Dames sur Le Passetemps des
   Chiens et Oiseaux* 48, 63
*Débat des Herauts d'Armes de France et
   d'Angleterre* 6 n.34
Deer 29
   attitude towards 13
   management of 33, 34, 77–8, 105,
   105 n.41, 106, 121
Défenses **15**, 18–20

214

INDEX

Devantière 7, 53, 181, 186–7
Dewanter 99–100, 187
Diana, goddess of hunting 50–1, 96, 117, 154
Diane de France, Madame de Castres 46–7, 50, 52
Diane de Poitiers 42, 64, 117
  development of Anet 50–1
  enamel of, hunting with Henry II 64–5
  hunting activities 50–1, 53
  influence on Mary 50
Diurnal of Remarkable Occurrents 150
Douglas, James, fourth earl of Morton 96, 140
Douglas Burn 89
Doune Castle 145
Driving game 18–25, 30
  comparison of, in France and Scotland 28–9
  comparison with *par force* hunting in France 28
  in France 18–20, **19**
  in Scotland 21–5, **23**, 107–9, 125, 128, 132–6
Drummond, David, second Lord Drummond 127, 144

Eclaron 70
Ecology 33, 34, 104
Edmonstone, Archibald, forester of Menteith 90
Edmonstone, William, of Duntreath 122, 124
Ehingen, Georg von 90, 165
Elboeuf, René, de Lorraine, Marquis of 116
Élisabeth de France, queen of Spain 42, 52, 53
Elizabeth I, queen of England 8,
  and hunting 69, 69 n.67, 109, 157, 161, 186–7
  and Mary, Queen of Scots 69, 106, 111, 115, 157ff, 186–7
Elrick **23**, 24, 26–7, 135

Elrig'ic an Toiseach 128
Equestrianism 45–6, 49, 52–3
  significance of 8–9, 53, 101
  see also riding astride; side-facing saddle; side-saddle
Erskine, John, sixth Lord Erskine, earl of Mar 145
Estates General, Orleans 1560 73
Ettrick Forest 37, 38, 76, 93
Ewesdoors 90

Falconry 48
  suitability for women 48
Falkland 11, 76, 93, 101–2
  compartmentalisation of park 104
  deer fold in park 105
  development of park and palace 102–6
  hunting in park 94, 115, 106–8
  livestock in park 105, 107, 108, 109
  management of woodland in park 94, 105, 106
  park pale 104–5
  Queen's seat 108
Fence month 24
Feria, Gomez Suarez, count of, ambassador 61
Fernie, Andrew, hereditary forester of Falkland 107
Ferrières, Henri de, author of *Livre du Roy Modus* 14, 18–20, 48
Fionn MacCumaill 17, 24, 25, 80
Fleming, James, fifth Lord Fleming 153
Fontainebleau 36, 37, 42, 62, 64
Fordun, Johannis de, chronicler 93
Forester, Duncan 24
Forests, royal 4, 31, 36, 122
  managing 32–38, 122, 124, 144
  see also Boulogne; Blois; Ettrick; Glenfinglas; Glenartney; Retz
Forster, Sir John, warden of English Middle Marches 143 n.34, 147

215

INDEX

Francis I, king of France   21, 32, 33, 35, 54, 58, 90–1, 185
  boar hunt at Amboise   21
  hunting with ladies of the court   53, 185
Francis II, king of France   10, 42, 46
  character   56–7
  frequency of hunts   58–9, 68–9
  and his councils   57, 70
  illness   57
  progresses with Mary   59–63, 70–1, *see also under* Mary, Queen of Scots
Fouilloux, Jacques du, author of *La Vénerie et L'Adolescence*   66–8
Free forest grant   32, 36, 120
Free warren grant   32
French court
  daily routine   58
  role of hunting at   47, 58

Gaelic influence on hunting in Scotland   25–8, 88–9, 115, 125, 136, 167
  see also elrick; highland dress; tartan; hunting mounds; lunkarts; *see also under* Highlands and highlanders
Gaelic literature   25, 88, *see also* Fionn MacCumaill; *Oran na Comhachaig*
Garennes   32
Glenartney Forest   24, 39, 76, 87, 122, 146
  description of   143
  hunt hall   83, 146, 174ff
  hunting house in   122, 144, 174ff
  James V hunts in   76, 82
  Mary hunts in   122, 143ff
  provisions for hunting in   78, 87
  size of hunting parties in   78
Glenfinglas Forest   39, 76
  description of   123–4, 123 n.25
  dispute over forestership   122
  James V hunts in   76, 82, 93

Mary hunts in   124–5
provisions for hunts in   78, 87, 124
size of hunting parties in   78
Glen Tilt   76, 87
  description of   127–8
  hunt in 1532 in   83–5, 91–2, 128
  hunt of 1564 in   132–6
  James V's 'palice' in   83–5, 129, 154–5
  provisions for hunting in   78
  see also lunkarts
Goat houses   177, 179
Golf   1, 100
Gordon, George, fifth earl of Huntly   139ff, 146
Gordon, George, fourth earl of Huntly   96, 100, 111
Gordon, Robert, of Straloch   123, 170
Gorges, Sir Thomas   163
Gorton, colonel Graeme of   178
Grandes chasses   54, 58, 71
Gray, Patrick, fourth Lord Gray   142
Grazing   3, 33, 34, 36, 105, 121, 124, 130, 144, 178
Greater game   13–14
Guise, Charles de, cardinal of Lorraine   29 n.68, 41, 56, 68
Guise family   56, 65, 68, 71, 75, 160, 161
Guise, François de, duke of   41, 49, 110
Guise, Marie de, wife of James V   41, 49, 62, 93–4, 103, 109, 131, 144
Guns   33, 121–2, 142

Haie   20
Hall house   82
Hamilton, James, duke of Châtelherault, regent of Scotland   33, 41, 59, 59 n.18, 96, 139
Hamilton, James, third earl of Arran   96, 115
Hamilton, John, archbishop of St Andrews   110

216

INDEX

Hare   14, 16, 30
Hay, *see haie*
Hay, William, of Yester   142
Henry II, king of France   35, 36, 37, 41, 47, 54, 58, 62, 65, 117
Henry VIII, king of England   41
Hepburn, Elizabeth, prioress of Haddington   79, 93
Hepburn, James, fourth earl of Bothwell   115, 140ff, 146ff
Highlands and highlanders (of Scotland)
    attitude towards   89, 113, 114–15, 155, 166
    dress   88–9, 113–14
Histoire de Guillaume le Maréchal   184
Holyrood Abbey, foundation story of   21–23
Hose, *see breeches*
Hunting
    accommodation for   80–3, *see also* hunt hall; hunting house; pavilions; Glen Tilt
    and diplomacy   55, 68–9, 69–70, 90–1, 115, 116
    as an elite pastime   29, 31–2, 58, 125–6, 164
    and fair play   29–30
    and image of Stuart monarchy   153, 165–6
    as a male pursuit   6, 47–8, 53, 97–8, 100, 101, 116
    methods   14–25
        see also chasing game; *chasse aux toiles*; coursing game; driving game; *par force*
    mounds   25–6, 108, 125, 132, 135
    as a performance   4–5, 54, 119, 137, 138, 153–4
    reserves
        and conservation   29, 33, 34
        and ecology   33, 34, 104
        management of   32–8, 60, 94, 119, 124
        see also grazing; poaching; wood-

cutting; deer
    political significance of   4, 31, 38–40, 92, 126
    rights   31–2
    seasons   29, 30
    seats   22, 23, 24
    treatises   45, *see also Master of Game*; Budé; Ferrières; Fouilloux
    see also Gaelic influence on hunting; women hunting; political and social role of hunting

Inverness   120, 127

James II, king of Scotland   80, 102, 104, 105, 165
James III, king of Scotland   80, 81, 103, 109, 118, 144
James IV, king of Scotland   38, 103, 107, 109, 124, 144, 166
    hunts in Glenartney   76, 105
James V, king of Scotland   35, 36, 38, 89–90, 90–1, 97, 103, 119, 122, 128, 144
    composition of his hunting parties   79
    escape from Falkland Palace   107
    and Falkland Palace   103ff, 109
    hunts in Glen Tilt   83, 91, 128
    hunts in 'Meggatland'   76
    provision for hunting parties   78, 85, 87–8
    size of his hunting parties   78–9
James VI, king of Scotland
    baptism of   142, 148–55
    and hunting   107, 152
Jeu de maille   1, 100, 102, 104
Jeu de paume   1, 58, 102
Judicial raid/hunt   78, 94,
    to Jedburgh   89, 141, 147
    to Megget   78, 89–90, 111
    to the North-East (of Scotland)   100, 111
Justice ayre   37, 40, 111, 141, 147, 147 n.55

217

INDEX

Kincardine Castle (Perth and
    Kinross)   121, 152
Kindrochit Castle   76, 81
King Hart   93
Knollys, Sir Francis   156, 157
Knox, John   97, 100, 112

Langholm   90
La Vénerie et L'Adolescence, see
    Fouilloux, Jacques du
Lesley, John, historian and bishop of
    Ross   22, 98, 112, 114, 119, 140,
    149, 152, 166
    description of a drive   22–4
Leslie, Andrew, fifth earl of
    Rothes   110, 116, 139, 140
Lesser game   12–13, 33
Les Très Riches Heures du duc de
    Berry   182
Limousin, Leonard
    enamel of Henry II and Diane de
        Poitiers by   64
Lindsay, David, of the Mount   149
Lindsay, Patrick, of the Byres   116
Livre de Chasse, see Phoebus, Gaston
Livre du roy Modus et de la Royne
    Ratio, see Ferrières, Henri de
Loches   59, 61, 90–1
Louis XI, king of France   182
Lunkart(s)   128
    description of   129, 132, 171–2
    site of, in Glen Tilt   128–9,
        169–174

MacGregor, Duncan   136
MacGregor, Gregor   113
MacGregors   113, 122, 136
    and letter of Fire and Sword   126
    and Mary's attempts to deal
        with   126, 136–7
Macmillan Cross   18
Maillebois   61
Maitland, William, of
    Lethington   112, 115, 137, 140,
    146, 147

Maîtres des eaux et forêts   36
Marchenoir   61
Margaret, daughter of James I, king of
    Scotland   182
Margaret Tudor, wife of James IV   24,
    41, 93, 98, 182, 183
Marguerite de Parma   53, 68
Marguerite of Austria   8
Mar hunt in 1618   79, 87, 113,
    130–1, 135
Marie de Burgundy, wife of
    Maximilian I   62, 185
Marie de Gueldres, wife of James
    II   93, 94, 104
Marie of Hungary   185
Mary, Queen of Scots
    at Anet   51
    and archery   1, 109, 158, 159
    and baptism of James VI   148–55,
        165
    books belonging to   45, 74
    courage of   137
    and court festivities   54–5, 101,
        119, 148–9, 165
    and court of session   118
    dower lands in France   74, 161
    education   10, 43–7, 50
        humanist elements   10, 43–4
        Latin exercises   44, 46–7
        learning to hunt   44–7
    effect of hunting on health
        of   156–7, 161
    equestrianism of   52–3, 98–100,
        182, 183–4
    geldings of   59, 106
    hackneys of   45–6
    hawking
        in England   157, 160, 161
        in France   44, 72
        in Scotland   110, 116
    and highland dress   113–14
    hunting dress of   53, 99–100, 114,
        187
    and hunting house   122, 144–6
    hunting in England

218

Bolton (1568–9) 157
Chartley Park (Summer
1585) 162, 163
Chatsworth (Aug. 1570) 158
Sheffield Park (pre-May
1571, April 1582, October
1582) 158–9, 160, 161
Tixall Park (Summer 1585) 163
Tutbury Castle (Aug.
1585) 162
hunting in France
from Bar-le-duc to Fontainebleau
(Oct. 1559) 70–1
from Blois to Amboise (Feb.
1560) 61
Chambord (Dec. 1559) 60, 61
Chenonceau (March 1560) 61
Loches (Nov. 1559) 59
in Sologne, Beauce and
Perche to Maillebois (June
1560) 61
hunting in Scotland
in Argyll (July 1563) 112
Falkland Park (March 1562,
1563) 106, 110, 115
Glenartney (Aug. 1566) 143–7
Glenfingas (Sept. 1564) 122–6
Glen Tilt (Aug. 1564) 132–6
Megget and Traquair
(1566) 121, 141–3
in North-East Fife (March
1563) 110
from Perth to Aberdeen (Aug.
1562) 111–12
Stirling Park (April 1565, Dec.
1566) 139 n.1, 151ff
hunting methods of 24, 52, 59,
110, 113, 135–6, 157, 162, 163
judicial raid/hunts of 111–12
learning court protocol 54–5
letter to Catherine de Medici in
c.1553 46, 46 n.30
and lunkarts 128, 129–32, 173–4
male role as hunter 6, 53, 100, 116
and management of royal

forests 122, 144
and parliament of 1563 96, 117,
118, 121
portrayed at Carberry Hill 98, **99**
portrayed in tapestry with
Francis 63–5
portrayed in treatise of Du
Fouilloux 65–8, **67**
provision for hunts 124, 132
and 'the queen's majesty' 118–19
and timber for artillery 121
triumph in honour of 75, 154–5
Master of Game 24–5, 45, 108
Matilda, empress of England 185
Maximilian I, Holy Roman Emperor,
62
Meall na h'Elrig 135
Meggetland 77–8, 79, 89, 142
Melville, James, of Halhill 149
Menteith 76, 79, 126
Menzies, James, of Weem 136
Menzies, Robert, of Weem 92
Moncrieffe Wood 121
Monimail 110
Montluc, Jean de, bishop of
Valois 57
Montmorency, Anne de, constable of
France 50, 56, 71, 73
Montoire 61
Morée 61
Morgan, Thomas 162
Moryson, Fynes, travel writer,181–2
Murray, William, of Abercairny 114

Nau, Claude 140, 141, 143, 182
Naughton 110

Occupatio 31
Ogilvie, James, fifth Lord Ogilvie of
Airlie 112
Oran na Comhachaig 18, 25, 27, 30
Ordinances of French kings
1516 32, 33, 35
1544 35
Ormiston, James, of that ilk 98

INDEX

Orléans, Charles, duke of 91

Par-force hunting 14–16, 29, 48–9, 58, 126
  assembly 5, 14, 49, 51, 62
  curée and unmaking 16, 52
  défenses 16
  relays 15–16, 51
  quest 14
Parks
  managing 32, 60, 104–6
  see Chambord; Chenonceau; Falkland; Stirling; Villers Cotterêts
Paulet, Sir Amyas 161, 162
Pavilions 82, 131
Phoebus, Gaston, comte de Foix, author of *Livre de Chasse* 45
  description of drives by 18–20
  description of *par-force* hunt by 14
  dislike of use of nets 29
Pictish stones 17, 92, 94, 183
Pitlethie 94, 98, 110, 115
Pitscottie, Robert Lindsay of, historian 30, 83, 84, 87, 89, 91, 98, 106–7, 166
Planche, Regnier de la 56
Poaching 33
  penalties in France 33
  penalties in Scotland 33, 121–2, 124, 144
Political and social role of hunting 2–3, 8
  in France 51, 53, 54, 55
  under Francis II 64–5, 69, 71–3
  under James V 79, 89, 91–2
  under Mary, Queen of Scots 97, 115, 116, 119, 137–8, 147–8, 152
    at baptism of James VI 152, 155
    in Glenartney 146
    in Glenfinglas 126, 136
    in Megget 142
Pont, Timothy, map-maker 11, 83, 84, 124, 125, 128, 130, 169, 170, 174
Proclamations about
  guns 121, 142
  poaching 33, 94, 121–2, 124, 144
Purlieu 122

Queen Mary's Psalter 7

Randolph, Thomas, ambassador 98, 100, 112, 115
Reformation 37, 73
Res nullius 31
Retz, Forêt de 42, 73, 185
Riccio, David 98, 100, 139
Riding astride 8
  in France 48, 53, 181
  in Scotland 98, 182
Ridolfi plots 158, 159
Ritter 98–9
Romorantin, Edict of 57
Ronsard, French poet 48
Rose, Hugh, of Kilravock 120
'Rough Wooing' 41
Royal progresses
  Francis I 58,
  Francis II 58ff
  Henry II 58
  importance of 69–70, 70–1, 116
  James V 89, 94
  Mary, Queen of Scots 109–10, 110 n.62, 115, 142, 147
Rum, island of 27–8
Russel, Francis, earl of Bedford 149, 152
Russy, Forêt de 42
Ruthven, Patrick, third Lord Ruthven 127

Sadler, Sir Ralph 161
Saint André, Jacques d'Albon, maréchal of France 70–1
Scrope, Henry, ninth Lord Scrope, warden of English west marches 147

220

INDEX

Scrope, William, author of *The Art of Deer Stalking* 134, 135
Sempill, Robert, third Lord Sempill 153
Seton House 100
Sheep houses 177–9
Sheffield Castle and Park 158–61
Shielings 171, 173
Shrewsbury, earl of, *see* Talbot
Side-facing saddle 8
  in France 52, 53, 65, 182–3
  in Scotland 98, 182
Side-saddle 8
  in France 53, 185–6
  origins of 184
  in Scotland 100, 186
Solis, Virgil, engraver 6, 8, 64
Somer, Sir John 162
Stable 20, 21, **23**, *see* tinchell
St Andrews 41, 93, 110, 115, 116
St Germain-en-Laye 42
St Leger 62
Stewart, Henry, Lord Darnley 12, 101, 111, 139, 140, 146
Stewart, James, earl of Moray 96, 110ff, 115, 139ff, 146ff
Stewart, James, of Beith 122
Stewart, James, steward of Menteith 144, 145, 146
Stewart, Jean, countess of Argyll 112
Stewart, John, third earl of Atholl 83, 91
Stewart, John, fourth earl of Atholl 96, 127, 135, 137, 140ff, 146ff, 153
Stewart, John, of Traquair 143
Stewart, Matthew, fourth earl of Lennox 127, 139
Stirling Castle and Park 102
  baptism of James VI at 148–55
  and designed landscape 149
  and King Arthur 149–50
  round table at 149–50
Strathbraan 76, 80

Strathearn 76, 122, 177, 179
Strathfillan 76

Talbot, George, sixth earl of Shrewsbury 157ff
Tapestry
  Chasses de Maximilien 6, 8, 48, 64
  Devonshire Hunting Tapestries 6, 8, 48
  of Mary and Francis 63–5
Taylor, John, the Water Poet 113, 114
Taymouth Book of Hours 7
Tempesta, Antonio, engraver 44, 182
Tenant-foresters 37–8
Throckmorton, Nicholas, ambassador 44, 68, 69 n.67, 72, 75
Throckmorton plot 161
Tinchell 22, **23**, 28, 31, 77, 79, 92, 119, 125
  in Glenartney 77
  in Glen Tilt 133–4
Tixall Park 163
Toils 20, 21, 28, 31, 49, 52, 109
Torwood Forest 24, 93
Traquair House 139, 143
Treaty of Cateau Cambrésis 1559 69
Treaty of Edinburgh 1560 75, 97
Tutbury Castle and Parks 156, 157, 161, 162

Vallery 70
Vaux de Cernay, abbey of 62
Venison as royal food 87, 90
Vénerie 48, 50
Venus, goddess of love 48, 68
Vincennes, chateau de 73
Villers Cotterêts, chateau de 42, 69, 102
  park of 46, 47

Walsingham, Francis 160, 162, 163

221

INDEX

Warenne, Ada de, mother of William
 I 92
West-Highland stones 18
White bull hunts 152–3
Women hunting 6–9, 21, 47–9,
 51–2, 62, 64, 92–4
Wood-cutting, penalties for 35
Woodland management 34–6, 105,
 119–21
 coppicing 35, 73, 105, 106

efficiency of 36, 39, 120–1
enforcement of 35
in France 34–5, 36, 73–4
and growth of royal authority 38–
 40
and public interest 36, 38, 40
in Scotland 35–6, 37, 94, 105,
 119–21
and shortage of timber 34–5
Wyntoun, Andrew of, chronicler 22

St Andrews Studies in Scottish History
Previously published

I
Elite Women and Polite Society in Eighteenth-Century Scotland
Katharine Glover

II
Regency in Sixteenth-Century Scotland
Amy Blakeway

III
Scotland, England and France after the Loss of Normandy, 1204–1296
'Auld Amitie'
M. A. Pollock

IV
Children and Youth in Premodern Scotland
Edited by Janay Nugent and Elizabeth Ewan

V
Medieval St Andrews
Church, Cult, City
Edited by Michael Brown and Katie Stevenson

VI
The Life and Works of Robert Baillie (1602–1662)
Politics, Religion and Record-Keeping in the British Civil Wars
Alexander D. Campbell

VII
The Parish and the Chapel in Medieval Britain and Norway
Sarah E. Thomas

VIII
A Protestant Lord in James VI's Scotland
George Keith, Fifth Earl Marischal (1554–1623)
Miles Kerr-Peterson

IX
The Clergy in Early Modern Scotland
Edited by Chris R. Langley, Catherine E. McMillan and Russell Newton

X
Kingship, Lordship and Sanctity in Medieval Britain
Essays in Honour of Alexander Grant
Edited by Steve Boardman and David Ditchburn

XI
Rethinking the Renaissance and Reformation in Scotland
Essays in Honour of Roger A. Mason
Edited by Steven J. Reid

XII
Life at the Margins in Early Modern Scotland
Edited by Allan Kennedy and Susanne Weston

XIII
Death and the Royal Succession in Scotland, c.1214–c.1543
Ritual, Ceremony and Power
Lucinda H. S. Dean

XIV
The Life, Poems, and Letters of Peter Goldman (1587/8–1627): A Dundee
Physician in the Republic of Letters
William Poole

XV
The Advancement of Learning in Stuart Scotland, 1679–89
Hugh Ouston